A TASTE OF LOVE

Theodora FitzGibbon was the most extraordinary woman. If you read her autobiography you realise how many lives she led. And in fact how many people she was all rolled into one. She was a beauty, she was a deb, she knew all the crowned heads of Europe. She met and married extraordinary people along the way. She was a great cook. She went to a finishing school to learn amazingly useful things, such as how to walk backwards away from royalty and how to eat a biscuit without making crumbs.

Maeve Binchy

The Author

Theodora FitzGibbon was born in London and educated in England and France. She was the author of more than thirty books, most of which were about food, and included her encyclopedic *The Food of the Western World*, which took her fifteen years to complete and covered some thirty-four countries and thirty-two languages. Probably her best-known book is *A Taste of Ireland*. Her Saturday column in *The Irish Times*, which appeared for twenty years and became as legendary as everything else about her, was witty, pithy, filled with extracurricular food knowledge and as avidly talked about as it was read. She had an unfailing instinct for putting both recipes and sentences together, and knew more than anyone how to be entertaining while doing both. She published two volumes of autobiography, *With Love* in 1982 and *Love Lies a Loss* in 1985, which are combined in this new publication *A Taste of Love*. She died in 1991.

A TASTE OF LOVE

The Autobiographies

THEODORA FITZGIBBON

Gill & Macmillan

Gill & Macmillan
Hume Avenue, Park West, Dublin 12
www.gillmacmillanbooks.ie

978 07171 6686 2

Chapters One to Twenty-seven are from *With Love: An
Autobiography 1938–1946*, first published in Great Britain
in 1982 by Century Publishing Co. Ltd. It contained the
following dedication:
'With love to Caitlin and in memoriam Peter and Dylan'.

Chapters Twenty-eight to Forty-eight are from *Love Lies
a Loss: An Autobiography 1946–1959*, first published in
Great Britain in 1985 by Century Publishing Co. Ltd. It
contained the following dedication:
'To all my dear friends in this book, especially George,
with love'.

Print origination by O'K Graphic Design, Dublin
Printed and bound by CPI Group (UK) Ltd, Croydon,
CR0 4YY

This book is typeset in Adobe Garamond 10.75/14 pt

The paper used in this book comes from the wood pulp
of managed forests. For every tree felled, at least one tree
is planted, thereby renewing natural resources.

A CIP catalogue record for this book is available from the
British Library.

5 4 3 2 1

CONTENTS

FOREWORD

Theodora FitzGibbon was legendary in both her own and many another's lifetime. Majestically present in company – Picasso admired her long arms – she made her mark on several decades of the twentieth century and had lived several lives, all of them exhilaratingly, before becoming an immediately superb cookery writer in 1952.

Her cookery writing, including a Saturday column in *The Irish Times* which appeared for twenty years, was witty, pithy and filled with extracurricular knowledge. As avidly talked about as it was read, it became – predictably – as legendary as everything else about her.

Theodora FitzGibbon was thirty-six years old when she took up cookery writing: a woman who had lived, loved and taken on the world on her own terms. She continued to do so with inimitable brio for nearly another forty years until she died, in Killiney, County Dublin, in 1991.

Joan Eileen Rosling – or it might have been Joanne Eileen Winifred, or even Joanna Eileen Theodora – was born in London, in 1916. A dab hand at creating her own legend, she was variously vague and imaginative with detail, especially about her name and about when and where she was born. But facts are facts, and they declare that her beginnings were in Bethnal Green in 1916, where her grandmother had set up a slum clinic at the turn of the century.

A Taste of Love tells it all: the names she used before settling on Theodora; how betting on horses got her expelled from the Sacre Coeur convent in Bruges; the cookery lessons given her by the former Queen Natalie of Serbia; and the food-chomping travels with her rakish father in Europe, the Middle East and India, until, at eighteen, he left her with £1,000 to make her way in the world.

As 'Karen Petersen' she became an actor, touring England and France and playing in the West End. She modelled, appeared in films, socialised with Balthus, Cocteau, Dali and Picasso, and escaped wartime Paris by bicycle and boat to live in Chelsea during the Blitz. She kept company with Freud, Bacon and Soviet spy Donald Maclean.

In between times she met and fell in love with Irish-American writer Constantine FitzGibbon. They married at Chelsea Registry Office in 1944 and divorced fifteen, famously stormy, years later. A year after that she married the Irish filmmaker and archivist George Morrison. They lived together in Dalkey, County Dublin, with Theodora, always happy in her Irish domicile, declaring to the *Guardian* newspaper before she died in 1991 that she had 'never understood the English, nor they me'.

Her cookery writing, in particular, is her legacy. She wrote twenty-six books about food in which her recipes, her love of food and lusty approach to the business of good dining were extensions of how she lived her life. All were acclaimed, many were award winning. An encyclopedia, *The Food of the Western World*, took her fifteen years to write and looked at the food of thirty-four countries and thirty-two languages. Her books for the series *A Taste of* . . . became instant classics. *A Taste of Ireland* (1968) had a drisheen recipe using pig's blood with cream, alongside her usual mix of food history, sociology and geography, and was, without a doubt, the best of them all. Not that Theodora was *all* about cream and the delights of fat in recipes: *Eat Well and Live Longer* (1968) was about *not* using animal fats.

Theodora FitzGibbon's knowledge of Irish food and cooking was encyclopedic and her defence of Irish cooking resounding. She roundly declared that the Irish kitchen had a lot to be proud of; she told how the country's fresh ingredients had been put to imaginative use for centuries, before being forgotten in the rush to 'progress' and the mushy peas of the mid-twentieth century. Irish butchery had its day when she wrote, 'people who say that there is no such thing as Irish cooking completely forget that butchering in Ireland is different from that in any other country' (*A Word on Irish Butchery*). In *Irish Traditional Food – Irish Recipes from 16th to 20th Century* (1983) she demonstrated definitively that Irish soup, game, meat, vegetable, bread, biscuits and drink recipes can hold their own anywhere, anytime.

Her only novel, *The Flight of the Kingfisher* (1967), became an acclaimed television play. Her two-part autobiography, *With Love* (1982) and *Love Lies a Loss* (1985) was, fittingly and with élan, the last thing she wrote. By publishing it now in one, delightful volume, Gill & Macmillan has done Theodora FitzGibbon and the twenty-first century a service.

Rose Doyle
December 2014

PART ONE

Peter's Book
1938–1943

PROLOGUE

The first time I saw him was in the Café Flore, Paris, in 1938. Usually I went to the Deux Magots next door, or when I wanted to indulge my taste for red plush, gold, and painted mirrors, the Brasserie Lipp opposite.

His appearance and manner attracted me as much as his looks. He was a large man with a beautifully shaped head: his hair, which was dark brown, inclined to chestnut at the sides, started high on his forehead, and was worn long enough to curl gently in the nape of his neck. Immaculately so. A prominent nose, under which was a well-trimmed long, silky moustache, a well-shaped full mouth, and the most extraordinary eyes. They were deep reddish brown, very large, but set slightly slanting in his face. Their expression was one of sleepy amusement. The eyebrows followed the shape of the eyes, and did not come down at the corners, so that they gave him a curiously Mephistophelean look. He was beautifully dressed in a dark striped suit, cream silk shirt, a buttonhole, and I think a monocle hung around his neck. He looked magnificent. I had never seen anyone even remotely like him.

I never did again, until I saw Josef Kheifit's haunting film *The Lady with the Little Dog* in 1961. The leading actor, Alexander Batalov, looked remarkably like he did then, and not only looked, but had a similar walk, and manner.

He had a very elegantly bound book open in front of him, and from time to time he would look up, and mark his place with the tip of his finger at the bottom of the book. His hands were very large, but he used them delicately. He glanced at me, then looked away. I then opened my book, Stanislavsky's *My Life in Art*, which was my bible, and made a pretence of reading. After a while he was joined by a very striking looking woman, beautifully dressed, over whom he fussed, and attended. They drank champagne, which made me feel thirsty, and quite took the gold from the autumn morning. From time to time friends would pass their table, stop and talk for a few minutes, then go on their way. The friends looked interesting too, and it all seemed marvellously urbane. So much so that the young man who was taking me to Fontainebleau that afternoon got very short shrift through no fault of his own.

At that time I had only a few acquaintances in Paris, mostly friends of my father's or relatives of people I knew in Ireland. They didn't interest me greatly, nor I them. But I loved Paris. I used all the money I got for my birthday or Christmas to get over there on various pretexts. Old school-friends; study; anything that came into my head and would satisfy my family. I was used to, and liked, being alone, and wandering about a strange and fascinating city thrilled me. Until this day I had had one consuming desire: to be a very good actress; and it was to this end that I was in Paris now. It was the time of Louis Jouvet, Jean Gabin, Madeleine Ozeray, Françoise Rosay, Marie Bell, Danielle Darrieux, and many great names of the French theatre. Jean Cocteau was a magician who could write plays, novels, poems or films with equal facility. I spent all available time and money at the theatre or cinema, sometimes going straight from one to the other. The rest of the time I went to the Louvre, sat in cafés, or just wandered about.

My theatrical career wasn't going the way I wanted it to at all. Owing to my being quite tall and blonde, I was always cast as the 'other woman', a figure prominent in the plays of those years. In fact, I can't think of a successful contemporary play without her. After doing this in good repertory companies like Coventry or Birmingham, it reached the nadir when I was again cast as the 'other woman' in a film with Elisabeth Bergner. I was then eighteen and playing a woman of forty, whilst Miss Bergner seemed about forty, and was playing a girl of eighteen. It seemed to me that I was too young to be playing character parts, but no others came my way. To my knowledge I had never met an 'other woman', at least not the kind of character that was portrayed in my scripts. Nowadays the 'other woman' is often the central character, and a much more human person.

The pattern of my day was changed: I went to the Flore and studied someone who was more fascinating to me than Louis Jouvet. Sometimes there would be a large party at his table. All the women were beautiful and the men, if not all handsome, were worth looking at. There was always conversation and a certain amount of laughter, presumably when pearls of wit fell from one of the lips. It was tantalizing, but full of interest, rather like watching a silent film. There was no opportunity to get into this magic circle: the membership was obviously limited. I started going there earlier and earlier in the hope that he would be alone again but, when he was, I could think of no way to introduce myself. The wildest schemes flitted into my mind, and flitted out again equally quickly. One day he did drop an envelope on the floor and I went to pick it up, but alas, he retrieved it first. I was rewarded with a nod. On the day when he wasn't there in the morning, I went back again in the evening and asked Pascal the waiter what his name was, but he couldn't make out which *monsieur* I was talking about. I couldn't even make out his nationality, as I was never quite near enough to hear his accent. He spoke both French and English to his companions, and he could have been either, or even Russian.

One day I sat deliberately quite far away, so that I could point him out to Pascal and get his name. Pascal was good at that, but he came back with a very unsatisfactory answer: it sounded like 'Poulum', and meant nothing to me, nor did it give any clue as to his nationality. Nevertheless, the day came when Pascal summoned me, bent low over me, and said he had found out that 'Poulum' took photographs, good photographs too, so he'd heard. It was all a bit disappointing, and for a day I let the Flore get on without me. Pascal took quite an interest in me on account of this, and never missed a chance to try to bring about a meeting, but either he was too intimidating for Pascal, or there were too many of those beauties about. The beauties came in all sizes and colours. Their clothes were outstanding, and in some cases *outré*, but looked right on them. The accepted dress for young women in the morning in those days was the tailor-made suit, or *le tailleur*, as the French called it. Almost my entire wardrobe consisted of *les tailleurs* in various materials which, after seeing Garbo and Marlene Dietrich at the cinema, I enlivened alternately with a large floppy hat or a small black beret according to the mood I was in. My black tailor-made I had inherited from a rather chic friend of my mother's. It had a wrap-over skirt, which when one crossed one's legs showed a large amount of calf. This was thought very dashing, and it was my favourite. However, even that must have looked tame compared to some of those beauties' outfits.

If I am giving the impression that I was a lonely young girl tossing on my bed at night, I must correct it. I was twenty years old, quite considerably travelled, had had a certain amount of success, and was in the middle of a nice cosy uncomplicated love affair in London. This all took place during my two weeks away, for reassessment of myself and other people – a habit started very early on in life, and still kept to. Anyway this watching and waiting was not my style, and I was getting a bit impatient. The effect that this man seen across a café had on me was not one of immediate love or desire: it was fascination. A curious feeling, and one that has never happened to me again.

For the next few days I had little time to indulge in my new pastime as some Irish friends arrived in Paris, and we did all the things that young and gay people like to do at any time. I got home too late to get up in time to get to the Flore before lunch, and the whole episode took on an air of unreality, almost of having happened in another century.

On the way home from a party the night before I left Paris, we stopped at the Flore for a nightcap and something to eat. It all looked very different at three in the morning: the change was quite startling. As we were leaving about an hour later, he came in with a crowd of people. They were in elaborate fancy dress: one woman looked exquisite as a black cat, and a magnificently tall, tawny-haired woman shimmered in gold. There was a man in an elegant Domino costume. He was dressed in tails, with a red-lined black cloak. Under his arm he carried a large eagle's head made out of *papier mâché*. It was this bizarre memory that stayed with me during the long London winter.

CHAPTER ONE

In fact the winter wasn't long at all. The spectre of the 'other woman' was well and truly laid, mainly due to my being cast in the first play written by Anatole de Grunwald, later to become extremely well known in film circles as a producer. He was a gentle, slim, dark-haired man in his twenties; shy in manner, he nevertheless was able to make a point firmly when he wished. When he became successful during the war, he was kind and helpful, and got me several small parts in films. A charming companion, and one I would have liked to have seen more of, but the partner in my cosy love affair had taken a very jealous turn, and hated to let me out of his sight. This I found very tiring, so I wriggled out of that situation as gracefully as I could.

When I wasn't working in the theatre, I worked as a mannequin, as modelling was called then. The top mannequins were always almost six feet tall but, owing to having very slender legs and arms and a small head, I looked at least three inches taller than I was. I found being a mannequin very unsatisfactory after acting as I hadn't got a clothes-horse mentality. That is, until I found Ronald Traquair, a young Scotsman with a *salon* in Grosvenor Street.

A *salon* is just about all he had: the other rooms in which he lived were almost bare of furniture, and often there wasn't enough money to go round. This made the whole procedure much more interesting, and I really felt I had to sell the clothes for him. They were made of rich velvets, brocades and silks; they were beautiful and romantic, and I looked good in them. I only worked part-time for him, usually when he had an important client or when he had the money. Sometimes he would show his clothes at night, and I would rush from rehearsals to Grosvenor Street. John Gielgud and John Perry often brought clients to see the clothes. Afterwards, if the killing had been good, we would go out and buy a bottle of whisky for twelve shillings and sixpence, and come back and queen it in the downy-cushioned chairs of the *salon*, with the log fire burning discreetly; we were sometimes joined by the chief cutter, a dear little woman who was crippled, and who adored Traquair. He was very good looking, but wasn't a ladies man. Nevertheless we were very fond of each other.

On Grand National day 1939 I put ten shillings on Marmaduke Jinks which came home at fifty to one. I took Traquair out to dinner, and found I had plenty left to get to Paris for Easter. The fare was about three pounds, and one could live comfortably in Paris on five pounds a week. I never saw Traquair again, as he was killed in a car accident shortly afterwards.

———

The strong sweet-sour smell of Paris; the aroma of garlic and olive oil; the taste of Pernod; the gritty feeling of French cigarettes between one's lips; the vitality and realism of the people: the city where to excrete was human, and to urinate, if not divine, at least a natural function. All this contrasted vividly with the lavender and dust smell of London. The weather was cold and clear, with a watery spring sun which bathed the buildings in a pale gold light. It was crowded with visitors, and it was often hard to find a table on one's own in the cafés. Pascal was delighted to see me again, and would look round for a suitable table for me to sit at. His choice was not always mine, but I didn't like to hurt his feelings.

On the third day I was there Pascal was standing near the door of the Flore, and looked quite excited when he saw me. He fussed over me so much that I didn't notice where I was going. He sat me down at a small table alongside the glass partition at the side, dusted the table vigorously and enquired about my order. I looked up and saw who was at the next table, not an arm's length from me. But could it be? Yes, it was 'Poulum', but 'Poulum' wearing a different coat.

My eyes started their examination at marble table-top level. A large drawing pad took up most of the table, and as he drew I saw that he was left-handed, but those large, surgeon's hands went swiftly across the paper. The cuff above the hand was frayed and dirty; the suit was shiny and covered in what looked like a grey powder; the monocle and buttonhole were gone; the hair still curled, but not immaculately; the moustache needed trimming, but it was undoubtedly 'Poulum'. He looked up and smiled. I smiled back; he was much more approachable in these clothes. He settled himself in the chair, and took a swallow of the red wine he was drinking.

'I wonder,' he said: 'I wonder if you would mind sitting at my table as you distract me sitting where you are?'

I moved at his request. He went on sketching, and try as I might I couldn't see what he was drawing. We sat in silence for some time and I was beginning to feel uncomfortable, when he closed the drawing pad and turned towards me. I looked up and met his gaze, trying desperately not to blink. He put his head to one side and the enormous eyes roamed all over my face. They had an amusing, quizzical expression. It seemed to go on for a very long time. Then in a soft, pleasantly drawling voice, he said:

'You're a very pretty girl, but you won't do.'

My heart contracted. 'Won't do for what?'

'For some very boring photographs I have to take.'

'But I thought . . .' I had been about to say that I thought he was a photographer, then stopped suddenly, as this would assume too much knowledge.

'But you thought what, my dear?' he said in an amused voice.

I stuttered, and said I thought he was an artist, a painter, anything that came into my head.

He seemed rather pleased by this, and seemed not to have noticed my awkwardness. His head went right down on one side, almost to his shoulder.

'Well, I suppose I am, but there are still those boring photographs. Let's talk about something else. You, for instance.'

He was surprisingly easy to talk to, and appeared to be interested in what I was saying. Once he laughed quite loudly at some observation I made, although I didn't think it was all that funny. Drinks came and went; perhaps we were a little bit tipsy. I had that odd feeling that I had known him for years and that we had just picked up a conversation where it had left off some time ago, the way you can with very old friends. It got very late, and suddenly my young belly gave a loud rumble.

'Heavens, you *must* be hungry; come back and have luncheon at my place.'

Pascal was summoned, and smiled benignly over us. It was quite embarrassing, and I was frightened he would say something about last year. There were endless saucers to be counted, and I offered to pay my share, but was airily waved aside.

We left the Flore, turned right, and he strode rapidly on – so quickly that I was sure I would lose him amongst the crowds; but he was very tall and easy to pick out. We turned right again; he still walked quickly with his head down slightly, as if he had forgotten that I was with him. Then he stopped dead, turned round and faced me square on. My head came about level with his chin. He bent down and said:

'I don't think I have very much to eat at home.' He said this apologetically, and his eyes held mine.

'Well, we'll buy something on the way there.'

'An excellent idea, except that I haven't any money left.'

It was agreed that I would buy the food from a *charcuterie*, as he had bought the drinks earlier. We picked out some good-looking terrine, pâté de marcassin, and cornichons, then we stopped several times again and bought bread, butter, cheese, and chicorée frisée. The episode had an air of unreality: I couldn't believe that I was with 'Poulum', even though it wasn't the 'Poulum' of last year. Neither of us had thought to enquire the other's name, so he was still 'Poulum' to me. Once we had done the shopping he walked at a normal pace, and there was an air of intimacy, almost of secrecy, between us. On passing a wine shop I said:

'Let's buy a bottle of champagne.'

'Champagne?' He said it as if I had said, 'Let's go up in a balloon.'

It was on the tip of my tongue to say, 'But you love champagne.' I desisted, but we bought it, and carried all our parcels like children at Christmas.

I don't know what sort of 'place' I had thought of 'Poulum' as living in; there hadn't been any time to think. We were beside an old hotel and it was there we stopped. A small beady-eyed man who looked as if he never went out gave us a key. We walked up endless flights of stairs, and when it seemed there couldn't be any more, we were there.

The room was an attic of large proportions, with a skylight on one side. It was cold, the patterned wallpaper was peeling and almost the entire floor space was covered with pieces of screwed-up paper. They looked like surrealist children's boats. The bed hadn't been made for some time, was rumpled, crumpled and littered with tubes of paint, more pieces of paper and a beautiful silk dressing gown rolled into a ball. There were the ashes of a fire in the grate, empty wine bottles, stained glasses, dirty plates, and more tubes of paint on the shelf above the fireplace. An easel stood in the centre of the room, and on it was a half-finished painting of a large room, empty except for a trestle table. The walls and floor of the room were painted in very delicate rainbow colours, each hue merging into the next. The contrast between the painted room and the actual one was startling. There was a sagging armchair by the fireplace and a hard chair with a cane bottom by the easel. Stacks of disordered newspapers were in one corner and a small pile of logs. The other furniture was sparse and battered.

Halfway across the room he turned, and with a grand sweep of the arm pointed to the armchair.

'Do sit down. I'll have a fire going in a minute.'

He went about the room, picking up the pieces of paper, which he arranged pyramid fashion on top of some books on a chest of drawers. I attempted to help him, but was waved aside.

'Don't you do it: I know where they go.'

It seemed impossible that anyone would know where they went, but nevertheless the careful arrangement went on. I shivered slightly, involuntarily.

'I'll light the fire then . . .'

But I was not allowed to touch anything. He behaved as if it was a very grand apartment, which only needed a switch to transform it. I eyed the food on the bed, and my belly made another ominous rumble.

'Goodness, I'm forgetting you've probably a healthy young appetite. We'll just wash up a few plates. I don't like the servants poking about, they disturb all my things.'

It was difficult to know what to answer, so I said nothing but busied myself in preparing the meal. The table was covered with paints and a palette, so I spread it out on the floor in front of the now crackling fire. He sat in the armchair and I sat on the floor, and we ate and ate and ate – so quickly, that we forgot the champagne, and had finished a bottle of red wine that was open.

'Oh, the champagne . . . well, we can have it with our dessert.'

The dessert was one wizened apple which we ate, bite and bite about, between us. The after-glow of the food and the warmth of the fire turned the room into the one on the easel. I felt sleepy and must have looked it, for he said:

'Do lie down on the bed, I'll make a space for you. I want to do some more to this painting before the light goes.'

When I woke up it was quite dark, and he was sitting in front of the fire with his chin resting on one hand. It was a characteristic pose. Cigarette smoke curled in the dim red glow. As I stirred, he moved over to the bed and switched on a lamp. He sat on the side, and took the lobe of my ear between his finger and thumb.

'It was pleasant having a sleeping muse in my room,' he said.

His hand moved about my face, and took hold of my chin, which he raised up to face the light. My hair, which I wore in a coil in the nape of my neck, had come undone and fell about my shoulders. A hairpin dug in my neck at the back. He wound my hair round his fingers, put it back behind my ears and turned my face in profile. It was as though he was examining a piece of sculpture.

'Surely your hair can't really be that gold colour.'

It was, and he drew his lips together.

'You have very pretty ears . . . and blue veins behind your eyes like my mother had. I've never seen anyone with those blue veins except her.' He sighed, and I luxuriated under the flattery.

'You look almost transparent in this light. Pity, I like dirty, black-haired women.'

I sat up, and said I must be going.

'Going – but where on earth do you think you're going to? I thought you were going to be my muse.'

'But . . . I don't even know your name, and I'm going back to London the day after tomorrow.'

'We can soon change all that; what on earth does a pretty girl like you want to live in London for?'

They were all very difficult questions to answer, so I suggested that we went out to have a drink. I had the feeling that I was playing a part in a play, and hadn't learnt the lines.

'I haven't any money until next week,' he said sadly.

I turned out my handbag on the bed, and we counted what I had left.

'Heavens, you *are* a rich little creature. This will last us for weeks if we go carefully.'

It was all said so gently, and with such obvious child-like pleasure, that I laughed aloud. I wondered briefly how he was going to survive until the money came next week, and what had happened to all those beauties, but I said nothing, got up and started to coil up my hair.

'Don't screw it all up like that. Leave it hanging down, it looks beautiful.'

'But, I can't just go round with it hanging all down my back like a child.'

'It makes you look pre-Raphaelite.'

I went out with it all hanging down my back like a child, and felt acutely uncomfortable to begin with. Nobody at that time had long hair falling all over the place. Either tight curls or short hair was the fashion, and I didn't know quite what a pre-Raphaelite was, except it sounded quite nice.

We went to a nearby café and sat there for hours, talking entirely about ourselves. He seemed to regard me as some sort of freak, and kept picking out a word from my conversation and rolling it about his lips, like a wine taster exploring.

'Actress . . . Irish . . . Tipperary . . . twenty-one . . . Russian . . . H'm, m'm . . .'

Then he looked at me and said:

'I don't believe a word of it.'

'Why would I make up a story to tell you? It's not a very exciting one at that.'

'Oh, don't ask me to explain what goes on in the mind of an imaginative little creature like you.'

He treated me as if I was a strange little animal that he should be wary of. When he said something nice, it was retracted in the next sentence, as if he thought I might take some advantage, or even bite. His whole manner would change from one of concern to one of making me concerned. You had to be quick, and you had to be right. One moment he was a mature man of forty, and the next like a schoolboy. It was like seeing different facets of a room in a piece of cut crystal.

The next day we went to the Flore, and Pascal beamed over me, asked how I was and at the same time cast a knowing eye.

'You seem to be very well known here, why haven't I seen you before?' he asked. He said this in a very proprietory way.

'I haven't been to Paris since last year.'

I hoped that this would provoke some explanation for his apparent change of fortune.

'Oh, last year,' he sighed, 'that seems like ten years ago to me.'

———

The days lengthened into weeks: I wrote to my maternal grandmother in London, and made some feasible suggestions as to why I should stay in Paris. Grandma, who had brought me up, was nobody's fool, and answered rather shrewdly, saying no doubt my French would be useful to me 'later on', but to be certain not to get trapped as she wouldn't trust those Germans an inch, especially that Hitler. She did, however, enclose a pure white, crinkly five-pound note. I bought a much needed pair of silk stockings, and the rest went on food and drink.

The atmosphere in Paris was tense in certain quarters. Hitler had occupied Prague; rumours were circulating that Poland would be next, which were reinforced when Chamberlain said that 'in that event, the British and French governments would lend all support in their power'. When one dared to think about the prospect, it was exceptionally gloomy. Poison gas, bombs, the huge casualty lists of the 1914–18 war ran in front of one's eyes like a piece of film. At my age, it was pleasanter to hope and to do all the things that might be denied me later on. The horrors were put at the back of one's mind, and it was only when more and more men appeared in army uniform on the streets that the horrors pushed themselves forward. There was after all the feeling of safety induced by the impregnable Maginot Line.

The day-to-day excitement of my life overshadowed everything. I helped to take the 'boring photographs', which weren't in the least so, and I showed such aptitude that he wanted to teach me more about it. But, if anything, I wanted to be on the other side of the camera, although I liked helping to fix lights and process the film. The photographs 'Poulum' took were not in the least boring; they were quite remarkable: not only for their imaginative qualities, but also for the technical surprises and innovations he employed. I had never seen anything like them, and they look as good today as they did then. Most of the portrait photographs of the thirties were set pieces, with the sitters looking as they thought they looked: heavy retouching and stiff poses. His photographs were startling because they captured their subjects spontaneously in their environments, a thing at that time hardly to be found in the work of any British photographer, though characteristic of the work of Cartier-Bresson. Not that his photographs resembled those of Cartier-Bresson in style, for 'Poulum' had a quite individual way of using a single light, and sometimes a surrealist style of allowing large areas to fall into complete shadow from which salient features would emerge strikingly illuminated, with remarkable dramatic interest.

He was a passionate surrealist, as were most of his friends and the painters he admired. He taught me to understand the gaiety and perspicacity of surrealism, for which I have always been grateful. The big surrealist exhibition of 1936 was still talked about; Mariette Oppenheim with her fur tea-cups and saucers was a good friend of his, and a very attractive girl. I got to know many of the 'beauties' and they weren't frightening: particularly Eleonor, or Leonor Fini, the cat-woman of the previous year, a brilliant and original painter, and Lady Iya Abdy, the beautiful tawny-haired Russian, photographs of whom were in all the glossy magazines.

The smell of paint and linseed oil; the studios of the painters, each one as individual as the individual artist . . .

Eugene Berman, the Russian painter, was always in a dressing gown with daubs of paint over it (I never saw him out of doors). When one's visit had lasted long enough he would say:

'Well, I must draw the curtains now and get back to my painting!'

I loved his dark, desolate landscapes and ruins.

Max Ernst, then in his forties, had an impish sense of fun . . . We once spent several hours going across Paris without treading on a line in the paving stones. His studio was a rectangular room with heavy dark furniture, relieved by a few comfortable Second Empire chairs. It contrasted strongly with the rococo style prevalent in the apartment of Salvador Dali – huge gilt looking-glasses, ornate but beautiful plaster work, and Gesso decoration on the large doors. A surrealist touch was a full-size stuffed polar bear which stood in one corner of a dark panelled room, where several vivid and unforgettable Dali pictures hung.

The young, saturnine-looking Balthus, whose name was Balthasar Klossowsky, and his beautiful Swiss wife Nuche, lived in the sixteenth-century palace of the Archbishops of Rouen, in Paris. He was a young man, a pupil of André Derain's and highly thought of. He painted his wife and also did a number of drawings to illustrate *Wuthering Heights*. Curiously he had been partly educated in Yorkshire and was an enthusiastic Anglophile. He couldn't understand my being critical of the English, so I had to give him a brief rundown of Irish history, at which 'Poulum' sniffed and told him not to believe a word of it.

When brought to the sixteenth-century house on the Quai de Saint Augustin to meet Picasso, the huge barn-like studio with the tiered stove at one end and the vast canvases propped here, there and everywhere overawed me, so I said very little and was hardly noticed, I thought. Then Picasso came over to me and examined me with eyes burning like the hot Spanish sun, and in a staccato voice said:

'Vos bras sont très beaux.'

From then on, if I wasn't there, he would ask where was the girl with the beautiful arms.

Giacometti, the sculptor, André Derain, Tristan Zara, Christian (Bébé) Bérard – all of them were living and working in the Paris of those prewar days. (If many of these names are now household words, it was not the case then. At a collected exhibition of their work, at Mayer's Gallery in London, just before this time, half the pictures were unsold, and those purchased went for very little.)

There were not only painters, but men of letters, such as André Breton, Louis Aragon, Henri de Montherlant, Jean Cocteau, André Mesens, and Antoine de Saint-Exupéry, who was a man of action and charm, and a superb writer. *Vol de Nuit* is a perfect example of his lucid and beautiful prose; and his tiny dark-haired wife, Consuelo, was a particular friend.

Such then was the intellectual atmosphere, as I saw it, in Paris in 1939. It is not being overdramatic to say that it changed my life, for from then on I have associated myself entirely with creative people.

CHAPTER TWO

lthough it was stimulating and exciting, it was not all honey. There was often no money at all, and we existed on dry bread rubbed with garlic. The garlic taste remained long after the bread had been digested, and gave one the feeling of having eaten more recently. As a change, we had bread smeared with mustard, when there was any mustard. I couldn't go past the local *charcuterie* because it made my mouth water so, and always had to take a much more circuitous route. It seemed not to affect 'Poulum' at all, or if it did he never mentioned it. There was to be no compromise; one painted and nothing else mattered. From time to time small sums of money appeared; I never knew from where or how much they were. The bills were paid, or something given on account; we had perhaps one good meal, a bottle of wine; canvas and paints were bought, and then back to the bread and garlic. One was always hungrier the day after the meal, which bears out Rabelais's words: 'Appetite comes with eating!'

He liked me to be in the room when he painted, so I tidied it up as much as I was allowed. I did the bed one day when he was out. It yielded a rich hoard of old tubes of paint, several empty matchboxes, two forks, a saucer and what looked like the skin of a kipper or dried herring. It looked very nice when I had finished, for I had found a faded cover in the wardrobe and put it on. I sat back in the armchair to admire my handiwork. But not for long! When he came home and saw it, instead of praising me, he was furious. His face went quite red with temper and he stripped the covers down.

'I hate made beds,' he shouted, 'there's something so squalid about them.'

I was too astonished to speak, but rushed over and wrestled with the bed clothes the other side. I treated that old bed like a treasured possession that had to be guarded.

'Squalid!' I yelled. '*You* are ostentatious in your squalidness.'

He stopped and turned quickly. 'What did you say?'

'I said you were ostentatious in your squalidness.'

'That's a very good line,' he said. 'I must remember it.'

I didn't tell him then that it came from W. B. Yeats's *A Vision* because I was too angry.

It was our first quarrel, and I went for my coat.

'But you can't go just because I don't like tidy beds.' He took me by the shoulders, and shook me very gently. 'You can't . . .'

It was finally agreed that the bed could be made, but must be ruffled, or preferably lain on straight away, so that it didn't look like the bed of a *petit-bourgeois* family.

I would lie on it and read his books. The elegantly leather-bound one that I remembered from last year was Benjamin Constant's *Adolphe*.

With the exception of *Le Sofa* by Crébillon, in which the sofa tells the story of all the love affairs it has witnessed, his library read like a list of French classics: Daudet, the Goncourt Brothers, Diderot, Flaubert, Stendhal, Turgenev, and Prosper Merimée. The latter's short stories of werewolves were new to me and I revelled in them. There was also a marvellous book called *Maldoror*, written, I think, by the Frenchman Count Lautréamont. It was weird and exciting, and highly thought of by the Surrealists. The only English book was *New Writing* edited by John Lehmann, and a current copy of *Horizon* magazine edited by Cyril Connolly and financed to a certain extent by Peter Watson, both of whom 'Poulum' knew. Once he came back with a volume of Racine's plays which was pushed into my hand with the words:

'If you're going to be an actress, you'd better start learning some of this.'

I found the alexandrines a bit heavy going.

Being a very fast reader I was often accused of 'not having read them properly', and would be tested on certain passages. My French wasn't all that good to start with, and I got seriously caught out over *la diligence* in one of Daudet's books: how could I have guessed it meant stage-coach? From then on the lessons got more intense, and when it was too dark to paint we often sat for hours over my instruction. I certainly learned more than I had done at various convents all over the place; but then convents are like Hilton Hotels – they vary little from country to country.

It was the hunger that made me think about ways of getting food. Always thin, I was becoming quite emaciated. I found that I couldn't read a passage about a meal without almost drooling. When the next sum of money turned up, I commandeered a small part of it and suggested that we should cook over the fire. This was thought marvellously practical, and he even made some sort of little trivet out of strong wire to hold a saucepan. I bought all the materials for a real curry, the most flavoursome meal I could think of.

'A curry? Like all those dreadful Anglo-Indians in Hove?'

'No, not like the Anglo-Indians in Hove, but like the Indian Indians in India. It won't be hot and peppery.'

'Well . . .' his nose twisted round disapprovingly. 'Well, perhaps just this once.'

I got all the spices and ground them up by hand: the smell from the cardamoms, coriander, cumin, mace, cloves, cinnamon, ginger, turmeric and peppers was like a magnificent *hors d'oeuvre*. A great pot of *dal*, Indian lentil soup, bubbled and spat over the glowing wood.

We ate until our bellies swelled up like poisoned pups. He had to admit it was good, although he did rather take the gilt off it by saying that next time I must try my hand with a *boeuf à la mode*. I wasn't too sure how to do that, so I kept quiet.

But from then on we had at least one hot meal a day: Irish stew, creamy and delicious, not swimming in liquid; bortsch; vegetable soups; and little chunks of meat grilled over the fire on skewers in true Cossack fashion. Actually, he didn't really approve of food that wasn't French, but it was difficult to perform *haute cuisine* dishes over that cramped little fire. The extra food gave me back my customary energy: my mind became more alert, and lying on the bed reading French classics most of the day began to pall. Being a muse was a rather sedentary occupation.

I pressed the black *tailleur*, bought a gay scarf, slapped on the black beret à la Dietrich, and went off to look for a job. The fact that I hadn't got a *carte de travail* didn't deter me. That would come, no doubt. I chose Molyneux first of all, because he was the acknowledged master of *le tailleur*. It took a bit of getting past the scented *vendeuse*, but I burbled on about Traquair and several other people I had worked for in London, and eventually I was promised an appointment.

As it turned out he was a charming Irish gentleman, whose name was pronounced *Molynoox*, and it was the French-Scottish name of the Auld Alliance, Traquair, that had stimulated his interest. He was, in fact, looking for the 'English Rose' type. Thank God my family in Tipperary never knew!

The job was on a temporary basis until the season was over in June. It wasn't demanding, and the money was nice. I could still be a muse on Sundays and Mondays, which was enough for anyone. I was delighted to be able to write some concrete news to my grandmother, who was getting restive. 'Poulum' didn't like my being away for most of the day, but we had very sybaritic weekends which made up for it.

Our relationship was in many ways an odd one, as one might expect from living with so curious a person. He could on occasions be very off-putting, almost intimidating and, at other times, warm, tender and full of spontaneous gaiety. Always outspoken, there were however many things I could not ask him: he would tell you so much, and then shut down suddenly, inexplicably, as though he was frightened to reveal too much of himself to another person. He was more afraid than I realized, but then I was not without some apprehension myself, and at that age one is still finding out a lot about oneself. He was particularly reticent when discussing his relationships with women, although he did tell me of eating baked jacket potatoes and caviare with one of his girls. The usual clichés of love or sex could not be applied to him. Generally undemonstrative, he would then astound one by being almost sentimental. Sometimes I would think he loved me, and at other times he seemed quite indifferent. But if I suggested returning to England he would get fussed, his shoulders would hunch up so that his neck almost disappeared, his eyes would become even larger and fill with a melancholy expression. I did not know his age, nor did I enquire, but I assumed it was about forty. These are small details, but ones not usually withheld in an intimate relationship.

His mind worked quite slowly, but logically. If I asked a question of an intellectual nature he would consider it for some minutes, even hours, and several times he said he would think about it and let me know in a few days' time. Then surely, in two or three days when I had almost forgotten asking it, he would come up with a long, detailed and comprehensive answer. He liked to instruct, and what he taught me I have never forgotten.

I did however find out what the crumpled pieces of paper were for. He was at that time experimenting with *trompe l'œil* painting. Whole canvases were painted of them, and were so realistic that once I went to pick them up.

Young people when they relax usually adopt untidy attitudes. Sitting up straight in a chair smacks of childhood training, and is a sign of inhibition in the young, or approaching middle age in older people. While I was curled up on the bed and listening to him talk, he would often stroke my hair, my shoulder or behind my ear. Then I would stretch out and luxuriate. I behaved like a cat, he said, and therefore he would call me Puss. Always after that, I was known as Puss or Pussy, although I don't think I was catlike in other ways.

Very early on I found I could make him laugh. Not the laughter associated with polite conversation, but so that the tears would come out of his eyes. He had a delighted, delightful laugh that made one feel good. It was always the comic situation that provoked it. Anecdotes about my family in Ireland were certain successes, although he always said he didn't believe a word of them. To him Ireland was as remote as Siberia. Certainly he never realized how close to the truth are the stories of Somerville and Ross. He must have thought I was much more imaginative than in fact I am, as I come from a rum, very individual family. My great-great-uncle coined his own money in Cloughjordan, King's County, in the 1870s and always used it. As children we would play with some of the coins. Now, alas, only pennies are left, but we all still have a total disregard for the coin of the realm!

He in turn would regale me by talking about his friends so vividly that I would think I had met them. Only once he spoke of his family. He said his mother had been wildly impractical with money and, when remonstrated with by his father for spending too much on housekeeping, had fed them both on nothing but rice pudding for three days.

Some days when I was working he would drink with his friends in the Flore. I was seldom brought out, but when I suggested a meeting, he would say that he would like to be alone with me, as he hadn't seen me all day. In many ways it was like living in the nineteenth century, when a person's public and private activities were markedly separate.

At the back of my mind I knew that I would have to return to England sometime, even if only for a visit. I had come away initially for a long weekend, and now it was months. I could not go on making excuses indefinitely. The news in Europe was disquieting: there were prolonged and unsatisfactory negotiations with Russia, and Hitler was a real and very near menace.

A letter arrived from my agent saying that a play I had toured in was being brought to London. I must come back for rehearsals. I did not envisage the reaction the letter would have when I showed it. First, utter sadness, the shoulders hunched, and tears; then impatience and temper. Finally he walked out of the little room I had come to love. I walked about it all night, touching the objects I knew were a part of him; stoking the fire, doing anything that would make the night shorter. He was not back by the time I had to leave in the morning. I came back again in the evening; the empty room mocked me. Had the actions been reversed, I would of course have stayed. It was a difficult decision, one that I would not like to have to make again. I left a long letter saying that I would come over for a few days when I knew what was happening, and that I was taking the copy of Prosper Merimée with me as a hostage.

My letter was unanswered.

CHAPTER THREE

Peter Rose Pulham, for that was his name, was born in England in 1910. His mother was Scottish, and his father's family came from Pulham in Norfolk. He was very proud that his family was mentioned in Fuller's 'Worthies', the finest work of the seventeenth-century English historian Thomas Fuller, called *The History of the Worthies of England*.

His mother died when he was twelve years old, and it undoubtedly had an adverse effect on him. His memories of her were affectionate and romantic, but cautious.

Of his early life and schooling I know nothing. He disliked school so much that he could never bear to talk about it. At the age of nineteen he went to Worcester College, Oxford, and read, I think, English literature. He loved Oxford, and when talking of his days there it was always summer: sparkling and magical. Many of the friends he made there, such as Desmond Ryan and Graham Eyres Monsell, were his friends for life. His descriptions of Oxford were almost Proustian, and were told with the same meticulous affection.

He came down from Oxford in his early twenties, without getting a degree, having decided he wanted to take photographs. He seldom talked of unpleasant periods of his life, for he had no self-pity, but I gathered that this decision displeased his banker father, who gave him a comparatively small sum of money (about a hundred pounds) to go ahead, but told him not to expect any more.

Painstakingly he taught himself to take photographs, and his original, individual style was almost immediately recognized and acclaimed. It became the fashionable thing to be photographed by Rose Pulham, and many a well-known English beauty sat for him. He worked for some years with *Harper's Bazaar* in both London and Paris. The long Regency windows of his Berkeley Square apartment opened on to a balcony above the green trees of the gardens below: the air was soft and quiet in the evenings when the traffic ceased. Weekends were spent in the houses of the rich. For several years he was content. He had success and the feeling of well-being it brings. He was still experimenting with techniques in his work, and enjoyed the company of the women he desired and the friends he wanted. A lot of money was made, and equally quickly spent. Tchelitchew drew his portrait: he was a handsome man in his twenties, charming and witty. Life was fair.

Success is a tyrant. It can be like climbing a beanstalk which waves perilously when you are at the top. The world of advertising reaches out to an original creative talent, then proceeds to superimpose its own imprint over it, thus restricting the mind of the creator. The bridle is slipped on, and whilst that is hardly noticed, the girths are tightened on the saddle, feet are put into the stirrups, and the faceless rider has acquired spurs or a whip. In those circumstances there are two courses ahead: to trot gently around the ring like a fat-backed circus pony, or to dig in your toes, refuse and unseat the rider.

The latter course was taken by Peter. He was asked to take more and more photographs which were not to his liking, so quite firmly, and suddenly, he dug in his toes.

He said he had taken all the photographs he ever wanted to take, and henceforth the visual side of his imagination would be applied to painting. He would finish only those photographs he was contracted for. Carefully, laboriously, he taught himself to paint, as he had previously taught himself to take photographs. He prepared himself for years of arduous lonely work. He would ask no one to undergo this with him; if they were prepared to share his hardships that was another matter, but they must not expect a comfortable bourgeois life. There would be no compromise.

Painting was to become the enduring preoccupation of his life. Everything else was secondary.

This was the man, at the age of twenty-eight, that I met in 1939.

CHAPTER FOUR

B ack in London *Goodbye Mr Chips* was playing to packed houses in the cinema, whilst H. G. Wells's *The Shape of Things to Come* enjoyed a more restricted audience. Will Hay, Moore Marriott and Graham Moffat cavorted in *Ask a Policeman*. Professor Joad argued endlessly on the wireless, Dodie Smith's play was still running, Margaret Lockwood was the reigning British film star, and the hit song was 'Deep Purple'.

The summer air was hot and heavy, trembling with the unease that means thunder. The streets were crowded, guttural voices of German refugees mingling with the familiar cockney or other English accents. It was much more tense than Paris had been: middle-aged people with vivid memories of the First World War showed their worry on their faces, and young men were uncertain as to whether to enlist in the army or take up their careers. Leaflets on how to detect poison gas or handle incendiary bombs were distributed; gas-masks, for those who had not got them at the time of the Munich crisis, were issued; air-raid shelters were being erected, trenches dug, and Anderson shelters like corrugated kennels were put up in suburban gardens. There were advertisements for air-raid wardens on a voluntary basis, also fire-watchers, and Red Cross personnel.

My mother had a German-Jewish refugee girl staying with her in London, who told us horrifying stories of life in Germany. It cast a gloom over the usually cheerful house as she sat in the evenings sorting out the innumerable railway tickets she had bought in Germany, to spend the money she could not bring, and deciding which one to sell next.

It was hard to concentrate on anything. The lines of the play seemed more banal than I remembered them, and I frequently thought of giving it up. But money had to be earned, and this was the best way for me to do it. I felt trapped.

I worried about Peter, and wrote saying that I would do the play for three months and then come back. He replied with a curt little note:

Dear Pussy,
Please do not worry about me for I am quite all right, and painting well. I miss you very much, but don't hurry back as I will probably have changed my mind by the time you get here . . .

We rehearsed in the empty Aldwych Theatre. Romney Brent, the American actor, was the producer, and I lived in the enclosed world of the theatre which seemed more real than the strange outside one. The play opened at the Richmond Theatre on August Bank Holiday Monday, as a try-out to London. The notices were, on the whole, good but there were complications about the London theatre. We were to be 'on call', and 'they' would let us know. A restless lethargy settled on me: the fear of rejection if I went to Paris; uncertainty, unhappiness and possibly no success in London.

I took the crowded mail-boat to Ireland with its smell of stout, and frying bacon and eggs: the soft voices of my countrymen, even the songs they sang in the saloon, soothed me.

Desolate dignified Dublin in the early hours of the morning. Kingsbridge station, Portarlington first stop, Limerick Junction, strangely enough in Tipperary, then Limerick. The battered old AC motor: the avenue of chestnut trees at Annesgrove, the tiger-skin rugs, the old rocking horse, sweet, lined, welcoming faces. The smell of a sweating horse, wet leather, the old jennet, turf fires burning, hams boiling, bread baking, all as evocative as the smell of paint and linseed oil.

Dash, Beauty, Trixie, Finn, bounded towards me with frenzied greetings. Old Dolly's muzzle under my arm; Slieve Kimalta, the Hill of the Sorrows, mist-enshrouded, from the bedroom window. The vividness of the far-stretching acres at Ballymackey which my ancestors had trod for over three hundred years. Raking the ashes at four in the morning, hot whisky, and talk, talk, talk.

'Would you not stay?'

Would that I could.

———

In London the strange wailing noise of the air-raid siren sounded, monotonously disturbing the stillness, and alarming the blackbirds. Rita Mayer, the German girl, straight away clapped on her gas-mask. The flaps of rubber around her cheeks made loud farting noises as she breathed.

'For heaven's sake, tell her to take it off. There's no gas, and it looks so depressing.'

'I don't know how to say it in German.'

'You were taught by German nuns . . . a year in Vienna . . .'

'But we didn't learn the German for gas and gas-masks.'

'Keinen gas. Nehmen Sie es ab.'

But as long as she stayed with us the gas-mask was put on when the siren went.

My mother and I said that if we were going to be bombed we would like to see what hit us, so we took a whisky and soda into the garden and sat under the beech tree. From time to time Rita's gas-masked head would appear at the window. She looked very sinister. The quiet was menacing, as though the whole of London held its breath. Even the birds were silent.

Was it the same in Paris?

'Let's have another . . .'

The voice made me start, and moving to replenish the glasses, the cheerful noise of the all-clear blew.

All day long the numbness continued. Stories circulated that half London had been destroyed, we were lucky. In fact a civilian plane had arrived from France, unannounced, but owing to censorship we were not to know that for many years. Orders and instructions were relayed at intervals on the wireless, as the radio was then called. Check the blackout curtains; no torches or even smoking in the streets; theatres and cinemas closed; identity cards; rationing details to be given later. Register; volunteer; evacuation of women and children; tighten our belts.

Oh darling, will I never see you again?

Waiting, always waiting. Waiting for news, for buses, for trains, the stations teeming with evacuees going out and coming back. Waiting for bombs that never fell; gas. Waiting for casualties in dreary improvised rooms. Worst of all, waiting in queues: for food, for forms to be filled in, for things that would never happen. The misery of doing nothing, waiting to be told what to do. Maybe.

It became known as the Great Bore War.

As all wars are going to be over by Christmas, everyone tried to live as normal a life as was allowed. With all theatres still closed in London, I went back to being a mannequin in the daytime, with a voluntary war job some evenings. The approaching winter, early darkness and frost, made travelling on the infrequent buses – all services had been cut to conserve petrol – much more exhausting than a full day's work. All young men and women were compelled to register for the forces. New ministries were suddenly opened, to deal with National Service, shipping, blockade, food and propaganda. Old ministries were moved, overnight it seemed, to the West Country or Wales. Many rich people went to their country houses to find them commandeered for the forces or evacuees. Some went to Canada or the United States, for money could still be moved out of England. The Civil Service, never popular with the masses, was having a field day. Uninspiring and sometimes incomprehensible posters, such as 'YOUR resolution will bring US victory', appeared on walls. Social order must be maintained, and we were told to carry with us our gas-masks, read official instructions, and proceed *quietly* with our affairs! The Civil Service's idea of affairs was not mine.

Lord Gort was Commander-in-Chief of the British Expeditionary Force in France; the French garrisoned the Maginot Line. There was no fighting, for the blockade would win the war. All we had to do was wait, presumably as quietly as possible. In December the German pocket battleship *Graf Spee*, which had been raiding cargo ships in the south Atlantic, was fired on and damaged by British ships, then forced into Montevideo harbour where she was scuttled on Hitler's orders. Britannia ruled the waves all right, and Montevideo was a long way away.

About this time in the phoney war I met Yvonne Chudleigh. She was working at the same place as I was, and at first sight we smilingly pussy-footed around each other like cats. In fact, even when I knew her better, she was so unlike me that it was remarkable we got on so well.

For she was a prototype John Betjeman girl: blonde, tall, attractive to look at and devoted to playing tennis. Far from being an intellectual, her close friends called her 'Bonehead'. She deliberately made remarks designed to provoke astonishment and laughter. That was her great charm: warmth, and being basically so sure that she didn't mind making a fool of herself. It made everyone else feel better, not superior, but better and gayer. For of course she was not foolish at all. Although a few years younger than me, she knew exactly what she wanted, and in the nicest possible way went ahead and got it. If she couldn't discuss metaphysical problems with the next man, she could cook a good simple dinner, make excellent and original clothes, and amuse. Yvonne also had that most under-rated of qualities, common sense. She had two brothers, both in their twenties: Neil, who at nineteen married a French women ten years his senior, survived the war in the Royal Air Force, had children, and lived happily ever after; and Derek, who had made a disastrous marriage which had just ended in divorce. When I met him he was working as a journalist, wanted to write a book, but was unable to settle down to it, as he was awaiting his call-up papers.

They all came from Chudleigh in Devonshire, and their ancestor was the famous, or infamous, and beautiful maid-of-honour Elizabeth Chudleigh, who in 1744 had secretly married Augustus John Hervey, afterwards Third Earl of Bristol. When he succeeded to the title, Hervey sought to divorce her. She appears to have been heartily sick of him by then, and to avoid scandal Elizabeth declared herself unmarried and was thus pronounced a spinster by the court. Within a month she had married the Second Duke of Kingston, with whom she had been living, and shocked licentious London society in a number of ways, but particularly by appearing at a ball in a transparent dress with little or nothing on underneath. Kingston died four years later. His nephew, who wished to inherit the money, declared her a bigamist, and Elizabeth hurried back from Rome where she was being received with honour by Pope Clement XIV and was tried in the House of Lords in 1776. She was found guilty but retained the fortune. Thereafter she lived briefly in Calais, then St Petersburg, on an estate which she called 'Chudleigh'. She died in Paris in 1788. There was a little of Elizabeth Chudleigh in all of them.

Yvonne and Derek had a penthouse flat in Chelsea, and were looking for someone to share it with them. Yvonne and I worked together; I was deadly sick of the long bus journeys, and the ticket sorting at home. It was the obvious answer, so for nearly six months we three lived a pleasant and uninhibited life together.

CHAPTER FIVE

In 1939 the small London borough of Chelsea still retained some of the pastoral quality of earlier days. Although the famous eighteenth- and nineteenth-century pleasure gardens of Ranelagh and the Cremorne were no more, old men still talked vividly of them, as though they had closed the year before. Charles II's old hunting lodge was transformed into the Pheasantry drinking club, and that of Henry VIII was a children's kindergarten, but it did not require great imagination to visualize the marshy land running down to the river being inhabited by mallard, snipe and woodcock.

The King's Road on the northern side was named after Charles II, and a dilapidated terrace of houses between Manresa Road and Carlyle Square were said to have been built to house the court mistresses. They stood back from the road, with pretty trees in front, leaning with a drunken air, slightly disreputably to one side.

Chelsea is bounded on the southern side by the Thames, and Sir Joseph Bazalgette's beautiful embankment, interspersed with the Battersea, Albert, and Chelsea bridges, and it is along this stretch that the Royal Hospital was instituted by Charles II at Nell Gwynne's behest, for invalid and old soldiers. The scarlet and blue uniforms are still worn by the pensioners.

In Saxon times it was called Cealchythe, and a synod was held there in 785; in the sixteenth century it was Chelcith, which became Chelsea. For many hundreds of years it attracted writers, painters and craftsmen, and it was perhaps unique in that rich and poor lived side by side.

The tomb of Sir Thomas More, the author of *Utopia*, lies in the close of Chelsea Old Church. In the seventeenth century Chelsea housed the painter Sir John Lawrence, and the poet laureate Thomas Shadwell. The eighteenth century brought the opening of the china porcelain factory, and the famous Chelsea china. Other celebrated inhabitants included the Irish physician and collector Sir Hans Sloane, Francis Atterbury, and Dean Jonathan Swift; Steele and Smollett, who lived in Monmouth House, Lawrence Street; later the painters Turner, Whistler, Rossetti, Sir John Lavery, and the writers Oscar Wilde, Carlyle and Leigh Hunt; Brunel the engineer, and many others.

Sir John Danvers introduced the Italian method of gardening so admired by Francis Bacon, in 1630, and later it was Sir Hans Sloane who gave the land to the Apothecaries Company for the Physick Gardens in Swan Walk.

All over this small part of London, street names commemorate the famous inhabitants: even the telephone exchange was Flaxman, named after one of Josiah Wedgwood's designers.

It was through Derek Chudleigh that I first knew Chelsea, for it was natural that we should be attracted to each other. We were both personable young people with similar interests. He knew a lot about the theatre, and encouraged me. With him I strolled about the pretty streets, past Don Saltero's, the eighteenth-century coffee house on Cheyne Walk, to Paradise Walk, up Tite Street passing Wilde's house, along the King's Road, sometimes drinking beer in pubs like the Markham, the Six Bells with its beautiful bowling green – the click of the woods as the Chelsea pensioners played their weekly game of bowls – down to Boris the delicatessen, a drink at the Cadogan, then across the road to Old Church Street, left into Justice Walk where, ironically, the notorious Judge Jefferies once lived, to emerge in Lawrence Street, with the tall lurching Monmouth House facing, and then to the right, the neat gardens with the statue of Carlyle in his square-topped shoes. Opposite, the spheres of gas-light, no longer lit in the blackout, on the tree-lined embankment; the fast flowing Thames; and the Battersea factories across the river. It had a grandeur and beauty such as I had only seen in Paris. Paris, and all that it had come to mean, I tried not to think about.

Yvonne and Derek made it possible, for indeed the flat was often so crammed with people that it was difficult to think at all. London can be a lonely city, and many residents in large blocks of flats never know their neighbours at all. This was not the case in Chesil Court, for very soon, through Yvonne it must have been, we knew quite a lot of people.

Arthur Barbosa looked like a Portuguese version of the man on the cover of *Esquire*, with shiny black boot-button eyes and a black curled moustache, always elaborately dressed in silk shirts, embroidered waistcoats, curly brimmed hats, and a long black overcoat. He had a vast knowledge of old military uniforms, and painted friezes and murals, using the uniforms in battle scenes. They were meticulous and exquisite. He moseyed about London, finding out what everyone was up to, and had the strange vice of having to start the day with brandy mixed with Moussec, a sparkling wine, sold in small bottles, popular at the time. He was sometimes known as 'King' Barbosa, for his knowledge of uniforms made him the instigator of the King Club. This very exclusive club met once a year: a King and Queen with an entire court were chosen, and all were dressed in the chosen period, when a ball was given. Some of the photographs taken on these occasions were used in Cecil Beaton's amusing spoof book, *My Royal Past*. Alas, the rigours of wartime put an end to this harmless but enjoyable annual entertainment. There was something very endearing about Barbosa.

Barbosa's wife, Rachel, worked in one of the ministries. We were all a bit terrified of her caustic tongue, but she did have good reasons, sometimes. She was called, unwittily, by us, the un-civil servant.

Mechtild Nawaisky was Polish and worked as art editor on *Lilliput* magazine. I unfortunately christened her 'no more whisky', which was shortened to Whisky. She hated this uncharacteristic appellation, and begged everyone to call her Mechtild, but Whisky she was and Whisky she stayed.

There was also James Dowdall, and his wife, Louise. James was a droll-looking Scot with enormous, drooping-at-the-corners brown eyes. I don't know what he did before he went into the Cameron Highlanders, but his father was a judge who spent his time rewriting the Bible, usually while reading the lesson in an Oxfordshire church. Jimmy was an excellent cook, and marvellous aromas of garlic and herbs came from the kitchen. He knew a lot about jazz and jazz musicians, and it was probably through him that we all got to know Arthur Young, whose band played at Hatchett's Restaurant in Piccadilly. Several members of this band had been with the Hot Club de France: Stephane Grappelli, the violinist, and the famous guitarist Django Reinhardt. Other members of this quintet were Tony Spurgeon and Chappie d'Amato.

Arthur Young, with his twinkling blue eyes behind small gold-rimmed spectacles, was more like a huge, blond, jovial doctor than a musician. His wife was an extremely pretty German actress called Karen Verne, who married the film actor Peter Lorre in Hollywood after the war.

Many times after the restaurant closed in the early hours of the morning, the whole band would come back to the flat and play a jam session until it was almost time for us to go to work. There were seldom complaints from the other tenants. That was the best thing about a penthouse.

Yvonne had a retinue of varied young men: from rugger buggers (her phrase) to elegant young officers, some on leave from France. For the first and only time in my life I lived the sort of existence that all only children imagine all big families do, but don't. We danced at nightclubs like The Nest, Coconut Grove and a gorgeous new one called The Suivi which had a pale-blue quilted satin ceiling. With the theatres still closed we enjoyed restaurants like the Café de Paris or Quaglino's, with a floor show, and particularly when it was the superb female impersonator Douglas Byng.

We used adjectives such as 'heavenly', 'divine' and 'marvellous'. We yelled at each other when the last drop of shampoo had been used, the last pair of someone else's stockings laddered, and when the frock *you* wanted to wear was staked by a friend who had come up from the country. The gramophone was on most of the time we were home, and it was always someone else's turn to put the record on. We played Jelly Roll Morton, Benny Goodman, Louis Armstrong, Jack Teagarden, Fats Waller and Red Nichols as we jigged about the flat to 'Honeysuckle Rose', 'Tiger Rag', 'Beale Street Blues' or 'Melancholy Baby'. The modern songs we liked best were 'O Johnny', 'Deep in the Heart of Texas' and 'Beat me Daddy, Eight to the Bar', which had the couplet:

> Now Mr Paganini,
> Don't you be a meanie . . .

Also an excellent song, called 'I Get Along Without You Very Well', which, for obvious reasons, was withdrawn.

The young officers on leave from France brought back presents of scent, or records of Tino Rossi, and of course Jean Sablon:

> Vous qui passez sans me voir,
> Pourquoi?

Derek was not in the least like his sister either in looks or personality: tall, dark-haired, with deep-set brown eyes which completely disappeared when he smiled, which was often; a loose limbed walk, as if he was double-jointed – not conventionally handsome, but attractive, and winning. He was a more introverted person than Yvonne, very even-tempered and extremely kind. He loved women and I think rather enjoyed having several around him. He was not in the least overwhelmed by us, and of course we behaved all the better for his presence. He could be quietly amusing, and we both spent quite a lot of time laughing at, and with, Yvonne. Despite the differences in all our natures, there were no personality clashes. Derek wrote very charming short stories of an allegorical kind, and often in the evenings when Yvonne was out he would tap away at his typewriter, whilst I read or caught up on my sleep. We both enjoyed the books of James Branch Cabell and Thomas Wolfe. Or we would have friends to dinner, and with food rationing becoming stringent, stuff and braise unrationed sheeps' hearts, or make mountains of spaghetti with a rich garlicky sauce. The big L-shaped room, with its balcony overlooking the rooftops of Chelsea and the river, was warm with central heating. The walnut wood piano and the period furniture gleamed invitingly.

Opposite this rather flossy block of flats was an excellent workman's diner.

Bare well-scrubbed tables, dark high-backed settles to sit on, and a good solid meal of hot meat pie, or a 'cut-off-the-joint with veg' for a shilling; sausages, egg and chips, tenpence. It was unpretentious, friendly, and the food was well cooked and sustaining. There was the Blue Cockatoo on Chelsea Embankment when one was feeling flush and able to spend two-and-six on a three-course meal. Old Maggie, the waitress, missed nothing. A young man I knew, dining there with two girl friends he couldn't make his mind up about, lost both of them when Maggie appeared after the meat course, and said pointedly to him:

'Tart or Fool, sir?'

The small neighbourhood shops were usually staffed by their owners or members of the family. They were understanding, and willing to give credit up to a pound, but no more. They knew to a penny what the traffic would bear and didn't want us to get into debt. Vic, of Bullards, and Jack of Jax's Stores: kind, sad-eyed middle-aged men, who had been through the 1914–1918 war, and thought the Jerries still had something up their sleeve. The 'secret weapon' was much speculated on. They had a twinkle in their eyes, and often a rationed can of meat or a packet of cigarettes was smuggled across the counter and into one's bag with a wink.

A horse-meat shop opened in Chelsea Manor Street, called the Continental Butcher. At first it was hardly patronized, but later on when food was very scarce there were queues outside all the way past Jax's Stores, which didn't please Jack any.

Chelsea was still a place for artists to live. Many of the pubs were willing to take a painting they liked in exchange for drinks, and writers or painters were not treated with contempt, or as odd-balls, as happened in most parts of England, but were, in fact, helped and encouraged by the working man, who was proud to share, even vicariously, the traditions of Chelsea life.

At midday on Saturdays and Sundays we usually went to the Six Bells in the King's Road and drank gin and lime, or beer, according to the money we had. Friends knew we would be there and joined us when they felt like it. The saloon was a big, long, high-ceilinged room with the bar running two thirds of the way down. On the other side was the public bar and partitioned off, at the bottom, a billiards room, which had a small hatch through to the bar and the Saloon. Tall glass doors at the end opened out on to the velvety bowling green. There were stools at the old-fashioned, heavy mahogany bar, and small chairs and tables on the left-hand side. The clientele was mixed, but painters like Adrian Daintrey, Mervyn Peake, James Proudfoot, who painted me looking like a large tawny tiger, and the Royal Academician, Egerton Cooper, were nearly always there, as well as writers such as Henry Savage, musicians and actors.

On this Saturday morning we were with Barbosa, Rex Harrison and his agreeable first wife Colette, whom I liked on first meeting but had little chance to know better, as she was mostly with her small son and her family in Cornwall. Her younger sister was a friend of Yvonne's, as they came from nearby the Chudleigh home. Rex Harrison was a friend of Barbosa's. He was rather sleek in those days, with an interesting and distinctive face which somehow reminded me of one of those elegant pedigree cats one sees photographs of at cat shows but never encounters in real life. His conversation was easy, amusing and polished, and it is not difficult to see how the word debonair became the cliché for describing him. I think he certainly encouraged it, and the parts he played opposite Vivien Leigh, especially in *St Martin's Lane*, fostered this image. He gave women the impression that he was sizing them up and filing away for future reference. I only met him a few times, as I think he went into the air force shortly afterwards, but I enjoyed his company. I was also not in the least surprised when, some time later, I heard that the German actress Lilli Palmer had supplanted Colette.

On this clear, cold, winter morning the conversation crackled and hissed like a well-seasoned winter log burning brightly. The war hadn't amounted to much so far, and for us it meant an earlier emancipation from family life. We were young, reasonably uncommitted, except for Derek who was expecting to be conscripted any day. Barbosa's boot-button eyes gleamed and glinted as we talked and laughed about whatever caught our fancy for the moment.

It was nearing closing time. Elbows were jostled, drinks spilt, the pitch of conversation raised, as the frenetic English onslaught on the bar for 'last orders please' took over. I was being pushed from behind, and as I turned angrily round, a pleasantly drawling voice said:

'Well, you do seem to be having a gay time, Pussy.'

CHAPTER SIX

I f this was a novel, it would all be plain sailing from now on, but in my experience nature seldom imitates art. Peter had arrived from Paris two days previously and telephoned my mother, from whom there was no reply. He was obviously pleased to see me, playful and teasing in manner, but preoccupied. It was difficult to find time to see him alone on account of my work on most days as a mannequin, until a merciful attack of tonsilitis gave me a few days off.

He was sitting by the fire in the Six Bells when I went in, and he sprang up, almost running to greet me. He was wearing a long charcoal-coloured riding jacket over dark corduroy trousers. I remarked that he was back in time for the hunting season.

'Hunting?'

'Your jacket. It's what is *de rigueur* for riding to hounds.'

He had no idea what it was, but was attracted by the deep pockets. He could almost go away for the weekend with it. It was somehow comic to see him in riding clothes.

The conversation was on a superficial, bantering level. He kept on saying how much he liked 'my young man', which was unanswerable and offputting. Anthony Powell in one of his *Dance to the Music of Time* novels writes that teasing is a sign of inner misery, and I wish I could have known that then. He enquired about the play I had been in, and I in turn enquired about his painting. Normally a chatterbox, I found it difficult to frame a sentence. He insisted that we drink the expensive Pimm's no. 4, as he said it was a celebration. It was suggested that we had a light lunch at his place. The pattern was the same as the first time I met him, yet I was much more uneasy.

The delicatessen shop was a bit of a disappointment, as all the good things were rationed and neither of us had our books with us. Boris, despite his name, had a very cockney accent, and showed bewilderment when Peter called the homely gherkin *cornichon*, and the black pudding *boudin*. We settled for the cornichons, some little squares of mystery called unattractively 'faggot', potato salad, bread and a carton of cottage cheese.

The room was on the top floor of one of the tall houses in Oakley Street. It was at the back, and looked out on to the large and beautiful garden of Crewe

House. The leafless winter trees made intricate lacy patterns against the pinkish snow-cloud sky. There was a gas fire with a shilling-in-the-slot meter at the side. The room was neat and clean, and on the bed was a spotless, unruffled, heavy white counterpane. In the middle of the threadbare rug was what looked like an old-fashioned carpet-bag lying open, and from it spilled shirts, tubes of paint, several French paper-backed books and a bottle of brandy. On a long table under one of the windows a new, slightly different version of the multi-coloured room painting leaned against the window ledge. A copy of Huysmans's *À Rebours* was on the table. There were no knives or forks, so the meal was eaten by means of a penknife, and the tops of the cartons containing the gherkins and potato salad folded over to form a scoop. The brandy was drunk neat out of a tooth glass. We sat on hard wood kitchen chairs; the gas fire hissed and warmed the room quickly. It was all a little bit eerie, doing similar things in such different surroundings and behaving as though we had just met.

He had come back to England for just so long as it would take him to arrange that his money be sent to France, and to see his friends. Why didn't I come back with him? Hesitantly, I mentioned the war . . . Oh, that made no difference; if one had been living in France, it was quite easy to get back.

'Germans?'

They would never come into Paris. There was the Maginot Line, and everyone knew that they would have done so by now if they were going to. Of course, I did have that young man . . . he could offer me nothing, whereas the young man might marry me.

But I didn't want to marry anyone.

In that case, why not come back? It would take a little while for the bureaucrats to sort things out, and I could think it over. The phrases were said dispassionately, but even so I might have agreed on the spot had I not turned my chair slightly to avoid my legs being burnt by the gas fire. On the back of the door we had come in through hung the most beautiful blue, purple and chartreuse-yellow woman's tweed coat.

Why it should have had such a sudden chilling effect on me I shall never know. But it hung there like a warning signal. Naturally impetuous, it stayed me. What friends? What money? Why hadn't he written? Recriminating, insinuating thoughts crept into my head, but never once did it occur to me to ask to whom the coat belonged. My head ached, and for the first time that day my throat was sore again and my voice husky.

Back at Chesil Court, Yvonne chided me for going out, and made me go to bed. Derek came home and brought me bowls of hot soup. For two days I had a high temperature, and then Yvonne and Derek succumbed. We three groaned and shivered, dragged about in dressing gowns, occasionally administered to by Barbosa, and once surprisingly by Peter, who came and made us some tea, a beverage he heartily disapproved of, and said so. Yvonne's malady turned out to be German measles, so we were all in quarantine. It was one way, for me, of not facing up to the situation.

When we were all better Peter and I met almost every day, usually in the company of other people, but not always. Once or twice he kept apart with a very pretty dark-haired woman, and I thought of 'I like dirty, black-haired women.' This one didn't seem dirty enough, but one never knew. I was always depressingly clean-looking, no matter how hard I tried – like William Blake the poet and painter, whose wife once sharply reprimanded someone for saying that Blake should take more baths by commenting:

'Mr Blake don't dirt!'

It was extremely difficult for a young woman used to a certain amount of adulation from men to understand someone of Peter's temperament. He never made an overt gesture to give me the confidence that he really wanted me. Most of the time I spent with him, I was teased unmercifully, and only when I had lost my temper, and was going, did he say something affectionate as a parting shot. My mixed Irish, Cornish and Russian ancestry didn't understand it, and this made me uncharacteristically shy. Also, although I had lived a lot in England, I was not conversant with Englishmen in love. The banter and the teasing were his version of the 'stiff upper lip', and foreign to me. My roaring ranting crew of a family had few sexual inhibitions, and followed their hearts sometimes to the point of eccentricity.

Peter still fascinated me in many ways, but no matter how close one got to him, he was yet elusive. With his curious nature, it seemed that the ordinary emotions which many people experience were side-tracked, or put aside for a further investigation which might never take place. It could have been that subconsciously we knew, for this particular time in our lives, that we needed each other. We were linked, not by *une grande passion*, but by something that would hold us, even tenuously, together for the rest of our lives.

Perhaps it was that all the old bureaucrats had been sent to the West Country or Wales, for the new bureaucrats didn't take long in making up their minds that it was all right for Peter to go back to France. Quite casually, one day in March 1940, he announced that he was leaving the next day, and that he expected me to follow shortly.

Soon after this Derek was called up and went into the King's Royal Rifle Corps, the Sixtieth it was called, as a rifleman. Quite often I made the depressing, slow train journey down to places like Tidworth, Luggershall, Andover, and

Middle Wallop to see him – endless army huts; thick, chipped china, and Naafi food swimming in grease, which Derek seemed not to mind, so hungry was he from unaccustomed route-marches and other strenuous army training.

Thousands of young men filled these camps, all looking enviously at the ones who had a girl with them. It was a myth of the time that saltpetre or bromide was put in the tea to stop them feeling sexy.

Was it?

Did it?

The small country pubs nearby were filled to standing room only, pints of beer awash on the floors and tables. The anxiety of getting a late pass or, if lucky, an all-night one . . . disagreeable landladies who demanded ration books or identity cards to make certain that 'no immorality was going on under their roof' . . . the smell of sweat; the stench of urinals; rough wool of new uniforms; the noise of army boots walking along the street. Barracks called Jellahabad or Allahabad, so far removed from their musky Eastern counterparts.

'Did you know that the Sixtieth march 120 to the minute?'

'What does that mean?'

'One hundred and twenty paces to the minute.'

'It seems very fast.'

'It is.'

The long journey home on Sunday night, the train filled with twittering girls, giggling about what Charlie or Jack said; women and children, tired and unhappy at leaving their loved ones, wondering how to make do on the curtailed army pay; and the let-down feeling after spending the weekend in such alien and uncomfortable surroundings. What a sigh of relief they must have given when they got home and settled down in an old but comfortable armchair, to listen to Tommy Handley in *ITMA*, or the late news on the wireless.

For the news had become more and more disquieting. Finland had been invaded by the Russians, but on 21 March she conceded to Soviet demands and made peace. 'Arms for Finland' was dropped in favour of an expeditionary force to Norway and Sweden. Chamberlain announced that 'Hitler has missed the bus', whilst Hitler was in fact planning a full-scale invasion of Denmark and Norway timed for 8 April. The recovery of Narvik, the Norwegian port, from which iron ore was shipped to Germany, was the current open secret. Chamberlain's government was uneasy: there were speculations as to whether the Labour and Liberal parties would serve under Lord Halifax or Winston Churchill. On 9 May, Churchill became Prime Minister. The next day Holland and Belgium were invaded by Hitler. On 13 May, Churchill made his now famous speech combining and paraphrasing the words of both Garibaldi in

1849 and Clemenceau in 1917, in which he said:

'I have nothing to offer but blood, toil, tears and sweat . . . What is our aim? I can answer in one word: Victory . . .'

Around 14 May the Germans broke through the allied forces in Belgium at Sedan, which cut off the British Expeditionary Forces, and on 15 May the Dutch army surrendered. Queen Wilhelmina came to England, with her bicycle, and set up her government here.

The war had truly begun: the days of the jam sessions were over. The penthouse was quiet, for the elegant young men were far away, destination unknown, some never to return. Yvonne had fallen in love with a naval officer whom she subsequently married. By then I had already taken the long road back.

In France, Daladier had been replaced as Prime Minister by Paul Reynaud: France and England had agreed not to make a separate peace as the German panzer divisions prepared to launch their attack on France, but there was little to stop them. On 16 May, Churchill was in Paris for one of the many consultations with General Gamelin, who three days later was replaced by Weygand, an elderly general who had served under Marshal Foch. Calais fell after a fierce battle, and Belgium capitulated, thus trapping almost a third of a million men and their equipment. Operation Dynamo, the evacuation of Dunkirk, began on 27 May, when nearly nine hundred British ships of all descriptions, from destroyers to river pleasure-boats, rescued the BEF and many French soldiers. The last men were brought away on 3 June, but fog prevented evacuation from St Valéry, where the entire Fifty-first division was lost. Spirits were low, for there was little force left to defend France: Weygand and the elderly General Pétain talked of an armistice. On 9 June the French government left Paris for Tours and Briare; the next day Italy declared war on France. On the 13th Churchill was again in France, and the French government left Tours for Bordeaux. On 14 June the Germans entered Paris, and Italy invaded the south of France.

The ordinary citizen knew only the barest of these facts, for newspapers were but a single sheet. To many French people it appeared that the British had saved themselves at Dunkirk. That nearly 140,000 French soldiers had been taken off, who formed the nucleus of the Free French army in England, was not known. Rumours slithered about like snakes, and the blazing summer sun, instead of inspiring leisurely holiday thoughts, only increased the feeling of oppression and fear.

Fear affects people in different ways. It is easy afterwards to say, 'I was not afraid' because one acted calmly, but it is surely only the statement of a very insensitive person or a moron. Fear is not cowardice, it is one of the most natural human emotions and manifests itself in many ways. For most people, death is less fearful than, and preferable to, torture or total disablement. Fear is many faceted: it makes the young old, and the old younger; it can cause betrayal, separation and incredible bravery. Physically, it can produce sweating with heat or shivering with cold. Fear is the unknown, and it may be said to have had Paris in its grip on 14 June 1940, when the German army entered that city.

It was through a misunderstanding, and the chaos on the roads outside Paris, that Peter and I were separated. Events happened too quickly for us to know what was going on, and all I knew was that he had gone to pick up his money in Tours. Then we would make our plans when he came back. That the government and other official bodies had left Tours was still a secret. Even early that morning the heat was intense, the pavements shimmering, the air stifling. Everything was closed: no bread or milk, the café on the corner locked up. That huge humming city shuttered itself up and was silent, for even the small amount of traffic seemed noiseless.

Telephone calls; always with no reply. As I was walking along the street to contact some friend, a strong arm covered in black hairs pulled me into a doorway, and a voice muttered, 'Les Boches . . .' as an armoured car drove in the middle of the street, its smiling passengers dressed in field grey. I didn't recognize it as German, never having seen one before, and thought it was a new branch of the French army. All morning I walked like a skulking dog across that city, keeping to the walls or shop doorways. Always the same answer from the concierge:

'They have left.'

K. had also left, but his half-German boy-friend had stayed. In the hallway of the magnificent house on the Ile de St Louis were two bicycles. Upstairs we drank delicious brandy from exquisite glasses.

'We must get away. This morning I saw an armoured car . . .'

'I can't. K. has left me all his belongings. I have never had anything of my own before. Look around at the beauty, the comfort. I can't leave it.'

'But if they arrest you, or shoot you? There are bicycles downstairs.'

'No. I will be safe. I speak German. You go. I have maps and some money for you.'

'Oh, come with me, please, please . . . you won't be safe.'

'Where could we go?'

'Anywhere, away, to Tours, further south; we could perhaps come back.'

'No, I can't leave it all. I will be safe. K. and I were going to take a trip together. I have all the maps and equipment. You take it.'

'Come with me for a few days, and then see . . .'

'No. I will stay and look after his things.'

He produced a light canvas bag and insisted on packing it for me. Had I gone back to my rooms I would have found Peter's message. He came with me on the other bicycle to the Porte de Versailles, and we had a final drink at a café there. Again I tried to persuade him. No. Dear, brave little blond figure, smiling and waving as I set off. Did he live to enjoy his luxury? Who knows?

The city streets were empty, but the country roads were crammed with every available vehicle: hand-carts laden with bundles, old and new cars left on the roadside without petrol. All faces showed anxiety, and sweat poured down people's cheeks like tears. Get out of this confusion, take small roads, go across fields, hurry, go south, anywhere, away from crowds and confusion.

'The world is in a state of chassis': why suddenly think of *Juno and the Paycock*? Why not? Try to remember the names of all the characters. Juno and the Paycock, that's easy. What was the Paycock's name? Doyle, Boyle? Joxer Daly, Mary, Johnny the boring one, Maisie Mulligan – no, something like it, begins with M; Jerry Devine, Mrs Tancred, funny name for an Irishwoman. 'The blinds is down Joxer, the blinds is down!' Maisie Madigan, that's it; Bentham: 'Take away this murdherin' hate . . .' getting too near the knuckle. Think of the lines of the last play you were in: 'Must we have the worst table in the room?' Mother of God, I can't go on talking to myself like this – but it helps, like waking up in the night in the middle of a bad dream, and saying 'think of something nice'. Think of the books you like: all rather depressing ones. Music then: Scarlatti, Vivaldi, Mahler, Mozart of course, except for *Don Juan*: makes me feel uneasy when he's in hell. Hum some of the melodies. Can't go on humming da-di-da-di-di-di-da to myself. I'm very hungry, but for God's sake don't start thinking about food. My bum's sore from bicycling. This damned racing bike's very tiring, all that bending forward. Should be easier if it's for racing. Take away this murdherin' heat . . . my skirt's like a second navy-blue skin.

That postman and his wife were very kind. I've still got some of the bread and sausage left. Their son's trousers fit me perfectly: a bit hot, but much more comfortable on this man's bike. Next time I get to a pair of scissors I'll cut them off and make shorts of them. It's so hot, and I'm so tired. Must be the hottest summer on record. Always talking about the weather like the English. Slieve Kimalta, nice cold Hill of the Sorrows; *bas in Eireann*, death in Ireland: funny thing to have in a drinking toast. *Les anglais s'amuserent tristement* . . . the Irish as well it seems. Who said it? Talleyrand? No, he said about the English having three hundred religions and only one sauce. What sauce? Bread sauce? Mint sauce? That's two already. Bit of a cod, Talleyrand saying that about the sauce; I can think of at least six without trying. Brandy butter? Is it a sauce? Of course it is. One thing I wouldn't like now is Christmas pudding, makes me feel hotter to even think about it.

Where on earth did Peter get to? Not at Donald's flat or at Consuelo's. Hope to God he gets away, he wouldn't be able to cope, just put the Germans' backs up, even more than they are already. My darling, we seem born to be separated. If you were here now the time would go like magic, as we talked or argued. Proust for instance: can't get further than *Swann's Way*, means nothing to me. Much rather have gusty old Joyce. At least Bloom thinks about sex and pigs' kidneys; better than those bloody madeleines and duchesses. I wish T. had come with me. I feel unhappy at having left him. I did try, but he was so set on staying. Perhaps he'll find some German officer who likes him. Hope so. Wouldn't like to be an adolescent queer: bad enough being an adolescent anyway without extra complications tacked on.

I'm more frightened when night falls. Thank God the dawn comes early. The slightest sound is terrifying when it's dark. Why? Pain is worse at night too. Why are we scared of the dark? It can be very cosy and friendly if you're with someone you love. I'll go right on until the last minute of light, and then get up at dawn again. I can lie down somewhere in the heat of the afternoon. Can't cycle then, too hot. Noises all day, sound like cars backfiring: in the night they are always guns, no matter how hard I try to stop thinking so. Fear stops you feeling sexy. Good thing at present. Oh please dear Mother of God help me to get to Bordeaux soon. Don't pray just because you're frightened, it doesn't count. Think of all the millions of people praying right now: must be like a blocked telephone exchange. How peaceful it was lying on that old haystack staring up at the blue, blue sky, the colour of flax flowers, the sweet smell, and the friendly crackly sound it made when I moved. I felt safe for the first time when I saw that aeroplane fly over, until I saw the swastika painted on the side. Did I imagine it? Didn't wait to check. Couldn't see my arse for dust as they say in England. How many days have I been going? Nine, ten? I'm a lovely golden brown, for the first time ever. Suntan with tears. As long as I live I'll never forget the trees of France. Poplars, plane trees, and those trees pruned in that funny bunchy way. What's the word for it? Pollarded. There was a fat brown mare lying dead under one; she was just like dear old Dolly. A belly full of lead instead of a furry, gawky foal inside. That must have happened during the machine gunning which at first I thought was a hail storm.

Bordeaux, bordeaux, bordeau, bordea, borde, bord, it makes the wheels go round faster. *Enfin*, Bordeaux. Go to the biggest hotel, that's what your father always said, if you're broke or in trouble. Beautiful city: Place de l'Opera, not much activity, but a few people. What do I say? 'Ou est l'Ambassade de Grande Bretagne?' Sounds like a sentence from an old-fashioned phrase book. Wish there was an Irish Embassy.

'Ou est l'Ambassade . . .'

'Gone? But where . . . when?'

'Angleterre.'

Sit down and think what to do. At least you're not alone here but you must look odd: frayed cut-down trousers, sweaty, hair nearly white with sun, shoes white with dust which is burnt on. Ask more questions. Find out something. Go all over, make a nuisance of yourself. St Jean de Luz. What's there? A ship. How on earth do I get there? Find the road out of Bordeaux: look at T.'s map. It's like lavatory paper now with creases; wish they'd make them so they fold properly. Soldiers: smile – girls are supposed to smile at soldiers.

'My papers?'

'Yes, here . . .'

'Wait.'

'Why? I have to find my husband – no, lover, father, son, brother. Please, please.'

I thought he'd never let me go. Kept staring at my passport as though it held the key to hidden treasure. Expected to have the red carpet laid out for me in Bordeaux. Thought Donald Maclean and I would have that blow-out at the Chapon Fin, and I'd be treated like a bloody heroine. Instead of which sore bike bum again. At least I'm away from the Germans – didn't realize I'd been just that bit ahead of them. Good thing I didn't know. When you get to St Jean de Luz make straight for the port. Not far now.

Oh the joy, the exquisite joy of having arrived. The quay is crowded. Comforting blue-suited officials actually worried about me. Park your bicycle, go and have a drink, but for heaven's sake don't miss the boat. Talk to someone, instead of to yourself.

People hung about in groups, standing up, holding their limited possessions. They seemed hardly to talk to each other, so weary were they. Weary from worry as much as physical tiredness, and many were English: middle-aged couples who had probably retired and come to live in France. There they stood under the scorching sun waiting to be told what to do. Conversation was limited to polite replies to unanswerable questions, for no one knew anything for certain. I wandered about with my hold-all slung over my shoulder feeling lost and alone without my bicycle. It had become my friend, the recipient of many confidences during the long journey. It was difficult to see through the knots

of people, so I weaved through them towards the sea. Occasional phrases in
English made me smile:

'Oh, Jennifer, you can't want to go again . . .'

'Yes I do, Mummie.'

Anna Wickham's poem which starts 'O give me back my rigorous English
Sunday' flitted across my mind. Well, they would soon be enjoying it.

A group of Basque fishermen, strong and sturdy like bronzed Welshmen,
stood talking and gesticulating by one of the bollards. I moved nearer to avoid
the glum groups. A large red-bearded man was sitting on the ground, his back
resting against the bollard, waving a bottle and laughing. This seemed more
jolly, so I went closer. I edged round the fishermen and approached him from
the side.

'Well, you do seem to be having a gay time, Peter.'

He jumped so, that I thought he would roll off into the sea. He beamed, the
red whiskers twitching up like a pleased tom-cat.

'Oh, Pussy, you are clever to arrive on my birthday.'

It was 26 June.

Later that night we embarked. The smell of kippers and boiled cabbage on
the ship was as strong as in an English theatrical boarding house, and never was
it more welcome. With three bottles of Pernod exchanged for our bicycles, we
sailed early in the morning, after a terrifying strafing by German planes, on the
perilous journey back to the comparative safety of England.

CHAPTER SEVEN

We arrived at Southampton looking like a road-show version of Svengali and Trilby, with a smack of an out-of-season Peter Pan thrown in. There were two queues: one for British citizens and one for aliens. Peter, as a French resident, went in the aliens' queue and I the other. He got ten pounds and a camelhair overcoat made for a giant, for even with his six feet three inches it came down to his ankles: a curious gift with the temperature in the eighties, but it was to come in useful later on. I got my passport stamped and a push in the backside from Jennifer who was behind me. No doubt she wanted 'to go again'.

At Waterloo I swapped a few French cigarettes for the twopence to phone my mother. After a preliminary remark to the effect that bad pennies usually return, she was glad to hear from me.

'Are you alone?'

'No.'

'Well, I suppose you'd better both come out. If Rita isn't there, the key is in the usual place.'

As we had no English money we took a taxi, stopped at a bank near my mother's house, and tried to change our francs. There wasn't any call for them, so we got rather short shrift until I got the manager. On promise of repayment, he lent me ten pounds, a large sum in those days, which was very kind of him, especially as at that particular moment I had no way of repaying. But I didn't bring that up.

Jason, the dog, was delighted to see me. He sniffed suspiciously and growled around Peter's ankles, but then he was that kind of dog. Even the cat stretched, yawned, winked at me and extended a condescending paw. Boy Boy was the nicest cat we ever had. Rita was out. I rang my grandmother, who said she would send my aunt's housekeeper Mrs Hayhoe over with a bottle of whisky. My grandmother was a great believer in the powers of a bottle of whisky. Mrs Hayhoe went back with the story that my mother had someone staying there who 'put her in mind of Edward VII'. Peter seemed very nervous. I suppose it was the idea of 'mother': everyone's dumpling, apple cheeks withal.

My mother was in her middle forties, but looked much younger. Her great asset was that she was unshockable and loved being amused, especially by men.

For something over twenty years she had worked at a clinic founded by my grandmother at the turn of the century in the slums of London, and she said that nothing that human beings did, either good or bad, could surprise her. At this time she was also working several nights of the week at a first-aid post, after which she had a long journey home. No wonder she wanted to relax and be amused when she got there.

Peter thought she was very beautiful and said so frequently. For some time I thought he was going to make the remark that had dogged me since I was six: 'She'll never have half the looks of the mother', but thank God he avoided it. They got on well together, despite the difference in their outlooks. In an attempt to find Peter some clothes left by former male members of the family, I unearthed several sequined or beaded shifts – the only word I can use – worn by my mother in the early twenties. Peter insisted we put them on, and on a hand-wound gramophone we played scratchy records of 'Bye Bye Blackbird', 'Black Bottom Stomp' and 'See Me Dance the Charleston'. My mother's attempt to teach Peter the Black Bottom and the Charleston made me laugh so much that I had to go and stand in the hall. Even today the thought of it produces that giggly feeling in my stomach. Rita Mayer's huge sad eyes, with the tragedy of centuries in them, boggled as we jigged and Charlestoned around, carpets flung back, until we were exhausted. One day Peter started to mow the grass. My mother said:

'Do stop him, he doesn't look right doing that.'

Friends called when they heard I was home, and of them all Peter liked Sophie the best. Sophie was not her real name, but Peter called her that, as he said she had a face such as one would find on a Victorian cameo, and Sophie she still is. We had known each other since we were five years old, and she liked being with me because, as she said, 'there was always trouble about'. We were both brought up by our grandmothers, but Sophie also had to contend with two maiden aunts, one with the glorious name of Zenobia, and a maiden great-aunt, in the same household. It was a bit oppressive for a young child, which is no doubt why she liked my trouble-finding proclivities, for by herself she had a passive nature.

Her grandfather, Mr Warren, and my grandfather Theodore Andrew, dressed in morning suits, high hats and canes, went for a stroll with the dog, Mick, each morning. This was in the middle twenties. No one quite knew where they went until Mick gave them away. My grandmother and I were out shopping one morning when we saw Mick sitting outside a pub called The Haymaker, quite a distance from where we lived. It was beneath Grandma's dignity to go in, and unthinkable to send me. A beery customer came out.

Quick as a trice Grandma said:

'Do you know who this poor dog belongs to? I think it's lost.'

'Not a bit of it, Ma . . . that's old Mick, Mr Warren's dog. The guvnor's inside as he is every morning, God bless him. Old Mick has his arrowroot biscuit reg'lar: won't give us no peace till he gets it. Good boy Mick.'

Mick wagged his tail half-heartedly and looked sheepishly at us.

My grandfather, when taxed with this outrageous deceit, said that it was the best place to discuss theological problems that interested them both. They couldn't do it at home, as there were too many women about! My grandfather never really liked dogs after that.

Sophie was still living with the maiden aunts: Mick, grandfather, grandmother and great-aunt Anna were all dead, but it didn't make the big old house any more cheerful. She was dying to get away and find some trouble of her own – at which, as it turned out, late-starter notwithstanding, she became adept. We decided to share a flat in Chelsea together, and in order to facilitate my finding one, Sophie being at work all day, Peter suggested we would meanwhile put up at the Cavendish Hotel in Jermyn Street. It all sounded rather grand, and I couldn't see how we would afford to live in such an expensive district, but with Peter one asked no questions.

———

Much has been written, and even more spoken, about Rosa Lewis who owned the Cavendish Hotel. She was unknown to me, and if I had read Evelyn Waugh's *Vile Bodies*, I did not for a moment think that the character of Lottie Crump had a real-life counterpart.

Jermyn Street, running parallel to Piccadilly, is narrow and discreet, and was then almost unchanged in outlook since Edwardian days. That is, it catered entirely for men: Mrs White still made the best men's hats (my father frequently sent from Tipperary for them); Paxton and Whitfield were the finest grocers for delicacies that men enjoyed, and had the largest stock of cheeses in London; there were various shops for boots, ties, cravats, socks, and silk scarves; expensive jewellers, and antique shops with *objets d'art* to please the most discriminating or exacting mistress; apartments, called chambers, for men only, and if all else failed, Fortnum and Mason's side entrance on the corner, where you could get kitted out for game-hunting in darkest Africa.

Strolling up from St James's, the Cavendish was on the right-hand side, a pleasant brick building with a front entrance like a private house, a discreet brass plate with the name at the side. Inside, the Edwardian atmosphere continued. The hotel was run entirely for men: women generally, unless they were titled, were only tolerated because men liked to have them around. I don't think Rosa thought much of modern girls: she said they only came in to have a pee and pick someone up. At this time she would have been in her seventies: tall, erect, with silver-white hair, a ruddy complexion devoid of any make-up, and penetrating large blue eyes with as much warmth in them as a seagull's. She was always dressed in a long-skirted suit, cut like a riding habit, in various colours, with a white cambric man's handkerchief knotted around her neck.

Stories about her were copious and conflicting. She had been Edward VII's mistress – or was it her mother? – Lord Ribblesdale's, or Sir William Eden's; or a French duke's. Her mother had been cook to a French nobleman, and Rosa as a pretty girl, in this aristocratic household, had . . . The most likely was that as a young girl she had married a dull Welshman called Lewis, and they had separated. She then trained a troupe, if that is the right word, of pretty girls to serve at the tables of the rich, she being responsible for the food. The truth does not matter. Whatever Rosa's early life had been, it had given her an undying love for the aristocracy and their way of living. Champagne was drunk all day long, and most of the night too, for Rosa never went to bed if there was a party on. When she slept is a mystery, for she was about first thing in the morning. There were always at least six or eight 'regulars', one usually being a rich American of impeccable family, whom she had met, or his father, at one of the grand houses before the 1914–1918 war, or on her visit to the United States in the 1920s.

Ex-kings were especially welcome, as were dashing young blades of good, preferably noble, family. In fact 'blades' were expected to be dashing and were cold-shouldered if they were not. After Evelyn Waugh had immortalized her in *Vile Bodies*, a portrait which did not amuse her, writers were allowed only under scrutiny, and anyone she disliked was referred to as a writer and usually asked to leave. Painters, on the other hand, were both liked and encouraged, and if they were knighted or honoured, like her special friends the Irishman William Orpen, Alfred Munnings or Augustus John, so much the better.

It was not an hotel in the ordinary sense of the word, although there were many innocents who haphazardly chose it to stay in. I often wondered what they made of it. For Rosa was a Robin Hood of hoteliers. The rich got very large bills, and the poor none at all. Rosa decided who could pay and who couldn't, and there was no use arguing with her for you would be told, in the fruitiest cockney, to get out. Like a true Edwardian, her conversation was pungent and spiced with references to tarts, backsides and chamber pots. The servants, if such they can be called, were varied, and led by Moon, an extremely old, bent headwaiter, porter, odd-job man, who was reputed to have been the Duke of Blank's butler in former days. He was so slow and so deaf that it was pointless to ask for anything. You got what he thought you should have. I once asked for some brown bread and butter and after half an hour was given a large brandy. There were several elderly, bearded housemaids, dressed in nineteenth-century clothes, and a young boy, his face shining like lard, wrapped in an enormous green baize apron. He had no name, but answered to 'Cheeky'. The one who did most of the work was called Charles Ingram, and he was unmercifully teased by Rosa. There was also Edith, or Edie. I didn't know quite what her function was: small, shy, brown-haired, with eyes like a partridge, she was usually to be seen carrying round, and consulting, a large heavy ledger – no doubt trying, with Sisyphean labour, to balance the books. Rosa for many years had a succession of West Highland white terriers, all called Kippy. There was a small marble slab low down on the wall near the floor, in the main room, known as the Elinor Glyn, commemorating the death of the last one. It had been the dog's favourite place for lifting his leg. There was another one of these slabs outside the front door. The main dish served went under the name of Game Pie, but the nearest it got to that in wartime was rook. This was always on the go, and served for breakfast, lunch and dinner. I only once had a change of breakfast diet: it was a chunk of smoked haddock, which tasted like fish flannel, and I was glad to go back to the unspecified game pie.

Having two very strong-minded grandmothers, I had had a little experience in handling self-willed old ladies. For several days we both watched each other, and although I was technically staying in the hotel, I was not yet wholly accepted by Rosa. One morning, grudgingly, she said:

'You're quite a nice girl, not like that saucy tart Francesca: go and put your name down in the hall.'

For there had been no signing of the hotel register on arrival. At the Cavendish you signed when you left, like a visitors' book in a private house. I was very glad, for if Rosa took one of her unpredictable dislikes to you there was no way of getting round her. To put it mildly, 'you had had it'.

It was impossible at any hour of the day or night to creep in without Rosa spotting you, for her sanctuary was a medium-sized room just inside the front door on the right as you came in. This resembled the comfortable study of a man of varied interests but little intellectual ability: leather armchairs, Rosa's winged armchair, a desk, heavy pieces of furniture of mixed antiquity, the walls plastered with signed portrait photographs, sporting prints, caricatures by 'Spy', yachting pictures, vintage motor-cars, old and young men riding or leading in the winners of well-known races. The regulars spent most of the time in this room, only moving to the Elinor Glyn at the back of the hotel at night, if there was a party. This weird collection of an old lady's life interested me, and I spent some hours looking at it. I was, therefore, both surprised and delighted to see a photograph of my father leading in his horse, Victor Noir.

'That's Adam . . .'

Rosa was behind me, champagne bottle in hand.

'What's that to you, Miss Christabel?' Rosa always called me that, for she never bothered to remember anyone's name, preferring to christen them herself.

'He's my father!'

Rosa was delighted to be able to give me a label. Most of her introductions were in the nature of Lord What's-his-name, Lady Thingummy, Pullman (Pulham) who-takes-all-the-photographs; Lulu Waugh (Evelyn Waugh) who-writes-all-the-books. Now it was Miss Christabel, whose father-owns-all-the-horses. Elderly mahogany-faced gentlemen would sidle up and ask me for racing tips, for most of the regulars were great gamblers. Rosa too liked her daily flutter. I hated to think that their fortunes were made or lost by my haphazard predictions, but they were so insistent.

Once Rosa had been able to place me I was guarded like an Infanta. For Miss Christabel, although I did not know it at the time, was not a very friendly appellation. There had been a lawsuit regarding paternity in the 1920s, and one of the protagonists was Mrs Christabel Russell. A jingle of the time was:

I'm Mrs Russell's baby,
Blue eyes and curly hair,
I'm looking for my Daddy,
All over Leicester Square.

This rhyme I learned subsequently from my father, who was enchanted to hear of my brief connection with Rosa Lewis. For all the high jinks at the Cavendish, Rosa had quite a strict moral code. It was all right to 'carry on' if you were unmarried, but any sign of rumpling the 'sanctity of the home' was treated very roughly. A newly married young Guards officer on leave, with his young wife pregnant in the country, was pursued by Francesca, or someone like her. She was told loudly and firmly in front of us all:

'Get your fat tart's arse out of my house.'

On another occasion, hearing one man say to another, 'May I speak to your wife?', Rosa misheard it as, 'May I sleep with your wife?', and the trio were out sharply, without realizing why.

At this stage of the war, after Dunkirk and the fall of France, anyone whom

Rosa liked was given the kindest of welcomes. With vivid memories of the earlier, bloody war, she became hostess to endless children of the fathers and mothers she had known in the past. Frequently she mixed them up, and addressed them by their parents' names, but there was a jeroboam of champagne, called a cherrybum by Rosa, to speed them on their way. Edie usually retired to bed about midnight, taking the ledger with her. One morning at about three o'clock, Rosa went off to the dispensary to get another cherrybum. Her old handsome face was flushed, and she looked tired, so I followed, thinking I could at least carry back the wine. In the dim, torch-lit dispensary she was bending over with her back to me, pouring one bottle through a funnel into another. A harmless enough deception in the early hours of the morning, especially as the source of champagne from France had been cut off. She turned, saw me and spat out:

'Get out of here, you bloody little spy.'

'Rosa dear, I only came to help you carry back the bottle. I promise you . . .'

'All right, all right, don't make a song and dance about it. Hold this bloody torch.'

From then on we were in league, and many times thereafter I heard the crisp voice saying:

'Come on, Miss Christabel, get off your backside and fetch another bottle.'

For Peter and me it was like being on leave, after the gruelling journey through France with fear and apprehension as travelling companions. Although we were outwardly gay, there were times of deep depression. Peter had only the rag-bag jumble of clothes he stood up in. All his possessions and paintings he had had to leave behind, and the sole prospect was conscription into one of the forces, to which he was violently opposed. The only sure work for an actress was with ENSA, entertaining the troops. I would willingly have done this, but my talents did not lie in singing or dancing, which were what was wanted. Peter worried about his friends in France, especially those who had already been pronounced 'decadent' by the Germans, such as Max Ernst and Giacometti. For this reason he was always delighted when English people he knew turned up, which they often did in the evenings at the Cavendish, for entertainment was limited at this stage of the war – all cinemas being closed by nine o'clock at night (there was just time to see *Gone with the Wind* if one went in after lunch), likewise the few theatres like the Windmill which ran a non-stop girlie show. They were a marvellously assorted mixture of people: amongst them the handsome Hamish Erskine, soon to be reported missing; outrageous, delicious, homosexual sauce-box Brian Howard, on whom Evelyn Waugh modelled his characters Ambrose Silk in *Put Out More Flags* and Anthony Blanche in *Brideshead Revisited*. Brian joined the air force in his forties, as an aircraftsman, and when asked by a pompous air force officer in the Ritz Bar for his name and number, replied:

'My name is Mrs Smith!'

I was always very fond of Brian, also his young Irish friend Sam Langford, who came from Tralee, and I delighted Rosa by calling him 'The Rose of Tralee'.

Dashing Lord Shimi Lovat – who, kilted, and with bagpipes playing, led the commando raid on Dieppe in 1942 – was another of the regulars.

Witty Daphne Bath, gentle and tender as only big women, in every sense of the word, can be, seemed goddess-like to me. She was one of Rosa's 'specials', for Rosa had cooked for her grandmother, Mrs Harry McCalmont, when she entertained the Prince of Wales, later Edward VII, at her country house. Now Daphne Fielding, she has written an enchanting book, *The Duchess of Jermyn Street*, about the life and times of Rosa Lewis.

And there was Crabbe: his first name was Lionel, but he was always called Crabbe. He looked like a younger, more genial version of the sailor on the Player's cigarette package. He was at this time an AB in the navy, dressed in bell-bottomed trousers, and was most engaging; quite small, but so perfectly in proportion that he didn't look a short man. He seemed delighted that Peter had a girl who was looking after him, as he put it, and kept telling me that he had bought an early Pulham painting of which he was very proud. A little before this he had come into a small inheritance which he had decided to blow on a celebration at the Cavendish. Of course, he well overspent it, and Rosa in one of her unpredictable moods had made him seriously work off the debt. This he did for several weeks with good humour. Many times later he came to Chelsea to visit us, and it was always a special treat to see him, for he was bold, brave and amusing. He survived the war, but disappeared in April 1956, when he was last seen diving as a frogman under the *Ordzhonikidze*, the Russian cruiser, during the visit of Bulganin and Khruschev to England. The Cavendish was a very romantic house. There were endless passages all leading to the same place, and many suites (I never saw a single room), which were very charming. Besides the old-fashioned huge bath-tubs, where the supply of hot water was capricious, the rooms were crammed with furniture of all descriptions, for Rosa was a great collector. She had a large Daimler motor-car, and for many years had resolutely attended auctions of the houses of the nobility. She was an emotional buyer and bought indiscriminately. With the war on, and many rich families abandoning their London houses, which were often used as offices, Rosa felt it her duty to buy up as much as she could. She was always delighted with her purchases.

As my main object in moving into central London had been to find a job and a flat, I was out most of the day, on those days when there hadn't been too many cherrybums the night before. As often happens, on this particular day I had found both, was utterly exhausted, and crept past Rosa's parlour to my room. At first I thought I must have mistaken the number, for as I opened the door it only went halfway. I groped for the light switch, and was confronted with a staircase. For a moment I thought I had lost my reason and went out to check the room number. I sat down in the corridor, wearily wondering whether I had the energy for the Elinor Glyn that night. Dammit, no, I said to myself, walk up the stairs and see what happens. So I walked up the staircase, round the corner, down the other side and eventually found my bed. The next morning when I awakened, there was Rosa sitting on the top half of the staircase with my breakfast tray (game pie again) on her lap.

'What d'you think of it? Beautiful carving isn't it? Got it cheap from Lord What's-his-name's town house.'

Dear Rosa, how many hundreds of people she must have cheered in her life. Given them a welcome taste of lotus-eating and gaiety, even the grandchildren of her original friends. She stayed at the Cavendish all through the war, leaving only for a few days to stay at a nearby hotel when the Cavendish was twice badly bombed during the Blitz. On each occasion a hamper of champagne accompanied her. A few times she went to the air-raid shelter at the Ritz Hotel, but generally, as did many elderly people, she preferred to stay in her battle-scarred home, until the last year of the war, when severe illness made her go to a nursing home. But this was not to Rosa's liking, and she was back in a few weeks, with a new 'Kippy', the fourth terrier in succession. She died peacefully in 1952, aged eighty-five, at her beloved Cavendish.

When I unpacked my small amount of luggage in the new flat, there was, snuggled in a spotless white napkin, a cherrybum.

Requiescat in pace.

CHAPTER EIGHT

The flat was in King's Mansions, Lawrence Street, Chelsea, a block built about 1910 which ran from Justice Walk to a small pub with a garden, the Crossed Keys. It had four medium-sized rooms and was fully, if drably, furnished. Rents had dropped considerably owing to the evacuation of many people to the country, so for this 'mansion' flat we paid two pounds a week. Reasonable enough – but the most Sophie or I could hope to earn a week, working a nine-hour day and Saturday mornings, was four pounds in a regular job. Temporary work was slightly better paid, but it was chancy. Photographic modelling at two to three pounds a day was almost non-existent, as all paper was rationed: the few magazines published were extremely slender, and newspapers consisted of a single folded sheet. When this temporary work turned up it was always a great temptation to take it and plead illness, but the day's pay was docked from the weekly pay packet unless you had been working with the firm for a year.

Peter couldn't paint as he had no money to buy canvas, brushes or colours. Sophie and I would go to Green and Stone's, the artists' shop, in the King's Road on Saturday afternoons and buy him a tube of paint or a brush between us, so that he could build up a little stock. For this reason many of the pictures he painted then are in monochrome. Once he took some money from the joint housekeeping to buy a tube of viridian green. He said he couldn't resist it, and would live on bread and garlic until he had made up for it. The garlic was the remains of a large bulb he had brought from France. The last clove I planted in a wooden box: it flourished, so for the rest of the war we had a small but continuous supply. All available pieces of wood or hardboard were commandeered to paint on, and two rather gloomy Victorian paintings already in the flat were treated and painted over, as were second-hand pictures bought for a shilling or so in one of the many Chelsea junk shops. Canvas was both expensive and scarce. My mother bought him a second-hand easel which lasted for over twenty years.

At this time we were told to expect an invasion and to stock up our larders accordingly. This was difficult for people with limited incomes like us, for tinned food was expensive, often at black-market prices, when unrationed. We were always hungry for the rations were meagre. One person's weekly rations consisted of one ounce of butter, four ounces of margarine, one ounce of cheese, and between one shilling and one and threepence worth of meat, with a few rashers of bacon. One egg weekly in summer; the winter was unpredictable. Egg powder, that is dried powdered egg, was expected to make up the deficit. The small amounts of sugar (½ lb) and tea (¼ lb) we often swapped, illegally, for cheese which was of the uninteresting 'mousetrap' variety, and best made into Welsh rarebit with a little beer. Tinned fish and meats were on a points system, so many points being allocated each month. A tin of stewed steak or corned beef took two thirds of the allowance. Unless you were pregnant, or a child, milk was only two and a half pints per person a week. Vegetables and fruit were ration-free, but limited and seasonal (in 1941 I queued for an hour to get onions from the greengrocer). Fish was also unrationed, but with mines and U-boats at large it wasn't plentiful, and sometimes didn't seem all that fresh. Chicken was expensive and kept 'under the counter' (a current phrase) for good customers. Technically all offal was free, but as the war progressed it was difficult to find. When I remarked to the butcher that all the animals seemed to be born without tongues, tails, hearts, kidneys, livers or balls, he winked at me, a great arm went under the counter, and he flung up a half-frozen oxtail. I had never cooked one before, but even today I can taste the thick gravy and see our grease-spattered lips as we chewed on the bones. Unrationed rabbit was the salvation for many people in a low-income group. I made big jellied pies with a scrap of bacon and onion; braised rabbit in dark beer with prunes, which made it taste vaguely like pheasant; or with cider and tomatoes; or with curry spices or paprika; or stuffed and baked rabbit, when we would pretend it was chicken; and if it was very young, Peter would joint it, and we would fry it in a crisp batter. Frying was quite difficult, as lard was rationed and olive oil only obtainable at a chemist on a doctor's prescription, so sometimes we were reduced to liquid paraffin. At least we didn't suffer from constipation! Another 'filler' was pasta, which could be bought freshly made in Soho; rice disappeared as the war went on, and even in Chinese restaurants spaghetti cut to look like rice or pearl barley was served. Housekeeping was made more difficult by the hours spent in queues. Local shopping was done by Peter, who became very good at it – except for the butcher, who gave me bigger cuts, so I bought the meat on Saturday afternoons. I also spread the ration books over different shops, for each one would give a mite over, which added up on three books. Indiscriminate shopping where you saw the best food was not allowed, for you registered at a certain shop, and it involved great bureaucratic difficulties to get the book changed. Soho was still well stocked, and Sophie or I would dash down in our lunch hour for coffee beans, smoked fish, pasta, or herbs and spices with which to dickey up the monotonous fare.

My mother would come over some weekends with tins of food 'for the invasion', also packets of dried milk powder. Little did she know we were so hungry that often she had hardly got to the top of the road before we had eaten them, usually out of the tins. The milk powder we didn't quite know what to do with, so that was our only invasion hoard. We didn't complain, because it was the life we wanted to live, and we had hardly known about housekeeping under any other circumstances. For those who took the challenge, it produced good, imaginative cooks who, once the war was over, felt they were in clover.

Even with these limitations we entertained frequently. Peter's heart was still in France, so he would describe French dishes vividly to Sophie and me and we would try to emulate them from his description, for at that time he was no cook himself. One of our first guests was the young diplomatist Donald Maclean. Until the fall of France he had been a secretary at the British Embassy in Paris, and enjoyed the company of the writers, painters and their friends who met regularly in the Café Flore. He was particularly kind to Peter, for when the Embassy moved from Paris during the German advance, and Peter was undecided about leaving, he left him his apartment in the rue Bellechasse, the rent having been paid beforehand. He had found us again through Isabel Delmer, later wife of the conductor and composer Constant Lambert, who sometimes referred to her as 'barmaid at the Mermaid'. Isabel was extremely striking to look at, with a strong, beautifully moulded face, large brown eyes full of mobility, and long dark hair worn straight. She was the model for Epstein's *Isabel*, which portrait bronze is like her in both character and looks. She had verve. Peter had a lot in common with her, for they were both painters. Isabel was married to the journalist and writer Sefton Delmer, but I think by this time they had separated, for I never saw them together. Constant Lambert's description of Isabel sums her up succinctly: 'drawing corks, nudes, and conclusions'.

The hot summer had continued through August, so that Donald and Isabel were able to sunbathe on the roof of King's Mansions. I was still working, therefore Peter had asked them to lunch one Saturday. Isabel had a previous engagement.

Donald was then about twenty-seven years old, boyish looking mainly due to his slimness and immense height, for with his six feet five inches he dwarfed even Peter. He was not particularly boyish in manner, as he could talk well on a variety of subjects, and had a pleasant but not overpowering sense of humour. His excellent manners put everyone at their ease, and Sophie, who sometimes felt out on a limb with some of our friends, took to him at once, for his attitude to women was friendly and uninhibited. Light brown hair fell slightly over one side of his forehead, above the handsome face with a cleft chin and full lips, which nevertheless had a hint of Scottish doggedness about it.

He was delighted we had survived the collapse of France, and as pleased with our new flat as we were. The wine he brought went well with the meal, and we talked naturally and easily about all the things that appealed to us. For there was no need for Donald ever to hide his feelings in our company, and this he knew. We seldom discussed politics because we weren't particularly interested in them, but his outlook always seemed to be, at the most, humanitarian, rather than dogmatic. He wanted to know what Peter was painting: there was very little, owing to the difficulty of buying materials. This he sensed, without being told, and at some time during the day he pressed several pounds into my hand, to 'surprise Peter', as he put it. He was remarkably sensitive and thoughtful for a man of his years. Yet, for all his easygoing nature, he gave the impression of having strength of mind and tenacity.

This warm afternoon early in September as we sat over the luncheon table with our coffee, looking out of the window on to the clock tower of Chelsea Old Church, he talked of his young American wife, Melinda. Neither Peter nor I had at that time met her, for although they were married in Paris, she had (I think) gone back to her family in the United States when it looked as though France would become a battlefield. But she was coming back quite soon, and he was looking for somewhere for them to live, and then we must come to dinner. He waxed so enthusiastic over her that Sophie, who found him very attractive until then, could bear it no longer, and went and did the washing up, for he was obviously very much in love.

I brought out the coffee cups, and as I walked along the hall, there was a ring at the front door, which I answered. In the dim passageway stood a medium-sized, slightly pear-shaped young man, in a tweed overcoat several sizes too big for him, and a green pork-pie hat. He had prominent tawny-agate eyes like marbles, in a round cherubic face.

'Is this Mr Pulham's residence?'

It was said in a rather uneasy, plummy voice which didn't suit the clothes, and the combination made me wary, for he had, or so it appeared to me, the plausible manner of a debt collector.

'What name shall I say?'

'Mr Thomas.'

Peter said it was a bore; he didn't know anyone called Thomas, but as he hadn't any debts in this country, he might as well see him. I went back to give Sophie a hand, and immediately Peter called us, and there were sounds of chuckling.

'Pussy, do hurry up, it's Dylan.'

I had not met Dylan Thomas, although I had heard about him from Peter, and was familiar with his poems in *Horizon* magazine. He had come, reluctantly, to London to look for work; Caitlin, his wife, had gone with the baby to stay with Dylan's mother and father in Wales. There was nothing like enough money to support them all in London whilst he found a job. How he discovered Peter I shall never know, for the idea of my taking the almost penniless Dylan for a dun obscured such questioning. Fantasies were built around the character of 'Dylan the dun', until eventually he became larger than life and burst, but by then we were all in a rollicking mood, for Dylan had that marvellous quality of being able to invest any character with comedy when he felt like it. He said it gave him fresh heart in his quest for work. We were very relaxed and happy; his fertile imagination had captured us all.

It was around five o'clock, the wine was all gone, and we began to think of going out for drinks at a pub. The air-raid siren had sounded a little earlier, but a warning about a week previously had amounted to very little, so we took no notice. It was, after all, still daylight. Out in the street, the sun was setting, and there was a faraway drone of aeroplanes and the sound of anti-aircraft guns. We decided to go to the King's Head and Eight Bells, a small pub on Chelsea Embankment, instead of the Six Bells. As we turned the corner there was in the sky a monstrous tower, looking like a giant puffball of smoke, away to the east. Even though it was too far off, the density of it made one's nostrils twitch with the imagined smell. We turned into the pub, normally empty at this hour, but the great menacing grey column in the east had brought many people out in search of news. The saloon bar of the pub had a long refectory table by the stairs, and several people sat there silently. It was old-fashioned in design, and over the bar, reaching almost to the counter, were panels of cut glass, with small windows on hinges which were swivelled open to give the orders. Through these foot-wide apertures the frightened eyes of the proprietors met one's own.

We decided to play a game of shove-ha'penny, a pub game of those days. It was convenient because both Peter and Sophie were left-handed, so we didn't have to keep changing sides as we spun the metal discs up the board. Men in tin hats, which we had all been issued with some time ago, came in from time to time with communiqués. When darkness came, the smoke had turned into a red bank of flames. It seemed as if they would flick out their fiery tongues and embrace the whole of London.

At about six thirty the 'all clear' sounded, and by then the sky was the colour of a blood orange, a seething, flaming mass. Donald said he would try to get home now; Dylan stayed quietly by my side. Against the now black sky, the fires shone doubly bright. After a year of the blackout it was weird to have light again, but it was an ominous brightness. It was not my night on fire-watching duty, but I thought I should report just in case. Donald walked with me to the post a few streets away. There we learned that the London docks and neighbouring boroughs had been pounded and set on fire. No, they did not want me, but would summon me if necessary. Donald brought me to the corner and went on his way.

Inside the pub, everybody was speculating as to what had happened on this sunny, Saturday, September afternoon. Jokes were made to relieve the tension; beer mugs were put down more noisily to shut out other sounds. We were glued together by dread. All our eyes were rounder, the pupils enlarged, and although we laughed, our lips twitched with alarm.

A little before nine o'clock the siren went again, and using the fires as beacons, the Luftwaffe sent wave after wave of bombers into the holocaust, until three o'clock next morning. Poplar, Bermondsey, West Ham and other places in the East End were bombed until they resembled desolate heaps of rubble, and at least a thousand people had been killed, many others trapped, wounded and made homeless. The planes flew up the Thames, which was lit up like a horrifying pantomime, past London Bridge, Victoria, Chelsea, dropping their deadly cargo indiscriminately. Nearby the flat, a gas main was hit, and a jet of white flame shot up into the darkness like a brightly lit geyser.

We did not know it then, but the winter of the bombs, or the Blitz as it was called, had begun.

CHAPTER NINE

The next day, Sunday 8 September, there was no gas to cook the breakfast with, so in a combined operation we made toast and coffee over an electric fire lying on its back, and cooked kippers on the flat part of an electric iron. For some time after this we smelt strongly of fish when we pressed our clothes, but at least we ate that day. Dylan had spent what was left of the night on the sitting-room sofa. The morning was bright with a hazy sunshine: the clouds low, and slightly oppressive. The government communiqué on the wireless said: 'Fires were caused among industrial targets. Damage was done to lighting, and other public services, and some dislocation to communications was caused. Attacks have also been directed against the docks. Information as to casualties is not yet available.'

'That,' said Dylan, 'is the understatement of all time.'

Sophie and I went for our customary Sunday morning walk in Battersea Park. Some of the trees were beginning to turn colour, and the swans paddled majestically downstream, looking more indignant than usual. The moonal pheasant strutted about the cage in the ornamental garden, its plumage shining and flashing like precious stones. The early autumn day was quiet, the air balmy, and it was difficult to reconcile the peace of the morning with the noisy, fire-drenched hell of the night before. Looking to the east, a pall seemed to hang just above the horizon. We strolled back across Albert Bridge, then up Oakley Street to join the others at the Six Bells. Everyone in the pub had theories: the invasion had begun; a great naval battle had been fought off Dover; the East End of London and the docks were finished, and this assault would be followed up by gas attacks. The cardboard boxes that civilian gas-masks had been issued in were slung over many shoulders, as were tin helmets. I telephoned my mother, who had been up all night tending to the wounded, organizing food and housing, for there had also been a smaller raid on the East End on the Friday. No, although the suffering and desolation were heartbreaking, they were far from finished. It was impossible to feel really frightened because it was all on such a vast scale. She was catching a few hours' sleep at home before reporting again that night. The East Enders who had implicit faith in Lord Haw-Haw's broadcasts (a traitor who relayed details of raids to come, from Germany on the radio) knew there would be another raid tonight. I was to be sure to go to a shelter. She had too much to do to worry about herself, and anyway had survived the First World War in France. Now she must sleep.

I was able to scotch a lot of the rumours, but even so the outlook was not exactly cheering. We decided to forgo the belly-swilling beer and club together for a bottle of whisky, which at pub prices was about a pound. It was a good decision to have made. The Sunday was indeed rigorous, that afternoon, as we sat and talked, each listening intently, and carefully avoiding our true thoughts. Dylan had an appointment the next day with Donald Taylor of Strand Films, who was making documentary films for the Ministry of Information. This started us talking about the cinema, which had had an enormous influence on Dylan, as it had on me, and we both knew quite a lot about it – particularly the early silent cinema, where as small children we had been entranced by the wonderful world of imagery, in which anything could happen: *Der Golem*, *Dr Mabuse*, *The Cat and the Canary*, *The Cabinet of Dr Caligari*, and in the thirties, James Whale's *The Old Dark House*. The latter we knew almost by heart, and during the afternoon we entertained Sophie and Peter by re-enacting large parts of it, squabbling for the best bits, which Dylan insisted on doing, because he said they were men's parts anyway. Thus was our fear sublimated into remembering, and acting out past childhood terrors, for on the far side of fear there is no fear, only endurance and hope.

The sirens sounded that night as darkness fell, and again we heard the throbbing, monotonous but unmistakable drone of the German bombers. Should we go to the shelter in the Embankment Gardens? We would go and see what it was like, and we weren't long in making up our minds. The long oblong concrete building was lit only by blue-painted electric bulbs, which gave an eerie light. Wooden benches were placed along the damp walls, and if they were occupied, you stood in the middle. People talked in whispers, and it was too dark to read or even knit. It was cold and dank, although outside the air was still warm. Peter made a joke, and someone 'shushed' him as though we were in church. I, for one, decided to take my chance outside rather than spend seven or eight hours under such dismal conditions. The others agreed with me, and it was the only time during the war that I went into a shelter. Out of doors, where you could see what was happening, or in a noisy distracting pub, was much better. That evening we took the latter course, and when the pub closed at ten o'clock we came home, finished the whisky, and did excerpts from *Der Golem* and *Dr Mabuse*. We did not, as it may seem, spend the war in a drunken stupor: we really drank very little, rarely more than a few pints of beer a night, for it was all we could afford.

Although the Blitz was to continue intermittently for eight months, the next ten days were the most intense in the Battle of London, for the city was bombed heavily both by day and night. The savagery of these diurnal attacks left no part of London unscathed. There seemed little to prevent annihilation, for the barrage balloons, in which so much trust had been put, only prevented dive-bombing. They did not stop high-level bombing. There were but few fighter aeroplanes, and only occasional gunfire. The whole city reeked of smoke and the dusty plaster-like smell of rubble. For the first three days we had not adapted ourselves to living under a constant threat of death or mutilation: we followed our working lives as best we could with two or three hours' sleep, for the crump of exploding bombs, even in another part of London, was deafening and disturbing. But another more deafening sound was to occur towards the end of the week. All Thursday afternoon, bombs whined down through the sky, and it was impossible to clear the wrecked buildings of buried people before nightfall, when rescue work was brought almost to a standstill owing to the total blackout. The bombers came back to be greeted with a roar of anti-aircraft fire, which sounded like a mad Wagnerian orchestra. The preliminary shock to our ears was terrifying, until it was realized that we were in fact hitting back. For the first time that week, groups of people stood out of doors watching German planes caught in searchlight beams, and saw the twinkling shell-bursts like fireworks in the sky. That large, jagged, murderous-looking pieces of shrapnel fell around them did not matter. In fact they were collected like seashells and displayed on mantelpieces like trophies. It became known as the 'barrage', and the noise was sweet music to our ears. The 'barrage' did not stop the raids, but it prevented concentrated attacks. From now on the loads were more widely, therefore more thinly, distributed.

Dylan was the most frightened of us all and, once he was assured of a job from Donald Taylor, he sensibly went back to Wales. Henceforth when he came to London, our bell would ring at the most unexpected times, and we were always delighted to see him. For Sophie and me, Peter was the bulwark, for apart from hunching his shoulders and occasionally glaring with rage, he never showed his fear. He was determined not to let the bombing interfere with his work, and used backgrounds of fire for his still-life paintings. The air raids had the curious effect of making me hungry, violently so, and if there was nothing else I would wolf down slices of bread, or cold potato, after which I fell fast asleep no matter how much din was going on outside. This reaction infuriated Sophie and Peter, so much so that Peter started my 'instruction course' again, in an attempt to keep me awake. Vasari's *Lives*, and Leonardo da Vinci's *Journal* were pushed into my hands, usually to little avail. But whether we liked it or not, our lives were changed for us, and such is the resilience of human beings that it happened quite gradually in the space of a week or two.

In the First World War large numbers of the population felt safe from the Zeppelin raids in the newly built underground railway stations. Many of the now homeless people, and thousands with homes, who left them during the afternoon, camped on the platforms of the London Underground. The railway authorities at first discouraged these squatters but, as the raids fanned out to envelop the whole city, the operation was organized by voluntary helpers, and this troglodyte existence, immortalized by Henry Moore in his shelter drawings, became the normal life of many Londoners. Seats and bunks were booked with foresight, like a permanent box during the opera season: deck-chairs, meals cooked on paraffin stoves, men and women wrapped in shawls, or with newspapers over their heads, like a surrealist picnic party; perambulators filled with clocks and vases won at funfairs, and bundles of old clothes which, when one got close to them, were people. The trains came rapidly out of the tunnels like snub-nosed centipedes, passengers got in and out before the centipedes vanished again, whilst the private life of large numbers of people was enacted on the platform. Several hundred families lived there rent-free permanently, enjoying the light, heat, medical attention, and cheap meals from the canteens. This was known as the 'deep-shelter mentality'. It was both depressing and fascinating; also rather horrible. But for the long diversions taken by buses to avoid craters or delayed-action bombs, which could be triggered off by a heavy vehicle passing, I would not have travelled by tube after the first weeks, for the smell alone was off-putting.

In big cities the moon is hardly noticed amidst the tall buildings, yet we became moon-conscious. A full moon, previously welcome in the blackout, as it bathed everything in clear light, was dreaded, for it meant a raid with three to four hundred planes, and was known as a 'bomber's moon'. We learned to look at the heavens as well as the gutter, for both could be treacherous. Certain unusual sounds became immediately identifiable: the noise like iron bedsteads rattling as if thrown from a height betokened a canister of incendiary bombs, and the sound as of heavy surf breaking on shingle meant heavy lorries driving over a solid bed of broken glass. A whole new vocabulary opened up: UXBs, unexploded bombs; DAs, delayed-action bombs; canisters, not tea-caddies but containers full of incendiary bombs; an 'incident' was not a trivial thing any more, but a badly bombed building; rest centres, a euphemism for a bare room where you were given a cup of tea after being bombed; stirrup pumps; chandeliers, which were multiple flares dropped before a bomb; siren suits – one-piece garments zipped up the front, worn during raids, so that one was fully dressed; and blast, no longer a mild swear-word, but the shock-waves caused by detonation of explosives.

Despite all the horrors, the Blitz was not entirely destructive, for it produced a marked change in the attitude of British people to one another. Experiencing a common danger made for a friendliness, almost a love, amongst total strangers. People were concerned with helping their neighbours: there was a joke or a laugh to keep their spirits up, and a sharing of scarce commodities. The last pinch of tea, or a bottle of whisky, was offered by people one had never seen before and might never see again. Everybody was in love with life and living. In apartment houses, the owner of the basement rooms expected to share his or her bedroom with perhaps five or six people of mixed sexes. Once you have lain on a bed, even platonically, with someone for several months, it is impossible to ignore them thereafter. A painter friend of mine, Francis Butterfield, told me he would miss his oddly assorted harem when the bombing stopped. Men felt masculine for, whatever some women might say, it was with the male sex they felt safest.

Social and sexual distinctions were swept away and, when a dramatic change such as that takes place, it never goes back in quite the same way. Whatever dreariness and anxiety the middle-aged and old people felt, for the young it was undeniably exciting and stimulating. It was God's gift to naughty girls, for from the moment the sirens went, they were not expected to get home until morning when the 'all clear' sounded. In fact, they were urged to stay where they were. When it came to the pinch, where their parents were concerned, fate was far preferable to death. Certain restaurants, such as Hatchett's and the Hungaria, and all hotels provided beds for their customers. Girls went out for dinner with their night attire, toothbrushes and make-up. Young people were reluctant to contemplate death without having shared their bodies with someone else. It was sex at its sweetest: not for money or marriage, but for love of being alive and wanting to give. Many married hastily when love was kindled by flames, and many of those marriages are today still snug in their happy philoprogenitive cocoons. An interesting point is that crime and nervous disorders actually declined throughout this tense period.

Instinct or intuition played a singular part in one's daily life, and it was unwise to ignore it. If you felt 'safe' in a certain place, you went there regularly. During a bad raid I usually had this feeling in the Six Bells and, when that closed, in a basement drinking club called the Gateways in Bramerton Street. There were several of these late drinking clubs in Chelsea (late meant until 11.30 pm): the Studio, next to the Town Hall, the Pheasantry, and one in a private house in Upper Cheyne Row called, appropriately, the Crater Club! The raids were very bad in Chelsea before and after Christmas: the weather was beastly cold, food scarce, and what festivity there was took place in the pubs. But this after-Christmas night I wanted to stay home, read by the fire, and finish the remains of the meagre Christmas food and drink.

The anti-aircraft guns rattled the windows and the clear, frosty air intensified the whine of the bombs, which were very close. The German bombers liked clear, frosty nights. Although not heavy smokers, when a raid was bad we chain-smoked, and by ten o'clock were down to our last. The pub next door was shut, for it was closing time, and the old couple who ran it never gave a moment overtime, so there was nothing for it but to walk up to the slot machine in the King's Road. Peter offered to go, but on those nights I preferred to be with him. Luckily we had a shilling, for twenty Player's cigarettes were 11½d, the halfpenny change being enclosed in the packet. The night was bright with a full moon, searchlights and the now customary glow of fires. Large pieces of shrapnel were clearly visible on the pavements as we walked up Glebe Place. The King's Road was full of activity: clanging ambulances, fire-engines and wardens racing up towards the Town Hall. We hurried on to find a cordon around the Six Bells, and massive chunks of heavy masonry on the ground. The front part upstairs had been hit, and toppled into both the road and the garden a matter of minutes before closing time. People were trapped in the back. We helped to clear the rubble and brick; it was hard work and made us hot, despite the cold. A small entrance was made and the stretcher bearers, wardens and war reserve police went through. The lights still blazed, and someone yelled, 'Turn that bloody light off.'

Several dazed but unhurt people were led out by torchlight; one had a bottle of brandy which was passed round, and we all had a swig. Some were 'regulars' who recognized us. The one with the purloined bottle said jauntily:

'What happened to you tonight that you didn't cop this lot?'

There were more inside, trapped, probably dead, as they had been sitting near the front door. Curly, the Irish barman, had gone down to the cellar and was found, his rimless spectacles still on his snub nose, but he was stone dead, an unbroken bottle in his hand. Almost-full pints of beer were standing unspilt on tables in front of customers who stared at them with unseeing eyes, for they too were dead from the blast. Similar occurrences happened every day all over London, and one learned never to persuade anyone against their will to go to a certain place.

It was towards the end of this same Christmas week that the great fire and bombing raid on the City of London took place, when the Guildhall, eight beautiful Wren churches, Guy's Hospital and hundreds of office buildings were hit, but as it was on Sunday, the latter were mercifully empty. Fire watchers saw twenty-eight incendiary bombs fall on the roof of St Paul's Cathedral, and bounce off the dome. One was blazing, and miraculously fell outwards, where it was extinguished. Indeed, amidst the wall of flame and smoke the only clear sky was around the cathedral. Londoners with a newfound love of their city watched its survival from rooftops both near and far away. With tears running down their cheeks, they said in one voice:

'The old church stood it . . .'

There was also a macabre sort of humour: a government notice told us to beware of toffee tins with a tartan design bearing the name of a well-known caterer, and also to look for a bomb with a spring which jumped out like a jack-in-the-box, and could blow off a limb. It had the delicate name of 'butterfly bomb'. One windy night, Arthur Mallett, a helper at my fire-watching station, told us of a weird, scraping, dome-like 'thing' which had chased him up Old Church Street. As he ran, so did it, faster and still faster. He turned the first corner he came to, and saw it race on about fifty yards, then stop in the middle of the street. He waited for some minutes to see if it exploded, then, curiosity getting the better of him, he cautiously approached the demonic device. In the clear moonlight, he saw it was dustbin lid.

'You can laugh at it now,' he said, 'but by Christ, I never did then.'

CHAPTER TEN

The winter was as cold as the summer had been hot. Peter had no warm clothes except the camelhair overcoat given to him when we landed at Southampton in July. Coal was expensive, and the ration wasn't enough to keep a fire going all day. It was too cold for him to sit and paint with no heating. Sophie had a large soft dark brown blanket, and one evening when she was out I made it into a sort of monk's habit for Peter to wear over his clothes whilst painting. She was very cross at first over the loss of her blanket, but in a mysterious way she acquired two more, and asked me to make one for each of us. We must have looked like a queer religious order when callers came to the door. Twenty-five years ahead of fashion, my go-ahead grandmother knitted me some brightly coloured woollen stockings. Peter was delighted and said they were just the thing for an intellectual's moll. Truth to tell, although they were gorgeously warm, I felt a bit like Minnie Mouse.

The day came when I arrived at work to find a police cordon around the area; they refused to let me pass, because it was unsafe with UXBs. The place was like a wilderness, with craters and the usual mounds of stone and broken glass. This was serious, for not only did I have no job but I never got paid for that week nor, more important, could I retrieve my insurance cards. To get new ones entailed endless waiting in queues, doctor's certificates and other hocus pocus. We were truly hungry that week, trying to eke out Sophie's wages, until I pawned a family ring I had been given for my twenty-first birthday which seemed much longer than two years before.

The next job was quite horrible, with a wholesale dress firm. The owner was appallingly sex starved; no doubt his wife was safe in the country, and he made grabs at me, usually when my head and arms were trapped in taking off some of the horrible clothes I had to model. I left after three days, and then worked for someone called Wally Craps. The least said about that the better.

We were right down to our last sixpence, for youth pays in the present. It is only in middle age that you pay in arrears. The rent was owing, and the only cigarettes we had were rolled from butts. On a desperate last chance I tried calling on my theatrical agent: 'No, nothing suitable . . .', but as I was leaving the office, Anatole (Tolly) de Grunwald, whose first play I had been in just before the war, came in. Miracles do happen, for the next day I was at one of the out-of-London studios, with a small but good part in a film about Nazi Germany called *Freedom Radio*, scripted by Tolly, and directed by Anthony Asquith. They had worked together previously, on *French without Tears*. Diana Wynyard and one of my childhood heroes, Clive Brook, played the leads.

The outdoor scenes were shot in a replica of the stadium where Hitler gave his rabble-rousing speeches. During the shooting the air-raid warning went, and we looked up to see a solitary German plane above. What can the pilot have thought when he saw hundreds of swastika banners flying in the remote English countryside?

With all the high drama going on in real life, I had almost forgotten how much acting meant to me. It seemed such a long, long time since I had watched Louis Jouvet and Madeleine Ozeray with such fascination. On account of the difficulties of even a simple railway journey, I stayed at a nearby hotel, yet still managed to come home with what seemed a fortune in good folding money. Film money is always like fairy gold, and like fairy gold it melts away, but this didn't before we bought sweaters, silk stockings, paints, canvas, food, coal, redeemed my ring, and I also managed to hide five pounds against the wettest of rainy days. This action, when that day turned up, I was never allowed to forget. For ever after Peter was convinced I had something stashed away. Alas, it was often only shillings.

The film business is not known for its high moral standards, but after the grabbing garment-men, it was like a Trappist monastery. My agent bucked up a bit after my getting that part, but there was pathetically little work going. A Midland repertory company I had worked for earlier wrote and said they were inviting 'guest artists' to act in well-established successes such as Robert Sherwood's *Petrified Forest*, *Idiot's Delight* and an excellent spine-chilling thriller called *Black Limelight*, and would I like to be included?

There was a lull in the London bombing, otherwise I wouldn't have accepted, and I left Peter and Sophie. What I didn't know was that there was a lull because the bombers had switched to the provincial cities, but they were scattered, often isolated raids and not comparable to those on London. In several cases I had played the same part a few years before, but I was a very quick study, so a bare week's rehearsal was enough for me to be word perfect. It was hard work, for in those days repertory theatres played two houses a night: one at 6.00 pm and the second at 8.30. The contract was for two weeks playing at a time, in various cities.

The lodgings varied, but I can never forget Mrs Pigg, a kindly woman who resembled her namesake but slightly. The sparse meat-ration was eked out by massive helpings of glutinous tripe and onions which, when served to us cold after the theatre, emitted a loud farting noise as it was cut up.

At the end of the first two weeks I intended to go home after the late performance on Saturday night, coming back for the first house on Monday. Provincial cities in wartime are not the ideal places for spending leisure hours. The so-called milk train would get me to London at about 4.30 am. It all sounded perfect. However, Birmingham was heavily bombed that night, and our train sat just outside the city until the 'all clear' went at about 4.00 am. There was no heating, nothing to eat, dim blue lighting, and the bombing made it too noisy to sleep.

Sophie and Peter were particularly pleased to see me, for it transpired that Sophie's firm had closed down. She had fallen in love with a soldier, and was behaving disgracefully according to Peter. They hadn't eaten anything for two days except the 'invasion' dried milk powder, made up with water.

'I not only feel like a baby,' said Sophie, 'but I'm beginning to smell like a baby.'

We all went out to a slap-up lunch at the Queen's Restaurant in Sloane Square and afterwards slept like babies. It was lovely to be home, if only for a little over a day.

There was a limit to the length of time one could live so strenuous a life: I stood it for about another month, and when I finally arrived home Peter said dramatically:

'Sophie's disappeared. I hope she hasn't gone to the bad.'

'Why couldn't she go to the bad here?'

She had actually gone back to Aunt Zenobia until she found another job. I don't think she could stand Peter's forcible feeding with the dried milk powder.

During the following months, Peter and I were closer together than ever before. We had become adjusted to each other, and he showed great tenderness towards me. On 14 February he painted a valentine which he left on my pillow, an unusual gesture for him to make. Small household tasks were done to save me trouble. We bought loose tobacco, and Peter rolled the daily cigarette supply. He made me a window box for the garlic and a few other herbs I was growing. He did whatever he thought would give me pleasure. When Crabbe came down for the evening and bought a painting, he kept only a few shillings for himself. If I had early film calls he would waken me with coffee and come to the station with me. Often he was waiting at the bus stop when I came home, standing in the cold and reading a book, for the time of my arrival was uncertain. Then we would sometimes go to the Lord Nelson pub, since the Six Bells was closed after the bombing, and have a few pints of bitter beer, which at that time was eightpence a pint.

The Nelson was not as pleasant as the Six Bells, but we were sure of seeing our friends there amongst the many strange faces. It was at the Nelson that I met Neville Heath, the multiple sex-killer, dressed in his phoney air-force uniform on phoney leaves. Full of bonhomie, he seemed: the epitome of a fighter pilot; yet he was not attractive to me, for which one can only be thankful! Barbosa was often there, as was Peter's friend Adrian Daintrey, the actor Basil Langton when he was home on leave, and Dylan when he was in London, and there were pretty girls and plain girls with the painter Raymond Myerscough Walker. We all crammed in, standing room only if you were late, the barman, who had a very large head, shouting at closing time:

'This is a pub, not a club!'

Or, otherwise in the evenings, Peter would rehearse the lines of my part with me, sometimes commenting:

'Goodness me, this dialogue is bad! I don't know how you can say it.'

He suggested that for every bad play I did, I should learn one good one, which he chose. It was an excellent antidote to the bombing which had now started again even more viciously than before. Apart from the war, life was seductive during this strange springtime.

'"But I, who never knew how to entreat, Nor never needed that I should entreat – Am starved for meat, giddy for lack of sleep; With oaths kept waking, and with . . ."'

'Oh do put a little more expression in it, Pussy.'

'I can't, I'm hungry, and so tired. You know the air raids always make me hungry, and the raid's been on for four hours.'

'Well, read to the end of this part, then we'll see what there is to eat.'

'"What say you to a piece of beef and mustard?"'

'"A dish that I do love to feed upon . . ."'

'"Aye, but the mustard is too hot a little."'

'"Why then the beef and let the mustard rest . . ."'

'"Why then the mustard without the beef—"'

'Peter, this is torture. And it's like our bread and mustard in Paris, I didn't know it was in Shakespeare.'

'Everything is in either Shakespeare or the Bible. Just go on until Petruchio comes in.'

'"Go, get thee gone, thou false—"'

There was a thud as if a gigantic sack of coal had been dropped, making the room shudder; almost immediately another thud, and a tremendous explosion. The window blew in and a dense cloud of greenish dust moved slowly through the gaping hole, forming into the shape of a weird monster. Peter flung himself on top of me on the bed, his eyes wide and dark with fear. His face and lips, pressed on to mine, tasted gritty.

'Dear Pussy, dear Pussy.'

There was a noise like exceptionally heavy rain, and his weight became almost unbearable. The bedside light was still on: the clock said twenty-five past one. All the furniture had moved, not far – it had all just moved round about a foot, except for the chair with my clothes on it, which had been under the window. There was no sign of that. I could move only my head, for the bed was covered with lumps of plaster, broken glass, wood and what looked like small stones. Peter's face was thickly covered with greenish-white dust, his eyes luminous, and large by contrast, like a clown's. Puffs of dust came out of the monkish habit as he clawed furiously at the rubble to free me. Sweat formed on his forehead, making the dust look like stale, clotted, theatrical make-up.

'I'm all right, darling, I think. But what happened? There were those thuds, it didn't sound like a bomb.'

'Well, if it wasn't a bomb, I don't know what has brought the ceiling and walls down. You're right, though, it wasn't the usual long shriek.'

'Should we turn the light out?'

'In a minute, when I've got you free.'

'Find me a coat or something, all my clothes have disappeared. There's a torch under my pillow.'

Through the open window came the sound of excited voices. I turned my head to look out, and saw leaping flames quite nearby.

'I can see fires.'

'That's not unusual.'

'But it is. Normally all I can see is the church clock tower.'

He framed his face in his hands and peered out through the fog-like dust.

'I can't see the church either. I think it's gone. There are fires everywhere. I must get you out, Pussy.'

Dressed in a long orange chiffon nightdress, brown brogue shoes and my top-coat, I switched off the light and by torchlight we crept along the corridor. Peter picked up his overcoat from the bathroom floor, where it had been blown. It was like walking on a shingly beach. There was no front door, just a frame, and a pile of glass and wood.

'Cigarettes. Damn, look in the sitting room.'

From the first floor somebody shouted up:

'Come down slowly by the wall, the stairs may not be there.' Peter went first and held my hand tightly. Ahead of us we heard footsteps on the stone staircase, which was littered with debris.

'Some of the banisters have gone. Go slowly, sit down if necessary, and come down that way.'

We sat down, slithering on our bottoms like children.

In the street were the occupants from the lower floors, wardens, ambulances, nurses, firemen and police, all lit by torchlight, the wardens with their log-sheets hanging round their necks. Someone tried to herd me into an ambulance but I pulled away, and Peter and I went into the Crossed Keys, which was wide open, the door and one wall blown into the bar. The elderly couple who ran it, never known for their generosity, were sitting down sipping brandy, covered in white plaster, looking dazed and very, very old, amongst the people gathered there. A local resident was in charge and gave us all a drink.

'The old church has gone!'

This was repeated frequently: that they were alive seemed incomprehensible.

We soon left, and went towards the remains of Chelsea Old Church to see if we could help. The nurses' home of the Cheyne Hospital for Children had the top floor blown off: a neat nurse's bedroom, the ceiling light still shining, looked like a stage set. A warden perilously climbed up the bombed staircase and switched it off, although there was a flaming gas main burning around the corner which floodlit the entire area. The church was nothing but an immense heap of timber and stone, flames licking through it; a large vaulted tomb with a stone urn on top rose up undamaged in the front. The New Café Lombard and all the large and small houses at that end of Old Church Street had been flung together into a giant mountain of shale-like destruction, all lit by the fires and the gas main. Under that fantastic mountain were people, some still alive. Heavy stones were flung aside like pebbles: the local grocer of the street, Mr Cremonesi, put his hand down through a space and felt warm flesh. A naked unhurt woman was pulled up. An old lady appeared, staggering, from the far side of the mountain, having been flung at least thirty yards and then covered with glass, wood and bricks, from which she had extricated herself. She seemed unhurt. A curious rattling sound like a time-bomb made us cautious: a battered tin was moving on a piece of stick. Below, the young woman had forced it through the bricks to attract attention. She was rescued by a war reserve policeman. A sixteen-year-old girl, pinned, only her head showing, talked to a rescue worker: she was freed, but died several hours later.

Young and old brought buckets of water to supply stirrup pumps to douse the fires. The dust was like a great fog. Charred papers and smouldering wood choked the helpers. Still the raid continued with whining bombs, cracking, thudding guns, droning aeroplanes, both German and our own night-fighters. Huge chandeliers of flares hanging in the sky like Roman candles illuminated the bomber's targets. Our hands were cut and bleeding, and when I saw the blood on Peter's hands I felt suddenly sick and faint. He led me down to the Embankment. Although the day had been warm, a breeze came off the river and it was chill. He held me close to warm me. Several wardens, police and onlookers were there talking. Two land-mines had been parachuted down on the church, which was why the usual whining sound was absent. All the fire-watchers at my post had been killed except Arthur Mallett who had previously been chased by the dustbin lid. One of the mines had landed beside him and the other fire-watchers.

'For Christ's sake, run!' he had cried.

He had run so fast he couldn't stop in time to turn the corner into Old Church Street with the others.

'Bugger this, right ho, I'll carry straight on,' he had said to himself. He'd crouched behind a small iron post, seconds before the second mine landed, which also detonated the first one.

'Blimey,' he said laconically, 'that lot's gone.' All he had lost was the trouser on his right leg. Now he wanted a cup of tea, and to find his sister, so over the mountain he went, and met her halfway in that pitiful no-man's-land.

The Thames was at low tide, factories in flames opposite, as we smoked our cigarettes leaning over the wall near the steps leading down to the river. Bombs were dropping all round, but we were too exhausted to bother. So long as we could see them, we said. Down on the silty river-bank a man was walking about.

'There's a man down there, Peter.'

'Probably a fireman looking for an unexploded bomb.'

'Well, he's coming towards the steps. Let's go down and see. It's cold standing here.'

It was light enough to walk easily down the stone steps, and we were about halfway down as he was coming up. Over Peter's shoulder, I said:

'Looks like air force uniform. Hope it's one of ours!'

'Don't be so imaginative, Pussy.'

As they met face to face I heard:

'Leutnant—' and some German numerals followed.

Peter stood aside, and the German airman stood on the steps between us.

'Ich sprache Deutsch,' I said.

He repeated only what he had said to Peter, and we walked up in silence to the top.

The airman looked about twenty-three, the same age as myself; his face was pale with terror. He did and said nothing, just stood with his arm at his side, as is understandable when someone has just parachuted into an area which he has been bombing. Wardens and firemen came round; in fact one fireman had a hose ready in case he attacked us. Nobody knew quite what to do with this man who had dropped from the sky. The airman suddenly lurched forward, as a man who none of us had seen kicked him hard in the backside. The man then rushed to the front and wrenched a pistol from a pocket on the pilot's flying suit. Peter, usually slow-moving, quickly stretched out his long arms and wrested it away. It all happened so quickly, in the dim light, that only those close by realized what was going on. Two war reserve policemen materialized from nowhere, and quite quietly they marched off the German airman between them. Someone said: 'Like a drunk and disorderly on a Saturday night' – except that the captive marched firmly and erectly, and there was no disorder.

Without speaking to each other, Peter and I followed at a distance. We had been shocked by the pistol episode: death on the ground was more real and immediate than from the skies; and despite all our horrors of the long night, we both knew that the young boy was frightened too. In a funny way, he was 'our parachutist' and we wanted to see him in safe keeping. What can he have been thinking as he walked through the ruined streets, fires blazing in all of them, bombs still raining down?

The policemen marched him into Chelsea Police Station, and we were just leaving when other policemen came out and spoke to us. We went in, and reported as accurately as we could. At about four o'clock in the morning, two more parachute mines exploded nearby – one in front of the police station, and the other behind, but the block of flats, Cranmer Court, took the brunt. They gave us a cup of strong sweet tea, which tasted like nectar. The orange chiffon nightdress was in flitters up to my knees from the rubble shifting. We borrowed a pair of scissors and cut it straight. Even so we must have looked a comical couple, still covered in dust, blood and dirt. A few minutes before five o'clock the 'all clear' went, after eight hours of continuous bombing. It was the second heaviest raid on London, and became known as 'the Wednesday'. Eighteen hospitals and thirteen churches had been hit, one thousand people killed, and two thousand seriously injured. Many others were to have reactions later on. On the way back in the early dawn light women were sweeping away the glass and rubble from their front doors, as if it was snow. Everywhere there was the acrid smell of smoke.

Dressed in borrowed clothes I was half an hour late for work. Nobody was interested in my bomb story: they had become like fishermen's tales. I was the 'one who got away'. The day was interminably long, and I dreaded going back to our bomb-shattered home. There were large holes in all the walls, no ceilings in the bedrooms, no windows or front door. Everything when I had left was thick with plastery dust and shattered glass. With the curious illogicality of blast, two eggs in a bowl on the kitchen table were unbroken, lying amid a shower of debris. Peter greeted me like the *patron* of a good restaurant when wearily I came home. I walked from room to room with amazement: he had put the beds in the front, least damaged room, swept away the worst of the wood and plaster, and nailed some transparent material over the doors and windows.

'Not a flat any longer, Pussy, a bed-sitting room, but I can paint in the broken-down one in the back. There's nobody else in the whole block but ourselves.'

What we didn't know was that whilst we had been dealing with the German airman everyone else had been rehoused in a centrally heated block of flats for a nominal rent. Nevertheless, we felt a sense of achievement at having made something from what appeared to be ruins.

Three nights later the heaviest raid of the Blitz, known as 'the Saturday', took place, when seven hundred and twelve planes unloaded over a thousand tons of high explosives and four and a half thousand canisters of incendiary bombs in this area. That night as we looked at each other, standing face to face, we found our knees knocking together.

'I thought it was only a figure of speech, like hair standing on end,' said Peter.

Just after he spoke, I was suddenly lifted across the room by a blast. It was the most extraordinary sensation, as though one had acquired wings. I was gently deposited by the book-case, and we both sat on the floor laughing until the tears came out of our eyes. Peter said his first thought was that I had become holy and was levitating.

This was only a fraction, a few 'incidents' in one of the ninety-five boroughs that were bombarded that winter and spring in London, when over twenty thousand Londoners were killed. Although we didn't know it then, the Blitz, or the Winter of the Bombs, was to end as savagely as it had begun, on Sunday 11 May. On this night the Cavendish was badly damaged. When we heard about it several days later, Peter went up to find out what had happened to Rosa. He found the hotel shattered: her front parlour and large parts of the building a shambles. Rosa had gone off with her hamper of champagne to the Hyde Park Hotel for a few days; the faithful Charles Ingram was almost in tears, for Rosa's imperious parting words were:

'Everything has to be put back as it was by the end of the week . . . *everything*: d'you understand?'

There were but two days left to complete this Augean task.

Yes, the Blitz was over, but it was not the end of the bombing.

CHAPTER ELEVEN

Often in times of trouble, completely unexpected people come to one's aid. So it was when I was seriously ill, an aftermath of the bombing of Chelsea Old Church. Lady Mary Montagu had been no more than a pleasant drinking companion, in either a pub or the Crater Club. She was at this time in her thirties, small, plumpish, with a light melodious voice. She had very pretty well-shaped legs and hands, of which she was proud, and was pleased when one commented on them.

'They're American legs and hands,' she used to say, quite firmly, brooking no argument, although we had no idea what she meant. Later it was explained that she had an American mother.

Her high heels tapped on the stone staircase announcing her arrival, for with no real doors all sounds could be heard quite clearly. She took one look at my white face and the bomb-struck room, and tapped out again. When she came back, there were bustling noises in the kitchen, and eventually in came a tray with the most superb piece of fresh poached salmon and new potatoes, all swimming in butter. No salmon I have ever eaten since tasted so delicious.

'I've asked my doctor to call: you don't look right to me. Where's Peter?'

'He had to go to a tribunal about his call-up.'

'Golly, I can't see him in the army.'

'Neither can he see himself.'

The doctor was beautifully dressed, languid in manner, his skin paper-thin and as milk-white as a baby's bottom. He popped a thermometer in my mouth and then proceeded to ask me questions. It didn't matter that I couldn't answer them, for he walked about the room humming to himself as if composing a piece of music. He was clearly wondering how Mary, a duke's daughter, had got into such weird company. War made strange bed-fellows.

'M'mm, you'll have to go to hospital: beds are very scarce. I'll let Lady Mary know.'

He departed as languidly as he had come, never once having laid an examining finger on me.

Donald Maclean came to see me carrying a huge bunch of gladioli and some cigarettes: 'for me only'.

Forty white, perfectly made beds in the Women's public ward of a hospital was not Peter's style, or for that matter mine, but with shoulders hunched and eyes on the ground he strode in to see me, bringing a copy of *Horizon* magazine. When he had gone the woman in the bed on my left said:

'Made me feel all queer when he looked at me, lovely.'

The woman on the right said:

'Don't 'e talk nice?'

Although they had apparently kept their eyes straight in front of them, they hadn't missed a trick.

When I got home the gladioli were dead, their water stinking; the bed rivalled the Paris one, and the flat looked worse than the morning after the bombing. Mary found me in tears, said we must move, and she would set about finding us a place. In any case the landlord wanted us to go so that he could put in a full claim for war damage.

Although the population in Chelsea had fallen from nearly 60,000 to 16,000 people during the Blitz, there were few furnished flats to rent as most people had moved to the country or suburbs taking their furniture with them. We hadn't a stick between us unless you counted the easel, but again Mary came to our help. All her furniture was in store, and without a second's hesitation it was handed over on a long loan. For seventeen shillings and sixpence a week, we took the top half of a house in Oakley Street, and lived resplendent with the ducal furniture. Except for the basement flat, the rest was empty, although Matthew Smith the painter had a studio on the first floor, but did not live there.

It was difficult to express personally the kindness Mary showed to us, for she did not hang about waiting to be thanked or intrude in our life once she had set us up. She brought me back to health, took care of me when I needed it most, for which I can but simply write a few inadequate words with love and gratitude. Those who knew her then will know that I was not the only person whom she benefited during those lean years, and not only people, for stray or neglected animals were also fed and looked after. It was through Mary we met Shane Leslie (now Sir Shane Leslie), the witty conversationalist and writer, for she had spent part of her childhood with him in the north of Ireland, at her family's castle, Tandragee, in Armagh. Shane Leslie, always kilted, was a full-time air-raid warden in London, and it was he who, when the bomb fell near the Cavendish Hotel, hurried round to find Rosa safe, sitting outside the hotel, enjoying a cup of tea with a bishop, as though she was at a garden party. He said he never thought to find her in such unlikely company, although he knew of her fondness for the cloth.

'A bishop in the Cavendish: the Day of Judgement must have come!'

By now we had all given up the Lord Nelson, and congregated in the small comfortable King's Head and Eight Bells, known to us as the Eight Bells, on Embankment Gardens. The long refectory table was usually 'held' by glares from Peter for us and our friends, and as the summer progressed we would take our pewter tankards of beer outside and drink by Carlyle's statue in the gardens. One evening Mary, who had great faith in Peter's knowledge of etiquette, said:

'How do you start a letter to a duke?'

'But your father is a duke, Mary.'

'Yes, I know, but when I write, I just say, Dear Dadda . . .'

It was decided that for someone who had met her father, 'Dear Duke' was the correct beginning. We none of us, including Mary, thought it sounded right, but that was how Mary's young man started his letter.

The imminent call-up was extremely unsettling. Peter had not become a 'conscientious objector' in the true sense, for he was prepared to take work not in the armed forces. Having been through the Blitz, he opted for the Auxiliary Fire Service. This, however, the tribunal had to think over and would let him know. Naturally he wanted to get as much painting done as possible before he was drafted. He had almost finished for the time being with the crumpled pieces of paper, been through eggs and other spheroid objects, and now had a desire to paint not human, but animal skulls. Rabbit heads were boiled and washed: no, not the right shape, or big enough. I consulted my butcher friend, who clearly thought I had gone mad and didn't mind saying so. His carcasses came without heads, but he might be able to get me a sheep's head. When it came it was split down the middle ready for cooking, which rendered it useless for painting. However we had several meals from it, after endless boning, skinning and skimming. In any case Peter had decided that a sheep's head wasn't the right shape or size either. What he envisaged was something like a horse's head, and he did rather keep on about it.

The 'continental butcher' thought I was even madder than the other one.

''Orse's 'ead? No call for 'em, ducks. 'Ere's a lovely 'orse tongue for you.'

Thinking of Dolly, and all the other horses who had nuzzled my pocket for sugar, I felt quite sick when he slapped the dripping, horny tongue on the counter.

'Don't want to eat it? Blimey, surely you don't want it for decoration?'

Explaining as carefully as I could the reason for this strange request, a gleam of comprehension came into his eye.

'Oh, artists.' He drawled out the word so that it ended with a hissing noise. 'I've got yer now, ducks, fer one of them gruesome pictures.'

He gave me the name and telephone number of a knacker's yard near King's Cross Station.

Yes, they had one, and would clean it for me.

Never, if you can possibly avoid it, ever go to a knacker's yard. The stench of blood which sticks in the gullet, queer thuds and shuffling sounds, occasional shouts, even the slamming of a door combine to make the flesh prickle and creep. After a few minutes we came out and stood in the road, then went to a convenient pub.

'It must be awful for you, Pussy. I've never had any contact with horses, but my stomach's turning over. Let's leave it.'

'Well, we're here now, and I ordered it. I saw an office on the right as we went in. Go in there. I'll stay here . . . do make sure it's cleaned, darling.'

It was cleaned after a fashion, but bits of flesh and hair clung to parts of the jaw, making it look like something from a horror film. We could still smell the yard when we came home on the bus with our grisly parcel. We imagined that people were avoiding us, especially when a man changed his seat and moved further down the bus. The day was warm and humid, which didn't help any.

'Let's stop at a chemist and get some ammonia or something to soak it in. Then we can put it on the roof to dry in the sunshine. It's got a frightful gluey smell at present.'

During the course of this Saturday afternoon we soaked, washed and scrubbed the noble skull, and even cleaned the teeth, which we found lifted in and out. It looked superb, like an unglazed T'ang head: the nostrils taut and almost quivering. One could imagine Ghenghis Khan having ridden it. I was standing on a chair, which was on another chair, preparing to spring up into the loft which led to the roof, when Dylan arrived. He was more goggle-eyed than usual when he saw what we were doing. Like many imaginative people he revelled in horrors.

'Pass me up those back teeth, Peter, we'll dry them before we put them back.'

Dylan made that characteristic sound of his: a cross between a snort and a snigger.

'Vernon would love this: it's like the Mari Lywd.* Most people bury their bodies in the basement, you put yours on the roof. You're like animal Burke and Hares. Payday yesterday, where shall we go? There's Tambimuttu at the Wheatsheaf, Ivan Moffat at the French pub, or Augustus John round the corner at the Eight Bells.'

We settled for the Eight Bells, as we'd already had a long journey that day.

This summer of 1941, Dylan called whenever he was in London working with Donald Taylor and Ivan Moffatt for Strand Films, from whom he drew a regular income of between eight and ten pounds a week. He and Caitlin with

---

*Vernon Watkins, poet, who wrote *The Ballad of the Mari Lywd* about a ghostly horse's head.

their young son Llewelyn were staying with Frances Hughes, wife of Richard Hughes, the author, at Laugharne Castle in Wales. The wartime journey could take anything up to twelve hours in an unheated train, so sometimes he would spend as much as a week with us; other times he would spend a night, then disappear and reappear a few days later in quite different clothes, for he had the habit of discarding his own dirty shirts, ties, even trousers, and replenishing them with whatever of his hosts' took his fancy. Peter was almost the only person he couldn't do this with for Peter's entire wardrobe was more sparse than Dylan's. Once Dylan and I spent hours with Ivan Moffatt in the Swiss pub in Soho and, when Ivan was getting a drink, I suggested that we must get back to Chelsea soon. Dylan sniggered and said he couldn't leave until Ivan did because he had his trousers on. They must have reached almost to his chin, for Ivan was a much taller, slimmer young man.

Dylan as a dinner guest was like the Master of Hounds in *Handley Cross*:

> He will bring his nightcap with him,
> for where the MFH dines he sleeps,
> and where the MFH sleeps he breakfasts.

His favourite breakfast was ice-cream and a fizzy non-alcoholic drink as a starter. Once when there was no lemonade to be got, he put a dollop of ice-cream into a light fizzy beer and seemed to enjoy it. Peter would bring back the ice-cream when he went to buy the newspaper at the corner shop. Dylan always had a craving for sweets, and the only food or drink I ever had to dole out gradually was the chocolate ration, otherwise a month's supply would go in minutes.

Far too much has been written about Dylan's drinking. In those days he drank very little more than, if indeed as much as, all his friends and contemporaries. He had no capacity for strong drink, so less made him seem drunker. Also he had a vivid imagination, and was a born and brilliant actor. He would play the drunken young poet to perfection, and revert instantly to being as we knew him, once we were home. He could be drunk with words and images, keeping us enchanted until the early hours of the morning, with nothing stronger to drink than cocoa or lemonade. I was quite certain he had some sort of liver complaint, for he would be horribly sick some mornings, retching up a bright yellow bile.

'It's in good colour this morning,' he would say cheerily as he left the bathroom.

For someone like myself used to very heavy drinkers amongst my family in Ireland, what Dylan drank all day they would have considered a normal morning's drinking. And they were all men who worked well, rode hard and were not thought to be at all unusual. My father and his nine brothers always believed that when they drank beer or stout they were practically on the wagon, and that was Dylan's main tipple.

His magic, for that he had, lay in the ability to make both himself and other people laugh. We would perhaps be sitting gloomily wondering where to get a shilling to put in the gas-meter and, within a half an hour of Dylan's arrival, be laughing fit to bust, and not only superficially for he would have stimulated our imaginations. We might sometimes play my father's word game: a word was picked, say 'down', and rapidly going round the company each person said a word connected with it: falling, going, hanging, sitting, lying, eider, at heel, at heart, County Down. There it could stop, and we would perhaps talk of the beautiful neglected novels of Forrest Reid, who lived in poverty in County Down: *Peter Waring*, *The Bracknels* (now called *Denis Bracknel*), *Uncle Stephen*; or of Charles Williams, the Northern Irish don, whose book *All Hallows' Eve* had frightened the bejasus out of us, and the marvellous opening sentence from his *The Place of the Lion*.

'From the top of the bank, behind a sparse hedge of thorn, the lioness stared at the Hertfordshire road.'

The function of the game was not in the game itself, but in the way it cleared the mind and provoked discussion in a new field.

The resonance and beauty of Dylan's voice was, in itself, beguiling. His accent was not English, nor was it the sing-song Welsh of the music hall; 'cut-glass Welsh' he used to call it. Even though a cigarette usually hung from the corner of his lips, his words were clearly audible. The word 'always', which he used frequently, he pronounced 'ollways', and words like 'daughter' or 'laughter' he intoned on the first syllable. It is easy to see how the shilling for the meter was quickly forgotten for Dylan could enchant and 'put a girdle round about the earth in forty minutes'.

Outside the Eight Bells was parked a large, rather magnificent open motor-car. I think it was a twenties Bugatti for it had a long barrel-shaped bonnet and a shining exhaust pipe nestling along the running board. Such a car was a rare sight in wartime, because of its petrol consumption, and particularly in Chelsea. Inside the pub, the crisp, clipped, clean young man who owned it was sitting with Augustus John. They looked as out of place together, as did the shining old Bugatti outside the shabby pub. Augustus was staring in front of him, the keen blue eyes of the Celt watching everything and everyone relentlessly, his gingery-grey beard occasionally twitching in acknowledgement of the clean young man's remarks, for generally he hated small talk and would affect an even greater deafness than he had. He insisted I sit opposite him, and went on staring, now, at me. I began to feel like a giant species of butterfly pinned to the chair. Peter, Dylan and the clean young man were talking about Henry Green's novel *Loving*, which had just come out. It appeared that Augustus's deafness excluded him from the conversation until he boomed out, so that the whole pub was stunned into silence:

'I suppose he'll call the next one *Fucking*!'

Then back to the silence and the staring, for the next half an hour. He behaved and looked like a querulous old man of seventy: he was in fact fifty-nine. I told him about the horse's skull, now drying, rampant on our roof. This he liked, although between times he glared at Peter as though annoyed he hadn't thought of it himself. The pub had run out of their daily allocation of his particular drink so he wanted to go to the Chelsea Arts Club. The undauntable clean young man said he would drive us all there.

Augustus sat in the front, Peter, Dylan and I in the back. It was like being in a chariot and we behaved accordingly. Even Augustus was cheered by the expressions on the faces of the passers-by, and several times lifted his stick in royal recognition. We arrived at our destination only too soon, for it was a different situation at the elegant door of the long, low, white-painted club. Women were not allowed in: Peter said he would go in for ten minutes and join me at the Cadogan on the corner. As they filed past, the doorman's arm came down like a frontier barrier, cutting Dylan off from the rest.

'You're barred, Mr Thomas.'

'Barred?' This was said in a hurt, full voice worthy of Sir Henry Irving. 'On what grounds?'

'A complaint was lodged by one of the members on the occasion of your last visit. I can't discuss it further.'

Peter wanted to come out too, but the official stood squarely between him and us. We said we would wait in the motor and make faces at the members through the window.

Dylan and I sat in the front seats like naughty children. We hooted the large old-fashioned rubber bulb horn, switched on lights, pretended to drive, and lit our cigarettes with the glowing gadget meant for lighting cigars. And like children we soon tired of our tricks.

'What did you do the last time you were there?'

'I called Sir G— a hoary blue-nosed old baboon.' He rolled the sentence around his mouth, giving the simple words a spite they do not have on paper.

'Perhaps he thought you meant "whorey"?'

Dylan sniggered, and said:

'He's too deaf to hear anything, but so vain, and such a bad painter.'

The ten minutes were up and we were restless. Opposite the club was a row of beautiful five-storeyed Regency houses. Leaning up against one was a very long ladder, reaching to the roof.

'Wouldn't it be marvellous to be so brave that you could run up that ladder to the top?'

'It's easy,' I said, 'let's do it. Then they'll wonder where we are when they come out.'

We sprang out of the car and I kicked off my shoes before starting up the ladder at great speed, Dylan behind me. I got to the third floor past a small balcony, when I looked down. Dylan had retreated and was sitting in the gutter, his back to the ladder with his head in his hands. It was the looking down that did it, for not only did I get *vertige*, but the ladder appeared to be swaying outwards in an alarming fashion.

'Dylan, it's falling outwards, for God's sake come and hold it, I'm frightened.'

Still he sat there head in hands. I flattened myself against the ladder willing it to stop, but still it swayed, in . . . out . . . in . . . out . . . surely in a second it would go, and my brains would be dashed out on the pavement.

'You cowardly little Welsh swine, come and hold it,' I roared. Still he went on sitting. I tried to take one hand off and grab the iron railings just below me, but this seemed to make the ladder sway even more. I was quite transfixed, face pressed between two rungs, my bare insteps aching as they clung round the slippery wood for what seemed like aeons. It was far worse than bombs, for there was endless time for dreadful speculation and contemplation. At last I heard Peter's voice:

'But where is she?'

Augustus, Peter and the young man came over.

'Do come down, Pussy,' Peter entreated, as if I were a cat in a tree.

'I've got *vertige*, I can't move down, but hold the ladder, Peter, and I'll try.'

Even with the ladder being held, it still swayed at that height. Augustus advanced to the front door and knocked the knocker. An immaculate middle-aged man who looked like a general opened the door. Augustus said:

'There's a young woman up your ladder.'

'Dear, dear,' he clicked, 'we must get her down.'

I could hear them talking at the ladder's foot, making strategic suggestions. It was the 'general' who took charge, and at once suggested a solution for the situation.

'Well, the mountain will have to come to Mahommed,' he said briskly as they all went inside, leaving me, as I thought, to my horrible fate. Then the long windows behind the balcony opened, and out on the foot-wide shelf stood the 'general'.

'Well, well, m'dear, soon have you on terra firma. Hold on to this.' He produced what looked like a looped saddle girth.

'That's right, now lean hard against the ladder, and slip it over your head. That's a good girl . . . now, one arm, now the other.'

He gave me great assurance as I hooked myself into this harness.

'Now lean over towards me and give me your hand. I've got you, you can't fall . . .'

I was slung over the balcony by one strong pull and then lifted to safety. The 'general' led me downstairs like a pony, the harness still on me, to a superbly furnished drawing room where his elegant grey-haired wife was serving huge goblets of brandy and soda to the others.

'I've got her . . .' he crowed delightedly.

His wife in a sweet soft voice said: 'I'm so glad, the poor child.'

And I too was given a beautiful goblet of brandy.

Nobody, least of all the 'general' or his lady, thought to ask what I was doing up their ladder. I was just beginning to feel all right when I looked down and saw I had put a black footprint of what looked like paint on the off-white carpet. My feet too had got filthy climbing over the balcony. I sat with one foot on top of the other, pressing down on the black mark, but they were too well bred to notice, or to say anything if they had.

We spent the most pleasant hour there: seven strange and oddly assorted people, all conversing as easily and naturally as if by gold-edged white-carded invitation. I never heard their name and never saw them again, but their gentle kindness remains with me to this day.

Peter and I walked home after I had retrieved my shoes; Dylan said he would be back later. The clean young man and Augustus sped away in the metal chariot, waving grandly to our host and hostess. By the time Dylan came back to Oakley Street, the brandy-comfort gilt had worn off all of us. Stale beer tasted like rusty nails after it. Dylan and I glowered at each other. In his especially hurt voice he said:

'I didn't mind your calling me a coward, a swine, or Welsh, but I did object to "little".' He pouted and looked deeply injured.

This incensed me, and made me say many more abusive things, so that we were almost in tears, both of rage and of misery. Peter wandered about humped up with despair, urging us to make up our quarrel, but we were word-locked with tantrum. Finally he made us laugh and broke it up by saying:

'What else could we expect when we'd been playing skulls and ladders all day?'

As a reconciliation he made me give Dylan half my chocolate ration, which we ate dipped into mugs of hot 'invasion' milk powder.

It was the only quarrel Dylan and I ever had; we never again played skulls and ladders. The next day my grandmother came to luncheon.

CHAPTER TWELVE

My maternal grandmother, then in her eighty-first year, had two favourite words. One was 'initiative' and the other 'go'. Women were expected to be liberally endowed with both these qualities; men at one time in their life should have had them, but were vaguely suspect if they displayed them too ostentatiously. Many of the men in her family had met sudden deaths at an early age, and I'm convinced Grandma thought it was because they had too much 'go' or 'initiative'. She was fond of saying that they 'warmed both hands before the fire of life', which as a child puzzled me, but then so did many other figures of speech.

She was Cornish, a descendant of Henry Fielding, the eighteenth-century novelist. *Tom Jones* was given to me to read when I was about ten years old, and I thoroughly enjoyed it. He too had warmed both hands before the fire of life, for he died at forty-seven. She herself not only had plenty of go, but was very go-ahead, for Grandma repeatedly said you had to 'go with the times'. In 1913 she went to Australia to investigate the sudden death of her brother, taking her own deckchair, which she brought back in 1914, and it is still in use. Whilst there, she shocked the polite Perth society by getting down from her carriage when out for a drive to assist an aboriginal woman through a difficult childbirth. The woman put a thin silver bracelet on my grandmother's arm, which was never to be taken off. Many times as a child I asked her to tell me the story of the bracelet, the aboriginal woman's most treasured possession, and how Grandma's grey taffeta frock was covered in dust and blood when she went on to the tea-party.

Contrary to most elderly people she thought modern life and times wonderful. Very soon after the First World War we had a motor-car with a chauffeur called George Deare. Grandma called him George for, as she said, it would give a wrong impression if she said:

'Drive on, Deare.'

Not that she really cared at all for wrong impressions. Less than ten years later we were up in our first aeroplane at Hendon; goggles on in the open cockpit as we looped the loop with Alan Cobham's Flying Circus.

Every modern appliance or gadget was tried out, and many times if it didn't work to her liking she would set about redesigning it, and off we would go to the Patents Office. She must have registered more patents than most people had gadgets. She was a born inventor, mastered quite complicated electrical problems very early on, and studied architecture at seventy, when she wanted to build three small houses to live in instead of her one large one. Some of it was done, I think, to annoy my antiquarian grandfather, whose idea of heaven was to sit alone in his room illuminating manuscripts or writing long treatises in an exquisite copperplate hand, for he hated any modern innovation and even circled round the telephone with a wary eye as though it were an unpredictable animal. He would never answer it when it rang.

Although a woman of the strictest moral principles, at the turn of the century she had opened her large house as a home for unmarried mothers and, later on after the 1914 war, worked almost exclusively for the poverty-stricken classes in the slums of London. Children were taken from Dr Barnardo's orphanage and given love, kindness and help, shared with her own children, and later with me – for, not only did she look after me from the age of ten when I was asked to leave my first convent, but she also took in two Jewish children whose mother had died. At this time she must have been nearly seventy. She firmly believed that if you could speak good English and Latin you could 'go anywhere'. When the Daniels children arrived they were being instructed in Hebrew so in our holiday classes we all learned Latin and Hebrew. Grandma was rather pleased when I did better in Hebrew than the Jewish children.

Quite early on I found that she liked to oppose the popular view, and the quickest way to achieve one's own ends with her was to be in a strong minority group. In fact the more factions were against you, the more Grandma was for you, for she loved opposition, even remotely. This showed in her political preferences: always for the side that was out of office.

Despite a firm belief in God, she tried and found all accepted religions wanting, arguing remorselessly with priests, parsons and even rabbis. When her youngest daughter died, she took up spiritualism, believing that if anyone could get through to the 'other' world, she could. But not for her the little medium round the corner. Off we went, starting on a pirate bus (buses run by private companies which were very fast and cheap), to see Sir Arthur Conan Doyle the writer, who at that time was one of the chief spiritualists. Me with a grubby copy of *Sherlock Holmes* in my eleven-year-old hands. Grandma thought highly of Conan Doyle, mainly I think for his championing the innocence of Oscar Slater, who had been convicted of a crime he did not commit. I never got around to asking him to autograph my copy for on first sight I fell in love with his son, about five years older than me, who treated me with handsome disdain. I remember Conan Doyle as a large man with sad thoughtful eyes and a walrus moustache, giving us tea in the country house and tickets for the next large spiritualists' meeting at the Albert Hall. Much to my grandmother's annoyance, I was one of those picked out of the thousands of people present as having a Negro spirit guide with a message from the other world. She was convinced it was really for her: they had made a fatal mistake, and spiritualism was out.

If the thought of 'Mother' had induced nervousness in Peter, 'Grandmother' made him doubly so. Dylan Thomas on the other hand looked forward to the meeting and spruced himself up accordingly. A Muslim's Paradise is peopled with houris; Dylan's was a matriarchal Bardic society with ten grandmothers and several mothers, himself, his beautiful wife and children disporting themselves under their protective and watchful eyes. For he loved women of all ages, especially if they took care of him. The female pulchritude displayed in pub paintings by Alma Tadema or Fortunio Mantania made him groan with delight. He was amorous, and would make verbal passes at pretty girls and women as much out of affection or bravado as sex. His wife Caitlin was the princess from over the sea, his true love, then and always. When he became famous he was pursued by women who often mistook his love of women for love of themselves.

There were nearly sixty stairs to our part of the house, so Peter took the prettiest chair and put it in front of the window on the second floor.

'So that your grandmother can sit down and rest,' he said. Contrary to resting, Grandma remarked:

'Silly place to put that beautiful chair. If the window is blown in the upholstery will be ruined.' Whereupon she picked up the chair and proceeded up the remaining stairs, Peter tussling to get it away from her.

Her big red bag – she loved bright colours – was opened, and out came a bottle of whisky, fifty cigarettes and several tins of food. 'Just in case we had nothing decent to eat or drink.' Also a packet of her own cigarettes, Muratti's 'Lucky Dream', which were of different colours, gold-tipped and slightly scented. (The distinctive scent had given me away when I had tried my first cigarette many years ago.) There was no awkwardness at all; she behaved as if she had spent her life amongst penniless poets and painters, and she made it clear that she thought women who married too early without realizing their responsibilities were fools. When shown Peter's paintings she found them interesting and said one must go with the times. The horse's skull ones were much admired, and she liked the initiative shown in getting it. As I dished up the meal I heard her discussing Swansea, a town she knew well and didn't think much of, with Dylan. She told us the story of her sister's husband who had died near Swansea, and my great-aunt having all the floorboards taken up to see where he had hidden his money, since he distrusted banks. Alas, this treasure was never found and the farm never sold lest it should turn up. Dylan loved this tale of 'the rancour of years' as he put it.

After lunch I suggested a rest after the long journey, but the eyes as blue as larkspur petals flashed with contempt. Instead she glanced through the copy of *Horizon* which was lying on a small table. It was the July issue, with the first publication of *The Ballad of the Long-legged Bait*.

'This is by you; read it out to us.'

'It's very long,' said Dylan, 'over fifty verses, the longest poem I've ever written.'

'The longer the better, if it's good,' she said. 'I should like to hear it.'

The beautiful voice brought the smell of the sea and seaweed into the room; spray and salt and shells were outside the window. Any obscurities of modern poetry were hammered out on that 'mounting dolphin's day':

Goodbye, good luck, struck the sun and the moon,
To the fisherman lost on the land.
He stands alone at the door of his home,
With his long-legged heart in his hand.*

That evening we were to dine with Donald and Melinda Maclean at their flat near Regents Park. Peter found a rare taxi at the Albert Bridge rank, which we shared with my grandmother, but not before we had all promised to have lunch with her during the coming week, for as she put it: 'if she didn't see a bit of life, she would die of boredom.'

The Macleans' flat in Rossmore Court was small and rather characterless. It was the usual centrally heated box-like apartment of those days, with a combined dining-drawing room, and what could be termed a large larder, known as a kitchenette. A central table was laid for dinner, taking up what little space there was. Peter and Donald looked like giants in the cramped room. Melinda, small, dark, with a bird-like face, fluttered around us. Her features were a little too sharp for prettiness, but she had a charming, soft American voice, and she was a good hostess. It was a very conventional evening: dry martinis to start with and general conversation. Melinda spent some time in the kitchen, and from time to time Donald would uxoriously go to see if he could help. We were all brought out to see some dried onion flakes, the latest thing from America, and expressed our surprise and wonderment at them. When we got back to the

*Dylan Thomas; 'The Ballad of the Long-legged Bait', *Collected Poems*, J.M. Dent, London 1954.

sitting room Dylan said they looked like old men's toenails, which of course they did. However, when they turned up in the casserole which followed I don't think they were recognized as such. Good wine, salad, an excellent cheese, coffee and brandy. There were no explosions or conversational gaffes; nor was there over-drinking. A quiet, civilized evening which ended about midnight. Somehow we got a taxi home, and I remember Donald solicitously inquiring if we had enough money to pay for it.

At this time I had a very pleasant job with a firm I shall call Dorian Models. Mr Dorian, an erect grey-haired figure with a glass eye, was in love with his models. By that I mean the rather ordinary clothes he designed. He fondled them, gazed fixedly (the glass eye helped) at them, often making quick darts across the showroom to rub his hands lovingly down a sleeve or a skirt. To him they were animate children of his creation. I was something to hang them on. I don't think he could have described my face, for he never seemingly looked higher or lower than those parts of my body his clothes covered. He caressed his coats and dresses, cradling them over his arms when carrying them, and would never sell the models, only copies. What he liked best was to contemplate their beauty, on me, when there were no customers. So long as I was careful with his clothes, and showed them to the best advantage, my job was secure. Actually, it was rather hard work for me, as generally I only had to model when there were customers: at Dorian Models I was kept at it most of the day. Like all jealous parents he really wanted to prevent strangers coveting his clothes; accordingly, instead of displaying them in the window as was the usual, a discreet net curtain was hung from halfway up, to prevent prying eyes.

Dorian Models was near the comfortable, old-fashioned Berners Hotel, which was filled with good mahogany furniture and chairs you could sleep in. The customers were elderly people of good standing who lived in the country, and the staff were like well-trained butlers or footmen. I often went there to make a telephone call, or to have a coffee after my sandwich lunch. One day as I was leaving, a taxi drew up, and out of it stepped a very dapper little white-haired man with a round face like that of a highly intelligent blue-eyed baby. I recognized him as being Max Beerbohm, whose cartoons and books, especially *Seven Men*, I loved. He was at that time giving some very amusing talks on the radio, one of which started with: 'Ladies and gentlemen, or if you prefer it, Gdeevning . . .' I admired him intensely, but felt quite impotent in his presence. All I could think to do was to hurry up to him and say excitedly:

'I think you're marvellous!'

Then stricken with every kind of embarrassment I went back to Dorian Models. The next time I went to Berners Hotel, Max Beerbohm was sitting in the lounge, looking even smaller in the enormous chair. He came over to me, bowed, and said:

'I think you're marvellous, too.'

From then on we would often meet when he was in London, have coffee together and talk. It was at Berners Hotel that I was to lunch with my grandmother.

On that day I was sitting talking to the packer at Dorian Models when Mr Dorian, face unduly flushed, ran into the room.

'Quick, quick,' he cried jerkily, for he had a faint foreign accent, 'ring for the police, there are some suspicious characters peeping through the window. I have locked the front door.'

Kenneth the packer was a typical phlegmatic working-class Englishman, who could never be made to hurry even during an air raid. He finished tying an elaborate knot then turned slowly to face Mr Dorian, who was incoherent with alarm.

'What harm if the suspicious characters are *outside*, guv'nor?' he said laconically. 'All the stuff's inside. They haven't got a gun, have they?'

Mr Dorian was not placated, and became almost hysterical at the thought of a hold-up.

'They will steal our beautiful clothes at night. They are examining the place with searching eyes. Ring for the police and they will question them.'

'The place is well locked up at night, guv'nor, you do it yourself. The police couldn't question them before a burglary, it would give the game away.'

'All clothes are on ration now, they will make a fortune selling our models,' said Mr Dorian frantically.

'Well, let's have a look at these blokes,' answered Kenneth.

We three went through the workrooms of stitching girls to the showroom, Mr Dorian hiding one of his models displayed on a stand on the way. Sure enough, over the top of the net curtains two faces were pressed, noses squashed on the glass. One figure was very tall, and looked like a 1910 idea of a bolshevik; the other was quite small, so that only his cap, a bulbous nose and protruding eyes showed above the curtain rail. Kenneth and Mr Dorian were in front of me.

'Blimey,' said Kenneth, 'they are a queer-looking lot.'

I pressed forward, and indeed they did look villainous and rather intimidating with the light behind them. To my dismay I saw they were Dylan and Peter, who had come to pick me up before lunch. When Peter saw me, he waved.

'Now they are threatening us,' said Mr Dorian. 'I entreat you, Kenneth, ring for the police.' Mr Dorian was not going to let his beloved clothes out of his sight for an instant.

'No, no, they're friends of mine,' I cried out.

'Friends?' questioned Mr Dorian, clearly wondering if I was a fit person to employ with his treasured creations. 'Friends? Well, what are they doing assessing my stock?' He said this as carefully as only someone who was unfamiliar with the English language would.

'I'm meeting them for lunch.' Then, feeling I had to offer an explanation, I said:

'One is a famous poet, and the other a painter.'

Unexpectedly the artist in Mr Dorian showed itself.

'Ah, la vie de bohème,' he crooned sentimentally, 'but what a shock they gave me. Open the door, Kenneth; no doubt they would find interest, especially the painter, in our beautiful things.'

I doubted it, but in they came looking like Rimbaud and Verlaine on an off-day. However they both sensed an occasion and rose to it. Peter muttered something about *Harper's Bazaar*, which was immediately seized on by Mr Dorian – '. . . and you think they would be interested?' – whilst Dylan, never at a loss for a word, rhapsodized about the very ordinary clothes. All in all it was very successful, for I was given an extra half-hour for my lunch. Mr Dorian's relief at the safety of his brain-children quite overcame him. From then on, too, Kenneth used to pump me about the 'carry-ons', as he put it, of artists.

We were a bit late meeting my grandmother in the Scotch House, a pub opposite the hotel, but she quite understood, and enjoyed the story, for neither Dylan nor Peter knew until then what had happened. Dylan sat very close to her, put his arm through hers and said:

'Lend us a quid, Grannie.'

She did, without any hesitation.

CHAPTER THIRTEEN

Dylan and I were cinema-crazy and our taste was omnivorous. We journeyed off to Classic cinemas in outlying districts of London to be terrified all over again by Léni's *The Cat and the Canary*, *The Old Dark House*, *des Dr Mabuse*, *Das Testament*, or Lon Chaney and Mary Philbin with the long golden hair in *The Phantom of the Opera*. We would re-enact our childhood memories of *The Lost World* or *Dr Fu Manchu* as the images remained fresh in our minds.

The cinema was true magic for many children brought up in the 1920s and early 30s, and Dylan and I were not exceptions. It was much more exciting than present-day television: it was an adventure in itself getting the few pennies together for the ticket, and then entering the darkened auditorium, to be entranced in a very real, often monstrous and also comic world.

Peter seldom accompanied us, only liking French or Russian films with the exception of Garbo. In any case he had a curious social life which took place mainly whilst I was at work and therefore I hardly ever took part in it. His engagement book, had he kept one at that time, would have read like a section of *Debrett*, and off he would lumber in his frayed, faded clothes, looking as Dylan described him in a letter in 1941, 'shabby, humped elegant Pulham', for he had an old nervous habit of hunching his shoulders when entering a room. He would tell me later about grand luncheons or dinners, and the participants became as real to me as if I had met them. In later years when I met some of these people I would, quite naturally, recall an incident, and they would say: 'But were you there? Funny, I don't remember you . . .'

At about this stage of the war a government order decreed that no restaurant could charge more than five shillings for a meal. If you had the money you could also have such delicacies as oysters or smoked salmon when they were available at a very high price, but the basic meal could not exceed the very reasonable price, even for those days, of five shillings. It was done to prevent black-marketeering, which it did to a certain extent. On account of this decree, many impoverished or elderly people took to lunching at the Ritz or similar hotels, as much as a return to prewar graciousness as for the meal itself, which was often disguised Spam or a similar product. And very pleasant it was, sitting on a well-upholstered banquette looking out over the verdant Green Park.

Lady Sibyl Colefax, a well-known hostess for many years – after Edward VIII's abdication the following lines were circulated in London:

The Ladies Colefax and Cunard
Took it very, very hard

– gave a weekly luncheon at the Ritz for friends, and it was to one of these that Peter brought me. As we were walking down the long hallway to the dining room, Peter stopped for a moment, put his hand on my shoulder, then tore off the flapping sole of his shoe. This he deposited amongst the potted palms framing the entrance, and we majestically sailed in, he with his sock meeting the thick pile of the carpet.

It was a remarkable gathering, with more women than men. Apart from myself they were well on in years with the curiously intense beauty of women who have accepted life and are long past youth. Ada Leverson, Oscar Wilde's great friend and champion both before and after he came out of prison, whom he affectionately called 'The Sphinx', Edith Sitwell, wonderfully medieval-looking, her face and body so attenuated as to be almost transparent, and Elinor Glyn, the best-selling novelist of the turn of the century, the originator of the 'It' girl, looking like one of her own heroines, startlingly, luminously beautiful with her abundant red hair curling from under the brim of a large hat, green eyes, and skin like fine rose-tinted marble. I sat next to her and found it difficult to stop looking at her and listen to what Vyvyan Holland, Oscar Wilde's son, was saying in his soft beguiling voice on my other side. Osbert Sitwell was at the other end of the table and so transfixed was I that I remember little about him. The bombs and barricades were far away, if they had ever happened: it was like dining with dinosaurs. I do not know what we ate or drank, it was not important, but I do remember at the end of the meal the magnificent red head of Elinor Glyn bending towards me; the crystal-clear eyes which had missed nothing in a long life fixed their gaze on me and a voice, almost ethereal so light was it, said:

'To preserve your skin rub it hard with a firm brush or loofah. All over your body, as well as your face. Do this every day!'

This segment of conversation, like a fossil caught in Baltic amber, has remained in my mind, and many times as I look in my mirror that beautiful face, and the voice like an incantation, is vivid to me.

It was no doubt when Peter was attending one of those functions (the word that comes to mind) that Dylan and I went to see *M*, the Fritz Lang film about the Dusseldorf child murderer. Dylan at that time looked remarkably like the young Peter Lorre, who played the child murderer, and it may have been that, as much as it being based on fact, that made us quite cold and quiet with terror. It was only when I realized that the film was about to start again that I spoke:

'Let's go now, quickly, I couldn't stand it again.'

Usually we chattered away after going to the cinema, making up sequels or acting out parts of what we had seen, but this time we clutched each other's hands and made our way to the French pub in Soho. It was crowded and noisy, which was just what we wanted to shake us out of our present mood. Old Monsieur Berlemont with his grey handlebar moustache and twinkling eyes greeted us and, when for the second time my drink was spilled by someone jostling me, he pointed to a small round marble-topped table which was empty at the back of the pub, near the bar, under his collection of signed photographs of Maurice Chevalier and other celebrities who had visited his pub. Dylan and I were still very untalkative, itself an unusual occurrence, and when we did talk it was of serious matters like Caitlin wanting to come and live in London, for she and their son Llewelyn were still staying with Frances Hughes at Laugharne Castle. Mary Montagu had also indicated that she wanted her furniture back, so Peter and I were trying either to acquire some or get a furnished flat we could afford. For a few brief moments we thought of sharing a large flat or house together, but sensibly decided that as none of us had any money it would be straining our friendship too far. In any case paternity and Peter didn't seem to mix.

Opposite us at the further end of the alcove we were sitting in was a large man who sat looking like an angry tenant-farmer. From time to time his piercing brown eyes seemed to fix on us, trying almost to will us into looking at him, or possibly to engage us in conversation. Dylan was disturbed by this; he obviously recognized the man although he would tell me nothing. I thought of him as a 'pub bore' and was therefore not surprised when Dylan rummaged in his voluminous, magpie-cluttered pockets as a diversion and produced some dog-eared writing paper. He was in the habit of always carrying a pencil and paper with him, for not only did he jot down lines of poetry that he wished to remember, but he also drew very engaging little pictures or cartoons. This was to be a drawing in which we would both make contributions and see what turned out. A pleasant, distracting game which meant we weren't likely to catch the penetrating gaze of the angry tenant-farmer at the other end of the alcove. We started with a child's hoop which eventually formed the front plate of a large train engine, and so it went on.

We had completed, in so far as one ever completes, our doodle when the pot-boy came round emptying ashtrays, removing glasses and wiping the table-top with a wet cloth. He did the table in the middle, at which sat a lovesick pair of private soldiers, then on to the angry-looking man, who gave the lad a folded piece of paper, which he brought to us. Dylan unfolded the paper and laid it on the damp table. The cold terror we had known earlier that evening came back, for we were looking at a similar, very similar, drawing to the one we had just completed. It was dominated by a large steam train engine as was ours. The effect on us was weird and uncanny: it produced an inner trembling in me; Dylan, almost white-faced, stood up and hustled me out. Outside, the summer evening seemed chilly, and Dylan shivered.

'We'll get a taxi if we can and go back to Chelsea at once.' He sounded unaccustomedly curt.

'But how did he . . .?'

Dylan's eyes like large tawny marbles widened as he said:

'That was Aleister Crowley, the Black Magician; he killed Betty May's husband in Sicily. He even calls *himself* the "Great Beast". Let's get as far away from him as possible.'

It has always annoyed me that in our hurry we left both the drawings on the damp table-top. No doubt they were screwed up and thrown away.

Peter laughed heartily at the whole story, which made us feel a little foolish but nevertheless reassured.

'Telepathy? What twaddle.' He said emphatically. 'It's done by mirrors.'

Dylan and I looked at each other, by no means fully convinced. Peter on the other hand seemed immensely cheered up by our adventure. So much so that I thought something else must have happened to put him in such a good mood. His eyes had an amused, teasing look as he regarded the two of us, flopped out in the two armchairs, sipping flat beer.

'I've found us the most civilized place to live, Pussy. The drawing room is over forty feet long. It's Peter and Glur Quennell's old flat in Flood Street. You must go to the agents and fix up about it – I'm hopeless at all those business things.'

'What are we going to use for furniture?' Dylan sniggered. Peter waved his arm airily in the direction of his easel.

'We've got a bed and one or two things. Furniture doesn't matter unless it's very beautiful.'

'Won't it be very expensive?'

An annoyed look came over his face and he shrugged his shoulders, as he said that I must find out all those boring details. His enthusiasm had infected us for we spent some hours inventing a new and curious life for ourselves in a flat we would probably never live in. Yet when the time came to go to bed, we took the mattress from our bed and put it on the floor for Dylan, as he was still reluctant to go to wherever he was staying and to be alone after our strange adventure.

———

It was indeed the most spacious flat, taking in the two top floors of a small apartment block called Rossetti House. The entire building was empty, but in no way derelict, for there were recent traces of habitation as we peered through windows and peeped through keyholes of the flats on the intermediate floors. The drawing room was certainly at least forty feet long with superb parquet flooring; long floor-to-ceiling bookcases at one end, a large open hearth with a marble chimney-piece surmounted by a giant sheet of thick black glass at the other. It looked very swish and expensive. There were five large beautifully painted rooms, some with alcoves lit by concealed lighting, all with wall-to-wall carpeting.

'We can sit on the floor,' said Peter gaily. Upstairs, two more rooms, one with a dormer window in a deep recess almost the length of the wall. This recess was entirely filled with built-in cupboards and drawers on either side of a dressing table which had lights set into each side of the looking glass, as in a star's dressing room. This part shut down, so making the entire top a table about four feet wide. I envisaged myself sitting grandly at it as I put on my *maquillage*.

'H'm, a very good room for me to work in. I can use the top as a drawing table.'

'But it's a bedroom,' I said.

'There are plenty of other rooms to sleep in, but *this* is obviously the place to work.'

I said nothing for the time being, amusing myself by opening the many drawers, most of which were empty or containing small signs of occupation such as hair grips or safety pins. The contents of one drawer made me stop, determined to find the means of living there, for it was half-full of unopened jars of Elizabeth Arden's creams and unguents. When Peter wasn't looking I slipped one in my pocket; he had once made me bring back to the shop a large tomato I had taken when we were hungry. This was a real find for, apart from theatrical make-up which was only given to 'regular' customers, it was almost unobtainable and of very poor quality. We used Meltonian shoe cream for mascara (I had a brief week on moustache-wax which made my eyelashes look like furry spiders' legs), Trex or Spry cooking fat for cleansing cream (how many bearded ladies as a result?), calamine lotion as a powder base and sometimes even baby powder for face powder. Eye shadow was not fashionable then off the stage, but we put Vaseline on our eye-lids and lips to achieve that 'dewy' look. Often it trickled down if the room was hot, which looked as if one had been crying, and sympathy was often given as a result. We were far too sly to admit what in fact it was and sometimes pretended a sadness which did not exist. In an attempt to curl up the ends of my hair I was once surprised by Dylan as I was using a chunk of large macaroni, called *rigatoni*, with a hair grip. He was agog as he enquired:

'Are we going to eat it afterwards?'

———

I wanted to live in Rossetti House so badly that I became quite reconciled to moving there without furniture: surely we could get tea chests or strong boxes to use as tables and, as Peter rightly said, we did have a bed to sit or sleep on. But I knew without asking that even if the rent was reasonable the agents would want a month, if not more, rent in advance. If all else failed I would pawn my electric sewing machine, a twenty-first birthday present. When I saw the fat wooden case which housed it at the end of the book-case I felt reasonably secure.

Taking an hour off work to see the agents, I arrived home early to find Peter and Dylan just going out. It was too early for the pubs to be open, and Peter in front had a strange worried look on his face.

'We're just going up the road . . .' He hesitated and looked very guilty.

'All right, I'll come too. I want to tell you about the flat.' He shuffled about nervously.

'Come on, let's go. I can get the rations before the shops shut.' Peter's telltale eyes moved anxiously: he turned to Dylan.

'It's no good, I can't do it. I told you we shouldn't.' He moved back exposing Dylan, who was standing with his right arm behind his back.

'What have you got in your hand, Dylan?' My voice sounded shrill and school-mistressy to myself. He brought out his left hand.

'Nothing.'

'No, the other one.' I moved forward and pulled his arm. Out swung the fat wooden case, the weight swinging him round. In his hurt actor's voice, he said:

'We were only going to pawn it.'

'Pawn? You know I would never have seen it again. You, you thief!' I turned round to Peter. 'And you're as bad for allowing it.'

'Are you accusing me of stealing?'

'I most certainly am.'

Peter intervened: 'It was as much my fault as his, Pussy, I'm sorry . . . we had no money, and Dylan and I . . .'

I snatched the machine and ran up the stairs with it, not even noticing the weight. My relief at recovering my lifeline was so great that by the time they had followed me up I had quite overcome my temper. The episode was never referred to, and later that evening we went to the Eight Bells together as usual.

Dylan would disappear for three to four days at a time. We would assume he had gone back to Wales, which he did every week or so. I missed my cinema-going chum very much, but we were seldom alone for long, for once our friends knew that we were living in Chelsea, we had many unexpected callers, some on leave from various armed forces, which always underlined that we too would be called up before long.

As I came up the stairs one day I heard a woman's voice talking to Peter. Mary? Kenette? Isabel? No, when I got nearer it didn't sound like any of them. It had the quick phrasing and slightly rough intonation I associated with parts of Limerick and Clare. My God, I thought, one of my Irish cousins.

Inside, Peter was standing up by the fireplace and Dylan was sitting by the window. A spruce tidy Dylan in a white shirt the colour of fresh snow, with a new, rather flamboyant tie. (So that was why he had attempted to take my sewing machine.) In the other chair sat one of the most lovely young women I had ever encountered. She looked as though she had been fashioned from wonderful wax, translucent and pliable. Her colouring was magnificent: pink cheeks, a creamy skin and a superb mane of golden curly hair. It shone and flashed like a beacon, now red, now gold, and now the colour of ripened wheat. Tendrils, so beloved in certain literature, curled like filigree goldwork on her cheeks. She looked like the embodiment of all the heroines in literature, far removed from the sophisticated 'beauties' of the Paris days, the only truly natural beauty I had ever seen.

The beautiful head and body were set off by the rose-coloured velvet frock which had old and exquisite ecru lace at the neck and cuffs, so that she looked like a rich jewel nestling in a velvet-lined case. It was as though a seventeenth-century painting had come to life. Her manner was natural; it invoked no jealousy nor the feeling of competition common between good-looking women, for she seemed to me then far removed from the quirks of ordinary people.

This was my first meeting with Caitlin Thomas, and the beginning of an unforgettable friendship. In a few months' time, the winter of 1941 to 1942, they were both to live in London.

CHAPTER FOURTEEN

'Living in the style to which we are not accustomed. I must say I *do* like space,' said Peter as he walked up and down the long room in Rossetti House, whilst I sat on the floor watching the flames lick up from some salvaged wood burning in the large fireplace. I was sitting on the floor from choice, for there were several comfortable old leather armchairs my grandmother had rooted out of an attic. Several months before, we had solved the furniture problem by having my mother move in with us; it hadn't worked out and, when she moved to a smaller place a few streets away, quite a lot of her furniture had stayed with us. Even if we could have afforded it, there was almost none to be bought except horrible, cheap-looking new 'utility' (the government name) furniture which was allocated to young brides (marriage lines had to be produced) on a points system. A quarter's rent had been paid by my mother, which was very welcome for I had been extremely ill and needed a few weeks' rest after leaving the hospital. Now all we had to worry about was food, and this problem was immediately solved in what seemed a miraculous way.

Mysteriously two barrels appeared outside the front door upstairs. They were there when we came back from delivering some 'samples' – I had temporarily become a commercial traveller, Peter volunteering to carry the heavy cases around for me. We rolled them in, poked, prodded and wondered about the contents. Beer? No. Whatever was inside was solid not liquid. How on earth did one open them? Peter went to the café opposite Chesil Court to borrow chisels, hammers and other tools; for what seemed like hours his strong arms levered and broad shoulders heaved.

'It's fish, Pussy, hundreds of fish all packed on ice. Who on earth could have sent them?'

Sure enough he was right – fish fresher than any we had seen for years, large, dark blue eyes staring reproachfully at us: herrings, plaice, gurnets, dabs, whiting and many smaller fish we couldn't name, all tail- and head-entwined in crushed ice. For three days we 'fished' extensively. We had them fried, baked, grilled and curried and Peter even tried salting and smoking some in the large chimney, for as he rightly said they would go bad before we could eat them all. Finally we bartered a few pounds from one barrel (the other we left sealed) for tins of meat with Vic the grocer, but not before we had given a large *fruits de mer* dinner party (fish knives not being admitted, there was the complication of having to borrow dozens of forks) at which Donald and Melinda, Dylan and I think Caitlin, Mary Montagu, Crabbe, and Brian Howard were among the guests.

Ever since I had met Brian at the Cavendish the year before, he would appear, from time to time, like a genie. Brian and drama were synonymous: he was possibly the original one-man theatre for he resented other players. Having experienced this with prima donnas on the stage I knew just how to play to it: consequently we got on very well together. He was fond of calling me 'that wickéd girl' or 'that wickéd Madonna', although to my certain knowledge I did nothing in any way outrageous. Brian made it impossible to scene-steal, for then the curtain would be rung down abruptly. Most of the dramas had several acts of a tragicomic nature. He had the quality of making the simplest meal into a banquet: you could live a lifetime during one of them; eat, drink, laugh, quarrel, make up and still discuss ideas with gaiety and spontaneity.

When all the guests had gone, he declared he would stay the night, and he was shown into the room with pink-painted walls and ceiling. 'My dears! I should wake up in the morning like the rose-red cutie half as old as time! I couldn't possibly sleep a *wink* here.' We hurried around and made up a bed in a plain white room. He wasn't impressed and demanded another drink. Carefully we steered him away from truculence as the night lengthened. Even he was tired, wrung out by the evening's entertainment. The staircase up to our bedroom was narrow: we both stood on the bottom step close to each other to say goodnight. He stood there, a slim figure, his dark eyes burning in the handsome tortured face, the full petulant lips quivering, reluctant to be alone. With a last burst of energy he made a loud sobbing sound, his voice trembled as he blurted out:

'You're going upstairs to lie in each other's arms, and here am I, alone, just a silly old sissy.' He turned, slamming the door of the housemaid's bedroom.

When we got up in the morning his bed was empty. Carefully laid on the pillow was a note saying:

'My dears! the kitchen smells like Mac Fisheries on a bad day. Meet me in the downstairs bar of the Ritz at noon.'

Peter kept this assignation while I got on with my commercial travelling. As I opened the door on my return I heard Brian's voice imperiously saying:

'Where is that wickéd girl?' He rolled the word 'wicked' around his mouth as though it was an exotic edible stone. I looked down the long corridor to see Peter's large head peering round the corner. He looked put out.

'Thank goodness you've come,' he said tetchily, 'you can deal with that thing in the drawing room.'

'What thing?'

'Oh, I don't know what it's called, a chauffeur brought it, and said you knew about it. I can't understand why you didn't tell me.' These were quite sharp words for Peter; normally he accepted what I did. Since that day in Paris we had never quarrelled. I went into the drawing room, and standing forlornly, yet comically, in the middle of the huge room was Gwladys.

Gwladys was a *rara avis* in the true sense, for she was an actress-penguin. She had starred in a film called *To Brighton with a Bird* and it was in a film studio I had first met her, and her owner. A few months previously I had met the owner casually in the street, who expressed to me her concern at finding a home for Gwladys for two weeks whilst she went away. Gwladys hated other penguins, preferring human company, therefore a zoo was out of the question. On the spur of the moment I said I would look after her. The fish should have warned me, but having been in hospital had put it right out of my mind.

Brian's large inquiring eyes opened even wider when I brought Gwladys into the kitchen in my arms. He sipped his gin and said:

'I do hope, you wickéd girl, you're not going to behave like your namesake Empress Theodora did with the geese!'

Gwladys wriggled when she smelt the fish, so I put her on the floor. She waddled over to the open barrel and very rapidly swallowed down several large fish.

'It'll choke,' said Peter. 'Heavens, it's already eaten as much as I could and it's only a fraction of my size.'

They were both fascinated by the behaviour and appearance of this comical bird, although neither of them would have admitted it. Peter had put his glass on top of the unopened barrel and, after the fish, Gwladys walked over to it; in a flash the beak was in and the gin gone. She looked up at us, turned round and walked, unsteadily it seemed, out of the room. We followed her along the corridor, as unerringly she went into the bathroom, hoisted herself up on to the side of the bath and tugged at the tap with her beak. As the water gushed out she chortled, rolled and splashed about with ecstasy. Brian turned to Peter and said:

'Fancy having a mistress with a gin-drinking penguin. It's going to cost you something, my dear.'

It was a tumultuous two weeks for there were many times when, as Peter remarked, the flat looked like a second-rate lagoon. The gin (what little there was) had to be kept under lock and key as it was often broached; the bathroom door was kept locked, for once we came back to find the place awash, the floors intricately patterned with wet webbed footmarks. There was but little painting or commercial travelling done, for she was a full-time job. Nevertheless it was worth it when she sat on my lap in the evening, her beak nestled under my ear as I read my book. Peter liked the surrealist 'mother and child' effect, saying that it almost made him want to take photographs again, had he possessed a camera.

In the unaccountable way that things happen he was soon to get a camera. Maitland Pendock, at this time with the Ministry of Information, had been an ardent admirer of Peter's photographs for many years, and was distressed that he no longer took any. He had gone to the trouble of finding out from mutual friends where Peter lived, and appeared one evening with a Rolliflex camera which he placed strategically on a nearby table. Before long Peter was fiddling with the case and looking inside.

'It's like my old camera,' he said; then, putting the camera firmly back on the table, 'thank goodness I've given all that up.'

Maitland's thinning brown hair was blowing gently from the breeze through the open window. His kindly, round, blue-grey eyes glanced at me almost imperceptibly through his spectacles.

'I'll leave it just in case you feel like using it, Peter. I could sell any photographs you took, very easily. There's some film, too; it's impossible to buy these days. Now let's all go out and have a drink.'

During that summer Peter took in all about twenty photographs, mostly nudes of me, some of which were published in *Lilliput*, of which Mechtild Nawaisky ('no more whisky') was art editor. It was practically the only magazine at the time which had photographs. Later on they reprinted, at Mechtild's instigation, some of Peter's Paris photographs in a series called 'Surrealist Artists'. Inevitably the day came when he pawned the camera to buy canvas and paints. Maitland redeemed it, but it was seldom used. To be fair to Peter it must be stated that he was as painstaking a photographer as he was a painter. He always developed and printed his own negatives (he would tease Cecil Beaton by calling him an amateur when he sent his rolls of film to be processed) for he said that any fool could click a shutter but the true art was in the dark-room. Despite the blackout, fully equipped dark-rooms were not easy to find, as many were taken over by the War Ministry for printing photographs brought back by agents. The Russian photographer Edward Mandinian, who worked for the Free French Army in England, became a true friend when he lent him his studio in Ebury Street.

Meanwhile I was still going some evenings to the fire-watching post but as the incidents were fewer at this time, the work consisted mainly of checking with headquarters and making cups of tea when it was available.

The quarter's rent had long since been expended. We were sitting rather moodily rolling cigarettes from our 'butt' tin, when the cheerful ting of a taxi meter being stopped came from the road below us. We hung out of the windows to see Sophie, arms bulging with flowers, bottles and brown paper bags. She came bounding up the stairs looking blooming, extremely smart in new clothes. It was almost a year since we had seen her.

Yes, she had a new job, a good one at a large hotel in Park Lane, and the manager had taken a 'fancy' to her.

'I thought we'd have a party, just ourselves,' she said, as chickens, salad, salami, cheese, wine, whisky, gin and brandy were all disgorged from the large brown paper bags.

'But how did you get it all?'

'Arthur made me up a parcel. I nearly brought him too, but he's on duty. I'll bring him next time. Tonight, just us.'

We didn't know whether to eat (for we were permanently hungry) or drink first: I think we did both together, talking all the time. Peter's eyes had the lazy smile in them that always showed when he was happy or excited.

'Dear little Sophie, this is a change from the dried milk powder.'

She beamed with delight and filled up his wine glass.

'What a lovely flat. Is there room for me?'

Aunt Zenobia, phase two, was obviously over.

———

I suppose it was Gwladys who reminded me that I hadn't had an animal of my own for some time (for Jason had become my mother's dog), so I bought a brown standard poodle puppy, who to begin with was only tolerated by Peter because she was of French origin, always called by him a *caniche*, and also called, on account of her proclivities, *Merde*. Finally we settled on Mouche; she became the mother of almost all the brown poodles in Chelsea, and a much-loved animal.

———

The nearest we ever got to a holiday was to spend the evening on the terrace of The Doves pub at Hammersmith when Dylan, Caitlin and their small son were living in A. P. (now Sir Alan) Herbert's one-room studio. It was highly unsuitable for a family, so in early summer Caitlin reluctantly went back to a cottage they had rented at Talsarn in Cardiganshire. Once more Dylan made the endless journeys back and forth to London. He was writing a short novel about a man who lost an article of clothing each time he went through a new experience, ending up stark naked outside Paddington Station, the most high-class London station, as Dylan said. During that summer Caitlin became pregnant so he begged me to find them the impossible: a cheap furnished abode, for all they owned was a 'deck-chair with a hole in it, half a dozen books, a few toys and an old iron'. His great childhood friend, the musician Dan Jones (now Dr Daniel Jones the composer), had at some time lived in Wentworth Studios, Manresa Road, Chelsea; it was empty and seemed, by peering in through dirty windows, furnished. It became my job to find out who owned it (for Dan was away in the army) and to get the keys.

In early autumn they moved into the enormous square room with a partitioned-off kitchen, a bathroom built not later than the turn of the century and a glass skylight that leaked when it rained. The furniture may not have been entirely solid, the strips of carpet threadbare, but Caitlin soon made it into a real home: the large round table shining with polish, the Welsh dresser gleaming with assorted crockery. There were books everywhere (mostly Dan Jones's) along the walls on the floor, as well as in lurching bookcases; some large volumes, piled one on the other, made low tables. Dylan's drawings were *passe-partouted* and hung on the walls, along with reproductions of paintings that took Caitlin's fancy. Her Welsh-Irish stew, made mainly from vegetables, was permanently bubbling on the stove, a true *pot-au-feu*. There was always a ladleful for callers, a hunk of the grey wartime bread, and sometimes a glass of Guinness or pale ale. Indeed, it was difficult, even if one had just finished a meal, to resist the mouthwatering aroma.

Llewelyn had gone to stay with his grandmother, so Caitlin was able to accompany us in the evenings, for she was a conscientious mother and never left a young child alone. This may have accounted for a certain wildness sometimes when she did get out, for whilst we were enjoying ourselves she would be baby-sitting – and often understandably ready to throw the first thing to hand when we came back hours late and not entirely sober. Dylan would send me in first, hanging behind with a sickly smile on his face, an expression of mock astonishment which tended, if anything, to make Caitlin crosser. All in all she was very tolerant, far more so than I would have been under the same circumstances. For it was all work and worry, with very little play, to a vital and beautiful young woman in her twenties, who saw all her contemporaries enjoying themselves. Friends of later years can scarcely imagine the deprivations she underwent, both before and after this time; Dylan, the enchanting companion and friend, was far from the ideal husband.

Despite our concessions to the bourgeois life it was a summer of unease and restlessness. Towards the end of it Peter was called up in the fire service to a post in the East End of London, where some of his cockney colleagues called him 'Uncle'. This he seemed to like. What he liked more was that he worked for two days at the post, and then got two days off, which meant he could continue with his painting. The pay was a little over three pounds a week for both single and married men. The first week he grandly said he was going to make me an allowance, handing me a ten-shilling note. I can't remember getting any more, but he was able to pay for his fares, food at the post and some beer or cigarettes. Sophie had to fill in endless forms about her call-up. Having been *enceinte* at my call-up time, I was exempt.

Arthur continued to 'fancy' Sophie, and was most generous to all of us in the way of food or drink. He was a hard-working yet gentle man, who realized his good fortune at not being in the forces, and shared what he could with his friends. Sophie worked until almost midnight, and was therefore entitled to an evening meal. Arthur saw that it was a hefty one, enough for three in fact, so Sophie would eat sparingly and bring the rest home. She was really extremely brave; for many nights, quite unable to get any form of transport, she would run through Hyde Park (all the iron railings having been removed for scrap, to help the war effort), down Sloane Street, then the King's Road, in all a good two miles, carrying the food, and sometimes a small bottle, or a jar of soup withal. I got so that I couldn't sleep until she came back, for then she would jump into our bed, and the three of us, when Peter was home, would eat our midnight feast, dropping off like young animals when our bellies were full. Mouche would finish up the pieces if there were any left, for the food was of excellent quality. But if the meat was tough we would tease her, saying a rich armament-maker must have left it, and she would be indignant.

'They're not left-overs. I've got friendly with the chef, too!'

My alarm would go off at 7.30 a.m. and how reluctantly I crept out of the warm nest, leaving one, and sometimes two, snug figures.

We had a charming milkman who climbed the four flights of stairs with our milk; on Sundays he first put the kettle on, then gave Mouche a run and, when he came back, would have a cup of tea with us, sitting on the end of the bed. If Peter was there he would say:

'The guv'nor can make the tea while I'm out with the dog.' It was a lovely treat on the cold winter mornings.

More and more forms came for Sophie to fill in, all left unanswered.

'I think I'll join the Land Army. I like the country and animals.'

My friends Hugh and Nikki Price Jones, from whom I had bought Mouche, had a rather smart farm in Kent, with several land-girls, as they were called. But I could never get Sophie even to telephone them. She was maddeningly stubborn, never believing she would ever be conscripted, for as she used to say: 'I can't see myself in the army.' It came as a nasty shock when she was peremptorily told to report to a barracks in Oswestry, North Wales, in three weeks' time. The barracks square on a winter's morning and the army huts were a long way from the warm hotel, Arthur, and Rossetti House.

'I'll soon be back on leave,' she said shakily as Arthur took her to the station in a taxi.

But the leaves were few and far between, and Sophie was never a good correspondent. The rent was paid for a month, but on about a pound a week army pay she couldn't keep it up. Out of sentiment, Arthur paid it until the quarter's end, which coincided with her first week's leave. Back came Sophie disguised as a lance corporal.

Towards the end of the week she lay mulishly on the divan saying over and over:

'I will not go back to that bloody place. I'm just not going, so there.'

'Won't they arrest you, or something awful like that? I wouldn't like to think of you in irons, or a cell. Do they have cells for women?'

'I expect so. It's the most ghastly life you could imagine with all those bitchy women. You simply can't imagine what it's like. School was a picnic compared to it. They're the scum of the earth in my regiment: one even whipped a piece of my equipment when I was in the lavatory. I lost an evening out because I hadn't got the blasted silly whistle.'

'Do you feel ill? Perhaps we could get you out on health reasons?'

'I feel unnaturally healthy: except I think I'll go mad.'

This put an idea in my head, so for two days I coached Sophie in mute, staring madness. She looked quite alarming when she was playing well. I got a doctor none of us knew to come and see her; a very sensitive-looking Indian.

'I don't think I can go through with it,' she said, clutching at me, 'not in front of you, I shall giggle.'

'All the better if you do,' I replied.

The doctor rang the bell and when he came in I explained the appalling apathy and sickness that had struck my friend, so unfortunate, just as she was due to report back to the army.

Sophie's huge saucer eyes looked truly frightened when she saw him, and after endless examinations and questions he gave her a certificate for an extra week at home. I led him quickly out lest he notice the joy in her face, but in the hall he said:

'It's a sad case; if she isn't better in a week, we'll have to commit her for further investigation.'

'I don't care. Anything's better than the army. I'll go and be investigated,' Sophie said as she leapt out of bed and started making up her face.

She did indeed go for one investigation, but when it came to the pinch, the army seemed better than a looney bin, so back she went, resolutely determined to find a way out. It was agreed that I would let one of her two rooms (keeping the other one for the joyful return) as a bedsitter to meet the rent.

'I wonder what sort of lodger will apply for the room,' I said to Peter. He twisted his nose with distaste as he said:

'I think I shall move upstairs when they come, and I prefer the word *locataire*.'

CHAPTER FIFTEEN

I took the first *locataire* who called within an hour of my putting a notice in the paper-shop window. He was a medical student, delighted to find a landlady about the same age as himself. He didn't upset our lives half as much as we did his, for in a few months he had married a partly West Indian girl-friend of mine and given up medicine. Peter was an avuncular, beaming best man.

In fact the place turned out to be almost a marriage bureau, for the next one was a strange and beautiful girl called Margery Morrison, who later married John Davenport, one-time poet, literary critic, an old and good friend of both Peter and Dylan. Then Mechtild sent round a shy, pale, dark-haired girl with a sweet smile, and the most unbecoming hair style I have even seen. Her long hair was screwed into a small bun which rested on the top of her head like a small chocolate cake. When I met her coming out of the bathroom with long waving tresses reaching her shoulders, I only recognized her by the sweet smile. She was so quiet that we never knew whether she was in or out; her name was Mary Smith.

We both missed Sophie bouncing in and out, with her schoolgirl midnight feasts and her unpredictable moods. The milkman missed her too, for he said it wasn't proper him sitting on the bed with just me in it. When Peter was off duty, we usually went to the Eight Bells in the evening, but as we had a little more money to spare we would sometimes go up to Soho with Dylan and Caitlin, who was now hugely pregnant. There, we would drink, mostly in pubs, or one-room clubs such as the Colony, Horseshoe or Mandrake, with young, as yet little-known, painters like John Minton, John Banting, Lucien Freud or Francis Bacon; Peter always thought Francis looked like me, and was delighted to find that we had both been brought up in the same part of Ireland. Francis was always my favourite, a brilliant painter working under great difficulties, yet he was, and still is, totally without malice. His face, to the world, was one of gay equanimity; his troubles were not brought out for drinks.

On very slap-up occasions we would go to the back bar of the Café Royal where Jimmy the barman presided priest-like over a vaguely literary gathering. Dylan loved Peter's story of once seeing Chaliapin the great Russian singer there, towering over everyone, his deep, powerful, resonant voice ordering

'Kvass', then being promptly served with a glass of Bass. If we had even more money to spare we might go through to the huge dining room, resplendent with red velvet seats, glass chandeliers and marble-topped tables, to have a cheap meal. It was possible at one end of the room to order food of the snack variety; the other end catered for diners. We were always intrigued by one item permanently on the menu: *pie froid.* Was it *really* cold magpie? We so wanted to think it was that it was never ordered lest we be disappointed. On the back of a menu Peter drew us his impression of the sportsman who only hunted magpies for the Café Royal. Across the room we might see Augustus John with a girl, Brian Howard, Francis Rose the painter, Gerald Kersh the writer, looking wonderfully Assyrian, or any one of many friends. But more often it was the pubs: the Scotch House, the French and the Swiss, all crowded to overflowing, mostly with soldiers (some of them friends) from many parts of the world. Francis Butterfield, another painter friend of mine, told me of a hefty coloured soldier he saw hanging over the bar, staring at his reflection in the mirror opposite and saying:

'Ah don't want no more women; ah don't want no more liquor; ah jes wants maself.'

There were many times when I felt the same way!

———

One such evening in early March, Caitlin and I got separated from the others. The heat, noise and crush were worse than ever, and Caitlin became faint, her huge belly squashed by milling soldiers. I battled my way through the sweating bodies, my face rubbed by coarse khaki, my clothes slopped with beer, to find Peter. I had to shout loudly to make myself heard, and he gave me a few shillings for a taxi. There was no sign of Caitlin when I got back, but after more pushing and struggling I found her outside, leaning against the wall, the street heavily blacked-out, in a state of near collapse.

'Let's go to the Gargoyle' – a club owned by David Tennant – 'and have a brandy,' said Caitlin.

'I've only got just enough for a taxi if we can find one.'

'I've managed to wrench some housekeeping money . . .' She stopped. 'At least I *had* some housekeeping money . . .' She held up her open bag, empty of a purse. With my pocket torch we searched through it as best we could in the pitch-dark street.

'Oh, Cait, where could it be? I couldn't face that crowd again, and we'd never find it, there's no hope of even *seeing* the floor.'

She sighed, then in her clipped, quick voice she said:

'Easy come, easy go . . . I hope whoever finds it really needs it.'

A taxi drew up disgorging yet more soldiers, and after wheedling with the taxi driver, he reluctantly drove us back to Chelsea.

About a week later I met Dylan in the King's Road, outside the Sunlight Laundry. I was carrying a large wicker laundry basket, full of the *locataires'* dirty laundry.

'Cait has had a baby girl. We're going to call her Aeronwy.' His eyes rested on the basket.

'There's nothing much to put her in, when they come back from the hospital.'

On the pavement, we turned out the laundry and made a bundle of it. Dylan stayed outside with the basket. The gimlet-eyed manageress said:

'Where's the basket? There's five shillings deposit on it. You'll have to forfeit that.'

It was perhaps the cheapest and best bassinet ever purchased.

――――

If anything Peter painted more during his fire service days than in the apprehensive days before he joined. The two days off were spent painting from early morning until it became too dark to continue: vivid pictures of flames, twisted girders, or charred wood; the horse's head set against melancholy or burning backgrounds, or crashed-aeroplane-like shapes. His painting was stimulated by the announcement of an exhibition of firemen's paintings, to be held at Burlington House. This was the first chance he had had to exhibit since the war started. (There were but few exhibitions, but I do remember with pleasure one given of Jankel Adler's pictures – Jankel Adler was then living in England; the sensuous, rich, thick swirls of paint, the strength and power of those large canvases, were like a feast to colour-starved wartime eyes.) It was an exciting time for both of us, selecting and then finding appropriate frames for the pictures. Finally he decided on three paintings, one from each phase of his development.

The standard of paintings in the exhibition was remarkably high, and I remember particularly a picture by Leonard Rosoman, the thought of which today strikes an emotion in me. The exhibition was given mention in the press, an unusual occurrence in the thin double-sheet newspapers of the time. Two days after the opening, a letter was forwarded from Burlington House for Peter, inquiring the price of the crumpled-paper-aeroplane painting. The writing paper was first quality, die-stamped, with an address in Admiral's Walk, Hampstead. As Admiral's Walk was commonly known as 'Millionaire's Row' our hopes ran high when Peter went out to call. Alas, it was a young girl, a student, who was unable to afford more than five pounds. Nevertheless it spurred Peter on, encouraging him enormously. It also paid for the frame, more canvas, and gave us a good dinner, as well as boosting his reputation at the fire station. Two of his colleagues, namely Syd and Reg, became his champions. Part of Peter's fire service training was to jump from the top of a high building into a blanket. He was not at all cowardly, but expressed the fear to me that the blanket would split under his weight.

'The others seem such small men compared to me,' he would say ruefully.

One evening Syd and Reg were at the front door, small, almost wizened men in their early forties. One was carrying a green parrot in a cage.

'Is Uncle in?'

I replied he was, asked them in, stupidly poking my finger at the parrot, who straight away gave it a feeble peck and then in a shrill voice said:

'Bugger it, I've done it again.'

Syd apologized for the language 'in front of a lady' and explained at great length that he'd been picking up his mum's parrot who'd been staying with his auntie in Chelsea while his mum was with his daughter who'd just had a baby.

Peter, hearing the voices, came down to see them. When they saw him, Syd and Reg became tongue-tied, so to put them at their ease he showed them round his studio, giving Reg a small painting for his 'gran' who was bed-ridden and apparently a 'picture-fancier'. I offered them a glass of beer when they came downstairs, by now quite relaxed and chirping like sparrows. The parrot gave an eldritch-like shriek when it saw them.

'We wus thinking, me and Reg,' said Syd, 'about your blanket jump. We've decided to change our days off, so that we're there to hold the blanket. You'd feel safer with us, wouldn't you, Uncle?'

They appeared even smaller standing in front of Peter than they did on their own. The gesture touched us both deeply and brought a lump to our throats. For many months, as their days off coincided with Peter's, they would make the journey to Chelsea, to drink with us in the Eight Bells. They were delightful chums.

Chums and friends were what I missed most with Sophie and Peter away. The two days he was on duty seemed like two weeks, the large flat very empty, for the *locataires* lived their own lives. But for the bounding poodle to greet me on my return I would have been very lonely. If the weather was fine I would take her for long walks in Battersea Park, sometimes calling into the Eight

Bells for a glass of beer on my return; to begin with, it was strange sitting alone in our usual corner. Caitlin was feeding the baby, so seldom came out in the evenings. Acquaintances would ask me to join them, but I wanted my big kind man.

Although our relationship had never been a passionate one in the accepted sense, there was mutual affection and deep love between us. He was too indolent to be a sustained lover; what energy he had went into his work. Materially Peter gave me practically nothing: intellectually and spiritually he provided me with the qualities I lacked. By careful example he made me intellectually honest and truthful, giving me an appreciation of many things I might not have found for myself. He gave me much-needed security, not of the prosaic, monetary kind, but of understanding my purpose in life. He was, truly, my mentor and friend. He knew I was impulsively quick-tempered, so tried to avoid upsetting me. He seldom reproached me, and unless in a devilish mood, I did little to provoke him, for I could tell instantly, from the expression in his sad, dark eyes, if he was displeased. However, when in extreme poverty I cut off my long blonde hair and sold it to a wig-maker for five pounds, he demanded we go immediately to get it back. Part of it had already been used; the rest was bought back, and made into a kind of fly switch which was hung on the wall to remind me of my folly. In these days of wigs and hairpieces, it is once more being worn.

When I came home from a party in the early (or late) hours of the morning, he was sitting up in the monkish habit writing his journal (which he wrote in mirror-writing, like Leonardo da Vinci); he looked up, smiled and said:

'Goodness, I'm glad you're back. I was beginning to think you'd nipped off with someone.'

His faults were of omission: the maddening slowness and apathy when faced with something he did not, or would not, do. In the four years spent together, the greater part of my adult life thus far, we lived life ten times over: sharing the horrors of war, invasion, bombing, near starvation, and the bloodiness of botched birth. From this we kindled our own small fire at which we warmed our hearts.

———

Briefly I worked for the Free French army in London, but *mon colonel* was a zealous man, and a nine-hour day with only a half-day off a week, and one Sunday a month, strained even my francophilic feelings. I was glad when they transferred to Algiers, for then I was able to leave. As I became adjusted to the changing life I did see my old friends, sometimes unexpectedly.

The nights were often still peppered with gunshots and distant bombs, but the sound no longer wakened us. It was strange, small unaccustomed noises that penetrated sleep. I awoke to the whimpers, and then hesitant low growls turning to rumbles of the dog as I lifted my head from the pillow. A soft footfall: was it the *locataire*, or my sleep-bound imagination? Fumbling, I switched on the light; standing in the middle of the room was my cat-burglar friend, whom I shall call Nemo, in army uniform. The blackout curtain hanging over the open window flapped gently.

'Why ever didn't you ring the bell, Nemo? Do shut the window, or else the wardens will be here.'

'I wanted to keep my hand,' he smiled angelically, 'or, rather, my foot in. There's not much chance for practice these days.' He drew in his lithe, slim body. 'These four storeys, with a perfect drainpipe, were a challenge, my dear!'

The gaunt face was deeply tanned, and more handsome than I remembered it. From his hip pocket he took a flask.

'Let's have a good drink, and then go to a nightclub and have masses of bad drinks. I'll deliver you back in time for breakfast. In fact,' he delved into his tunic pockets, 'I've got some sausages, and,' he folded his hands over like a magician, 'two eggs.'

Off we went in a curious motor-car (I asked no questions) to the Nest, the dog as well, and drank whisky of 'Four Nations', very bad nations from the taste, but we danced, and talked, and drank, and got home in good time for breakfast.

The word 'cat-burglar', in common with 'Raffles the Gentleman Burglar', has gone out of currency in these days of knives and guns. Burglars used to be like snakes; they were more frightened of you than you were of them, and only attacked in self-defence. In any event, Nemo had once proved his worth by restoring the indiscreet letters of a young woman I knew, who was being blackmailed.

There were many pleasant times, especially when Peter's days off coincided with a weekend. I had taken a part-time temporary job, so as to have more free time, as we now had two *locataires*, and the large flat had to be cleaned and otherwise organized. Some evenings were spent with the tiny exquisite Grete Wyndham, estranged wife of Richard Wyndham the painter, in her delicate doll's house, which suited her to perfection, with its lovely Chirico paintings, and always a large ginger cat, called Teddy: it was, or it seemed, half the size of Grete. It was there I met Constant Lambert's first wife, Flo, her Javanese features looking exotically beautiful, set off by a prim VAD uniform. Simon Harcourt Smith, the diplomatist, lived in Lawrence Street, with his amusing wife Rosamond, then encased in plaster up to her waist after a car accident. When I first met her, sitting perched on the end of her bed, she said:

'Well, shall we talk about people we know, or shall we talk bawdy?'

There were unpredictable, richly amusing evenings with John Davenport; dinner with Philip Toynbee, on leave from the army, with his first wife, Ann, at the White Tower; a luncheon we gave at Rossetti House for Edouard Mesens, the Belgian poet and surrealist leader, who was working for the Belgians in England. From him we learned welcome news: Giacometti was safely in Switzerland, and Max Ernst had married Peggy Guggenheim, and was in New York. There were many others, all Peter's friends. Caitlin and Dylan, with the baby in the wicker basket, came to share a piece of meat the size of a spectacle case one Sunday. Dylan was enthralled by a story concerning an elderly Welsh woman of his acquaintance who had gone mad.

'She was seen pouring the milk on the ground outside the front door' – a considerable actor's pause – 'and then trying to put the cat into the milk bottle!' He drew in his breath and then gave his characteristic snort-snigger.

But the old pattern had broken: events had to be arranged ahead according to days off. There were fewer spontaneous meetings, for we were both on the side of authority. We no longer made arrangements as one person, but as two. Inevitably, I did make new friends as the months ran on, some of whom shared no part of my life with Peter. *Mon colonel* was equally zealous on his half-day off; his long, lean, agile Norman body springing up the four flights with a bottle of wine, but I did not see myself as *une fille du regiment*. Subsequently I heard he had written several highly praised books. I met Bertram Wedgwood, the Casanova of that large and distinguished family, who had recently returned from occupied France and who, although in his sixties, spent most of his time trying to get back as an agent. Through him I met other members of the Wedgwood family. Also a strikingly outrageous Austrian girl, Lieselotte Sworn, recently married to a Staffordshire surgeon.

'But he *had* to marry me, darling. I vas staying at his house for the veekend, vhen they said enemy aliens couldn't move from vhere they vere. You can't live in sin in Stafford.' The marriage was dissolved more than twenty-five years later, by the death of her husband.

Gavin de Beer (later Sir Gavin de Beer), eminent biologist and writer, then a captain in the Grenadier Guards, with the bluest eyes I have ever seen, and his gentle-voiced wife, Cicely: to my subsequent immense embarrassment, I spent the first evening I met him explaining the functions of the liver in the body. How it came about I cannot imagine; we laughed about it later, but why, oh why, couldn't someone have told me! Yvonne Chudleigh would appear like a blast of strong sea air from Cornwall, tell me the latest gossip, then disappear into a waiting taxi with the elegant young naval officer she was shortly to marry; Jane Donn Byrne, daughter of the Irish novelist, a Rosalind-like figure in the trousered uniform of the fire service; Geoffrey Sansom, with whom I spent pleasant evenings, and a day at the zoo – he was later reported missing, believed killed, after an air raid over Germany.

There were pub friends too: Felix Hope Nicholson wearing old, finely embroidered silk waistcoats, and his two good-looking sisters, Lauretta and Marie-Jacqueline; the Coopers, alike to look at, both lawyers. A charming elderly Irishman called Brading who came from Nenagh (near my family home) and whose family owned property which housed the Garda station. His married sister who lived there collected the rent from it. When she died during the war, he wrote them a polite letter (which he showed me) concerning the transfer of the property to his name. Some months later they replied, saying they had always paid the rent to Mrs — and they couldn't consider handing anything over to a stranger. Robert Herring, editor of *Life and Letters*, who lived opposite the Eight Bells, added a touch of colour when he joined us from time to time, dressed in a pillar-box red, nineteenth-century army uniform.

Some months after Pearl Harbor a new uniform appeared on the streets, and in the pubs of London: the curious parti-coloured (mushroom-pink trousers, and olive jacket) uniform of the American army officer. To begin with it was a rare sight, seen only in the West End of London, and as such it provoked certain interest. It was some time before this uniform was seen generally, particularly in the borough of Chelsea. For specialists of military uniforms (such as Barbosa) there appeared in the Eight Bells a puzzling anomaly.

A tall, extremely slender young man with penetrating yet friendly brown eyes, a pleasing, ready smile revealing very white teeth, and dark curly hair was dressed in the uniform of a British army officer, yet with badges both of rank and regiment unknown to us all. As we had long been told to look for German spies dressed as nuns (we would know them by their boots) and other like discrepancies, for a few days he and his companion, a tall, beautiful blonde with slanting eyes, were a subject for discussion, as they sat apart, talking quietly together. Standing next to them at the bar one evening, Peter heard the girl address him as Constantine.

'He must be a Russian officer,' said Peter authoritatively.

This remark carried a certain weight, and those regulars convinced we had a spy in our midst were silenced. When he looked around the pub, his cherubic smile was returned by the less fanatical clientele as their fears subsided. The ten-day wonder was over as they became 'regulars' themselves, sometimes in the company of a dramatically thin, black-haired girl, with eyes like a Byzantine empress, and a tall handsome blond man. They always left enormously long butts to their cigarettes, which Peter and I would carefully collect for our butt tin.

Several weeks later I was enjoying my drink and reading a book after walking the dog, when he came alone into the almost empty pub. I looked up and smiled as he walked to the bar, then bent down to attract the pub-owner's attention through the tiny glass aperture, to order his drink. I looked up again; surely the colour of his jacket and trousers were different? As he turned round, I saw he was dressed in an American olive army jacket, with unmistakably British khaki trousers. He leaned against the wall at the end of the bar, his long legs crossed at the ankles. An elderly man whom I hadn't seen before got up and went over to him, took his hand and pumped it up and down vigorously.

'You're the first Yankee soldier I've seen since 1918,' he said enthusiastically. 'You boys pulled us out of a tight corner in France then. Welcome back. I'd like to buy you a drink. What'll it be, whisky, gin?'

Towards the end of his speech, the old men's voice had acquired an accent he assumed to be American.

The young man gave a rather embarrassed smile. He tapped his toe on the ground as he said:

'Thank you so very much, I'll have a mild and bitter.' This was delivered in the purest tones of the accent known as Oxford English. The old man looked flabbergasted and not a little annoyed. He felt gypped, so sure was he the answer would be 'Scartch', delivered, with luck, in a Brooklyn accent. Two regulars exchanged significant glances.

The young man's name was Constantine FitzGibbon, and although American born, with an American mother, he had been brought up and educated in England, France and Germany. It is therefore not surprising that he spoke with an Oxford accent, having attended that scholastic settlement for some years. His curious succession of uniforms was explained by his transferring from the British army at a time when there were scarcely any American soldiers, and certainly not uniforms, in England. Later on when we became friends, Peter would tease Constantine by calling him the 'Middle-Western Max Beerbohm'. From now on I would occasionally join his party, at their request, if I was on my own. The Byzantine empress became a lifelong friend of mine; she was the actress Diana Graves, niece of Robert Graves the poet. Her father, an immensely well-groomed man, when adviser to the Tangier government, was known by his colleagues as 'Graves Superieur'. The handsome blond man was her husband, the actor Michael Gough. Sometimes they were joined by an extremely pretty girl, her superb figure set off by an immaculate uniform of the ATA. Her face and elegant figure seemed familiar to me as she walked across the pub, with the assurance that very attractive woman have, to greet Peter. She was one of the 'beauties' of those far-off Paris days, and Constantine's sister, Mimi.

This incidental meeting hastened our friendship, for in those alarming times of departure 'to destinations unknown', sometimes with no return, even the most unsentimental of us tended to cling to the friends and customs of the peaceful past. Perhaps quite erroneously, if you had known someone 'before', they had a verity not easily acquired by wartime acquaintances.

For some time Peter and I had been, almost imperceptibly to ourselves, growing apart. Some days of his off-duty time we didn't see each other at all; instead of being home to greet me in the evening, there would be a note saying he had gone to dine, with Isabel, Anna, Joan, Donald or one of a dozen other friends. This happened very gradually; I realized it only when I found myself making appointments for the days I knew he would be at home. There was no change in our attitude or feelings to each other, but the tough outer edge of the fibre that had bound us together for nearly five years was beginning, very gently, to fray; the kissing time was almost over. Yet he was to me, still, as Charles Lamb wrote of Thomas Fuller, my 'dear, fine, silly, old angel' and always would be.

———

It is difficult to know the precise moment when one becomes attracted to someone else. It is certainly some time before one is conscious of it and even then it is often not immediately realized or, if it is, it is pushed by safety-valve impulses into the back of the mind. Often if opportunity, fate, call it what you like, does not arise to nurture the attraction, it will lie fallow, eventually wither and die.

Constantine and the tall beautiful blonde with slanting eyes quarrelled and parted. Constantine spent more time in the Eight Bells, both with friends and alone. How or why it happened I shall never know, yet, in the course of an evening spent alone together, we found twelve hours later that we were passionately, irrevocably in love.

I told Peter of my feelings the next day. He hunched his shoulders, the eyes clouded slightly, as he said:

'I'm not really surprised, Pussy, I always thought he was just the chap for you. Promise me one thing: if we meet together, don't call both of us darling; behave as if we had just met.' He caressed my ear, and went to his studio.

When he was on duty I packed my personal belongings. There was a letter addressed to me propped in front of my carriage clock on the mantelpiece. I avoided opening it until I was finished. The two suitcases were heavy; I took the first one downstairs to the hall; on the way back I heard the phone ringing. It was Sophie.

'I came home on leave yesterday. Peter says you've gone off with an American. You haven't, have you? What are you up to?' We arranged to meet later in the day.

The front door was blocked by a tall figure in a dark overcoat, although the August day was warm. It was Donald Maclean. His manner was stern, his immense height overwhelming.

'I've come to talk to you about Peter. You can't seriously consider leaving him after all these years. He loves you, and needs you.'

I was almost in tears as I put my hand on his arm.

'Let's go and have a drink, Donald. I want desperately to talk to you.'

The sun was strong, casting long black shadows as we walked along Christchurch Gardens to an unfamiliar pub called The Surprise. The high ceiling inside, the open double doors, made it unusually bright, and I wished I had brought my dark glasses. As I talked, and he understood my inner turmoil, he became less forbidding, but still I couldn't convince him that what I was doing was right for both Peter and myself. He saw it only as self-justification. Finally I took Peter's crumpled letter from my handbag and handed it to him. He unfolded the long sheets torn from a sketching block, with Peter's distinctive left-handed writing, and read:

Friday Night.

My dear Pussy,
Unless I write now impromptu, if one can use the word of so prompted an action, I am sure I shall never do so; and I wish you to go away knowing that I know how much I am grateful to you, how much I owe you. Of myself, of course I speak: when I came back here to England I think I was as much in a state of collapse as France was: the war, other things, had entirely upset me and I was completely adrift and incapable of action; you rescued me and put me on my feet, made it possible for me to do the one thing I want to do but which without you would have been so much more difficult; you made it practically possible for me to paint and gave me the mental armistice from the war without which I would not have been able to continue; and I shall always be grateful to you.

I'm not in love with you and except for a brief spell (not when I first met you; much later) didn't see how I could be – I like dirty, black-haired women – but I do love you very much, and it would make me happy that you should be so. I've tried to love you – I would so much have liked to, I admire you so much, you have all that I lack: but I can't and you know I can't. I've been 'faithful' to you longer by a dozen times or so (not wholly by laziness, but because I wanted to be) than ever to anyone else; but it wasn't possible and I'm very glad indeed that you've found someone else, it seemed such a terrible shame that you should be wasted on an unresponsive person. Dear Pussy, I hope you'll be luckier this time, you do deserve it.

Love,

Peter.

P. S. (i) Can't I have 'Mouche'?

(ii) Don't keep saying 'I can't tell you . . .'

(iii) Can't I have 'Pinkie'? [the tall, beautiful blonde with the slanting eyes]

(iv) Will you give me the address of the shop at which you get the coffee?

(v) I like Constantine and rely on you to persuade him to behave as if I met you this evening with him.

(vi) Would you write and have printed a short circular which I can send or hand out to such people as Pendock, Mr Brading, Cooper's, Maybee's, answering in a nutshell such questions as 'How is, where is T—'?

(vii) Don't drink very much. Have some children, and be as good to everyone as you were to me.

Dear Pussy,

adieu

Peter.

The lock of golden-brown hair fell over his forehead, the steady hazel eyes looked at me, as Donald carefully folded the letter, put it into my hand and closed his large hands around mine.

'Forgive me for interfering,' he said. 'It's almost impossible to understand why people do things unless you know the whole story.'

PART TWO

Constantine's Book
1943–1946

CHAPTER SIXTEEN

'I am,' he said, 'the marrying sort; some men are, you know. Thanks to Mr A. P. Herbert,' he emphasized the word Mr, 'I can't marry you until at least next March.'

I watched his reflection in the large Empire looking-glass as I wondered how the inoffensive-looking, mild-eyed man we saw in the local pub could possibly stop Constantine from marrying. It passed through my mind briefly that he might have a persecution mania of which I had no experience. The tick of my clock seemed unnaturally loud for such a delicate instrument and appeared twice as fast as I remembered it.

'You do want to marry me, don't you?'

I replied with complete honesty that I hadn't thought about it. Due to my upbringing I considered marriage was for life and shouldn't be entered into hastily. The penetrating eyes fixed on me, then he smiled.

'Quite right too. Let's have another glass of your grandmother's delicious elder-flower wine. Put some gin in it, and make it good and strong.' The wine, like floral-tasting pee, was very strong on its own; nevertheless I complied with his wishes.

'What's A. P. Herbert got to do with our getting married?'

'He put through some ridiculous legislation saying you had to be married for three years before you can get a divorce. My three years doesn't expire until March. Damn fool,' he said, as though it had been especially designed to inconvenience him alone.

It was the late summer of 1943 and Constantine and I were living in a small charmingly furnished house in Godfrey Street, Chelsea. On one side there was the gaping void of a bombed house and on the other side our neighbour was Stephane Grappelli, whose hours of dexterous practice filtered through the walls and gave our house a marvellously weird sort of enchantment. This only took place during the daytime as he was playing in Piccadilly with the Hot Club de France in the evenings, at Hatchetts I think. He was very friendly, and when we expressed our enjoyment he would leave his door open for us to hear better on warm summer days.

My life had changed considerably: there were always people calling, the ping of the arriving taxi; the phone ringing constantly, the sweet smell of American

Peter Rose Pulham in 1938,
photographed by Howard Coster.

A studio photograph of
Theodora, 1939.

Pablo Picasso, photographed by Peter Rose Pulham, 1939. (*Courtesy of Mary Ryan*)

Jean Cocteau, photographed by Peter Rose Pulham, 1940. (*Courtesy of Mary Ryan*)

Theodora wearing a Traquair model dress, 1940, photographed by Tommy Hepworth.

'The Muse'. Theodora at Rossetti House, 1942, photographed by Peter Rose Pulham. (*Courtesy of Mary Ryan*)

Peter Rose Pulham in his studio at Rossetti House, 1943, photographed by Bill Brandt. (Horse's head in background.)

Chelsea Old Church, shortly after its destruction, 1941.

Constantine and Theodora, shortly after their wedding in Chelsea, 1944.

On a Wedding Anniversary.

At last, in a wrong rain,
The cold, original voices of the air
Cry, burning into a crowd,
And the hermit, imagined music sings
Unheard through the streets of the flares.

The bold birds fly again
From every true or crater-carrying cloud
Riding the risk of the night,
And every starfall question with their wings
Whether it be death or light.

The sky is torn across
This ragged anniversary of two
Who moved for three years in tune
Through the singing wards of the marriage house
And the long walks of their vows.

Now their love lies a loss
And Love r his patients roar on a chain;
The sun's brought down with a shout,
Three years drive headlong, and the mice run out
To see the raiding moon.

'On a Wedding Anniversary' – the original poem written by Dylan Thomas for Constantine and Theodora, of which a slightly different version appears in Dylan Thomas's *Collected Poems*. (*Courtesy of Caitlin Thomas*)

Norman Douglas, in the garden at the Crossed Keys pub, 1945, photographed by Sheila Curtis.

Dylan and Caitlin Thomas shortly after their marriage, 1937, photographed by John McNamara, Caitlin's brother. (*Photograph by courtesy of Constantine FitzGibbon*)

Mimi Mounsey, photographed by
Francis Goodman.

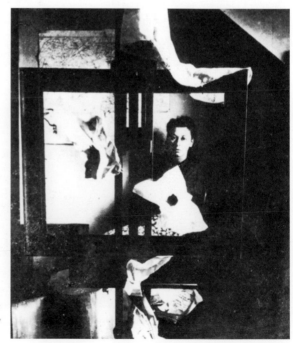

Mary Rose Pulham,
photographed by Peter Rose
Pulham. (*Courtesy of Mary
Ryan*)

Constantine (*left*) in Normandy, 1945.

Theodora in her youth, riding at Annesgrove, County Clare.

Constantine's mother, Georgette, in Bermuda, 1946.

Theodora by the tree at Tranquillity House.

Theodora with two dogs, Christmas 1947.

cigarettes and impromptu parties. As well as going to pubs we went to very different places like the rather grand American Club in Piccadilly, the Ritz and the Berkeley. The five-shilling limit on meals meant that almost everywhere was accessible. I had given up my job and concentrated on reading all Constantine's books as I had read Peter's, listening to music and making as comfortable a home as I could. Even Mouche became domestic and gave birth to six splendid poodle puppies.

There was, too, the difference of the life passionate as against the life affectionate. Constantine's paradoxical nature, which was in turn bohemian, puritan, yet sybaritic, inspired arguments, and in a way competition, which had never happened to me before. Yet there was always the sweetness of reconciliation: the long, lusty connubial Sunday mornings in the downy double bed; the noise of gunfire and bombs drowned by the gushing rushing tumultuous lovemaking.

Every day seemed to produce some new experience or excitement: I was living with a man who wanted to, and was convinced he could, do everything. My domesticity became ever-increasing. The search for food took more and more time, for with the many callers, some who stayed for hours, even days, meals had to be provided. I would make huge pots of onion soup, and when the horseflesh shop opened in Chelsea Manor Street not only the dogs profited but also ourselves, for I had no scruples about making enormous horse-liver pâtés and jellied tongues. Would everyone's enjoyment have been so great had they known, I wonder? I even made a rook pie one day, which was eagerly devoured.

On my shopping expeditions I often met Peter doing his shopping while Mary was at work, and sometimes we would have a drink together. It was during one of these meetings that he said hesitantly to me:

'How do you get married?'

'Why? Are you thinking of it?' I asked.

He mumbled something about Mary and then stopped. I explained that you had to get a licence, or go to a clergyman, whichever you wished.

'How much does it cost?' he asked.

I didn't really know but said that I would find out for him, and we arranged to meet in a pub the next day.

Over the months I had thought of him often and of how he would survive on his own, so I was exceedingly happy about Mary. The next day when we met I pushed an envelope into his hand, saying:

'Take this as a wedding present.'

It was the details and money for the licence. He smiled the sweet lazy smile of his and patted my knee.

'Dear Pussy, what would we all do without you?'

He had hardly finished speaking when the door opened and a beaming Donald Maclean came in, his face dropping slightly when he saw me.

'It's all right, Donald,' I said, 'we were just discussing Peter and Mary's wedding.'

He immediately relaxed and bought some drinks.

'Here's to it, isn't it marvellous news? All the world loves a wedding.'

'No, Donald: all the world loves a lover.'

He made a slight *moue* and it is that expression I remember, for it was the last time I ever saw him.

CHAPTER SEVENTEEN

Constantine had three sisters, all older than he was, and all different both in looks and personality. I think he felt closest to Mimi, the youngest one, for they had seen more of each other as children. Mimi was exquisitely pretty and a temptress. Whenever she appeared something unexpected, and frequently odd, happened. This you knew in advance, and if you went on any expedition with her you gave yourself up, wholeheartedly, to whatever took place. Mimi was married to Claud Mounsey, who was in the navy, and at this time she lived just a few minutes' walk away in Markham Street.

It was on a Sunday in March that Mimi arrived at Godfrey Street with Armor Archbold, her 'young man' of years ago, and a delicate, good-looking young woman: 'Flea' she seemed to be called. I don't think Constantine had seen Armor since the palmy days in the south of France before the war when he was about seventeen. Armor was now in the American Air Force, and it was a reunion *par excellence*.

After an extremely boozy lunch, Mimi decided she wanted to go swimming. This was the fifth year of a tedious war and the end of a long winter. But where to go to satisfy this curious desire? Flea Selsdon in a very quiet voice suggested her club. By this time we all wanted to swim very much indeed. The club was the Lansdowne in Berkeley Square, and we were bowed in. The swimming pool of course was closed for the winter, the lights out, and the water cold. Mimi, however, never daunted, said she wished to look at the swimming pool. This curious wish was granted, and we were led down to the pool, which was in complete darkness. A dim light was switched on, and with a look of complete incomprehension on the porter's face, there we were left.

It was a long pool, dark and cold: Armor, used to Miami and other warm watering-places, shivered. We of sterner stuff decided to look around. Mimi, Flea and I found a small room rather like in a girl's school with standing coat-rails and, on the numbered hooks, a great selection of bathing costumes. We looked them over, took our choice and quickly undressed to put them on. We couldn't find any men's costumes, so we took the most conservative of the ladies', for Armor and Constantine. On the way back to the swimming pool through a very dark corridor we encountered a very small old lady. I was ahead of the others and she stopped me. Thinking she wanted some directions I was about to say that I was a stranger there, when Mimi and Flea caught up with us. The old lady took my hand and, leaning forward, said in a very sonorous voice: 'It's the Ides of March. Never do anything unusual on the Ides of March!' We thanked her and hurried along. Of course we laughed about it, but it was weird; what was she doing down there, and why did she feel so anxious to impart to us her doleful message?

We had our swim, shivered, and while we were dressing it was discovered that Flea had forgotten to take off her earrings, rubies and diamonds, as I remember, and had lost one of them. Mimi and I put back the wet bathing clothes and dived into the pool to see if the earring was on the bottom. Perhaps Constantine did too, I can't remember. It was never found, so we dressed, and in a more subdued frame of mind went to have some warming drinks. Too many, no doubt, as later that night we were involved in a fight through someone making insulting remarks about American soldiers – a common occurrence in those days, and one which never failed to make us angry. By that I mean Mimi and me.

Two days later, on 21 March 1944, after a tremendous official wrangle with the army authorities, Constantine and I got married. The difficulty was that his divorce hadn't come through in time for him to give the three months' notice of marriage. One dialogue went as follows:

'It says here, captain, that you married Margaret Aye Moung in 1939, and now you want to marry Theodora Rosling. Can you explain this?'

'Haven't you ever heard of bigamy?'

Not the way to deal with humourless officials. It was eventually due to General Bradley that permission came through on the very day, but that is Constantine's story.

It was a pretty busy Ides of March that year.

———

Dylan Thomas and Teddy Rose were to have been our best men or witnesses or whatever they are called. Also Nikki Price-Jones had bought the wedding ring. (Sophie by this time had been conscripted into the ATS.) Rings were extremely difficult to get then, at least the kind I wanted was, and Nikki had been deputed or had volunteered to get one. She arrived at Godfrey Street about ten o'clock in the morning. The wedding was fixed for eleven o'clock at the Chelsea Registrar's Office where Constantine had been married to Margaret a few years before. No permission from the army had been granted by the time Nikki arrived, and frantic phone calls came from Constantine to go ahead no matter what. At 10.30 Teddy came, still no groom; at 10.45 Constantine arrived in a taxi waving a piece of paper and carrying two floral sprays. The one for me was quite the wrong colour, a deep red, to go with my cinnamon coat, so Nikki had to have that one, and I pinned a somewhat inferior but nevertheless more fittingly coloured one to my lapel. We got into the taxi and decided that before getting married we would have a drink at the Six Bells, which was opposite the registrar's office.

'Sorry, no spirits.' With what delight that used to be uttered. I had a glass of port and the others a half-pint of cold bitter. Mr Algernon Whiting was the registrar: a Victorian looking gentleman, and well named.

'Good morning, Mr FitzGibbon, it is indeed a pleasure to see you again.' ('My boys are doing well.')

This put us in a very giggly frame of mind. My mother hadn't yet appeared and neither had Dylan, but that was understandable as he was coming from Bosham in Sussex and trains were often a day late if there had been air raids *en route*.

Just as the simple ceremony was ending, my mother appeared in the doorway with her hat on back to front. She really did look very comical and we all burst out laughing.

'I hope you realize that this ceremony is binding?' said Mr Whiting, looking over the top of his spectacles.

We had arranged to have a reception in the Rivoli Bar of the Ritz Hotel. On no account would the Ritz allow the two large poodles, Mouche and her son, to share our nuptial celebrations, so they were left disconsolately at home. It was a pleasant party; you simply ordered what you wanted to drink, and my aunt, very handsomely, was going to pay the bill afterwards. What could have been better? Quite a lot of people who usually drank there at that time of the morning joined in our party and at least one old friend of Constantine's, Halsey Colchester, was among them. Generally, most of the guests drank Pimm's of one form or another. Constantine's father, who liked his drinks very strong, had a double Drambuie put into his. Two of these were inadvertently drunk by young Janie Donn Byrne, who behaved very oddly when she got back to her fire service post in Westminster.

Teddy had to go back to the army, but another American friend called Ferdinand Helm had taken his place by the time it came for luncheon. Constantine's family had all, curiously enough, gone off to see Tallulah Bankhead in *Lifeboat*, and so my family and Ferdie, Nikki and I went in to eat. But where was Constantine? A rapid search of all possible places proved fruitless. Well, we'd better start – oysters, a foolish choice after all that whisky Pimm's, but there you are. After at least twenty minutes, Constantine appeared.

'But where have you been?'

'To the bank to cash your aunt's cheque so that I could pay for the lunch.'

More wine and more oysters were ordered. A very punctilious flunkey then appeared, bent low over my new husband's shoulder, and in solemn tones announced: 'There is a personage in the bar, sir, who *says* he is a member of your party.'

We both went to see who it was, and there perched on a bar stool, wrapped so it appeared in two or three very long woollen scarves, sat Dylan. I still think of him as the best man no matter what.

———

As there were only two days' leave going, the honeymoon was spent in some rum dives, and usually with at least two other people if not more. After the wedding breakfast we did a round of those afternoon drinking clubs that mushroomed during the war. Pluto's, Maisie's, Eileen's and so on. It was in the latter that an incident took place which to this day I don't remember, but Dylan, Ferdie and Nikki all swore it happened.

I suppose that by this time I was 'over-excited' as my mother tactfully put it, but it appears that Constantine and I had an altercation and I threw my drink at him. He ducked and it landed smack on the brand-new hat of a tart sitting at the next table. According to all reports she behaved splendidly and on finding that it was our wedding day bought us a bottle of champagne. Well-intentioned though it was, it didn't mix with the oysters and everything else. Not that I'm blaming her for anything that happened later.

Sometime in the late afternoon we got back to Godfrey Street; to a house full of dog shit and biscuits as Dylan put it. There we found a case of Madeira sent by my grandmother. Even we couldn't broach it just then. At Nikki's persuasion I had a lie down. As I went up the stairs I heard Dylan declaring from Joyce's *Ulysses*, in that wonderful voice: 'The son unborn mars beauty: born, he brings pain, divides affection, increases care,' etc. Nikki, not realizing it was a quote, thought he was being prophetic.

Very much later, it seemed to me, I woke up to darkness. The faithful Nikki was still there, having fed the dogs and washed up endless dirty glasses. She had to catch a train to Kent. I enquired where everyone was. They had just left to go to the King's Head and Eight Bells, on Chelsea Embankment. The dog had gone too; she loved pubs and often went to them on her own. I got a taxi for

Nikki and then made my way towards the river.

I had got as far as the top of Upper Cheyne Row when I heard the sound of many voices singing to a guitar accompaniment. I hurried on in the blacked-out streets, and a little further down a wet dog's nose was put into my hand. It was Mouche, the poodle, begging me to join the fun. Although such a party might be a common occurrence today, in wartime London it was not.

Constantine, Dylan and Ferdie had made at least one stop before the Eight Bells. There they had encountered an elderly gentleman named Bill Gee with his guitar. He was a delightful character, and after an evening spent together we all went back to Godfrey Street. Bill Gee's trousers may well have been split from end to end, but as an entertainer he was superb. He told us that he lived with his eldest son. Dylan, the family man, asked him with an almost smile-in-the-voice tone one uses about children how old his son was. 'Fifty-seven.' At one point during the long night Dylan said to me: 'You are lucky, you have jesters, musicians and tumblers at your wedding. I didn't have any.'

Now Dylan was very frightened of air raids, and announced this during the night. At about four o'clock when we went to bed Dylan was tucked up on the sofa, and Bill Gee still in the armchair. When the sirens went, Bill Gee woke up and said: 'You don't have to be frightened, your old friend Bill Gee is here.' Dylan said that was the one air raid he *might* have slept through.

At eight o'clock in the morning I heard Bill Gee leave the house, strumming 'Daisy, Daisy, give me your answer do'. It was the only time I ever saw him, except for on Victory night the following year when there he was standing next to me at the bar of the Black Lion in Paulton's Square.

———

When I came downstairs the day after my wedding I found three rather green faces. The case of Madeira had been broached and wasn't the answer at all. Nobody either looked or felt very well. We went off to Fred's bar at the Royal Court Hotel in Sloane Square to have something like a gin fizz, or a Tom Collins, that didn't taste like drink. Robert Newton, the actor, with a face the colour of old mahogany, was already there having just ordered one of them. I sat on the bar stool next to him, Dylan on the other side of me. I looked from face to face. Dark mahogany on one side, and unripe melon on the other. 'There's men for you,' I thought. Annie Newton, Bob's wife, came in and Constantine said: 'Oh Annie, Theo and I have just got married.' Annie looked around at all the faces and replied: 'What gluttons for punishment we all are!'

Nevertheless that marriage lasted for nearly seventeen years.

CHAPTER EIGHTEEN

The next three or four months were perhaps the most idyllic I have ever spent. Constantine was the first 'young man' I had ever liked. He was twenty-four at the time, and we loved and laughed, and talked, and drank; but for the war everything would have been perfect. He used to say: 'Won't it be wonderful when the war's over, and we've nothing to worry about except money?'

I, who had determined not to marry until I was thirty, was enchanted by my new domesticity. The 'snail with the house on her back' had a house at last. For the first time there was money, although we were always broke by the end of the month. Shopping for the hard-to-find food could be done during the day, instead of in a rushed lunch-hour or on Saturday afternoons. I enjoyed finding out about food and how to cook it; in fact I enjoyed everything.

Most of all I loved listening to Constantine talk. His conversation was as bright and vivid as the sight of a kingfisher. Among our friends at that time were numbered some of the most interesting minds of our generation and, disliking compulsory education, I would say that any knowledge I have gained has been through listening to the conversation of intelligent men and women. I had read all Peter's books, and now I read most of Constantine's. Constantine's mind was like an Aladdin's cave to me. We used to love to argue, and often I would take a side that I didn't really believe in simply to enjoy the argument. Not for nothing had I been dubbed 'the intellectual's moll' by Peter.

What was Constantine like then? Very tall and slender, curly hair, and quick brown laughing eyes, with a natural, easy smile, would be the immediate impression. Charming, immensely full of life. Full of everything: love, ideas and a spontaneous gaiety which I have never found since. It was all new and wonderful. He was quite unlike anyone I had ever known.

He seemed so very mature that I never realized how hurt he had been by the failure of his first marriage. It wasn't entirely preoccupation with myself, as even now Constantine in periods of deep misery and unhappiness can, and will, exude the same gaiety if his mind is entranced. I simply didn't believe in his jealousy; I thought it was play-acting. Not that I did anything at that time to cause his jealousy, but it was there even without any cause. Perhaps the most alarming side-issue of jealousy is that it is contagious or infectious. I, who had never known it, was to become contaminated, and that was to lead to sorrow.

It was a warm early summer, and we would wander in the evenings through the pleasant Chelsea streets to one pub or another, whichever had the supply of beer. Constantine, although it was strictly prohibited, used to change from his army uniform to his prewar faded corduroys, and I would take off my shoes and walk barefoot beside him. There was a little wall about two feet high outside the Godfrey Street house, and this we would sometimes sit on. An American woman who lived in the same street talked to us there one evening. 'What war work are you going to do?' she asked me. Constantine answered for me: 'She's going to look after me, and have twelve sons, all named after Roman emperors.'

It didn't happen quite that way. But I did want to look after him, and I would have been quite happy to have the twelve sons, although I feel the one called Heliogabalus would have had a halter round his neck. We were, as Constantine's mother would say, 'on the crest'.

I have always felt, and still do, that women lost an awful lot by emancipation. True, they gained certain privileges, but by and large to be a woman in the correct sense of the word had been dissipated. I would no doubt have been a suffragist, but never a suffragette for instance. Had I been of an age in 1916 in Ireland I would certainly have been in the Cumann na mBan, and I hope the College of Surgeons with the Countess de Markiewicz. And in fact, Irish women, when all their men were in prison, carried on the revolution, and afterwards they went back, looked after their men, and in many cases had twelve sons, all named after saints. It is not an affectation when I say that I have never understood the English, nor they me. That is not to say that I haven't a few very good English friends – but I would never, for instance, have married an Englishman. Constantine *sounded* English, that is he had an educated English voice, but he was anything but English in his thought and behaviour. Indeed, how could he be? His mother was American, and his father half Irish and half Scottish; he was born in Massachusetts in America, and had served in the British army before transferring himself to the American forces.

One of the books he gave me to read was George Santayana's *The Last Puritan*. I thought then, and still do, that the main character is remarkably like Constantine.

Quite a lot of people during the war got married because of the fear that one or other of them (this was a civilians' war, as well as the soldiers') might be killed and never see each other again; also for economic reasons. The army allowance for wives was, I don't care what anybody says, an incentive. The curious thing about our marriage was that when it actually happened we were much poorer. It came about like this. Constantine had already been married: when he married me his income was cut by some twenty pounds a month, *because* he was living with his wife *under the same roof.*

————

Dylan and Caitlin came back to the Manresa Road studio for a few months, unable to put up with the 'damned banned area' of Bosham as Dylan put it. The German raids on London were preferable. It was then that the sustained friendship I had found with Caitlin in the autumn flourished still more. They had the baby, Aeronwy, with them, and also the poodle puppy Dombey that they had in fact bought from us for a nominal figure. I spent one whole day clipping and bathing the puppy, and when Caitlin came to collect him she was convinced it was another dog, and wanted Dombey back.

Up until the time I had met Caitlin my clothes were very similar to the ones I usually wear today. Coloured woollen stockings (nylons were new then, and unobtainable anyway), a straight skirt, and either a blouse or a sweater. This was my winter garb; in summer it would be a cotton dress usually gathered in at the waist as the dresses were then. Oh! and the snood. This was a wonderful invention for wartime England, when there were many disturbed nights, and no time to go to hairdressers (not that I ever did); they were made of a coarse fishnet, like a bag, and threaded with elastic. You popped all the back of your hair into them and there you were. It was a mark of defiance then for young women to have shoulder-length hair, as it meant that you weren't in the forces, and therefore not conforming. Until they became over-popular, they were both attractive and useful.

Caitlin's clothes, however, followed no fashion but made one. She knew a little woman who collected clothes made from beautiful velvets, Indian silk, damasks, nankeen, georgette, chiffon, ninon; a stream of beautiful names for forgotten materials. I never found out where this paragon lived, but occasionally Caitlin would give me one or another of these dresses which I particularly admired. I remember especially a midnight-blue velvet frock with a heart-shaped neckline which I wore when I got to New York in 1946 and which was admired by everyone. To this day I still have an enormously long, tattered raw silk, cream scarf, which I used to wear as a blouse, draped sari-fashion, and one little cushion is covered by a rose-pink velvet from one of the 'creations'.

Although we were both Irish, both blonde and from neighbouring counties in Ireland, we couldn't have been more different to look at. In fact it is a mystery how I could jam myself into Caitlin's clothes; I was a good two inches taller, bigger boned, and what used to be called 'classical-looking'. Nevertheless I did, to the amazement of both Constantine and, I think, Dylan. Once, Desmond Ryan's wife, Isabel, asked me if I was in fancy dress. I was delighted.

But if I was living the plush life it was far from that for Caitlin. How she managed I shall never know; there was little money, but always that delicious pot of Irish-Welsh stew on the stove, enough to feed ten people, and the studio was home.

We were all very quick-tempered in those days; it was a savage time, and I don't think Caitlin was any more so than the rest of us. We sincerely believed that to keep things to ourselves was wrong, and that marriage meant sharing everything. Perhaps I would behave differently now, but I doubt it. Although Caitlin could be fierce, she was no fiercer than I was with far less to be fierce about. I loved going round to their studio and noticing all the things that she had done, most of them no doubt missed by our menfolk. She had even planted the broken-down window-boxes with flowers.

Generally we would meet in the evenings for a few glasses of beer or Guinness. Spirits were never on sale in a pub unless you were a regular customer – then you might be given one – only in the hotels and flossier bars. In fact in a pub where you weren't known you had to bring your own glass! Our evening walks got longer and longer, but it was no doubt good for us. Whenever we gave a party it was my grandmother who supplied the booze; she was 'registered' with all the shops she had dealt with pre-war, and was allowed *one* bottle per month. Being the sane old granny who had 'lent the quid' a few years earlier, she always dibbed up, and we had our party. Occasionally Constantine got a bottle from the *PX*.

The Thomases and many other people would come to our house in Godfrey Street: Peter Rose Pulham and Mary, now married, John Davenport, Philip Lindsay, Vernon Watkins and quite a few American dons in the army. Generally, though, we spent part of the evening in a pub, and would then go back and eat in whoever's house was nearest, read poems aloud, play records, dance, or just talk. Dylan and I would often go alone to the Classic Cinema on the corner of Markham Street to see any old film which took our fancy. Once we were asked to leave as we sobbed so loudly.

One evening we were at Caitlin and Dylan's studio. The baby was being fretful, and although the stew was richly going strong, I had got some eggs from the country and we decided to have an enormous omelette as well. It is difficult to realize now that we were *always* hungry. There simply wasn't enough to eat. I whipped the eggs and looked round for something to fill the omelette with. Our ration that winter had been one pound of onions per person. I opened several cupboards and drawers, and in one I found a whole heap of shallots. Knowing that Caitlin and Dylan had been in Sussex, I thought they must have brought them up with them. I peeled, sliced and cooked them, made a magnificent dish and proudly bore it in. We all fell on it, and then seconds later started to feel not only odd, but sick. Caitlin questioned me as to where I had found the shallots: 'In that drawer.' Her reply was terse and to the point. 'You've taken my bloody tulip bulbs for the window-boxes.'

Never, never, no matter how hungry you are, eat a tulip-bulb omelette.

The studio was difficult for Dylan to work in, being only one large room partitioned off, so he would come round to Godfrey Street each morning, as bright and fresh as a home-baked bun, and work in our very small spare room. He wrote a poem there for our wedding anniversary differing from the finished poem in his *Collected Works*. We seldom ever drank at lunchtime; only on a special occasion.

We all seemed much older, we were at least twenty-five, than the footless days in King's Mansions, Oakley Street and Rossetti House. Somehow we had been able to make a pattern, no matter how small, of our way of living.

During all this time the air raids went on, but with less intensity than before. They didn't alarm me unduly unless they were very near. What did cause me to shiver was our mobile anti-aircraft guns, one of which was sited very close to Godfrey Street. The whole house would tremble as the noise reverberated through. Sometimes we would go outside, and see the German plane caught in the searchlights. Then to hear the guns was comforting, and not frightening.

One night they were particularly noisy and Constantine went out to see what was happening; perhaps the aeroplane would be shot down. I was reading and stayed in the sitting room. A little while later I could hear Constantine talking to someone. Then I realized it was to the dog who had no doubt followed him out.

'Come on in, oh, do come in, Mouche, I want to shut the door.' All this in the darkened corridor on account of the blackout.

He came into the room; I looked up, and placidly standing beside him was the most enormous St Bernard dog I have ever seen. There was a growl from behind our sofa, and Constantine looked down. I have never seen such a look of surprise on anyone's face. We were all, including Mouche, too dumbfounded to speak. Quite quietly the enormous creature turned round and, slowly and majestically, walked out of the room and out of our lives. We quickly went out into the street. No sign of any dog, large or small, and never did we see a St Bernard again in the vicinity.

There was a knock on the door some time afterwards, and there stood Sophie beaming and looking very healthy. She never wrote letters, and always just appeared when on leave. She came in and we had a drink.

'I've deserted,' she said. 'I simply couldn't stand all those bloody women a minute longer.' She was in civilian clothes but with no luggage.

'But how . . .?' I asked.

'It was simple. I traded in my watch for a ticket to the station-master, said I had lost my ticket.' After a second she added, 'I gave your name and address. Don't tell Con.'

We had just started to talk when a blue-coated figure passed the window. (Chelsea Police Station, where Peter and I had brought the German airman to a few years before, was just around the corner.)

'Quick, upstairs.'

Sure enough there was a heavy official knock at the door.

The police were looking for Lance Corporal Warren.

'But isn't she in Wales?'

'No. She's deserted.'

'How did you get my name and address?'

'The person in question falsely gave it as her own, to the station-master at Oswestry.'

'Oh dear, I'm afraid I know nothing about it, officer,' (he was a constable) 'but of course if I hear anything . . .'

'Sorry to trouble you, madam.' Here he hesitated and looked across the room. There were the two glasses we had been drinking from, one still half full. He looked at me again, squarely in the eyes. I opened my large blue eyes and looked squarely back.

'You will pass on any information, no matter how small, won't you?'

'Certainly, officer, but I'm sure there must be a good reason for this misdemeanour. You must excuse me – I have a friend staying here, she's just dressing, and then we are going out.'

Out went the law, and the sound of giggles came from upstairs.

'I heard every word he said. You were wonderful, you sounded so concerned for him.'

Sophie stayed for several weeks. We didn't tell Con to begin with, but she had no clothes, no money, and worst of all no ration book. To spread our rations around she and I would eat out at lunchtime. If Constantine thought it odd that she always dressed in my clothes, he didn't mention it. Nor did he mention the fact that whenever the policemen returning to the station passed us by, Sophie would hide behind the two of us. But after a few weeks he did say:

'What a long leave you've got, Sophie.'

It had to come out. He was quite horrified, and rightly pointed out that as an officer in a foreign army in a foreign country awful things could happen to him for 'harbouring' a deserter. Sophie couldn't stay with us any longer. We thought and thought. Finally, armed with several doctor's certificates, she went sadly back. I did have one postcard from her saying she was sick of peeling potatoes, but very shortly afterwards she got out on 'compassionate grounds', but that is Sophie's story.

CHAPTER NINETEEN

S*econd Front Now* was scrawled on all the walls, and although I didn't know it, it was shortly to take place. Constantine, as an Order of Battle man, worked late, and came home sometimes full of tension. One night in June he was reluctant to go to bed, and we stayed up talking until dawn. At six o'clock in the morning he switched on the wireless and we heard that a landing had been made on the coast of France. Our relief was tremendous, but for many days afterwards we waited for more news than was given us. Anxious hours and days were spent until it seemed that it had been successful.

Then I knew that Constantine would soon have to follow his generals to France. He wanted me to go down and stay with his mother in Berkshire. My family, including my grandmother, was still in London; my mother was working hard all day with the bewildered and mutilated people of the East End of London, and at an air-raid post at night, so I was reluctant to leave.

One sunny evening in midsummer, he went, dressed in battle-dress, with what looked like a new wooden gun over his shoulder. I'm assured it wasn't, but was the latest American model. The taxi was called, and as he drove off I saw his bunch of keys lying on the hall table. I ran after the taxi. No good. Wherever he went, he didn't have his keys with him.

At Constantine's insistence, I did eventually let the house and go down to Berkshire with the two dogs. I hadn't been at all well. No doubt due to the bombing at King's Mansions, I had miscarried, and needed a minor operation.

Church House, Hurley, had originally been a long row of almshouses, built about the time of James II, and made into a long grey house about the beginning of this century. From the outside, the rather derogatory word 'picturesque' could be applied to it. Inside, the large rooms were dark, bitterly cold, even in summer, and, to tell the truth, depressing. The garden was pretty whenever it was warm enough to sit in it and the Thames snaked along the end of it, periodically flooding over, reducing the ground floor of the house to dank silt. I believe that the previous occupants of the house had been a Protestant clergyman and his family, who no doubt lived on too small a salary, as all the old large fireplaces had been removed, and in their places 'all-night burning stoves' had been installed. Now these stoves are excellent if a steady, small heat is needed, but they are not the thing for a forty-foot-long drawing room which never, ever had a glimpse of the sun in it. Also, as fuel was difficult to come by, the doors, which when open gave out a welcoming glow, were usually kept closed to conserve the heat. In front of this useless contraption stood a highly polished brass stand called, I think, a footman.

It was on this that Mimi was always crouched whenever she was at Church House. Even if the doors were open, when Mimi (who was a tall girl) was sitting on the footman in front of this stove, it was impossible to see any fire at all. The family joke was to say: 'Is the fire in, Mimi?' To which she always replied: 'Oh, yes.' We, in the hinterland, put on yet another woolly.

The whole house was impractical. Although there was electric light, the cooking was done, for a minimum of eight people, on an enormous paraffin stove which belched out huge black clouds of smoke on a bad day. Only May, the cook, really understood its temperament.

But if this description of Church House makes it seem grim, the occupants were as colourful a group of people as could be found anywhere.

The atmosphere of the house was dominated by Georgette, Constantine's mother. This is not to say she was dominating, because she was not; nevertheless, she was an extremely strong and fascinating character. At that time I had met her only a few times and, as good-looking women of all ages all the world over do, we examined each other thoroughly, before committing ourselves to affection, dislike, indifference or whatever other emotion should arise. In fact, we needn't have bothered, as from almost the first day of my arrival until her death, through all the vicissitudes of remarriage, we have shared a great affection for each other. She was then a tall beautiful woman, with golden hair and golden eyes (like a marmalade cat, as Francis used to say), a gentle, soft smile, and one of the most musical laughs I have ever heard. It made you want to laugh to hear it. She had the manners of, and was, a 'grande dame'. The hardships and unhappiness she experienced only made her more humane in her relationships with other people. A magnificent woman, in all senses of the word, and one whose advice and friendship I valued for many many years.

She was marvellously paradoxical: the housekeeping varied between lavishness and penury accordingly. Mimi defiantly maintained she had once been given grass to eat, dressed with liquid paraffin. As meat was severely rationed I brought back some chickens from a shopping expedition, and was thought wonderfully practical, but I might just as well have been thought hopelessly extravagant. Once coming back exhausted from a cross-country bus trip she told me that the best way to overcome tiredness was to have a hot bath, then lie with one's feet higher than one's head and have two Pernod frappées. A bit difficult in wartime, but I found it successful later on.

Francis, Constantine's father, was staying at Church House during the summer I was there. He was a rotund, merry man, who told very funny stories at which he chuckled himself as he was telling them. His moods never seemed to change: as long as he had enough food, drink and company he seemed content, although he sometimes grumbled about his false teeth which didn't fit properly. It appears that in his brief spell in prison they had taken out all his teeth and given him ill-fitting dentures. This annoyed him, because he said they made him lisp when telling his stories. Before that he had had a perfect delivery. He would, of course, have liked to be immensely rich and give grand dinners and so on, but he never harped on it, and took life very inconsequentially. Whenever he got a cheque he would take me to Maidenhead, or another nearby town, and blow it on as good a lunch as we could find, endless liqueurs, with taxis all the way. Drink had little or no effect on him; but sometimes the stories got funnier. We were always late home, and he used to say: 'Let's wait until G. has gone to the Old Bell for her drink. She can be a bit sticky before she has her drink.' Often we waited far too long, but Francis would chuckle away no matter how 'sticky' Georgette was. He told me about his time in the French Foreign Legion and the British navy. His comment on the conversational standard in the latter was terse: 'Positive statement, flat denial and personal abuse.'

We would go for long walks along the river-bank, and sometimes be given a basket to pick mushrooms.

'But there aren't any,' Francis used to say, as I jumped over a hedge into a cow-pat. 'Let's go to the Dewdrop Inn or the Black Boy instead.'

We did, and got back late for dinner every time. Very soon we weren't asked to pick mushrooms. He was very boyish. On one of our walks with the two dogs, a sportsman was shooting on the opposite bank of the river. His quarry fell at our feet. Quickly Francis picked up the mallard, and we ran home with it, the sportsman shaking his fist at us from the other side. For the next few days we didn't take that walk, but we were always on the lookout for the fruits of the field. We also tapped the ARP brandy kept in the first-aid box, and very soon it wasn't kept there any more.

It was impossible to be cross with Francis, as Georgette knew so well. She told me that she had never seen him in a bad temper, which surely is unusual in many years of marriage. 'Not even', she said, 'when I was swatting flies in bed one morning, and by accident brought the fly-swatter down on his stomach.' Such a rough awakening did not provoke a word of anger, merely one of those infectious chuckles.

Constantine's eldest sister, Geraldine, was also staying at Church House. She was a beautiful woman, capable of making an extremely pertinent remark from time to time, but in those days preoccupied with looking after her baby daughter. The baby was being brought up as a vegetarian, as commodities like nut butter were ration-free, and she thrived on it. However, when teething time came and tears were frequent, I gave the baby a juicy chop bone to chew on. The tears cleared, and the little sore gums chomped on the bone. Unfortunately, Geraldine came in in the middle, snatched it from the baby's hand, and said indignantly to me: 'She's not a puppy, Theodora!' Francis loved that little *contretemps*.

I was at last notified that there was a bed for me at the Chelsea hospital where I was to have my operation. Constantine wrote from 'somewhere in France' that I was on no account to attempt the journey back from the hospital by the crowded train, but that I should hire a car and driver from Harrods. Constantine had great faith in Harrods.

CHAPTER TWENTY

Mimi came to see me in hospital, and when I told her the plan she said it was ridiculous to pay for a man to drive me to Hurley. She would find someone only too pleased to do it. It seemed a good idea. A certain naval commander was produced (Claud, Mimi's husband, was in the navy, and it all sounded terribly correct), and everything arranged with naval precision. The commander would pick me up at the hospital, bring me to see Mimi and Claud, and then transport me in the greatest luxury to my destination. So it happened. I met Mimi and Claud at a pub in Smith Street, Chelsea, and also a large chow dog that Mimi had found somewhere.

It was a great relief to be out of that clinical atmosphere, and I felt better than I had done for months. I was gay again. Several drinks later Mimi suggested that we drive to Norfolk where they were going to stay in a beautiful old house with Rosemary Langton, whose husband was David Langton, the actor, then away in the army. As an added attraction I was told that Peter and Mary Rose Pulham had a cottage nearby. Peter had gone back to as near to Pulham as he could.

'But what about the petrol?' I enquired. Oh that was all right, Claud's uncle was a rich farmer in Norfolk and everyone knew that farmers had a lot of petrol for their tractors which they didn't use. I still wasn't quite convinced; but they were all, including the naval commander, convincing. I had to telephone my mother-in-law, Georgette, and tell her of the change of plan. It would only take a few hours, in fact it was almost on the way to Berkshire, and I could ring from Norfolk. I looked at the naval commander, now on his fourth pink gin (he was obviously a regular regular). Yes, he was willing; he was only the driver.

An enormous amount of Mimi and Claud's luggage had to be collected and finally, wedged in the back of the car with some of it, Mimi, the chow and I set off.

The journey took much longer than I expected; indeed it was much farther away than I had thought. We arrived at dusk. Rosemary had no telephone; the chow was a present for her and took an instant dislike to her, her children and the country generally; there was no proper bed for the naval commander, not enough food to go round and nothing to drink except a bottle of whisky my grandmother had given me to bring to my mother-in-law. That went first. Then

I was anxious to telephone, so the naval commander took me to the nearest pub some three miles away. There was no line to Berkshire unless it was a 'priority' call. One only got these if one was in the forces or some civilian force such as the ARP.

There was a wasp's nest just outside the bedroom window; in the morning hundreds of the stripey creatures were circling around my face and head, dive-bombing with remarkable accuracy. I got a sting on the lip, and from then on kept under the clothes. The noise was appalling.

At breakfast, speaking thickly through my swollen lip, I started on about the telephone, the uncle and the petrol. Nobody paid any attention to me except Mimi, who said quite firmly that 'Mummie would understand,' and there was no hurry. Whereupon they went off to do the shopping, find the uncle, and I, on the grounds that I was just out of hospital, was left to mind the children. Hours later they came back, with very little shopping and no news about the uncle. They were all very gay, enjoying the weekend in the country. I got the naval commander to drive me again to the pub to telephone, unsuccessfully.

I found a bicycle in a shed, and that evening set off for the pub. Still no line to Berkshire unless I had 'priority'.

By the next morning I was very disconsolate. I saw no way of getting to Berkshire, and the naval commander whom I had hired showed even less interest in my plight than the others. I must have been an awful nuisance; also I wasn't feeling all that good. The elation at being out of hospital had passed; the bicycle ride of six miles had done me no good at all, and the wasp sting was painful. Force would do no good, so I started to cajole.

'Let's go over and see Peter and Mary,' I said. I felt Peter would understand and somehow be an ally, and after all Mary had worked at the American Embassy, or something like it, and – who knew – perhaps she had this divine right called 'priority'.

They lived in what appeared to be a tower; it was very picturesque and very primitive. They were delighted to see us all, quarts of beer were produced, and it was obvious that they were both a bit homesick for people, talk and excitement. Peter and Mary thought it very comical that I was in Norfolk and not Berkshire, and when I attempted to explain my predicament, Peter airily waved his hand, took a deep drink and said:

'Don't worry, Theo, you're so practical, of course you'll think of something. I *never* could.'

Mary had no 'priority'.

Much later that day we went to see the uncle. We were not all allowed to call, only Claud. The rest of the party were deposited in a seedy country hotel nearby. We made for the bar. Some hours later on Claud appeared, but no uncle. I heard him say to Mimi:

'He'll be along when she's gone out. It won't be long.'

I had already initiated the call to Berkshire, and there was some hope that it would come through in an unspecified number of hours. I felt more cheerful and enjoyed my drink. The alcohol was doing my wasp-sting a lot of good.

The door was flung open, and a good-looking dapper little man with huge brown eyes came in walking at a crouch, rather like Groucho Marx.

'Where's the car?' he said. 'We've got to get going. She'll be back soon.'

Mimi, Claud and the naval commander sprang to their feet, and I was hustled out despite protesting cries about the phone call.

'Uncle Roly will arrange all that,' said Mimi with remarkable confidence.

As soon as we were out of the village, Uncle Roly snapped into action. He gave directions, and the naval commander appeared to love taking them. Right, left, left fork, hairpin bend, and off we sped. Uncle Roly was clearly a man of action.

'*Stop*, we're here now,' and the hired limousine whined to a stop. A huge notice greeted us: *The Devil's Punchbowl. All Welcome.*

It was what looked like a large private house with a long avenue. We drove up, and a mild-faced brown-haired woman greeted Uncle Roly as though she were his long-lost housekeeper. I immediately felt that the brown-haired lady would be an ally. But once inside, the picture changed rapidly. All the downstairs rooms of this large house had, it appeared, been turned over to make a bar, restaurant, games room and so on for the American base nearby. It was packed. We made for the bar, and there the brown-haired lady left us, smiling kindly and saying: 'I know you'll be happy here.'

Uncle Roly was delightful company, and gave one a sense of well-being. Several American officers started a crap game on the floor, and it wasn't long before Mimi joined them.

'Come seven, come snake eyes,' was repeated over and over again. I took a throw, lost and retired. I didn't follow the game, so felt best out of it. There was no sign of the naval commander, and Claud and his uncle had a lot to talk about. I wandered about the house. Everywhere were soldiers, playing records, eating or just lounging about. I asked for the telephone, and put through my call once more. I would have to wait.

Coming back to the bar I found Uncle Roly alone. I asked him what the petrol situation was like in the country. He said he had no idea as he hadn't got a car. I thought this odd for a farmer, but maybe he had an efficient steward.

I was summoned to the phone: there was a three-hour delay. It was now about

6 p.m. and I was getting hungry. I pushed open a door, went down a long corridor and at the end heard kitchen-like sounds. There was the naval commander sitting down at the table finishing what must have been quite a substantial meal. The brown-haired lady was fussing over him. I told him about the phone call, and asked him to broach the subject of petrol to Uncle Roly. At this the brown-haired lady uttered an eldritch scream and then sat down in gales of laughter.

'Roly get you petrol?' she said. 'Roly *always* has to have people get things for him.' She said this with pride.

This was when I had what Mimi subsequently termed my first attack of hysteria. I was soothed and calmed by the brown-haired lady, given a cup of tea, and a promise by the naval commander that he would ask the Americans if there was a chance of any petrol.

'What a charming, efficient man,' said the brown-haired lady. 'I could do with someone like that here.' Then I told her my predicament about the telephone call, and was told it was always difficult to get cross-country calls, but London wasn't too bad. This gave me an idea; I would telephone my mother and get her to pass on a message. There was however no reply from my mother's number; she was obviously still at the first-aid post where she worked.

I was still rather shaken by the temperament I had displayed, and so forthwith explained the situation to Uncle Roly.

'Berkshire,' he drawled over the word, 'a lovely county, haven't been there for years. Wouldn't mind a trip there myself. Mmm, might consider it.'

'Petrol,' I said weakly.

'Oh, these American chaps are riddled with it, don't know what to do with it all. They'd give a pretty girl like you any amount.'

'But surely, not for me to drive away,' I replied.

'Shouldn't be surprised; whatever you might say about these chaps, they're damnably generous.'

It was now nine o'clock, time for the call to come through, and far too late to set out for Berkshire even if we had got any petrol.

I asked Uncle Roly when he was going home.

'Never, I hope,' he said. 'It's damned nice to have a weekend out. Mmm. Berkshire.'

The naval commander was still in the kitchen, this time cutting a large pile of sandwiches. I ravenously took one.

'I've got a job,' he said.

'Yes, you have.'

'No, I mean a real job. Mrs H. has hired me to be the manager.'

'But what about getting me to Berkshire?'

'Oh, I'll get that fixed up, and get back here as soon as possible.'

A ray of hope.

'But the car has to be taken back to Harrods,' I said, 'and what about the deposit?'

'That's gone now,' the naval commander answered cheerfully. 'And I expect you'll have to pay a good bit more for all these extra days. I'm on the track of some petrol.'

'Can Mrs H. put us all up here tonight?'

She had apparently 'fixed up' Mimi and Claud, and the naval commander had permanent and splendid quarters. No provision seemed to have been made for Uncle Roly or me. I wandered out into the large overgrown but beautiful garden. There was a dilapidated swing. I sat on it. A lonely-looking American soldier approached me. I thought of Constantine, and not for the first time wished, oh, how I wished, that he was here. We talked, and I told him about the petrol, and Berkshire.

'I wish you would stay here, nice girl,' he said, and kissed me gently on the cheek. I felt like crying and hurling myself into his arms, and being comforted.

'I'm in the office, and don't have nothing to do with the petrol, but you might try the loot. But later, please.' He pressed my arm.

I said I had to find my sister-in-law, and hurried away lest I broke down.

In the lounge, Uncle Roly was asleep on the large sofa. He was curled up, and looked even more like Groucho Marx than ever. He opened one eye and patted the sofa. 'Jump up,' he said as though speaking to a pet dog.

I went to the naval commander's quarters and found him sitting in a large armchair, relishing a glass of whisky. I said that I had nowhere to sleep and couldn't find anyone to ask. He said he expected they were all in bed. 'Try the lounge.'

I had, but Uncle Roly was sleeping there.

The rip-roaring weekend had been too much for me. I wept. Phone calls, petrol, beds, Berkshire, all tumbled out amidst sobs. Then the naval commander did a very sweet thing. He patted my head and shoulders and said:

'You can shake down in my bed. I shall be quite happy in this chair.'

I was led into the other room and left there. I took off my skirt and blouse, climbed into a bed of down and slept well for the first time since I had left Berkshire two weeks earlier.

The naval commander awakened me with a cup of tea and everything was shipshape. He was dead on the button in his new job.

'Breakfast in the dining room, and I've laid on some petrol. Got to get cracking. Mrs H. wants me back first thing tomorrow morning.'

Uncle Roly was at breakfast looking as spry as when he had first stepped into the dreary little hotel bar.

'Berkshire, mmm, and then London.'

He said this with the glee of a child at Christmas.

I found I had no money left, but the brown-haired lady cashed me a cheque. She said she hoped I would come again, she had enjoyed having me. I smiled wanly.

We had to go back to Rosemary's to get our luggage. Most of it seemed to belong to the naval commander, no doubt used to having all his belongings in one place. We told Rosemary where Mimi and Claud were and she said if she could find a babysitter she'd join them; it sounded fun. Perhaps Peter and Mary might come over?

The car was started and a dreadful noise like a big-end going deafened us. 'Good God,' said the commander, 'it was shipshape when we drove over.' My heart thumped; another hold-up. However, after investigation it was found that Simon, the older boy, had inserted a piece of metal in the rear wheel. After what seemed like hours it was extricated and we were ready.

Uncle Roly and I sat in the back, the naval commander with his luggage in the front. It was a hot August day. Many adventures overtook us on the journey, but it was nevertheless enjoyable. I found out a lot about Uncle Roly that I hadn't known before. He had apparently no money, and wasn't allowed to have any lest he should disappear just the way he was doing. He was as intent on London as any 'Tommy' in France in the First World War. But what was he going to live on in London? I enquired. He patted his breast pocket and smiled:

'I didn't forget to bring it,' he said, 'even though I was rushed.'

'But what?'

From his breast pocket he produced an enormous gold cigarette case. He patted it.

'She'll see me through,' he said, patting it again and putting it back.

As we got nearer and nearer to Hurley I began to feel sensations of panic. What could I say without involving Mimi and Claud? This was the fourth day I had been 'missing'. Straight from the hospital, too ill to come down by train, and then to turn up with two strange men, and one tipsy?

'I don't think I'd better ask you in, as I'm so late.'

'Pity,' said Uncle Roly. 'I would have liked to have met me nephew's in-laws.' He was by this time lying along the back of the car, and I had to sit forward.

'Another time,' I said, 'when we're not quite so rushed. The commander has to get to London.'

I crept in, hoping to get to my room and, I suppose, pretend I had been there for hours. But the dogs spotted me and were delighted to see me. I'd never been so pleased in my life to see them.

'Your mother has been very worried about your disappearance,' said Georgette, my mother-in-law. Francis appeared, beaming all over his face. He loved situations like this.

I explained about the telephone calls, Rosemary, Norfolk, petrol, carefully avoiding what I thought might look like a betrayal of Mimi.

'Oh, you were with Mimi,' said Georgette. 'I quite understand.' She did too, and it was never mentioned again. Mimi had been quite right.

CHAPTER TWENTY-ONE

The quiet country summer of 1944 passed slowly like the smile on a ploughboy's face. I went for walks with Francis and with my baby niece-in-law; we played games in the evening; I read, and wrote long letters to Constantine. Sometimes Mimi would come down for a few days. Quite a few evenings we would all have drinks in the Old Bell at Hurley, which was almost next door. A rich Russian gentleman who was staying there offered me a large diamond which he took out of his jacket pocket for my young dog. His offer was refused with great politeness although Francis said I should have taken it. Occasionally I went to London for a few days, and it seemed as though I had never lived there. I had become that most unlikely, for me, person: a grass war-widow.

———

One sad incident happened in Hurley. I was good at reading the Tarot cards, and sometimes I would read them for my sister-in-law or guests in the house. A strange little dark woman appeared one day, and that evening I read the pack for her. I never told her or anyone else what I saw that evening in those cards, but try as I might it always came out to her dying by her own hand. When she did so, about a month later, everyone else was most shocked and surprised. Had I told her, would it have hastened that event or stopped it? That I shall never know, but I have never read the Tarot since that evening, no matter how insistent people may be.

We also had several evenings of table-turning. It takes a war for people to want to know their future immediately. Usually, in fact I would say always, the table would give deliciously absurd answers, and we would all vote it the best parlour-game of all. But after one session, when it had been particularly nonsensical, Georgette said to it: 'Would you like to dance?' The most extraordinary thing was that it did: four people, still with their fingers meeting on the delicate top of the three-legged table, were danced about the room, and truly, out of the door and up two stairs, after which it and all of us collapsed, us with laughter. However, an incident occurred after one of those table-turning evenings. I went to bed, the two large dogs lying on their mats in the room. At some time during the night I was woken up by a strong, but so strong, smell of garlic. Now this was all the more unusual because in wartime England no garlic ever passed the portals of Church House, Hurley. Would that it had sometimes. As Rosemary used to say:

'We rise from our meals stiff with starch.'

I turned on the bedside lamp. Both the dogs were bristling and snarling about something, and anyone who knows standard poodles knows they never bristle or snarl. They paced about the edge of the room and were loth to come to my bedside. It was really terrifying. Eventually I got out of bed, and we all went for a walk around the garden. When I came back the overpowering smell had completely gone, and we settled down for the rest of the night. The next day I changed rooms with Francis, and we all of us slept soundly thereafter. But I don't remember any more table-turning after that.

———

My birthday has played an important part in my life. It has to be looked forward to, planned to a certain extent and enjoyed. Usually I am disappointed, and sometimes it has ended in tears. As a child I tried hard to get my feast day counted as an extra birthday, but it never really worked. Had it done so, it would have been perfect. For my feast day is in May, and my birthday in October. But the fivers never turned up in May; only chocolates, or some quite unsuitable piece of wearing apparel. It was dropped on both sides for the fraud it was.

This October I did not know what would happen. Parties were difficult to organize on account of the scarcity of drink, and my grandmother, the only true source of liquor, was still in London. I had decided that we would all have a few extra drinks at the Old Bell, and that would be that.

On the morning of Trafalgar Day, the telegraph boy from the post office next door arrived with a telegram for me:

'Expect me today. Will ring from London. All love, Constantine.'

But where had it been sent from? We all peered at it, but nothing but numbers filled the top of the form from next door. Could it be a misplaced joke? Georgette, whose first reaction to anything unexpected has always been a quick burst of annoyance, said:

'Oh, it's just like Connie to do something unexpected like this.'

All day we speculated and waited for the phone call. I was dressed and re-dressed in various clothes, and finally by six o'clock I was quite dejected. In desperation we all went to the Old Bell. May, the cook, came puffing in just as we were on the first drink.

'Phone . . . quick . . .'

Dressed in a borrowed suit I took the old overstuffed taxi to Maidenhead Station. The October mists swirled about us as in a bad Hollywood film. Trains came and went, but no London train. I was cold and the suit too tight. At last with a roar and a gasp it was there, and with it the 'dark slender boy'.

It appeared that his colonel had lost him in a poker game to the Sixth Army. Therefore Constantine thought the colonel owed him something, so asked him quite seriously if he could fly from Luxembourg, where they were then, to London for his wife's birthday. The colonel, whom I met much later on, told me he was so astonished that he said yes, and even lent him his personal plane and pilot to fly to Paris. However, that was only halfway. The rest of the story is Constantine's. But arrive he did, on my birthday, from the battleground of Europe in 1944.

My brief grass-widowhood was over.

Constantine had decided that the American Sixth Army was not for him. He would get himself attached to the British army, we would live again in London, and that was that. Such was his personality that one never for an instant doubted that it would happen, and it did, within the space of exactly one week.

Yes, the quiet country summer was certainly over.

CHAPTER TWENTY-TWO

House-hunting is always a depressing occupation, and in wartime London it was even worse, many of the 'desirable residences' still being thick with the dust of bomb-blast. Then I remembered a pretty studio house, set back in a small cul-de-sac off Upper Cheyne Row, from the days of house-hunting with Peter after leaving Oakley Street. It was indeed desirable, but we could never find either who owned it or the agent. I went to see if it still existed. While strolling around the front garden the door opened and out came a friend, Mary Tolstoi, who was married to a grandson of the writer.

'How nice to see you,' she said. 'Have you come to call? I do hope so.' I didn't like to give my actual purpose, but followed her in. It was a late autumn afternoon and a glowing fire was burning in the comfortable sitting room.

'Let's have some tea and make toast over the fire.'

A delightful idea, and during the course of it I told her how I had found the house empty a few years ago, but could never find its owners. I was so completely at home there, I felt it really should have been mine. But I didn't say so. Anyway it would probably have been far too expensive for us then, and this I did say.

'Oh no, it's only fifty pounds a year,' she replied. 'I got it from the agents at Harrods.'

That was the last place I would have gone to look for a house or flat, which made it seem more elusive and less 'mine'.

'But why so cheap? It's quite large and so very liveable-in.'

'Quite simple,' Mary answered. 'It's haunted, you see. But they're enchanting ghosts, so friendly and happy. Maybe if we're lucky they might be here today: a little later is their usual time. But it doesn't happen every day.'

Well used to Celtic tales, I didn't for one moment doubt what she was saying and more or less dismissed it from my mind. We went on talking until darkness fell, which was fairly early at this time of year. A very delicate chiming clock sounded, which reminded me I should be going. I looked up to the mantelshelf but there was no clock there and I looked round the room.

'Sh-sh,' she whispered, 'they will come any moment now. That's not my clock, for mine doesn't chime.'

I sat staring at the clockless shelf above the fire; then there was the sound of people chatting and skirts rustling. Once a small dog gave a yapping bark. The noise got louder as though a small party of people were going upstairs in the next room. There was light laughter and the happy buzz of conversation. They were obviously looking forward to a pleasant evening. Gradually it faded away as they reached wherever they were going. The whole thing took only a few minutes but seemed an age.

'Mary, it's extraordinary, but what's the other side of this wall?'

We went out and I saw there was nothing, just a small path to the back of the house. It was a charming experience. Mary had been right: they were delightful and happy and induced that feeling in their listeners. I often wondered how their presence would have affected my life with Peter.

Eventually we took half a house in Paulton's Square, Chelsea, belonging to Maurice and Bridget Richardson. Bridget's mother, Mrs Tisdall, had the top half. She was a pencil-thin outspoken elderly woman who lived with a companion as she had lost the use of one eye. When I commiserated with her, she said briskly:

'It's quite all right. I've seen all I want to see.'

We had no furniture, and it was impossible to buy any except on 'points' allocated to brides; 'utility' furniture it was called, and it was horrible. This did not deter us in the least. Our respective families combed their attics, spare rooms and woodsheds and soon we had a lot of certain things but none of vital commodities like beds. It was then that I remembered that all my furniture from Rossetti House, which was too big or not needed in Godfrey Street, I had lent to Sophie, now enjoying an uneasy domesticity in Oakley Street. One should never lend furniture to anyone. Once it has become part of another person's home and personality it never becomes yours again, and causes the most bitter resentment when you remove it. Some of it I never took, but I did swap a rather small single bed for my old double divan. We had a home of sorts again, but it was never even remotely as pleasant as Godfrey Street had been. Even when, later on, Mrs Tisdall went away for some months and we had the whole house, it wasn't our atmosphere, and being sensitive individuals it reacted on us. The idyll was over.

Nevertheless I made it as much like me as I could. We had five Orpington hens and two Khaki Campbell ducks in the garden, and later on eight poodle puppies. One of the ducks flew off and Constantine reported it to the police. Two days later they rang: it had been located twelve doors up. We went to get it, were led through the hall and went to go out into the garden.

'Oh no, it's in here,' said the woman, opening the door of a book-lined dining room. And sure enough there was my duck sitting in a leather armchair.

It never took to Paulton's Square any more than we did, but went on laying its daily egg with the others. As the egg ration then was one per month per person, I was the most popular girl around. That is, egg-wise.

One morning in bed I asked Constantine what he would do when the war was over. 'Be a writer, of course,' he said. He might just as well have said a balloonist, as it didn't seem then that the war would ever end. A glassed-in verandah was converted into a writing room, and some evenings he would go there and write surrealistic short stories. 'Old Uncle Onion-head' was my favourite, and many of them have since been published.

This was when my grandmother gave me the bicycle, and I used to go around on it at Constantine's behest to find out which pubs had their beer delivered and when. But generally our local was the Crossed Keys in Lawrence Street, with new owners since the Chelsea Old Church bombing, and the most gorgeous queen of all the barmaids called Dorothy. She was like a young dark-haired English Mae West, if such a person can be imagined. She flirted, yet kept all the gentlemen in their place. She was also quick, efficient and kindly. Owing to a misunderstanding, which took us years to find out about, we had been barred from the King's Head and Eight Bells. The ban was so stringent that when an Irish girl who had never been to London before took my dog Mouche in there one night, she was also refused a drink. Sometimes we went across the road to the Black Lion in Paulton's Square, but to begin with it was crowded with people we didn't know, and there was nowhere to sit.

If it seems that undue importance is being attached to pubs it must be explained that they were the only places in wartime London where one could entertain and be entertained cheaply, and find the companionship badly needed during the war. For people of our age with no solid, regular accounts behind us, it was difficult to come by even a bottle of sherry. Food was very scarce indeed, and food for the occasional dinner party had to be hunted for and often took many hours and much traipsing about. Many middle-aged people used to drinking at home found their only source of supply was the pubs. Bombs dropping on London could not be so easily heard when one was in them, and the company lessened apprehension. I loved pubs; they were new to me and I liked being able to find friends I wanted to see in a certain place at a certain time. Dylan had previously pointed out to me that the link between host and guest was a tenuous one, but that it never arose if one met in a pub.

The Irish country pubs I had known were not at all the same. In them all women were put into a small place resembling a railway carriage, and known quite erroneously as a 'snug'. Not that I'm saying anything against the snug for certain occasions.

CHAPTER TWENTY-THREE

Intermittent bombs were dropped throughout this time, but after D-Day, 6 June 1944, a new horror arrived. These were the pilotless flying bombs, called VIs and known almost affectionately as 'doodlebugs'. They arrived almost as soon as the siren sounded. A characteristic drone announced them. Then silence before the indiscriminate bomb fell. They nearly all fell on London, and over six thousand people were killed. Before they stopped at the end of August over one and a half million people had left London.

Among them were, Dylan, Caitlin and the baby, who left their flimsy studio home and went back to Wales. Early in August, Constantine had gone to France with the Americans. In September, Duncan Sandys, then in the Ministry of Defence, announced to our great relief: 'The battle for London is over.' However, he was almost immediately proved wrong, for the next day the first rockets (V2s) reached London. These were even more terrifying: there was no warning siren; it was useless taking shelter for it was all over so quickly. Over a thousand fell on London and killed nearly three thousand people. They were to continue, in desultory fashion, for over six months. It was a curious time and life became a valuable stroke of fortune, for we had no idea when death would fiendishly fall from the skies. Sometimes it seemed the war would go on all our lives, increasing in devilish intensity. Equally unnerving was the sinister thunderous noise of the death-laden flying fortresses passing overhead on their way to cities such as Dresden for intensive morale-breaking raids, in which some eighty thousand people are thought to have been killed.

I was beginning to feel bereft without Constantine and I also missed Caitlin, for not only had the studio-shack always been welcoming, but we would often meet in the King's Road when shopping, Caitlin and the baby Aeronwy colourfully dressed, the pram piled high with the rations, always a few bottles of Guinness or pale ale peeping out. The studio in Manresa Road was let to a painter friend of ours called Francis Butterfield. Despite the lack of any proper home, Dylan was writing a lot in Wales. It was during this year and the next he was to write his poems *Refusal to Mourn*, *This Side of Truth*, *A Winter's Tale* and *In my Craft or Sullen Art* as well as others which were to make him famous.

He had also written many BBC radio talks, later to be collected and published as *Quite Early One Morning*. They were relayed on the Welsh Service, which was not easy to get in London, but the quality of both his voice and the prose made many want to hear them. That kind and charming man Donald Taylor, whose company was Strand Films, had commissioned Dylan to write several short film scripts which necessitated frequent trips to London. Caitlin of course was usually left in Wales. Many times it would be to our flat in Paulton's Square that Dylan would come, always neat and spruce on arrival. He was an odd guest, for not only did he appear unexpectedly, but after two or three days he would disappear and we would assume he had gone back to Wales. However, sometimes he would turn up again, but always dressed in different clothes. As mentioned, this was an inherent and curious part of Dylan: he would slough his own clothes like a snake with his skin, and dress himself in whatever of his host's took his fancy. This proved difficult with Constantine, not only on account of the vast difference in height, but also because Constantine had few civilian clothes. Nevertheless, socks, ties and some shirts were there for the taking.

Sometimes he came with friends and it was through Dylan we met Vernon Watkins, another Welsh poet, at this time in the air force. They made an ill-assorted couple, Vernon being a very thin, ascetic-looking El Greco-like figure. Vernon had previously worked in a bank and Dylan told me he was extremely absent-minded, thinking mainly of his poems. One day he was counting out a pile of notes, as tellers seem so often to be doing, when he looked up and saw a customer awaiting him. Without further ado he pushed the pile of notes through to him. Luckily it was someone who knew him and just as quickly pushed them back. I think it was a surprise to all of us when he married the practical and robust Gwen and had several children.

It was at Paulton's Square that Dylan first told us about the radio play he was writing. It was about a Welsh village, peopled with what he called 'a good cross-section of Welsh characters'. He was going to call the village Buggerall, which of course he did, backwards, in *Under Milk Wood*. When we had talked for hours and Constantine had come home, we would go over to the Black Lion, our nearest pub, on the corner of Old Church Street and Paulton Street. Sometimes we would go further afield to the Crossed Keys, especially in summer, as it had a small garden.

Dolly Donn Byrne, widow of the Irish writer Donn Byrne, was in the local pub, the Black Lion, most evenings. She lived with her daughter Janie (who was to die so tragically just after the war) at number 9 Paulton's Square. Her other daughter and two sons were in the forces. The house was shared with Kathleen Raine the poet. Dolly had one of those india-rubber Irish faces that changed as quickly as the light on an Irish hillside. She was very talkative and very kind. Many the night a hungry writer was given a meal at Roma's café just opposite the pub. I think that *Wings of the Mornings* had just been made into a film, from her husband's novel, with Annabella starring in it, but there was always a drink, endless cigarettes (and better ones than the usually available, dreadful Clipper brand) and stories from Dolly.

However, it can't have been 'fairy gold' film money that made her so generous. She had four children and had taken a job way out of London at Lutterworth Press, at which she worked extremely hard. When talking about Donn Byrne she would say:

'Some Irish people have lost their country houses gambling. My husband made his that way.'

And it was quite true. In the twenties Donn Byrne had made a small fortune at Monte Carlo and bought a beautiful house on the Old Head of Kinsale, County Cork. I believe he had driven his car over a cliff there and died, but this she never talked about. Dolly could make you cross but, like so many Irish women I had known in my youth, you couldn't help but love her. Dolly was a good woman and a good friend.

Kathleen Raine was then married to the poet Charles Madge. She used to give Sunday-evening poetry readings, to which we were sometimes asked. She was a pretty brown-haired woman with a slight lisp and a quick smile. At her house, poets like George Barker, Dylan Thomas, Bernard Gutteridge, Bernard Spencer, Bill Empson, Pierre Emanuelle and many others met and read their poems. Constantine was never asked to read, much to his chagrin, so we didn't go there all that often. We had our own poetry readings at home; indeed I remember once Constantine being quite sharp with Janie Donn Byrne because she wasn't reading her poem with enough expression.

Many evenings until early in the morning we would play 'Russian plays' and this on lime juice and soda. The game consisted of improvised Chekov-style dramas in which I was always Natasha, Dylan my mother (stuffed with cushions and heavily made-up), Constantine was Sergei with his jacket on back to front and my fur hat on, and sometimes an overworked and exhausted journalist called John Thompson who had the flat on the top floor was roped in when he came home late, to play a very subsidiary role. It was all very satisfying, stimulated our imagination and used up our energy.

But it wasn't all Russian plays. One Sunday night we had a poker party instigated by Dolly and Constantine. Dylan, Janie and myself were only stringers, and apparently talked too much for the experts. Sometime around midnight a tremendous thunderstorm started and Dylan, overacting, said it was because we were card-playing on Sunday. He worked this up to such an extent that Constantine almost believed it and became unduly emotional. The poker party was quickly disbanded, and Dolly and Janie slunk out. Dylan and I were left to face the wrath of whatever God Constantine was then invoking. It had become quite out of hand, and I was alarmed. In the middle of one of Constantine's harangues, out of the corner of my eye I saw Dylan get down on all fours and begin to creep out of the room. The excellence of the idea imprinted itself quickly on my mind, because instantly I was down on all fours, and out of the room, in the hallway with Dylan. We stayed on the ground, whispering together and we could still hear Constantine in the sitting room continuing to give vent to his anger. He must after a minute or two have realized that we were no longer there because we could hear him saying:

'Well, where the devil are they?'

It might read curiously in print, but it caused Dylan and me, still on all fours and huddled in a corner of the hall, the greatest amusement, as indeed it did Constantine when he realized what had happened and how comical the whole situation was.

———

The winter of 1944 was unnecessarily spiteful. There was snow and hard frost for about a month, and the roads were so bad that no horse-drawn coal lorry was able to deliver the coal. This was when the little spiv boys would turn up with the logs, but if you weren't there to watch when they were putting them down the coal-shute you found you had about a dozen logs, instead of a hundred.

Unless you were in one of the women's forces, trousers were not usual for women to wear and difficult to buy without coupons, so I wore my jodhpurs and hunting jacket during the days of this hard spell. Bertram Wedgwood, who was well over seventy (he eventually got into the Red Cross and was one of the first into Belsen camp), and I hired a hand-cart and dragged back several hundred-weight of coal from a yard near Lot's Road, to Paulton's Square. Food was every day more scarce, and our ration that winter was again one pound of onions per person. Not that any of these things worried us: they were part of the life that we were living and intended to go on with for as long as we could. It must have been much harder for middle-aged or elderly people who had prewar standards to judge by, but for us it was life as life came. Paulton's Square, whatever else it might have been, was never dull. At breakfast time the Wrens from Crosby Hall at the bottom of the street drilled in front of us. Mouche hated these squadrons of women stomping about outside her house, and although not an aggressive dog her one ambition was to get out and chase them. This only happened once or twice but it pleased the girls very much, though not the officers, as a welcome break from routine.

Feeding a large standard poodle was sometimes a problem, but she more than earned her keep. She insisted on carrying the small torch we used during the blackout, and the light shone just where one needed it, on the pavement. At the kerb she would wait until we had reached it. Where the oncoming people thought the light was coming from must have posed quite a problem, until they passed by, sometimes loud in their praise, but the strong-minded Mouche was immune to their blandishments when doing her job. She also loved taxis and was adept at getting them. At that time only the driver's compartment was enclosed in the front, the remainder being free to put luggage in. Some taxi drivers had the habit of putting their glove over the meter while still on a rank. This meant they weren't working. Mouche was oblivious to the glove, and would jump up on to the luggage part and sit there, putting an appealing face through the driver's window. It almost always worked; in fact there was one taxi driver from Battersea who was so flattered that he used to take her for a ride when he had another fare and then bring her back to me. There were also the puppies, which sold quite lucratively. Con once said he had heard of men living on women, but he'd never heard of one living on a dog!

I bought horsemeat for her when available, but sometimes after queueing for an hour there would be only bones left, so I made a stew of them with flour dumplings. I did get whale meat twice which was much appreciated: when I tasted it once, I found it extremely rich. Ends of bread were baked in the oven and sometimes when there would be nothing else, she ate those with made-up dried milk powder and a few drops of cod liver oil. Then there were the pig bins: these were large drums situated in most streets where you put your edible waste. First thing in the morning Mouche would make a tour of these, but I don't think she got much, as they contained mostly vegetable peelings. She found many friends of her own, one being a dear old man from the workhouse who always had a few crusts for her in his pocket. She would go to Dovehouse Street where the workhouse was to wait for him. I think she was probably his only friend. In pubs there was sometimes an arrowroot biscuit; large ones were kept in jars on the bar, and these she liked with a drop of Guinness in the ashtray.

One day when Dylan was staying the subject of hypnotizing chickens with a white line came up. I went out with a piece of string and laid it out straight, then put the birds' beaks on it. It worked: both Dylan and Constantine, who were hiding behind trees in the garden, thought me very brave to pick up pecking birds like that. In a way, it was country life in the town. I thought a lot about Ireland and my father's family there, but it became more and more difficult to get back even for a short while.

On an evening in December I heard a taxi stop outside the house; I peered out and the man getting out appeared familiar, yet strange. Perhaps he was going next door where Ford Madox Ford's wife lived, as did Herma Briffault, wife of the French writer. Nevertheless my doorbell rang and I answered the door. It was my father.

CHAPTER TWENTY-FOUR

My father was the *pater nonfamilias* for we hardly ever saw him. His adult life was spent mostly in India and he would appear from time to time, years apart, without warning, for an indefinite stay. Nevertheless I was always delighted to see him for his arrival meant complete disorganization of whatever you were doing and tremendous excitement.

As a small child I had seen him perhaps half a dozen times and on every occasion something unusual happened. When he came to visit me at my convent school the nuns were charmed by him, and whereas other parents left in the afternoon, my father was still there being royally entertained in the evening. He had the ability to make everyone with him seem special. If that is called charm, he was endowed with it in a very natural way. He had a quick and ready wit, a remarkably hasty temper and a most infectious laugh.

His passions, in the true sense of the word, were beautiful horses and beautiful women, followed by good food and drink, the theatre and books. He had several children, only one being born in his own wedlock. He was definitely not the marrying sort. Nevertheless I never met anyone who didn't like him.

When I was very young he was like a myth to me and if someone had told me he was really Jupiter disguised in human form I wouldn't have been at all surprised. He would, it seemed, swoop down and carry me off to faraway places where everything looked and was quite different from anything I could have imagined. Very occasionally my mother came too, but usually it was just me. To an only child brought up in convents, when at the age of about eleven they expressed the wish that I should leave, and I went to live with my seventy-year-old maternal grandmother, it was an enchanted world he opened up for me. I believe he genuinely liked being with some children, for, surprisingly, late one night in the Gargoyle Club in Soho, the granite-faced Maurice Richardson told me he often had been taken out by him when he was about sixteen years old.

As I grew a little older the trips got longer. I was never treated as a child but as an equal, and was expected to behave accordingly. It was he who, when I was sixteen years old, gave me my first cigar as he said he didn't like smoking alone. He was also full of worldly advice, which even today I reflect on and sometimes follow. He gave me a leather-covered flask filled with whisky on my seventeenth birthday.

'Never,' he said, 'ever go on a journey, or to stay with friends, without it. There will always be the time when you will want a drink and they won't.'

I have profited many times by that advice, never more than during the war when trains stopped, sometimes all night, during an air raid. Today that same flask still goes with me.

When, as a girl, my grandmother thought I had made an undesirable friend and hoped to win my father to her way of thinking, he replied that she couldn't expect *us* to have the morals of a haberdasher!

However, he did draw the line at what he called 'curly-headed counter-jumpers' and I was warned never to get involved with one.

We travelled together over most of Europe, the Middle East and parts of India. We stayed in castles and cottages and everywhere we went he seemed to know people, albeit mostly pretty women. Once in France we rose at dawn and drove for miles to visit one such charmer who lived in a magnificent hilltop château where we stayed for two days. She had a chubby, angelic-looking baby boy of whom she was very proud. When we were driving away, my father turned to me and said:

'Do you think that baby looks like me?'

I replied that it had a certain similarity.

'Nonsense,' he snapped, 'all blond blue-eyed babies look like me. Did you look at his ears or eyebrows?'

I said it hadn't occurred to me, and the subject was never mentioned again.

His clothes were always of the finest materials and he expected his female companions to be so attired. Unlike most men he loved shopping with pretty women and if you found it hard to choose between two dresses, then he bought you both. I once went home with six new pairs of shoes. He was highly critical of what you wore, and one time when I thought I looked just right, he said:

'Where do you think you're going? To a dog show?'

But if you had nothing else suitable to wear, he would take you out to buy something really beautiful immediately.

It was largely due to him I discovered my immense interest in different foods, for not only did we travel to many countries to taste them, but his interest stimulated mine. He insisted that we ate the food of the country, even a sheep's eye in Arabia, a fearsome, huge object which I don't recommend. He disliked people who tried to stick to roast beef, and was a firm believer that 'travel reinforces prejudice' in many. All dishes he ate had to be what they purported to be. If it said Potage Dubarry on the menu, I pitied the waiter who didn't bring a good cauliflower soup. When a Sole Véronique was presented with a white sauce over it, and not the glazed juices, it would be thrown on the floor with the words:

'That's what I think of your Sole Véronique.'

However, simple well-cooked food was also enjoyed, particularly calf's head with vinaigrette sauce, a dish seldom seen today. It is no doubt due to this training that I so dislike dishes called Hawaiian or Polynesian simply because they have a slice of pineapple on them.

Having eaten a good dish he would assume I would either know, or find out, how to cook it, and after a while I learned to do just that. One time we were having friends to dinner and I complained about the smell of garlic on my fingers.

'The hand that cuts the garlic is the one that gets kissed the most often,' he said tersely.

He had a marvellous way of describing people in a sentence.

'The sort of person who would be *seen* cutting up a lettuce.'

His method of summing up a man was in these words:

'You can usually tell what a man is really like by the expression on his wife's face!'

How often have I seen the truth of that remark.

Once when someone's legitimacy was being questioned, he took a large swig of whisky before saying:

'It's a wise cork that knows its own pop!'

He gave me the taste very early on for perfection. To a child used to the severity of a convent (breaking the ice on the jug to wash in wintertime was normal), the luxury of first-class hotels was impressive, although I was also taught not to despise the humble.

However, sitting in the sumptuous Gritti Palace in Venice, he once remarked:

'Thank God, at least we *look* rich.'

He went through a lot of money during his lifetime, but as my half-sister said:

'It was worth it: we learnt a lot.'

On my eighteenth birthday he gave me a thousand pounds, which was a vast sum in those days, and told me not to expect anything more. From time to time I think lump sums were handed out to his ladies as well as to his children, but never when you expected it. I will never know how spontaneous those trips were, but I do know that after a certain time, perhaps sitting in an hotel somewhere, he would give that wonderful laugh and say: 'Time we went back to the ancestral home,' and off we would go back to Ireland the next day. The enchantment was over until the next time he swooped down.

During all those years I was only once given any indication of what to do in strange surroundings. That was when he told me not to talk so freely to the footman. A few words would do.

Like most Irishmen, eventually he went back to Ireland, and once on a visit I found he had ten pretty servant girls all called Brigit.

'But why do you want ten, all with the same name?' I asked.

'Simple,' he replied. 'If I shout Brigit down the stairs at least one of them answers.'

———

This night in Chelsea in 1945 there was no possibility of being carried off anywhere. He was, although I didn't know it, a dying man. Flashes of the old wit were displayed, but they were like sparklers instead of rockets. He asked for whisky, but alas we had none, only beer, which he shouldn't have drunk. He was delighted to meet Constantine and unexpectedly my mother also called. It was a domesticity we had never known together.

The difficulty of finding him a taxi in blacked-out London was solved by the arrival of Diana Graves and Michael Gough, for he was able to take theirs. Foolishly, in my joy at seeing him I forgot to ask where he was staying. Two days later he telephoned me, and in the middle of the conversation we were cut off. It was the last time I was ever to hear from him. Adam, for that was his name, had left my life as abruptly as he had entered it.

———

Some years later, when I had returned home from the other side of the world, I heard this story. As his funeral cortege was slowly going its winding way to Ballymackey cemetery, the mourners were startled to hear the clatter of horses' hooves in the narrow country lane.

Ahead of the hearse, a young chestnut thoroughbred horse had leapt a five-barred gate and was rearing up in front of the coffin. He was led back into the field and the gate shut. Twice more he raced along the fields, jumping hedges and gates, and the performance was repeated along the road. The mourners murmured among themselves:

'It's a sign. He would have liked that,' they said. 'God rest his soul.'

CHAPTER TWENTY-FIVE

Spring came early and with it our spirits revived, for not only were the days warmer and longer, but the course of the war seemed to take a turn in our favour. Warm days meant one needed less food and fewer clothes, for those too were on a 'coupon' system. Even the watery-thin sunlight meant we could dispense with wool or silk stockings (nylons were almost only obtainable through a member of the US forces) and heavy top-coats. The coupon allowance, like all the rations, was only the barest minimum. Elderly people who didn't buy much would sell these coupons for small sums of money. Maybe one of the reasons the GIs were so popular was that they were given vast quantities of coupons. Shops dealing in second-hand clothes opened up, and when the clothes were well cut they often sold for high prices, but were worth it for special occasions.

Warm days also meant going out more, and further afield. Harold Scott, the actor whom Bernard Shaw had in mind to play the Dauphin in *St Joan*, and the originator of the famous Riverside Nights with Elsa Lanchester, would call from time to time. Then we would sometimes take the tube to Tower Hill, by the Tower of London, have some drinks, then walk down the almost deserted, bombed dockland of St Katherine's Way, calling at some of the little pubs, until we reached the Prospect of Whitby. At this time it was almost entirely patronized by dock workers and their families. There was an ancient piano, and there Harold would play and in his light sweet voice sing old music-hall songs such as 'My Old Man Says Follow the Van' or 'The Boy I Love Is Up in the Gallery'. He was immensely popular and we were always assured of a warm welcome when he was there; sometimes even some hot wartime sausages would be handed round. It is curious that the only war song was 'Lili Marlene', a German one.

Harold was a remarkable person, a true bohemian in many ways. He always looked scruffy and penniless, yet to my knowledge he was seldom out of work over a span of at least fifty years. He was extremely well read, but his knowledge sat lightly on him. He was the most quietly entertaining person, and perhaps because of this he was usually with very pretty women.

Dylan was often in London writing his film scripts, and about this time he was collaborating with Philip Lindsay, the prolific historical novelist, brother of Jack and a member of the talented Australian family. Phil was a curious little man who resembled a small nocturnal animal with a large carbuncle on his forehead. He was in the Crossed Keys every evening, sitting by the fireplace drinking beer. Occasionally his correct-looking wife (who in fact wasn't correct at all) would be there for a little while, usually later in the evening to accompany him home. How he got all the writing done is still a mystery to me, but the long well-researched books would appear regularly despite the paper shortage.

Dylan and Phil were collaborating on a script about the life of Dickens. Dylan was anxious to use as far as possible Dickens's own words, but the collaborators did not always have the same ideas. One night or early morning Dylan and Phil were arguing about it in our house. Phil turned to me and said: 'Dylan's too f— intellectual, he ruins the bloody film.' In any case the film was never made. Another time Dylan turned up with a Welsh policeman called Walter Flower, and the art critic Tommy Earp. D. H. Lawrence once wrote these lines about Tommy after he had given Lawrence an unfavourable review of his exhibition of paintings.

> He can't write
> But he can chirp,
> His name is Tommy
> Tommy Earp.

I think Lawrence was wrong, for not only was Tommy a fine critic, far better than Lawrence was a painter, but also a much underestimated writer, as the following last verse of his poem *Five Christs* shows:

> Now, in the Rue de la Paix,
> In a shop-window,
> A small glass Christ,
> Fragile and expensive,
> 'A Dainty Christ for the Dressing-table'.

Tommy was an extremely tall, thin man with a long narrow head. He waved his arms about a lot and seemed to me like an enormous upright dragonfly. The reference to his 'chirping' was a comment on his voice – not a chirp, but high and fluting – with which he enunciated the most exact English with an exaggerated Oxford accent. I don't know what the quiet blond policeman made of it all, for although we drank a certain amount in the pubs, we also did the most elaborate dances (at which Tommy was very good) and improvised plays about Goethe, Dylan being the young Goethe, Tommy the old, me Lotte, and Constantine an unlikely Schiller.

——

Then a new figure came to live in Paulton's Square, and figure is an appropriate word for John Davenport. He was not a very tall man, but immensely wide with a Beethovenesque head. One had no difficulty in believing he had been a boxing blue at Cambridge, both for his build and his strength. He was, however, a man with a deep love and knowledge of literature, painting and music. He had a large circle of friends both in the intellectual and social milieu, and a ready and precise wit. For such an enormous man he had a very soft voice and the trick of dropping it when telling a story, so that you were literally sitting on the edge of your seat to hear it. John had spent some time in Hollywood in order to write a script for a Robert Donat film about the Young Pretender, which came to nothing as Donat broke his contract and left. He stayed on for a little, and used the money to collect such modern painters as Roualt, Picasso and Tanguy, which sold for very little then. Just before the war and at the beginning of it he entertained lavishly at his house in Gloucestershire.

Dylan and Caitlin had been his guests for over three months in 1940, and it was during this time that John and Dylan started writing a thriller together, subsequently published as *The Death of the King's Canary*, which was a *roman à clef*. John had written a book of poems at Cambridge, but subsequently he found himself with that condition most dreaded by writers, an increasing writing block. He did, however, write excellent, succinct literary criticism.

This then was the man who, having spent most of his fortune, came to live in a small flat in Dolly Donn Byrne and Kathleen Raine's house in Paulton's Square. He was often in the Black Lion or the Crossed Keys and we became great friends. Dolly adored him and had many amusing anecdotes about him. It appears that at this time he met Margery Morrison, who had been one of my *locataires* at Rossetti House. She was brought to the Paulton's Square flat to live. Dolly, eyes shining with delight, told of knocking on his door one day to ask a simple question, to which he replied: 'Come in.'

On entering she saw them both lying on the sofa *au naturel*; John raised himself up on his elbow and in his soft voice murmured:

'Dolly, I'm glad you called. I wanted you to meet Margery. She's a charming girl, her father was a captain in the Scots Greys.'

——

For some time past we had seen an elderly white-haired man in the Crossed Keys, usually in conversation with Desmond Ryan, flamboyant in his black Inverness cape. One evening I was sitting next to the white-haired man when he turned to me and almost querulously asked:

'What's your name then?'

'Theo FitzGibbon.'

'Nonsense,' he replied, 'that was my wife's name.'

And it was, although her name had been Theobaldina, but as it happened she was the daughter of Augustus FitzGibbon, Constantine's great-uncle and also a distant cousin of her husband.

This was the writer Norman Douglas, or 'Uncle Norman' as he became, author of *South Wind* and many even finer books, such as *Siren Land, Fountains in the Sand, Old Calabria* and some twenty others. He was at that time seventy-seven years old and was to be a constant friend until his death in 1952.

He had arrived in wartime London in 1941 after a circuitous journey across Europe from Italy, first to France and, when that was occupied by the Germans, to Portugal. He had thought he would never return to England again; certainly he couldn't have picked a worse time. Life was not easy even for regular inhabitants, but for an elderly hedonist it must have seemed even more dismal and restrictive. However, self-pity was not one of Norman's faults and whatever his private feelings may have been, he stimulated and fascinated all who met him by his scholarship and wit. Most of all he loved to shock and it was this mixture of immense and diverse knowledge, classicism, lucidity and bluntness to the point of bawdiness which made him perhaps the most interesting person I have ever met. He belonged more to the eighteenth or early nineteenth century than the twentieth and this carried through to his appearance.

When I first met him he looked remarkably robust for a man of his years: tall and broad with a strong physique, a large noble head covered with thick but silky white hair, which went well with his ruddy complexion, clear-cut features and shrewd but twinkling eyes. His friend in Florence, Reggie Turner, has described him as 'a mixture of Roman emperor and Roman cab-driver', which combined his distinction and shrewdness to perfection, as well as his heritage, a Scottish father and an Austrian mother. All his life he had been very active, climbing and walking miles, and this habit of walking, even in the blackout, continued well into his eighties. Almost nightly he would walk from his room in South Kensington to Chelsea to dine or drink with us or other friends. He would sometimes take my arm, but one knew better than to take his. One evening when we had been drinking in the Crossed Keys for many hours with Desmond Ryan and Brian Howard, we wandered towards our house at closing time. In the blackout there were sounds of a conversational scuffle between Norman and Brian.

'Do stop holding my arm, please.'

'But the steps are very difficult to see, Norman.'

'I had to live on nothing but carrots in Estoril for three weeks and my eyesight is much better than yours, duckums, I'm sure.'

While Constantine was working at his army duties during the day Norman would often call on me, his arrival heralded by a loud tapping on the window with his walking stick. Sometimes we would simply go for a drink and a pub lunch, and he would walk round Chelsea or Kensington first to see which provided the better value. As meals were still restricted to five shillings wherever you went, it was simply a question of sometimes finding a change of menu.

'Fish pie, shepherd's pie or sausage and mash, what are you having?' he would say. 'Whatever you have I shall have something different, for that way you get better helpings.'

And when we had finished he would invariably conclude by saying: 'Robbed, starved and poisoned, duckums,' and then make that extraordinary 'hah' sound which sounded like a minor explosion. Sometimes we would wander to the Queen's Restaurant in Sloane Square, or Caletta's, a homely little Italian restaurant where the cannelloni weren't bad, in the King's Road. It was Desmond Ryan who introduced us all to the Ladder Club in a mews off Bruton Street with its genial Irish owner, Mossie. She served quite good snacks, and it was warm, comfortable and there was always a fair supply of spirits to drink. Most important, she was open during the long bleak hours of the pub-less afternoon, closing early in the evening.

Norman had a great capacity for almost everything except humbug. He ate heartily, drank everything available, yet I never saw him even remotely drunk and no matter how long the evening he would insist on walking home. He could get very merry, however, and one evening, Norman, John Davenport, Constantine and I did a pub crawl of Chelsea and from each place we left Norman had acquired a new hat in exchange for one he had left behind, which he would slap on his head saying:

'This one's rather cinquecento, isn't it? Does it suit my style of beauty?'

He was never without his hat, stick, snuff box and pipe, and walking home he would stop to strike a match to refuel his pipe.

'I must light up my nose,' he would chuckle.

The constant pipe smoke turned the forelock of his white hair yellowish.

'How can I get rid of this yellow part?'

I gave him a blue-bag to dip into the rinsing water, but alas the first time he used too much.

'Rather smart, duckums, don't you think?' But after that he didn't bother so much about the yellow streak.

Nevertheless he could be most persistent about small things, forever asking where he could get a child's cash-box. I had no idea in wartime London, but he kept on until finally I found one in Hamleys, but I don't think it was quite right. When he wasn't smoking he was taking snuff and many times I made the journey to the Haymarket to the gracious eighteenth-century tobacconists Fribourg and Treyer to get the right kind for him.

He was an intensely curious man which is no doubt why he got on with so many different kinds of people. For although his knowledge on many subjects scientific and intellectual was vast, he enjoyed the company of friends with quite simple minds. It was through Norman that we came to know Viva and Willie King. Viva was a large friendly woman and Willie small, eccentric and erudite. Viva held a *salon* every Sunday afternoon where one was likely to meet some of the liveliest minds in England.

Viva and Willie adored Norman, Viva saying:

'He was so gay and amusing and Rabelaisian, I used to think of him as old Silenus – sometimes I used to look under the table for his goat's feet.'

Willie, who worked at the British Museum, became his literary executor. Viva once greeted Norman with:

'You're the best advertisement for the evil life.'

To which he replied:

'Humph, it's uphill work now, still I try to do my best.'

We went to Hampstead Heath together one Bank Holiday for he wanted to see the English enjoying themselves. We wandered over that vast heath, eating jellied eels (pronounced excellent), winkles (too much trouble for too little) and crab sandwiches.

'They should be good, my dear, so many dead bodies for them to feed on.'

Every so often he would stop and remark on a pretty girl, decrying those that had what he called 'the industrial eye'. Having heard a little about his unusual sex life I remarked on this interest, to get the sharp answer:

'Pretty girls are my business!'

We went to all the freak shows: the bearded lady; the 'mermaid'; the six-legged pony and the largest rat in the world, at which Norman said in a loud voice that it wasn't a rat at all but a European beaver. We walked and walked until I pleaded exhaustion, so we sat on the rather damp grass near to a large woman with two or three wild children. They all seemed quite out of hand and it was most unrestful. Then one tough, dirty little boy of about four years old charged up and said:

'I'm thirsty, Mum, give us a swig of the titty!'

'Well, he's enjoying himself at least,' said Norman. 'Come on, duckums, we've seen enough for one day.'

Norman was immensely interested in food and had been at one time a good cook. During his travels he had missed nothing, nor forgotten anything. He would sit in my kitchen while I was preparing meals and give me little tips, such as cutting tough meat up small, and putting a spoonful of grated chocolate into inferior coffee to improve the flavour. Mostly his tips were almost impossible to carry out as the ingredients weren't available, but he approved of a shashlik I made out of two meat rations one day for a luncheon of eight people. Sam Langford was helping me to cut up the meat, and went out into the garden to pick small twigs which he pared down to make skewers: 'Pick an aromatic wood,' said Norman, but alas we didn't have any. I did, however, have bay leaves and a rosemary bush, which he would pinch every time he went past saying they reminded him of Italy. Also I still had my homegrown garlic, which impressed him.

'Put plenty in, it's good for the stomach, and other things, my dear.'

We had no rice to accompany the shashlik so we broke up Soho-bought spaghetti quite small, and Norman told me to put a spoon of oil into the boiling water to stop it clumping together, something I have done ever since.

At the end of the lunch, with stuffed eggs from the hens first, Brian Howard said:

'Delicious. Why don't we have meals like this at home, Sam?'

To which Sam replied: 'Because we don't have a home, Brian.' For once he had no answer.

Norman told me how to cook a leg of lamb or mutton so that it tasted like wild boar, but I had neither leg of lamb nor the ingredients, which consisted of a litre of dry white wine, pinoli, candied peel and powdered dark chocolate. Later on I read it in his book *Birds and Beasts of the Greek Anthology* and then I did try it. His comments afterwards were:

'Not a dish for every day, someone may remark. Assuredly not. The longer one lives the more one realizes that nothing is a dish for every day.'

He would talk of his collection of aphrodisiac recipes and ask if I had any. Oysters and truffles were all I had heard of: he would look thoughtful and say a few would be nice now, duckums. His last book was this collection which he called *Venus in the Kitchen* and it was published posthumously in 1952 although he had been collecting for it for over twelve years. Some of it was maybe tongue-in-cheek, but I met at least one person who swore it had done him a lot of good.

During all this time Norman had very little money, and what he had was supplemented by giving Italian lessons, for he was an excellent linguist, speaking French, Italian and German fluently as well as having a good knowledge of other languages such as Russian, for in his early days he had been a diplomatist in St Petersburg.

It was particularly galling to see a pirated edition of his famous privately printed *Some Limericks*, with the succinct footnotes, being sold in thousands to the American forces, for which he got not one penny. Likewise the reprinting of *South Wind* earlier by Bennett Cerf in America, for which he received no money owing to copyright problems.

He had, however, written *An Almanac* in 1941, dedicated to the Honourable Neil Hogg of the British Embassy, Lisbon, as a token of thanks for his kindness in putting a room at his disposal in Lisbon after he left Italy in 1940. It was a charming book published by Chatto and Windus with an aphorism for every day of the year. The one for my birthday, 21 October, was: 'I always know when a man is drunk, even when I'm drunk myself.' In 1944 he was compiling *Late Harvest*, which was published by Lindsay Drummond after Nancy Cunard had introduced them. Owing to the paper shortage and other things it was not brought out until 1946.

The book contained, amongst other writings, the whole of *Summer Islands*, those two beautiful essays written earlier about the idyllic, magical islands and islets off the coast of Naples. Then he had said:

'I have shut up my little writing shop for good.'

Although then I had no thought of ever writing anything, there are many times when I think of his advice:

'Never stop writing at a sticky spot; always leave it in the middle of a good, flowing part, for then you will be able to continue easily.'

It does work.

For Norman, at seventy-seven years old, uprooted from all he knew and loved, living in one room in Kensington with his few treasured belongings in a small bag and a child's cash-box, during the bleak and dangerous years of wartime London, it must have seemed the most impossible dream that he would ever again see his beloved Italy.

CHAPTER TWENTY-SIX

We had learned never to plan anything ahead of time; too many places disappeared, friends never returned and our attempts at two brief holidays had resulted in either the trains not going, or the place we wished to go to being in a restricted area. The fact that you woke up in one piece was something to be thankful for, and we were. We continued to take advantage of the chance meeting, to enjoy life as we found it.

Nevertheless, as the spring came the four-page newspaper, still lamentably short of news, was eagerly read. In March, General Montgomery crossed the Rhine and, in early April, General Alexander's armies broke into the Po Valley. Paris was liberated on 25 August and Constantine with his great foresight and determination had managed to get himself transferred there, briefly, together with a letter of introduction to Nancy Cunard, who had gone back after the liberation, and one from Francis Rose, the painter, to Gertrude Stein. Norman worried about his flat in Florence and the fate of Emilio, who had been left in charge of it. The dream of getting back to Italy was not so distant. Yet he was inexpressibly sad, as he wrote to Nancy Cunard in France in 1945.

'I spend half my days now in climbing stairs and asking people whether they have a room to let. A dog's life . . . instead of my becoming used to this country, I get more homesick every day. Went for a solitary walk down the Serpentine this afternoon. Yesterday for a solitary walk in Battersea Park . . .'

There was, however, an excitement in the air for many, which became more so when the Allies landed in the south of France. However, there was still fighting in the Far East. It was not until the two dictators were dead that it appeared the fighting in Europe would stop. This all happened at the end of April when Mussolini and his mistress were shot by partisans and, on 30 April, Hitler killed his mistress, then committed suicide. On 8 May the long-awaited ending of the European war was announced.

It was an emotional time for almost everybody. Church bells rang out once more (during the war they were only to be rung to announce a gas attack), flood-lighting and drawn curtains took the place of the blackout, strangers hugged and kissed in the streets, and there was dancing and singing around the boarded-up Eros in Piccadilly Circus and in Trafalgar Square. The pubs were full, work seemed to stop for the day, but the few shops that opened gave good measure on the ration books. Desmond Ryan turned up with a battered car and said we should go to Piccadilly. Norman Douglas threw out anecdotes of peace day in 1918 with vivid descriptions of lovemaking in the streets. Yes, we would go: I said I would stand on the bonnet of the car the length of Piccadilly. Not quite though, for after about twenty yards I tripped forward and all I did was chip my front tooth, so I retired to a safer place inside.

What did we see? A thin crowd of people straggling towards the Circus and Augustus John, hands behind his back, looking furious, going in the opposite direction. Not enough licentiousness, I would imagine. We went on and at the Circus found thicker crowds, very good natured, singing and dancing. We decided to go to the Café Royal and enjoy the marble and plush. The lights were all blazing, it was very crowded, but at a table we saw Brian Howard and Sam Langford, whom we joined. The drink flowed as it had not done for nearly five years, and it was then that Sam and I decided to go out and climb lamp-posts. Like white Irish monkeys we shinned up the tall Regent Street stands and had a marvellous view of everything. Then back home, pubs all open after hours on the way, and a night-cap at the Black Lion. People there were discussing when Jack or Bill would be home, when rationing would be over, and when would the Japanese pack it in? Everyone had theories, none of which proved right as it turned out. It was after all only half the war which had ended but it was something to be going on with.

Nevertheless, some of the forces did come home but it was not always the homecoming they had dreamed about. Wives found that husbands who had left as young, almost innocent men returned as disillusioned, weary and war-shocked individuals unable to settle down to family life or to find a job. Wives too had changed after years of living alone bringing up a family; if they hadn't lived alone, that only complicated matters further and added to the frustration and feeling of uselessness. These were violent times and very few were untouched by them.

One such man who had been a commando officer behind the German lines in Greece returned home to his wife, a childhood friend of Dylan's, to a bungalow near the Thomases in New Quay, Cardiganshire. During an evening in the local pub, Dylan, a secretary Donald Taylor had sent down to help Dylan to finish an overdue film script, the officer and his wife were drinking together. Dylan's account was that a verbal skirmish took place between the secretary and the commando, who then taunted her with being Jewish, an unfortunate happening at any time but especially when the savagery of the concentration camps was being revealed. The secretary attacked him, and he hit back, to be forcibly removed from the pub by Dylan and the other male drinkers. He went on his own to another pub, drank heavily and thought of revenge.

Dylan and the wife went back to Caitlin at the flimsy bungalow they lived in and had a few more beers, no doubt trying to dismiss the incident from their minds. All of a sudden they were startled by sten-gun bullets coming through the walls. Caitlin with foresight pushed the babies up the wide chimney minutes before the door was kicked in. Dylan, with a bravery one wouldn't have connected with him, got the gun away, only to find that the man had a hand-grenade in his pocket. He threatened to pull the pin unless the gun was returned. Naturally Dylan complied with his wishes and, after trying to reason with him, left with his wife and children. The man was subsequently prosecuted for attempted murder, but released on the grounds of temporary insanity brought on by provocation.

Although a terrifying and upsetting experience, it was somehow not so surprising, for the climate of Britain at the end of the war was one of exhausted brutality, and it was maybe one amongst many other incidents.

Meanwhile, the euphoria gradually passing, we all went about the daily tasks, looking for food to eat, for rationing had in no way decreased, working, and relaxing at whichever pub had their beer ration. In July a general election brought the Labour Party to power, which caused great hopes amongst many of the returned forces. The atmosphere was once more excited and electric. The hungry thirties were still very real for many people and the Labour programme with promise of work and social security seemed attractive. Francis Rose told of a large luncheon he was at in one of London's big hotels: 'where, my dears, all the waiters were *quite* tipsy. The courses were all out of order, ice-cream served after the fish! Lady Colefax exclaimed, "Oh, delicious, a sorbet!"' But alas it was simply vanilla ice-cream. The working classes thought the time had come for them to inherit the earth.

There were murmurs that Constantine would soon be sent back to America and from July onwards it was merely a question of when. Norman Douglas had applied for a renewal of his passport to Italy, which he got, mainly perhaps due to the answer he gave to the interviewing official:

'So you want to go back to live in Italy?'

'No, I want to go back to die.'

We realized that we too would shortly be packing up, probably to go to some unknown part of America. We started to sell furniture and some books. Norman came round when we were sorting the books and said:

'Oh, I'll sign them for you; it'll make them much more valuable.'

He did sign them, not only his own books, but some of Hardy, Conrad and so on. 'Best wishes' from Thomas Hardy; 'A memorable meeting', Joseph

Conrad. Alas when we did come to sell some of them, the buyer said he couldn't give us full price as they had been defaced!

It was to be another year before Norman was to see Italy and Capri again. However, while we were all still together we would often meet during the summer months, in the garden of the Pier Hotel at the bottom of Oakley Street. One day Constantine and I had joined John Davenport and a rather tall, ill-looking American soldier to whom we were introduced. It was pleasant under the trees and even a hard pear falling on Con's head didn't disturb the tranquillity. We were joined by Norman well wrapped up in overcoat, scarf and hat despite the heat. He seemed in sombre mood and not very talkative. Then he looked up and in a loud voice said:

'I thought I was coming here to meet W. H. Auden.'

He hadn't beard John's soft-voiced introduction, but thought it amusing when he realized he had been talking to Auden for nearly an hour. Once more he was in an ebullient mood.

When the final victory did come it was at the terrible cost of the atomic bomb being dropped on innocent victims of American war-strategy. There were outcries about it, but to be fair I will say that the ordinary person did not realize, for we were never told then, the monstrous and lasting effect it was to have on so many people. A little under a month after the first bomb was dropped on Hiroshima, VJ-Day, as it was called, was officially celebrated on 2 September 1945.

This time the celebrations seemed more ordered and more restrained. The crowds, at least in Chelsea, were not so evident as after the European peace, but there were many private and street parties. The Black Lion announced they were giving us all a party in the pub and outside in Paulton's Street, and many pubs did likewise for their customers. How many of the pubs had been safe harbours for us during those long years, places of congeniality and friendliness; the hum of conversation, the warmth in winter, the kindness and cheerfulness shown by many publicans will never be forgotten by those who experienced it.

The weather was still very summer-like. Mouche the poodle, heavily pregnant, puffed about the house trying to find a cool spot; we opened a few hoarded tins for lunch and looked forward to the party the next day. At about five o'clock, almost as if he knew there would be a party, Dylan turned up with a rather dreary, adoring fan who hung on his every word and flattered him so outrageously that even he told her to stop. We told them of the party and through the window we could see benches being put in the street, huge barrels of beer being rolled out and put on to wooden trestles, then finally a piano. We had none of us ever been to a street party before and no children were ever more excited. Then, what were they doing now? Hanging up rather faded bunting left over from George VI's coronation.

At opening time precisely, Francis Butterfield arrived, to be followed by Norman, and over they all went, I saying I would follow when I had fed the dog and the poultry. Mouche puffed even more and refused her dinner. I thought she had caught our excitement, but within minutes the first little brown poodle puppy was born. I led her to her prepared bed and waited, but nothing more happened, so I comforted her and decided she would be better on her own for a bit. I went over to join the fun, and fun it was too. Free beer, the piano thumping out with whatever repertoire the pianist had. Dolly, Janie and most of our chums were there. Two enormous women were dancing and the young girls were doing their best to persuade fathers, uncles, anyone who would volunteer, to dance. First we sat on the benches, then, as the evening progressed, the kerbstone. I would keep going back to see to Mouche, until finally the eighth puppy was born. I gave her glucose and water and straightened up the nuzzling, wandering bunch. As dusk lengthened into evening we wandered inside the pub. It was there, at the bar, that I found myself standing next to Bill Gee, the guest of our wedding night. It took me a moment to recognize him, then he smiled and said:

'Hullo, my child, how's hubby?'

It became evident that the adoring fan was not going to be easily shaken off, so Dylan, supreme actor that he was, simulated such extreme drunkenness that I took him home where, although not sober, he perked up considerably.

'Has she gone?' he said conspiratorily.

'I've left her with Francis, he'll take care of her.'

'Good, let's have another drink.'

Norman had wandered off into the darkness muttering that it wasn't a patch on Armistice Night, but we had all enjoyed it. Constantine came home, with Francis, then we all had some supper and went to bed.

Much later, when we were all asleep, I woke up to find a cowering Dylan by the side of the bed.

'I think there's been a mistake,' he said. 'There's an awful noise of aeroplanes flying very low. I think it's a raid.'

I got up and went down to see what it was. Nothing, but after a while a faint buzzing sound.

'Dylan, it's the puppies nuzzling on the verandah just next to you.'

We went out to see them, and the noise did sound quite loud in the still night. Then, fascinated and reassured, he went back to bed with a bar of chocolate I had tucked away for just such a special occasion.

CHAPTER TWENTY-SEVEN

About two weeks later Constantine was sent to a port, prior to embarking for America, destination unknown, but he would write when he could. Meanwhile I was to see about finding homes for the puppies, hens and ducks, go to the American Express and Cook's, every shipping line and every airline I could find to 'put my name down'. That is just about what I did, for to this day I have never heard a word from any of them. Also I was to pack up the house and find somewhere to stay when I'd done it. When there seemed no urgency I tried to carry on as usual. I saw quite a lot of Norman Douglas who, like myself, just waited for news, any news of leaving England. Nothing. We wandered about having our fish pie or shepherd's pie at various pubs, and sometimes he would come to dinner with me, but now I had only one ration book and no eggs, as the poultry had gone.

Dolly Donn Byrne's two sons returned from the Far East and sometimes you would see a friend you had thought you'd never hear from again in the street or on a bus, thus giving the illusion that life had returned to a prewar level. But this was never to happen. Britain had changed greatly, and had taken an important leap forward in many ways into the twentieth century. After years of what had seemed like stagnation, people were anxious to progress. Many young men of my acquaintance had joined mounted regiments only to find them rapidly mechanized. The trend was from agriculture to industry.

Constantine had been sent to Camp Ritchie in Maryland, where he was interrogating captured German generals, such material being edited into a book for the United States Army. His letters made it sound a pleasant place and the work not arduous. When was I coming over? he wanted to know, to which of course I had no answer. He suggested I went to the United States Embassy to see what they had to say. This I did; they were attentive, but nothing had been decided, they said. They would let me know.

After the long hot summer, the winter of 1945 to 1946 was extremely hard and there was no relaxation in coal supplies or food. The house seemed comfortless and cheerless. For the first time I felt lonely. Dylan and Caitlin came up to stay a couple of times, separately, and once with the baby Aeronwy, now a sturdy two-year-old with the determination of a dictator and the strength of Hercules. She was not an easy child, but Caitlin seemed to go on placidly making her huge cauldron of soup. After a while I went to stay with my mother, taking the dogs with me. Maurice Richardson then complained about my leaving the Thomases in charge, so finally they went to stay in a flat found for them by Nicolette Devas, Caitlin's sister, in a basement in Markham Square, Chelsea, where they were for some time.

After a bleak Christmas I was ill again, and had to go to a very out-of-the-way hospital for an operation which left me very weak and dispirited. So in February, Constantine got compassionate leave to join me. He was at that time working with General Laegeler, ex-Chief of Staff of the Home Army in Germany, who replaced the gallant Count Stauffenberg who was hanged after his attempt on Hitler's life. General Laegeler remarked:

'I expect your General will lend you his private plane. I would to one of my officers.'

It was, however, the old army transport which flew him over for the few weeks he was here. Before he left I heard from the Embassy that they were in fact going to transport the 'fireside companions' as we seemed to be called.

The remaining things were either sold or stored with my family, including Mouche who was looked after by my grandmother until such time as I could send for her. All the puppies were in good homes, and really my clothes were so few and so old that they hardly seemed worth packing. I did take the most precious of my books with me.

From the moment the Embassy sent me four labels, three for my luggage and one to tie on the lapel of my coat, with a covering letter enclosing my 'orders', everything promised to be unusual. I had become that unlikely person for me, a 'GI bride'. Just before I left I had a cable from Constantine giving me an address in Park Avenue, and also sending me love and kisses from the Stork Club. Later I heard my grandmother telling her friends that her grandson-in-law was staying at the Stork *Hotel*.

I arrived at Waterloo Station, labelled and with my luggage, on 14 March 1946. My grandmother had pressed five pounds into my hand and a bottle of whisky for the journey. A porter said to me: 'You a bride, miss?' which rather amused me as I had at that time been married for two years. He led me to a special train which was to take us all, not to the boat, but to an army camp at Tidworth on Salisbury Plain. I settled in the first compartment I came to, and watched the leave-takings of the other 'brides'. One fond mother produced a hot-water bottle which was disdainfully handed back with the message 'where I'm going to everything's properly heated'. I wondered if it was.

The unheated train rattled slowly through the London suburbs. In Middlesex the first sign of fields appeared and I noticed a rather pretty farmhouse in the middle of a field, the small town about a mile away to the left. My reverie was disturbed by a dark girl, well wrapped in a travelling rug, sitting opposite me.

'My, I wouldn't like to live in that isolated spot,' she said in a very false American accent. I asked her where she was going to in America.

'Montana,' she replied calmly. I hadn't the heart to disillusion her.

It was dark when we arrived at Tidworth Camp. We were helped out of the bus by shadowy male figures. I heard the girl in front of me say, 'Thank you,' but as she came into the lamplight she wheeled round to me and cried:

'My mother would be furious with me if she knew I'd said thank you to a German.'

I saw then that our assistants were German prisoners. From then on the German prisoners looked after us entirely. In the bare room I shared with sixteen other 'brides', Fritz or Hans stood by while we made our beds and commiserated with us for the dust on the bare wooden boards. They cooked for us and served the food into our tin trays. We were frequently told over loudspeakers that we mustn't fraternize with them. My limited knowledge of German was a great nuisance as I found myself let in for many things. In this barrack room was a central old-fashioned coke stove around which we huddled in the evenings. I shared Grandmother's whisky with a chosen few.

It was all nightmarish. The beds were as hard as boards, the food uneatable; there were two baths only in an outhouse between two hundred of us. Also the American Army's passion for youth was a bit overwhelming: only one other girl apart from myself was in her middle twenties, all the others were teenagers, with the exception of one rather jolly old lady of about fifty, whom I took to be a relic of 1918.

We were not allowed out of the perimeter at all, and the Red Cross 'rest' room was built to hold about a quarter of us. The two public telephones it housed were besieged at all hours by long queues of girls shouting inanities like 'and we had tinned peaches for dinner' down the mouthpiece. Most of the time you couldn't get through, and if you did you couldn't hear what was said at the other end because of the noise in the 'rest' room.

On the third day of our stay we were herded into various rooms for vaccinations, medical inspections and interviews. It was refreshing to have something to do rather than just sitting in the cold barracks. However, some who had never been vaccinated before got very ill, and very homesick. By this time I had made the acquaintance of Joan Ogle, or 'Oggles' as she preferred to be called, who occupied the bed next to mine. I think I might have lost my sense of humour but for her.

She was a pretty girl of about nineteen, dark-haired and dark-eyed, with clear-cut features which bespoke her Italian blood. She had been bred in one of the toughest London city districts. Oggles swore incessantly, yet with such charm that it seemed like anyone else's normal conversation. She told me her grandmother said she remembered 'women with cleavers fighting bare to the waist on the street corners'. 'Bloody old liar' was Oggles's only comment. It was she who stood by me at the baggage inspection when it was made known that I was married to a captain and my address was Park Avenue. This information was stencilled in large white paint on the cases by the prisoners. Nobody, it appeared, had married an officer. That night Oggles said to me:

'My husband's only a private, first class. Do you think it matters?' I thought of saying that none of it would matter in a little while when everyone had been demobilized, but instead I said that my husband was only a captain in the Intelligence, not in the fighting line, and anyway we had been lent the flat, and it was way downtown and not up to much. Yes, it was despicable, but I valued Oggles's friendship.

Two days later, early in the morning we went by train to Southampton, labelled and numbered, to be shepherded on to what I thought was a very small ship to be crossing the Atlantic at that time of year. It was the SS *James Parker* and it was my wedding anniversary. After Tidworth Camp the ship, although small, was quite luxurious, although the cabins weren't really equipped to hold four of us and two babies. The saloon was well proportioned and would have been comfortable for half the number. Nevertheless it was considerably better than I had expected. Larger luggage was stowed in the hold. We were allowed, indeed there was only room for, one small case each, and one for each baby. After being allocated our cabins we were summoned by bells to go down to lunch.

The dining saloon was attractive and for the first time we had tables laid with cloths and proper cutlery. Remarkably there were also well-trained stewards. The food was plentiful and good considering the numbers they had to cater for, with mostly American dishes. All in all it was a pleasant surprise. It was interesting to wander over the ship, but that soon palled, especially as it got much, much colder. Reading, my main occupation, was out; there were too many people about all the time, and a scarcity of chairs. So it was that Oggles and I volunteered to do some work in the office.

The work was routine, making duplicate forms of the names and addresses we were to be dispatched to. A cheery little sergeant called Charlie was in charge of us, a small man with twinkling eyes behind spectacles, always smiling and ready with a quip. We were his favourites and one day he offered us a coke.

'Wouldn't drink the bloody stuff,' said Oggles determinedly. 'Haven't you got anything decent?'

'I think you'll like this one,' he replied. 'Try it and see.'

I took a deep swig and coughed violently. It had been half emptied and filled up with rum: delicious, especially on a dry ship. From then on, one or two was our daily ration, very much looked forward to.

Class-consciousness is something I had never been in contact with, but it soon became apparent when my luggage and labels were exhibited that it was rife on the ship. I suppose I got what was coming to me when I asked what the abbreviation for Staff Sergeant was, during our work-time.

'I expect you'd know how to abbreviate General,' was the only reply I got. Whereupon Oggles chipped in on my behalf with a mild obscenity.

After we passed the coast of Ireland at night, we struck a northern route. The ship was fairly stable, but at that time of year I felt we could be in for bad weather later on.

During that ten-day voyage I became an information bureau. Because I had been to America before I was expected to know in detail about all the cities and towns of every state. They seldom got my name right. Usually I was called Bedelia after the heroine of a current film; they knew it was long and ended with an 'a', that was all. I used to wonder and worry a little as to how some of them would make out, they had such odd ideas of what they were going to. One very pretty Welsh girl would spend long hours on her bunk gazing at her husband's photograph, which I thought omened well, until she confided that she had always hated tall men and her husband was six feet five inches. She wondered whether *it* was worth it; *it* being that she loved her busy home port of Cardiff and she was going to a box number in Iowa. There were large notices over the ship saying *Orientation Meetings*, with an arrow afterwards. The lieutenant in charge of the meetings told me of the poor attendances. I enquired among the girls and found that most of them thought that if they went to the meetings they would come out resembling Geisha girls.

I always regretted that Oggles wasn't in my cabin. There were three others and two babies but no Oggles. She did make an appearance one evening when I went to bed early because I had a slight cold. She opened the door and stood there with two lemons in her hand and a pot of hot water.

'Well, don't bloody say I never bloody well do a bloody thing for you.'

Dropping the lemons on my bunk, she left. The mothers enquired if my friend always talked like that. I murmured something and squeezed the lemons into the remaining whisky. Dear Oggles.

When we were being de-loused she left the powder in her hair and looked like Marie Antoinette on her way to the scaffold. 'Too much bloody brushing,' she commented when I asked why her hair still had a grey powdery look. Then there were the physical jerks. I refused to do them for several days until I saw the fifty-year-old bending at the knees and felt ashamed. Oggles got herself made a section leader under the impression she would be exempt from the 'bloody things', but found she wasn't and in the bargain had to round up the other girls. Her comments were choice.

The selection of films shown to us during the voyage was most unfortunate. The one that caused the most distress was called *Grapes Have Tender Vines*, which depicted a prosperous farm in Wisconsin, but not so prosperous, as it got flooded regularly every year. Groans went up from that part of the audience that was destined for the farming states, especially when Edward G. Robinson, who played the prosperous farmer, had to lie on the floor because his wife was sitting in the only chair. The other film was apparently made in Australia and called *The Man From Down Under*, starring Charles Laughton. It started in 1914 when Sergeant Laughton adopted two children in France, became an idle drunk in Australia with Binnie Barnes, and ended up killing with his bare fists six Japanese soldiers who, believe it or not, came down the chimney while he was in a semi-alcoholic stupor. If anything was guaranteed to set off our pent-up hysteria, that film was it. These films were shown at least four times. The other nights we had rough and competitive 'states' competitions, in which you had to sing a song connected with the state you were going to. This was a non-starter except for those going to Texas. We had an amateur dramatic show, given to us by the American Red Cross girls, and a horse-race with cardboard horses. It was eerie, like being at an old-fashioned Kindergarten school. For me it was a far cry from Paris or Chelsea, and very funny sometimes.

I was right about the weather; when the little Arctic owl landed on deck, it presaged a storm. We were fairly far out, past mid Atlantic, when it came, and it blew for two or three days. The small ship rolled and heaved, faces turned green and eventually, apart from the crew and Red Cross staff, only Oggles and I were still on our feet. Except for the banging of the storm, the ship was quiet for the first time; we had it almost to ourselves and Oggles was determined not to miss a meal. Unfortunately the dining saloon was on the deck below and to get to it we had to pass on the way huge bins full of vomit. This almost turned me up, but the next time we went Oggles was ready for them.

'Put a peg on your nose,' she said, and painfully snapped one over mine. Where she got them I will never know, but she was very resourceful.

The stewards, delighted with our strong stomachs, plied us with food and we would sit there for hours having second helpings of course after course. The games were suspended as there were not enough people, and Charlie's rum and coke in the afternoons was most welcome. It was almost like a regular crossing until we got back to our cabins with their heavy, sickly smell.

At last 30 March arrived and we started up the Hudson at about eight o'clock in the morning. A tug drew alongside with a coloured band on it playing 'Sentimental Journey'. Everyone was in tears including the Red Cross girls and we had to use all our powers of persuasion to get the brides to decide to leave the ship when it docked. Not that it was as easy as that to leave the ship. Unless your husband was there to claim you, you weren't allowed off. I was quite worried because I had been unable to send word of the exact sailing date and the Park Avenue address was unknown to me. I had very little hope of Constantine being there at nine o'clock to meet me. If you were met you had to pay your own fare to wherever your destination was, but if nobody turned up you had to stay on board for two days, then you got a free ticket. With no address they kept you on board until further inquiries were made.

At nine o'clock precisely, the immigration people came on board and questioned us. All those who had husbands meeting them were called out. My name wasn't on the list. I was beginning to feel I would never get off the ship, when Charlie appeared, cheerful as ever, and I told him what had happened. Oggles passed me in the queue, still looking a bit powdery, and said her bloody husband hadn't turned up, but Indiana was a bloody long way. Well, I thought, it won't be so bad if Oggles is here too. Then Charlie eased me out of my queue and took me to look through a porthole to see if Con was on the dock. No sign. I gave him Con's name, number, rank, address and in a panic even suggested he rang up the Stork Club. Eventually, by what means I don't know, he reappeared with a man in a smart uniform who checked a list then took me to a lower deck. Pointing through a porthole he said:

'Is that your husband?'

There were a lot of men in a sort of giant playpen, but following his direction, surprisingly, I saw him.

On getting off the boat there was the usual business about finding my luggage despite the indelible white stencilling. However, once again Charlie sorted it out for me and down the gangplank we went.

Constantine stepped forward from the other husbands and said:

'Darling, it's lovely to see you. Look, I've been promoted to Major, so we've got two things to celebrate.'

I hurried him away quickly lest one of the other GI brides should overhear. I had no Oggles with me and it had been bad enough being a captain's wife.

'How did you find me?'

'I rang up of course, but the fools first sent me to the wrong pier. I've only just arrived.'

'Where are we going to celebrate? At the apartment on Park Avenue?'

'For heaven's sake, no, that's Teddy Rose's place. I had to give some address otherwise they wouldn't have let you off.'

'But where . . .?'

'Oh, don't fuss, we'll find somewhere.'

It was the end of the month so the paycheque was a bit low. We took a taxi and Constantine went to an office which found accommodation for 'veterans'. He came out, eyes shining.

'It's marvellous, darling. I've taken us a suite at the Plaza Hotel overlooking the Park. Damn fine hotel, we're lucky to get in.'

'What are we using for money?' I enquired.

'It costs practically nothing. Apparently if any hotel has spare rooms they have to rent them at a nominal sum to service personnel. They only had this suite left.'

So it was that we arrived at what seemed like the bridal suite at the Plaza with our battered old luggage. It was very luxurious with huge bowls of flowers, such as I had never seen before, and fruit of all different kinds. At dinner that night the menu confused me; it was so vast and varied, I thought I would never decide: swordfish, kidneys in Madeira and fresh pineapple and bananas . . . m. m. mm, all things I hadn't had or even thought of for years. For the first time for many months there was warmth, plenty of food and drink, an atmosphere of gaiety and peace, and a soft, inviting-looking bed.

Tomorrow, we said, we would have to make plans: there was the New World to be explored, money to be found and a new way of life to be discovered.

CHAPTER TWENTY-EIGHT

There had been many sea voyages right from the beginning, for I had started to be born on a ship coming from France to England. Maybe it was preordained that my life would be lived in many countries. Each time there was not only the excitement of travelling, but the thought of the pleasures of discovering new countries and people. The time was when the cabin trunks seemed so large I could stand in them, then later I could only sit down on one side waiting for unfamiliar clothes to be arranged on hangers in the space. Each boat had a distinctive smell: the French steamer taking me to school had a rich, smoky odour like cigars; the English one smelled of fish; and the boat going to Ireland always reminded me of frying bacon and beer. It was a warm smell which made me feel I was almost home again. When I thought of my family in County Clare it was always the summer holidays, the ponies to ride, the companionship of cousins my own age, my father, who had influenced my life so much, and of the love they had all given me.

As I sat in the luxurious but impersonal hotel room in New York, where no traumas lingered to ruffle the *toile de jouy* curtains, and the silk-covered beds seemed as undefiled as a unicorn's virgin, my mind was filled with pictures from the past. The images were clear, the ships of my scattered childhood anchored in a harbour of my own memory.

Attempting to visualize what sort of new life I would live, in New York, I recalled all the anticipation in my journey on the P&O liner to India when I was sixteen. I had refused to go back to any school. My father was returning to India, and at the last minute he had said:

'Do you want to come out? You'll have to make your own arrangements. I'll leave money in the bank. You'll have to work too, running my house and seeing the horses are looked after properly. White women with nothing to do get ruined in India; too many servants, so they gossip all day to amuse themselves.'

When he had left I asked my mother what she thought, and she replied it was a long way if I didn't like it. But first, knowing my father, she suggested that I go to the bank and see whether the money was actually there. It was and I decided to go.

At first it was very exhilarating; the ship to be discovered thoroughly, as well as the passengers. The brief stops and shore excursions at various ports absorbed me. North Africa was like something out of the *Arabian Nights* and equally compelling. It was magical. I wished I could have stayed longer. The stultifying heat of the Red Sea; the joyous shoals of dolphin or flying fish. There were young officers to be flirted with, constant entertainment and nobody in charge of me. However, as the weeks went by I realized it was in fact a monotonous routine, that I was being treated more and more as a pretty child and not as a wayward young woman – to me, much more attractive. Families tended to encourage me into their tight middle-class circles, but this I avoided deftly. I was not allowed in the bars, not that I drank, but all the gay young people were there. I read most of the books in the ship's library, especially those about India, and I longed to get off the boat and explore this strange new country.

Always a recalcitrant child at school, I had refused to continue with geography once it reached the stage of isotherms and isobars.

'How are you going to know about other parts of the world if you don't learn geography?' they demanded.

'When I grow up,' I replied, 'I'm going to travel a lot and find out for myself.'

So it came about that, after reading and listening to travellers' tales of India, I determinedly disembarked when we reached the large, strange-looking port of Bombay. My destination was Calcutta.

It was very terrifying; I had never even contemplated such crowds of people, such confusion, such a babel of strange tongues, such a mixture of machines, vendors, porters, powerful smells. I was rescued by one of the young officers from the ship.

'Someone meeting you, then? Or are you travelling on?'

'I'm going on, but I don't know how to get to the station. Can I get a taxi?'

'Hold on, you stay there with your baggage. I'll fix something.'

I was very thankful when after some time I saw his spotless white uniform appear again and he arrived with two very thin but muscley Indians.

'I've got two cars; we'll go in one and the baggage in another. I'll come with you if you like.'

There was something to being a pretty child still, for he treated me like an enlightened ten-year-old. When we reached the big, dusty old station, he said he'd buy my ticket.

'Where are you going?'

'Calcutta.'

'Calcutta!' he almost shouted it. 'But that's the other side of India. You'll be in the train for days. Why didn't you stay on the boat?'

I begged him just to get my ticket and take me to the train. I was almost in tears and bitterly regretting having so precipitously left the safety of the floating hotel. I was astonished to see the size of the compartment; it was like a sitting room, something you could imagine Queen Victoria travelling in, with heavy furnishings and comfortable chairs like an English gentleman's club.

'How many others will be in here?' I asked.

'Oh, it's all yours, it's a bogie-car for long distances; you'll need it, I think. It's a long way, you know. Sure you'll be all right?'

I assured him I would be fine and we exchanged addresses in Calcutta. I was sad to see him go, and I waved from the window until the last glimpse of white uniform had disappeared into the homogeneous crowds.

Exploring the bogie-car was fun; the bed was covered with heavy, Indian material, and I found a little wash-place and a tiny galley-like kitchen. I wondered what it was for, as surely there was a restaurant car on a great train like this. However, at that time, as I soon discovered, there weren't communicating carriages. I was beginning to feel very hungry, and wondered how to get some food.

I had to wonder for nearly two days; I was frightened to leave my carriage lest the train started off again, or worse, in case I lost it to someone else, for there were people on the roof and hanging on the sides. I bought foods standing on the steps by the door – samosas, chappattis, nuts, fruit and some awful, over-sweet gummy things which gave me a dreadful thirst. I didn't know what to make of the countryside, but then I didn't know what I had expected. Some places were very arid: red, dusty earth with an occasional tired-looking shrub; then it would be greener with sheep and vivid red flowering trees amongst others which looked quite dead. Later I was to know them well, *gol mohurs*, 'the flame of the forest', which blossom profusely from the dead-looking trees around April or May. One day, emboldened, I walked on the platform towards a military looking man, and his wife and young daughter. They seemed astonished to hear I was on my own and invited me to their carriage for a meal, which I readily accepted. I was to go back at the next halt. My healthy young appetite did full justice to the large meal, which had been prepared by their bearer.

When I got back to my bogie, I found the most beautiful young Indian boy sitting on the steps, very poorly dressed. He got up as I approached.

'Missy Sahib need looking after?' he enquired tentatively.

I certainly did, and Hari, for that was his name, seemed agreeable to work for a very low salary. Hari was a most diligent and attentive servant. He tidied my compartment and gave me delicious meals with rice, chicken, Indian spices and vegetables. Sometimes he would find some eggs and some beer. When the train stopped he would run off like an eel and come back in a very little while, his arms full of food. He showed me how to open the heavy windows, for the heat was sometimes overpowering, and got the fan working. At night he slept on a mat in the hall.

We would talk together in the evenings, Hari squatting on the floor by the door. He came from the south, and wanted to find work in Calcutta. Sometimes I found his quick, rhythmic, light voice difficult to follow, then he would speak more slowly. His uncle had been in England, he told me, and when he was a little boy had taught him some English so that he could get a good position later on. The train rolled on, through villages and small towns, every station crowded with people all carrying bundles. It was as though the train and the passengers were a travelling theatre. At the smaller stops everyone, it seemed, came to look at us.

One day Hari came back with a bunch of very sweet-smelling flowers, probably picked from the stationmaster's cottage. He said it was frangipani but it didn't sound like that when he said it first. The scent permeated the whole car, disguising the dusty, slightly frowsty smell it had before. He was about my age, I think, and was already affianced, but needed money before he could marry. The journey had an air of enchantment with Hari there; I was glad I had left the ship, and it was certainly a far cry and better than going back to that convent. He would tell me tales of India in his singsong voice and, by the time we were approaching Calcutta, I felt I was returning, rather than just arriving.

As we were nearing our destination, he carefully repacked my cases and enquired where I was going to meet my father. I showed him the address. He said he knew where it was and would take me there. He did everything he could to make it easy for me, getting porters and an enormous but very old taxi cab which groaned loudly when the luggage was put in. The springs of the seats had long since broken; sitting almost on the floor we set off at a breakneck pace to the address I had. When we arrived he said he would go in first to enquire, and was soon back, the huge, black, liquid eyes looking sad:

'No Sahib, missy, we go on to next place. We will try the clubs.'

This was repeated several times, each time his face getting more and more sad. The traffic was appalling, people weaving in and out all over. We were bewildered and didn't know what to do. We sat, taxi driver as well, staring at each other wondering what on earth to do. Suddenly Hari looked up, face brightening.

'One more place, naughty place,' he said, and we set off again.

In fact it wasn't at all naughty but allowed women in, a great departure in those days. He came down the steps, smiling, those expressive eyes dancing.

'Sahib here, missy. Will you come in?'

So in I went, hot, dusty, but with a rising excitement. I was ushered into a large room with a verandah along one side covered by a creeper. There weren't many tables filled, but coming from the verandah side I heard that unmistakable laugh. Looking over I saw my father, another man and two rather pretty women. He was sitting with his side towards me as I walked to within about ten feet of the table.

'Hullo, Daddy,' I said.

He turned round, stared as if at a ghost, and said:

'What the bloody hell are you doing here?' Then he laughed, put out his arms and kissed me.

My arrival was, of course, quite unexpected. If I'd stayed on the ship and gone round Ceylon, I wouldn't have arrived for some time. He thought it was all rather splendid; the only thing was, he hadn't moved into his house yet. Oh, well! I could help with it. I told him about Hari, who was engaged on the spot to be a special bearer.

What had transported me back so naturally to India, I wondered? That voyage seemed closer and more real than the one I had taken a few days ago, with my strange G.I. bride travelling companions from England to the United States, in very overcrowded conditions. That journey was still stored in my memory, waiting to be re-examined, before it became part of my life.

———

The insistent ring of the telephone startled me back into the present, for I was still contemplating the magic spell that Ireland and India had cast over me. Who could be telephoning me in this strange country which I had not explored? Where, as yet, I had no friends?

PART THREE

Manhattan and Bermuda

CHAPTER TWENTY-NINE

In 1946, New York was an extraordinary experience, for it was quite unlike any city I had ever visited. It is now a cliché to speak of speed in connection with New York, but after the almost car-less, depopulated and still-rationed city of London, it was very noticeable. Not only were there crowds of people and automobiles, but they all seemed to be travelling very fast. They even spoke fast; asking a simple direction produced a few rapid sentences containing several numbers. Everyone said I couldn't get lost in New York, and, having wandered about Budapest, Belgrade, Rome and several other cities, I believed them. But somehow I did. In fact the only place I could find my way about was Greenwich Village, which had only street names.

This well-dressed motley crew never mooched along the streets chattering to each other; they walked purposefully, seemingly knowing exactly where they were going and why. This went on day and night. A friend assured me that thousands of New Yorkers preferred to live through the night and sleep all day. Restaurants, cafés, small grocery stores, and drug stores were open all night to look after them. Sometimes it seemed to me the streets were brighter at night, with all the blazing neon lights outside cinemas, theatres, clubs, and on advertisements, than on some days when the skyscrapers cast their long shadows. So, to me, there was always the noise of traffic and the smell of petrol, something I had never noticed about Chelsea or Paris once it was nighttime.

However, we were fortunate to be staying at the Plaza Hotel which overlooked Central Park on one side and always had a line of horse carriages parked outside should you wish to take a discreet drive. The horses were well looked after, my favourite being Geraldine, whom the cabby assured me couldn't find her way around the West Side. We had been installed in a splendid suite with positively no prospect of finding anywhere else. Still, I don't think we tried very hard, for the few friends we had in New York were determined to show us their city.

The Plaza Hotel was built early in this century with all the comfort and sumptuousness that its wealthy clients demanded. If they were to venture outside their large, lush houses, then they must feel at home. There was a Palm Lounge where a small orchestra softly played pieces like 'Tea for Two' as a background to the conversations of the hatted, befurred and jewelled ladies. There was the wood-panelled Oak Room, for gentlemen, a grill room, and a charming dining room where in the evening the best, and also the most appropriate, cabaret was performed. When we were there it was Paul Draper, the magical dancer, a nephew of Ruth Draper the great impersonator.

Our friends, mostly brother officers of Constantine's, included our wedding night guest Ferdinand Helm, and our best man Teddy Rose. Teddy was big and bluff in manner, an Old Etonian who had lived in Paris for years. Without doubt he was the best raconteur I knew. My go-ahead grandmother also gave me the names of two actor friends of hers. All were anxious for us to leave the placid delights of the Plaza and join them. Whatever you feel like eating you can have, they said. The best bortsch is in 3rd Avenue; the best Italian restaurant is on 2nd Avenue; fine French food at La Grenouille in the 60s, where the frogs' legs were as good as any in France. Or maybe Chinatown where our host insisted we drank only tea, yet on the way out we saw Chinese dining with a bottle of Scotch on the table! My favourite was a tiny Basque place in Greenwich Village called, I think, Jai Alai, where we had been taken by Peter Boyne, my grandmother's actor friend; I was able to indulge my quite unreasonable passion for kidneys. Swordfish steaks, snapper, fillet mignon, asparagus, we had them all. Teddy Rose entertained us in his Park Avenue apartment to a Lucullan feast of Maine lobsters. Constantine's colonel, Bill Jackson, took us to the theatre and I wore the purple velvet dress Caitlin Thomas had given me, which she had bought secondhand in London. I must have looked like something from a B-movie costume drama, but at least nobody else had anything like it. We went to the Metropolitan Museum and were drunk with looking, then drunk with dizziness at the top of Radio City. Ferdie Helm introduced us to editors and writers including the beautiful Jean Stafford, who was experiencing great unhappiness with her husband, the brilliant, outrageous and sometimes brutal Robert Lowell.

As I looked out of the hotel window overlooking Central Park, the scene was like a Willard Metcalf painting, and I thought of many things, few of them connected with New York. What on earth were we doing here? How long could this interlude go on? Opening the windows brought in the noise of traffic and the smell of fumes. I closed it quickly and picked up Prosper Merimée's *Le Soulier Satin*, which I had borrowed from Peter Rose Pulham in Paris so many lifetimes ago. Constantine had that morning a letter from his mother who was staying with one of her sisters at her house in Bermuda. It had enclosed a letter for Constantine from a downtown bank which requested him to call. He had left when I was having my bath, saying I was to meet him for lunch at the Russian restaurant on 3rd Avenue.

I moved moodily from the chair by the window and looked through the few wartime clothes I had brought with me. Was it cold out? How could you tell in these hot hotels? If it was, I definitely wasn't going to wear again that old mohair coat which smelt of goat when it got wet. I counted my money and decided to go out shopping. The prices all seemed amazingly high until I realized you had to divide everything by four (the dollar was around five shillings). Then they all seemed amazingly cheap, so I left the shop positively purring in a soft, pale green suit and a top-coat. It was known as a three-piece. I had just about two dollars left as I went to join Constantine for lunch.

At first we didn't recognize each other. He was standing at the bar in an extremely handsome tweed suit, sipping a large vodka. He beamed when his very short-sighted eyes focused on me.

'You look very smart,' we both said together. 'I almost didn't rec—' Then we both laughed.

'Have a drink and I'll tell you what's happened.'

It appeared that when Constantine was born in 1919 his godfather, Hamilton Benjamin, a rich man on the Stock Exchange, had given his godson $10,000. Ten years later the crash came and the money was almost worthless. However, a small sum had survived, had been forgotten by everyone, and had been collecting interest over the intervening quarter of a century, to make the very handy lump sum of about $1,000 in 1946.

'So, I went to Abercrombie and Fitch and got this. It's the first ready made I've ever had. Good isn't it?'

It was.

'I hope you've got some left because I bought this and I've only got $2,' I answered.

'Of course I have,' he replied rather scathingly. 'And I've been to a travel agent. We're going to Bermuda and I can write my novel.'

'But how? Where?'

'It's Mummy's letter this morning. Aunt Maud's got this big place in Bermuda with two cottages on it, and we're going to have one. We'll go down there in a few days when we've made the arrangements.'

'Sounds wonderful,' I said. 'Is it free? How do we get there?'

'We'll find all that out. Aunt Maud can't charge us much, if anything. Come on, let's order some of that good beef stroganoff.'

We met Ferdie Helm that night and he thought the news great. Could he come and stay? He wanted to work on his Alexander Pope thesis. Of course he could.

Constantine concentrated on getting us there and I was to pack our things. This sounds simple but the luggage was extremely battered by this time, and as usual we had acquired more secondhand books, which were decidedly heavy. This problem was soon solved in an army surplus store where we bought canvas bags and a very ugly but strong expanding suitcase, which I think still survives stuffed with old galley proofs. The boat was obviously a cheaper but slower method of getting to Bermuda, so we decided to take a flying boat from Baltimore; the only snag was that most of the luggage would have to go by ordinary boat. We had quite persuaded ourselves that hanging about in New York would eventually cost more than the difference between the fares. Perhaps we were right. Nevertheless we had to have some clothes for hot weather, and so rushed off to Orhbach's where for about $100 we bought what seemed like half the shop. The days of the Palm Lounge, the Oak Room and the Plaza Suite had ended as suddenly as they had begun.

Once more we bundled our things into taxis, some for the boat and the rest for the station at Baltimore. I remember crossing the immensely wide Delaware River, and finding Baltimore a most attractive city, with its tall brick houses with delicate iron railings either side of the steps leading to the highly polished and painted front doors. There was an impression of regularity and order which the bombings and blastings had destroyed in London. The streets were clean, quiet and peaceful as we made our way to the immigration office before embarking on the huge flying boat.

Inside the flying boat it was very spacious – much more like a liner than any modern aeroplane. There were small tables to eat at and large windows in the cabin, which was about twice the height of our aeroplanes. Stewards were dressed like ship stewards in short white coats. When the engines started the sea churned up alarmingly and made a lot of noise. Then, slowly, we were airborne, feeling not a little excited at going to a new place, and not a little relieved at having got off the merry-go-round of New York. Our hopes were as high as the flying boat coursing about the clouds. We ate a leisurely meal chosen from a menu, and it was some hours before we started to lose height, followed by the thundering splash and shudder of the landing at Perrott's Isle in Bermuda. On the dock the sun was strong and hot as we looked around, across water the colour of viridian green, to the white houses on the nearby mainland; then into a motor boat and a swift journey across the bay to the capital of this coral reef, Hamilton. It was quite an experience.

Constantine said we must telephone his mother to find out how to get to Somerset, so we took the light luggage we had and went to the nearest place which had a telephone, a waterfront bar. The streets seemed very empty: no cars anywhere and but few people. Soon he was back with the news that we were to take the train which went close by the house. The bar-owner called a carriage which seemed very small for us and the luggage, so I got in with the bags and Constantine said he would follow – for the horse couldn't go very fast. It was the smallest railway station imaginable, like something out of Toytown. The train, too, was very curious and very uncomfortable. The wooden-slatted seats were high and narrow. It looked and felt like some old relic of a distant and backward country. We found out later that it had been bought secondhand from the Belgian Congo, and it felt like it. It rattled and shook alarmingly like an old-fashioned tram, particularly so when crossing what seemed a very rickety bridge high up on stilts over the sea, which the single passenger told us was Somerset Sound.

'We must be near, then,' I said.

'I hope so; this is terrifying isn't it? There must be another way of getting to Aunt Maud's. Why couldn't we have come by boat?'

The passenger told us the last ferry for Somerset had left just before we had taken the train. The place at which he told us to alight turned out to be a halt with hardly a house in sight. Dusk, which falls quickly in these parts, would soon be down; and there we were, luggage dumped around us on the roadside, hot, thirsty and tired.

'Oh, Mummy's so hopelessly impractical – what are we supposed to do now?' Constantine stalked off in the direction of the nearest house while I waited with the bags. He came back looking very frustrated and cross.

'She said to take a carriage, though where she thinks we'll find one on the roadside I don't know. Anyway I told her, with the luggage we were too heavy for a horse, so she said she would ring the only taxi here. Apparently no cars are allowed in Bermuda, and taxis are few and far between. How in the name of God did people get all the furniture in their houses in the past?'

When it was quite dark and our spirits were very low, the taxi came, picked us up, whizzed round a few corners and we were there, but he couldn't take us up to the house because the drive was too steep. So we had to carry the bags, stumbling about for several minutes in the dark amongst bushes which appeared to have arms to grab you. The large, low whitewashed house, named Tranquillity, with its welcoming steps up to the door, was ablaze with light, and through the wire screen door we saw the two dear welcoming faces.

'Come in, have a whisky. You must be exhausted. Sit down.' It was all said at once.

'Mummy, why did you send us on that ghastly train? Why couldn't we have had a taxi from the beginning?'

'Oh, Connie, it's the best way. Much cheaper than a taxi, which is about five pounds.'

Like many elderly people who have a certain amount of money, Georgette would always practise funny little economies at the most awkward times, and then be wildly extravagant – or so it seemed to me – at other times.

Aunt Maud said we must be hungry; and yes, we were, very. Two trays were instantly produced with a plate on each, a few slices of spam (which we had thought never to see again), a little square of mousetrap cheese, two slices of bread and a little butter. Lavishly we spread the butter on the bread.

'I say, be careful with that butter. It's our ration for the week.'

Such was our introduction to Bermuda – a very different island from Manhattan.

———

The cottage was across a courtyard from the big house. It was small but adequate, since there were about three acres of grass lawns to sit, read and eat on. The unaccustomed April heat and sun woke us early and we walked around, thankful for the thin clothes we'd bought.

Glorious bushes of multi-coloured hibiscus, poinsettias, oleander and lilies set in clumps on the lawns were sometimes overshadowed by trees of tropical fruits from which flew vivid blue birds, the scarlet red cardinal bird, and the black cat-bird which made a noise like a mewing cat. High up in the sky, the long-tailed white tropic bird flew effortlessly. Through the trees we could glimpse the opalescent sea which graduated from a pale green to a deep, deep blue.

'It's like a paradise and everything's so green,' we said to each other as we wandered through a hedge into a small plantation of sweetcorn and crisp green lettuce.

Quite far away from the house was another whitewashed cottage of one large room with a bathroom and kitchen. This had been the studio of Clark Voorhees, Aunt Maud's husband, an American landscape painter who had died some years ago. As we neared the house we saw a small building with steps up to what must have been one room.

'I wonder what that is. Maybe a servant's room?' I said. Georgette told us it had been the buttery but wasn't used any more. We went up to look at it and Constantine said it would make a perfect writing room, so that is what it became. Aunt Maud suggested we go down to Mangrove Bay to see about our ration cards and also to hire some bicycles.

We wandered downhill along the sandy lanes, past round-moon gates and a few houses, many cedar trees, some festooned with spagnum moss hanging like a water nymph's hair, until we came to a small settlement overlooking the bay. It consisted of some little cottages, shops, a bar called the Loyalty Inn and the Mangrove Bay grocery stores.

'Let's get something good to eat,' said Constantine. 'You know Mummy can only just boil an egg and, if last night's supper is anything to go by, Aunt Maud's cooking is not much better.'

Alas the Mangrove Bay grocery store did not live up to its exotic name. It was rather depressing, with shelves full of American cereals with names like Cheerios or Brekkos, and rows of cans of clams, cans of tuna fish, Campbells soup and, of course, Spam.

'Aren't there any fresh foods?' we asked.

We were shown some fish, which raised our hopes, but these were either tagged or stamped, with purple ink in large letters, 'CHICAGO', a curious place to find fresh sea fish. We bought some bananas and cans of beer.

Further down we found a sad-looking black butcher who really didn't want to sell us anything, but finally parted with some pork chops and a few pigs' tongues. On the counter he had large bowls of intestines called chitterlings, which he said were good with mustard greens, but as I didn't know how to cook them and had never heard of mustard greens, I left them alone. The meagre rations of butter and cheese were a bit daunting after the plenty of New York, but maybe the rationing wouldn't last very long. We decided to buy two secondhand old-fashioned, high bicycles, on the grounds that we were going to live here. When I saw them I was sorry I couldn't have brought my brand-new Raleigh with me.

Then a drink at the Loyalty Inn before going home: they weren't a bit keen to serve us either, as it was a bar for coloured people, though we didn't realize that at the time. I think they felt that if they weren't allowed into white bars, why should we be served in theirs? However, they brought us a cold beer and Constantine told me about the novel he was going to write. Our life together, unimpeded by war, was just beginning. We had just enough money, with army back pay, to survive for several months, and we were starting out in a paradise of our own choice.

It is hard to describe Bermuda in 1946 without making every word a superlative. This tiny coral island set alone about eight hundred miles out in the Atlantic was so very beautiful to look at; it was just as Andrew Marvell's words described:

Where the remote Bermudas ride
In th' ocean's bosom unespied.

Some of the beaches were quite pink, made by the seas pounding up the fresh coral. If you owned any land there, house-building was simple. You dug a hole the size of the house you wanted, and the coral blocks were used to make the walls, the hole at the side being used for your water tank, as there were no fresh springs in Bermuda. There were no squalid settlements, for many of the islanders built their own houses this way. The climate all the year round was warm; at Christmas you could go on picnics and swim, and when rain and wind came occasionally, we were only delighted that the water tank (in which was housed a toad to catch the flies) was full again. There was only one kind of poisonous animal on the island, a large scorpion, and during our time there I saw only one. There were huge toads, which gathered round the street lights at nighttime, like Italians, as Con said, but they were quite harmless to people, although if attacked by a dog they could spurt a poison into the dog's mouth. There were masses of a certain cockroach-like animal which didn't bite, but in summer took to flight and could fly into you. There were huge spiders, quite harmless, which I found could be channelled into one place if you played some music. This they seemed to love and about two at a time would gather on the walls to listen. I grew rather fond of them.

The exotic-looking trees in time bore such fruit as pawpaw, loquats, guavas and tamarinds; these grew almost wild. Almost every garden had a banana plant where great bunches clustered. At night, the tree-frogs chuckled until dawn. The waters were so clear that large and brightly coloured fish could be seen close up to the shore, and there were sea-gardens of anenomes and corals. Fish with glorious names like yellowtail, angel fish, parrot fish and bonito seemed sometimes too beautiful to eat. We had sweet potatoes, Bermuda potatoes and the sweet Bermuda onion, as well as home-grown pale gold corn called Country Gentleman. We almost forgot what red meat tasted like and didn't mind a bit. Eggs from chickens fed on corn had orange yolks, and the birds themselves tasted almost like young pheasants. If we wanted something special we took the leisurely steamer to Hamilton, which had big hotels, cafés, bars, big stores, and shops which sold almost everything. It also had the island's only indoor cinema.

Constantine had fixed up the buttery with a table, chair and bookshelf. Most mornings, starting quite early, he would go there and write. Then we would perhaps take a picnic to nearby Long Beach, or a longer expedition to King's Point Islands where we would swim sometimes without our suits, for it was deserted, and afterwards make love on the warm sands. When the tide was out, little pools held tiny brightly striped fish called sergeant majors, and we would catch them in our glasses to look at them more closely before putting them back. In the evenings, sitting on the lawn with long cool drinks, Constantine would read aloud to us what he had written that day, and then we would have another long glass of the pale gold Martinique rum, which was a guinea a gallon, with some fresh lime juice in it.

In May, Aunt Maud said she would be soon going back to her house in New England and why didn't we move into her house and let Georgette have the cottage which was more suitable for one person? Before she left she gave a party for us to meet all the old families of Bermudians who lived in Somerset, such as the Gilberts, the Onions, the Misicks, as well as David Huxley, then attorney-general, with his wife Nancy, a childhood friend of Constantine's, and some American friends who had lived there for many years.

Two large tables laid with white damask cloths were set out on the front lawn, and on them were put bowls of deceptively innocent-tasting rum punch. Hibiscus blossoms were strewn around. Myrtle, the Negro maid, cooked all afternoon with her pretty little daughter; nobody else was allowed in the kitchen. It was all delightfully gracious and old-fashioned, as were the guests. Much later that evening Constantine, who never ate anything much more than a few peanuts at parties, told me he was feeling decidedly odd. His head felt quite clear, but his legs felt as if they would buckle under him. I told Georgette that the punch must have been stronger than we thought, and she mentioned it to Aunt Maud, who replied:

'Ah, well, with some it goes to their heads and with others it goes to their legs.' She had served that punch before.

CHAPTER THIRTY

Laughter and literature typified most of the next few months. In the larger house, which wasn't in fact so large but had big, airy rooms, we had friends from America to stay, notably Ferdinand Helm, who was there for some months. As well as working on his Alexander Pope thesis he was doing a key to Joyce's *Finnegans Wake* for his own pleasure. Quite rightly, he said the only way to understand it was to read it aloud, which he did very well. For some time after, phrases from the book were applied to various people in Bermuda: 'a woman of no appearance' was one, and 'Jerk the Beanstalk' fitted many a visitor. Sometimes we toyed with the idea that, instead of Marvell's 'remote Bermudas', it might have been more like 'Tristan da Cunha, isle of man-overboard'.

Ferdinand was a strange person, for he could be so charming and amusing, then, without warning, sentences vitriolic with venom and hatred would tumble out, many times without apparent reason. He seemed to have a museum of hatreds from which he would produce one piece every so often. I think he was very fond of Georgette, who was always kind and understanding even during his outbursts. He had a sort of camaraderie with Constantine, but I was the person he trusted with his fears. He told me he was bisexual, mainly because he was frightened of being rejected by women. Unprepossessing in appearance, he won both my affection and sympathy, although the latter was the last emotion I would have shown him openly. What *did* attract me was the brilliance of his thought, rapier sharp and full of originality. In many ways I think he associated himself with Pope, and would have wished to be as Pope wrote:

Happy the man, whose wish and care
A few paternal acres bound . . .

Alas, he never was.

Constantine was busily writing his novel, his day's work always being read to all of us. We thought it extremely good and looked forward eagerly to the evening drinks and the readings. I was very contented, for Aunt Maud had an excellent, although not large, library of American writers. Sitting in the shade of the lucky nut tree I would enjoy the books of Willa Cather and John Dos

Passos, Thomas Wolfe's *Look Homeward Angel*, William Faulkner's *Sanctuary*, and several works of Edith Wharton. Georgette told us Edith had been a friend of her father and mother in Lenox, Massachusetts, but the seven little girls (Georgette and her sisters) didn't approve of her at all, for she bitted her horses too tightly in the carriage for the sake of a smart equipage. The girls would run out to give the horses sugar, but the coachman told them they wouldn't be able to eat it. Ring Lardner was a favourite of mine, especially his superb *How to Write a Short Story*, and Ferdie had brought down some critical essays of Edmund Wilson's and also a book of Sherwood Anderson's. It was during this period of reading that I found an apt title for Constantine's book, a quotation from one of the Earl of Rochester's poems of the seventeenth century:

'Tis the Arabian bird alone
Lives chaste, because there is but one.

That evening we christened *The Arabian Bird*.

We still had our picnics although it was getting too hot for prolonged sitting in the sun. There were convenient rocks nearby where we always swam before lunch and sometimes later in the day as well. As the novel neared completion, Georgette and I took turns at typing it. Neither of us could type very fast, but somehow after endless hours it was finished; then we punched holes in the side and made it into a very handsome manuscript. And so with pride, pleasure, and relief it was despatched to a literary agent in London.

There were a great many cocktail parties, of which we enjoyed those of our friends the Misicks best. They had a pretty house near Somerset Bridge and were interested in writers and writing. There were several American bestseller writers in Bermuda then, including Munro Leaf, the creator of *Ferdinand the Bull*, and James Ramsey Ullman and his pretty wife Elaine. Jimmy and Elaine became great friends, and also their tiny monkey. Jimmy, although he looked like a genial businessman, was an adventurer at heart. He had a passion for mountains and mountain climbing which is no doubt why his first great success *The White Tower* had such veracity. Every book he wrote was a bestseller, book of the month, film, and everything that goes with that kind of success. Yet withal he remained unassuming, kindly, and determined to get as near the top of Mount Everest as he could.

In July my aunt wrote to say that our large poodle Mouche, whom I had left with my grandmother, was coming out on a Royal Mail Line ship. Con and I hired a carriage to meet the boat and we waited under the shade of some trees for it to dock. We could see Mouche, running around the decks, putting her paws on the rail and looking over.

'She's not kennelled,' I said.

'You know how clever she is, darling. Mouche could get round anyone.'

As soon as the gangplank was lowered she ran down, no lead, the captain behind her. She stopped at the bottom, obviously waiting for a friend. Right at the end came a small man in shirt sleeves and Mouche bounded up to him. Yes, she was very pleased to see us, but taking her friend by the wrist she brought him forward. It was the ship's carpenter, or 'Chippie', and he had had her in his cabin all through the journey.

'She liked the Azores,' he said. 'I thought a bit of *terra firma* would be good for her.'

She was very fat, but it might have been overgrown coat.

'How many meals a day did you give her?' I asked.

'It's difficult to say, you know. I'd always bring her a bit of what was going. She didn't like my mate being in the cabin, though.'

That evening we had the whole crew up to dinner. Not the captain, though. When he heard I had asked Chippie he refused, having accepted earlier on. He missed a fantastic evening, fresh corn from the garden, a roasted ham and many exotic fruits. Nobody got back to the ship until early morning. Mouche had certainly arrived, and had behaved like the dowager she was. It was a very happy time.

The small Catholic church was about a twenty-minute walk away over fields with just a few houses here and there. Mouche would walk with me to church, then sit outside, except when communion was given and she heard the shuffling of people walking. Then she would come in, walk down the aisle to find me, and sit in the pew with me. After that I always sat at the back. Father McPherson, the priest, had been a friend of Aunt Maud's and often called. I didn't catch his name at first; when I queried it he said:

'McPherson, son of a parson!'

He was a good jazz musician and loved to play on Aunt Maud's piano. The only Somerset taxi driver was expert on the guitar, so sometimes we had impromptu concerts. It was through Father McPherson we met Father Grace, our dear friend for many years.

The book finished, we had more time to explore the island on our bicycles – going out to Beebe's museum in St George's, or Prospero's Cave (it was generally held that Shakespeare had set *The Tempest* on the newly found island) with its stalactites and stalagmites; or perhaps to the sea gardens, where in glass-bottomed boats you could see the busy but clear underwater world. At Harrington Sound you could hire an old-fashioned diving helmet and be lowered down about twenty feet in your bathing suit to walk amongst the ever-moving inhabitants with their brilliant colours. Or there was Cambridge Beaches, a charming hotel development of small cottages, with a central building for meals or drinks if wanted. It was quite the nicest place to stay in Bermuda. However, as the idyllic summer ended, our money dwindled to an alarming degree. We waited eagerly for the English mail to hear about *The Arabian Bird*. At last a letter came from the agent saying, cursorily, that he couldn't handle it as it had no 'reader identity'! We were all stunned; for once I was without words and we all went about the house as though a dear friend had died. I wonder if anyone not connected with creative people ever realizes the shock that a rejection of their work means to them. The book, painting, sculpture or piece of music has been as much a part of them for months or even years as is an unborn child to a woman. It *is* them, for ultimately what has any artist to express but their own thoughts and personality?

Unusually, Constantine was very quiet. He put the manuscript into a drawer and went for a long walk with Mouche. He came back in quite a different mood and said, why didn't we spend our remaining money on a party? Then maybe he could find a job. Georgette, knowing the delicate coil on which her son's emotions balanced, was delighted, and as it happened it was a most fortunate decision. Constantine never again mentioned the unpublished novel to anyone. At the party I talked to a studious man, whom a friend had brought, and mentioned the need for Constantine to get a job if we were to stay in Bermuda.

'Oh, he'll soon find one,' he said, and paused: 'I'll give him a letter to Booker of the Saltus Grammar School. He's always looking for teachers.'

School? Teacher? Neither sounded like Con, still I did get the letter, which surprisingly delighted him.

'Let's go into Hamilton and see about it,' he said; 'though I didn't hang around at Oxford to get my degree. What on earth would I teach?'

'French?' I replied hesitantly. 'Or English maybe?'

Both the Saltus Grammar School and Bobbie Booker were like something from the pages of Evelyn Waugh. Perhaps Bobbie thought we had come to pay a social call, for a tray of delicious drinks was brought in, and then we were asked to lunch. Bobbie was a man of medium height with a very lined but humorous face. He spoke almost entirely in 1920s slang and kept calling me 'old thing'. As we got jollier, the asking for a job receded, and the daiquiris took over. Constantine, always a splendid raconteur, was at his best. Bobbie, probably homesick for England, was delighted. I was getting alarmed that nothing would be mentioned, and was trying hard to frame a sentence which wouldn't make it look as if I was taking over. Then unexpectedly at the end of a splendid meal, over coffee and brandy, Constantine asked:

'I suppose you haven't got a job going here, have you, sir?'

Bobbie thumped the table hard, so that the silver cream jug slopped over.

'Old chap, you wouldn't, would you? The last fella Gabitas Thring sent out I had to return [like a parcel?]. He was a raving lunatic.'

Nothing was asked about credentials and Constantine was to start at the beginning of the September term in a few weeks' time. As we were leaving we were asked to a party the following week and Bobbie whispered to me:

'You wouldn't like to be Matron, would you old thing?' I declined, but I did say I would help out with prizegiving at speech day.

The next morning the buttery was in use again. Georgette, delighted, led me into the huge old-fashioned larder and shut the door.

'Let's have a snifter to celebrate,' she said, handing me a glass of whisky, 'and not a word to Connie about writing again.'

That evening he read us part of an article he had started.

'I'll send it to the *Atlantic Monthly* when it's finished. It's the sort of thing they like.'

———

When term started he would cycle to the ferry each morning with sandwiches for lunch and in the late afternoon I would walk down to meet him on his return. The pupils were mixed Bermudian, American and Portuguese children, yet every morning they had to salute the Union Jack and sing 'Land of Hope and Glory'. They seemed to enjoy it in a puzzled sort of way. Constantine taught all subjects to eight- and nine-year-olds, but French and English to older boys. He even got them to learn a short Molière play, at which the Portuguese were so brilliant that the promised performance never came off, as the others were too slow at learning the French. He seemed to enjoy the school very much. It wasn't arduous work, and there were weekends, quite long evenings and long holidays to look forward to. Writing was done in the buttery from time to time, but he never discussed it as before.

The school brought many new friendships, mainly parents of boys there. Amongst them was Frederic Wakeman, who had just published a bestselling novel *The Hucksters*, and was negotiating the film rights. He lived near us with his wife Margaret and their two children, the little boy, Freddie, being one of Con's pupils. Fred was to play a prominent part in our lives. He was an interesting man with a lineless slightly Asiatic face, his brown hair worn in a crewcut. His Asiatic features were emphasized by his hairless chest and loose-limbed walk which reminded me of the movements of one of the larger members of the cat family. His first book, *Shore Leave*, about his experiences in the navy during the war, was excellent. After that he had gone into advertising, and *The Hucksters* was a vivid exposé of this. Overnight he was a celebrity; James Thurber referred to him as 'the millionaire novelist'; film companies vied with each other for the rights, but his Midwest astuteness took it all very calmly. The family lived very simply, Margaret's mother taking care of the two children. Margaret had been Fred's college sweetheart and I got the feeling that whereas he had read a great deal and missed nothing, Margaret had remained as she was when she left Missouri. However, she had a lively sense of humour. Fred was then working on a new novel, which was already sold, film rights as well. He had put a lot of his money into the New York publishing house of Rinehart, of which he was a director.

When Ferdie went back to New York, Fred and Margaret became our closest friends, and we were introduced to many of the people Fred knew. One evening we were asked to dinner at the Coral Beach Club, and when we arrived it was exciting to see that James Thurber was one of the party. By this time his sight was very bad, hardly noticeable, but since I was sitting next to him I saw he cut his food up quite small before starting to eat. I had just been reading and re-reading some of his books, and we talked mainly of large poodles, to which he was devoted. He told me the story of the strange dog at the front door of a house he was visiting, which followed him in, jumped with muddy paws all over the sofas and beds, then turned out not to belong to the house owner, who had thought it was his. That was the end of that friendship!

Then he turned to converse with the woman on his left. I don't know what they talked about to begin with, but in a silence that sometimes occurs at dinner parties I heard him say:

'What is the thing you have done in your life which you are most ashamed of?'

The woman was silent for too long. Not a word or a splutter did she make.

'Do you mean to tell me that you are so self-satisfied that it doesn't immediately occur to you?'

More silence, then a blather of talk. Ever since then I have had something ready for that question, but no one has ever asked me.

We used to meet Thurber fairly often on the ferry from Somerset; Mouche, who knew a poodle-lover when she saw one, was always going to greet him.

One hot afternoon when Constantine was at Saltus, a telegram came saying that my father was dead. I read it through as though I were studying the lines of a play. It was so very impersonal, the printed letters on strips of paper which said nothing except that he was dead: not where, or how or even when. I went into the bedroom and closed the louvres of the shutters to keep out the hot sun. I lay down on the heavy wooden half-tester bed and shivered slightly despite the heat, drawing a coverlet over me. I didn't sleep and no tears came, for it seemed impossible that the vital Jupiter man I had seen so little of had gone from my life.

I have no memory as to how long I was lying there, but the heat became very oppressive and a heavy sweet smell hung like a solid cloud above me. I was back in the hill station in Kashmir, India, in bed early in the morning. The previous day my father and I had been to a race-meeting in Rawalpindi and had come on for the night. This was long before the formation of Pakistan, in the days of the British Raj when the Afghans were fighting a bitter guerrilla war with the British. Around Peshawar was the North West Frontier, and driving through the Khyber Pass it was often necessary to lie flat on the floor of the car to avoid snipers' bullets. As a sixteen-year-old I found it exciting.

The drive had been long, hot and dusty in the open car; conversation had dwindled as we contemplated a bath, then dinner. At race meetings when it was very hot we often took a change of clothes with us, wringing out the sweat of the worn ones before packing them up. But high up, with the cold air from the Zasker Mountains, the evenings were pleasant and the nights cool. I wandered around the compound enjoying the air, then went in to sit on the verandah, the punka-wallah still working the fan with his foot. Dinner took a long time with many courses; my father, in the best of form, told outrageous stories which were no doubt a relief in this remote place. When the port came I excused myself and went to bed. The heavy smell of the Indian night, bursts of laughter, strange outside noises, all were soon forgotten as I went into a deep, youthful sleep.

When I arrived in the breakfast room my father was already there looking very cross, yet making a hearty meal. Maybe the night had gone on too long, and too much port had been drunk. No pleasantries were ever allowed at breakfast other than the simplest enquiry.

'Was your bed comfortable?' I asked.

'No, it wasn't,' he snapped at me with unaccustomed testiness, 'and I don't like people coming in to take my money in the middle of the night.'

'Who was it? One of the men at dinner last night?'

He relaxed slightly and told me he had woken up to see a tall, fair, thin young man with a high collar bending over his dressing table. Then the man had turned and my father saw his face quite clearly through the mosquito net.

As he was about to lift the net and get out of bed, the figure receded into the shadows.

While my father was talking, the commanding officer came in, then asked my father to meet him in the library after breakfast. I could come too, if I liked. I joined them when I had finished; they were looking at old photograph albums, heavy and ornate with brass corners. My father was talking, his voice as light and clear as ever. The colonel shut down the album with a snap and, taking up another, said:

'Look through this one and see if you recognize anyone.'

Turning the pages slowly, still looking annoyed, my father stopped suddenly.

'That's the fellow, but no, it can't be. He's got the wrong uniform on, must be his father.'

'No, that's the same man. It's a long story but, briefly, he gambled very heavily and got into very deep water, even regimental funds too, I think. It was about twenty-five years ago that he shot himself in the room you occupied. Very occasionally he does appear. I saw him myself once, always goes to that dressing table, looking for money, I suppose. Strange story, there's no telling when he will turn up. Feel sorry for the chap myself.'

Slowly and thoughtfully we left the room, the bearer put our luggage in the newly cleaned car and we went down the long hill.

It was not a dream for my eyes were wide open all the time. I knew for that brief period I had somehow been with my father again, and heard his voice quite clearly. I was content.

CHAPTER THIRTY-ONE

After a time the lack of mental stimulus in an island Eden is noticeable. Used as we were to the richly tapestried conversations of Dylan Thomas, Norman Douglas, John Davenport and many others, it was similar to being on an ocean liner stopping at ports to pick up people who are merely pleasure-bent. Although it had been without peer as a holiday, the mood unavoidably followed that we should be getting home now.

In 1946 there was a library set in the beautiful Par-la-Ville Gardens, Hamilton, riotous with tropical flowers. The small building had dark rooms and a very mixed selection of books. The gardens also housed a little open-air theatre (where Constantine would have staged the Molière), but in the two and a half years we were there a play was never performed. The only indoor cinema was also in Hamilton, which meant only a matinée for us as the last ferry and train left early. Outdoor cinemas showed rubbishy films which competed with aeroplane noise, flying beetles and cigarette smoke. There was no local radio, only crackles on Aunt Maud's old set. No transistors and, perhaps mercifully, no television. Local newspapers were just that, foreign ones always a day late and generally only available in Hamilton.

Therefore when one's own imagination and thought wanted a rest or a new injection it was to people one turned. We valued those few friends who wrote books, painted pictures, played music or had interests other than in sunbathing, swimming and cocktail parties at which conversation was at the level of, 'Aren't the tray ceilings charming?' 'Yes, we just love the hibiscus too.'

As Eugene O'Neill had written twenty years earlier:

Here in Bermuda one rarely gets the chance, especially now in the slack season, to say a word to a human being above the intellectual and spiritual level of a land crab, and this solitude gets damned oppressive at times. But it's a fine place to get work done . . . and that's why I'm here.

This reflection of O'Neill's was vividly emphasized for me once when a prominent businessman there asked where Constantine was one evening. I replied he was working on his book and didn't like social engagements at such times.

'Oh, I know just how he feels. Eugene O'Neill was just the same when he was here. On Fridays when I have to write the notes for the yacht club, I don't set foot out of the house either.'

After the war in Europe it had been unbelievably wonderful, but nearly six months of living in Bermuda, with very little money, made us realize we were not perhaps good candidates for paradise. The cast of Prospero's island had long since departed; only the beauty of the sets remained.

Cleon and Juliet Throckmorton were the most stimulating pair I have ever met. Being with them (and they were seldom apart) was like enjoying a marvellous surrealist exhibition, and then going on to the finest revue you had seen for years. Throck, as he was called, was in his late forties then, Juliet a few years younger. His round face under ruffled dark brown hair always looked good-humoured, his eyes twinkling, his generous mouth appearing to have a quip or a witty remark waiting to be said; yet behind the gentle eyes lurked the mask of tragedy. Although of medium height, he was broad-shouldered, inclined to fat, but he walked very lightly. The surprise was his high, rather squeaky voice which somehow added to the fun and made him an original. When I knew him better I asked him if he had always had that voice, for Throck was a man of many parts.

'I come from Snicker's Gap, Virginia,' he carolled. 'Everyone speaks like me in Snicker's Gap.'

Then he went to the telephone.

'Who are you ringing?' asked Juliet.

'I'm ringing the Snicker's Gap operator, so Theo can hear for herself.'

I did, and he was right.

Juliet was a very pretty woman with dark hair and laughing brown eyes. Her maiden name had been St John Brenon, her father having been Irish. She had met Throck in the late 1920s and her uninhibited manner was characteristic of those days. Even her simple clothes on a very slim body would not have been out of place in 1928 or so. Although I was in my twenties, there were days when the two of them made me feel old. Their fun was enchanting and we had another bond in common, the theatre.

When *Emperor Jones* opened at New York's Macdougal Street Theater on November 1st, 1920, it unveiled the work not only of a major new American playwright, Eugene O'Neill, but also of a new and important stage designer, Cleon Throckmorton.

That is what was printed in the *New York Times*, which also wrote:

In the nineteen-twenties Mr Throckmorton became so busy and so prominent that his name, it was said, appeared on Broadway playbills with a frequency exceeded chiefly by the Fire Commissioner.

Juliet told me that Throck had worked with O'Neill for many years at the Provincetown Players, set-designing for all of O'Neill's well-known plays. With Christopher Morley, the playwright and author, they had started the Hoboken Theatrical Company in New Jersey, which brought society and celebrities across the Hudson to see the plays. That was only at the beginning, for he designed sets for over six hundred plays, some of which were on exhibition at the Museum of Modern Art.

Never was anyone endowed with as much gaiety as Throck, who'd startle you with his imagination and his sometimes slapstick behaviour. His impersonation of Queen Victoria delighted us as much as it had Noel Coward. He also loved to play practical jokes, but I didn't know that to begin with. While Constantine talked to Fred Wakeman about books I would spend hours talking to Throck and Juliet about the theatre. Sometimes, late at night, he made it seem as if the theatre was nearby and we had just left it.

There were some very rich Bermudians, who called themselves 'the forty thieves'. Eldon Trimingham owned the large store, Gosling and Gilbert were liquor merchants, and there was also Sir Howard Trott, who did all sorts of things. They brought Throck to Bermuda to start a theatre company there, similar to the Provincetown Players. When I met him it seemed it would all take place and I would be in the company. Alas, well after a year later everything was to fall through. I don't think 'the forty thieves' saw much financial return in a theatre, and as the income tax in this Crown Colony was remarkably low they had no need to undertake any venture to make a tax loss. Failure, however, was in the future. At this time it was an exciting project to be discussed, enlarged and dreamed about. I would act, Con would write plays and Throck would design sets. Maybe this paradise would have its angels.

After some months of our idyllic life we, too, were to have an upheaval. Aunt Maud died, so Georgette went back to Massachusetts to stay with her younger sister, Constance. Aunt Maud's son, Clark Voorhees, and his wife and young daughter came down to stay. He was a sculptor and it was obvious they had very little money, young sculptors seldom making a very handsome living. With reluctance they said they must raise our very modest rent, an impossibility for us, as the school didn't pay very much. So unhappily we looked for somewhere else – but winter, the high season in Bermuda, was approaching and rents were at their highest. In the end we heard of a newly built cottage miles away, the other side of Hamilton, near Spanish Point. For lack of anything in our price range we took it. It was called The Small House, Cheriton, which made all the Bermudians smile, as 'the small house' was their euphemism for lavatory. I could have been more Anglo-Saxon about it.

The complete property, both a large, elegant house and the three-roomed cramped small house, was owned by a painter called Verpilleux and his wife. Despite his name he was English. He was quite genial with large brown eyes. The paintings which he turned out very regularly were larger-than-life portraits, painted in bright colours, of the sitters as they wanted to look. He had painted most of the rich Bermudians and people who owned property and came for the winter. I don't think he ever painted anything or anybody unless he had a good fat commission. He was always friendly, and he dressed, when working, in a spotless smock with a floppy bow. It was a theatrical sort of garb and far from that of any of the good modern painters I had known in Paris or London. Possibly his wife, rather a bossy little woman, thought cleanliness gave a good impression to his sitters, and no doubt it did. We were politely asked to drinks when we first arrived, and for devilment I mentioned names like Picasso, Max Ernest, Graham Sutherland and Victor Pasmore, at which he evinced no interest except to say he hadn't been in Europe for some time.

The house was kept impeccably; before one had even left the room cushions were plumped up. Once, when we went to lunch, Constantine dropped a lettuce leaf on the table when helping himself to salad, which caused consternation, and cleaning materials to be brought in.

Our cottage still smelt of new concrete floors, on to which rush mats had been laid. When Mouche had eleven poodle puppies I had a wired-in enclave with a kennel built for them in the garden. Nothing as natural as puppies in the house, yet later on, when the rush mats frayed and rotted on the damp concrete, it was thought I'd let them pee on them.

It was difficult to have more than four or five people in the small rooms, but there was quite a lot of rough ground in front of the cottage where we could at least have tea or drinks. The sea was nearly a mile away along a lane, but when you got there Spanish Point was quite attractive for picnics and swimming. It was certainly nearer for Saltus Grammar School, but the desk where Con could write was in the bedroom, and the atmosphere just wasn't right for us.

Our friends Gay Coulter and Lorna Temple lived fairly near and Constantine would often stop off there after school for drinks or tennis. Their house, Quickswood, was so much more attractive than ours. Their two small boys who were at the school would cycle up to us sometimes to play with the puppies. However, after we had sold the puppies ('Once more I'm living on a dog,' said Constantine) we had enough to entertain occasionally in a simple way. Father Tom Grace would often arrive with some steaks from the American base, always enough for at least two meals or a small dinner party. We lived very simply and were often strapped for money. There seemed to be no way of making any more, apart from Christmas time when I made Christmas cards to order, painstaking work which brought in very little and was very tedious.

Most of our friends lived near or in Somerset, yet we were several miles away on the other side of this narrow, curved island twenty-eight miles long. To get out to see them was a day's excursion and, unless we came back early, very expensive as the boat and train didn't run very late in the evening, so that meant a taxi home. Therefore, as drink was cheap, we asked friends to our house.

It was one such evening, when Fred, Margaret, the Quickswood girls, and a dull man called Murdoch were there, that I was talking to Fred about books.

'Why doesn't Connie write a book?' he asked. 'I'm sure it would be good.'

'But he has.' And I told him the story about what the London agent had said, which he said was meaningless crap.

'Let me read it, I'm going to New York in a few days' time and if it's any good I'll show it around.'

Knowing Constantine's reluctance even to talk about it, when I took it from the drawer I wrapped it in brown paper and put it under his jacket in the hall.

'Don't tell him I gave it to you,' I begged conspiratorially. 'If you like it, well that's different.'

The next afternoon he rang me and said he thought it was swell and was taking it to New York. He would be back on Saturday.

Still I said nothing.

On Sunday morning, as we were making up a picnic, the crunch of tyres stopping on the rough avenue alerted us.

'Why, it's Fred, he's up early. I wonder what he wants,' said Constantine.

Fred came in, his usually placid face alive with excitement. He cleared his throat, as was his habit before speaking:

'Well, Connie, I sold your book for you. They went overboard for it at Rineharts.'

'What book? How?'

Unable to keep quiet any longer, I blurted out the whole story; Fred, nearby, looked like a cat that had eaten *all* the canaries. He added that he had sat up all night reading the typescript, becoming convinced it was a seller. He'd be hearing from Rinehart in a few days and they were rushing through the printing. So *The Arabian Bird* was christened again, and toasted many times that day.

The change in Constantine was extraordinary, almost magical. His voice became lighter and the generous mouth couldn't stop smiling. That week when he came home he sat for hours in the small, dark bedroom, hunched over the desk writing, until I suggested moving it out to the small sitting room. After all, it was a writer's house now, what did we want a sitting room for? New novels were planned, discarded, then new ideas developed to be worked on. It would have done any publisher good to see the change wrought overnight. The letter came, giving very good terms and followed by the contract. That same week a letter also arrived from Edward Weekes of the *Atlantic Monthly* accepting the article, and offering what was to us the gigantic sum of $500. We were rich again, and life was sweet.

Constantine grew a small beard, which gave him a scholarly appearance. It might intimidate some of those little blighters at school, he mused, but I don't think it did. Now that all the puppies were sold, except one we were keeping called Flotow, we decided that the house had become too small and unpleasant. There were constant complaints from Mrs Verpilleux, who would dash in at odd hours and find something wrong. I think she wanted us to go, so she could find more compliant tenants. Penniless writers were not really her style. So many weekends we went over to Somerset, asked friends to look out for something and visited some of Aunt Maud's old acquaintances. Finally, a charming New England lady, Mrs Dodge (the same family as the motorcars), said that she had a cottage at present inhabited by a painter called Staempli and his wife who would soon be leaving.

The moment I saw Graysbank Cottage at Somerset Bridge it won my heart. It was situated right on the sea, in a sandy lane which led only to a jetty, at the end of which the ferry took up passengers. It was small, but the rooms were large and beautifully furnished. There was a large sitting room with a bay window overlooking Somerset Sound, and underneath, an equally large bedroom; there was a medium kitchen and bathroom, where salt water was piped for the loo, which meant it could always be pulled. Fresh water was often scarce. Adjoining the house was a well-built structure which had originally been a boat house, but was now another bedroom. The dining room was on the terrace which ran the length of the sea wall and there was a small changing room.

On the terrace was a little rock garden with very exotic plants; even an orchid *rothschildiana* flowered prolifically. Leading down from the terrace was a captive fish pond about fifteen feet square, fed by the tide, in which swam brightly coloured fish amidst huge conches. Across the sandy lane in the front was a wild overgrown garden full of loquat, guava, the fast-growing pawpaw trees, prickly pears and a passion fruit vine, as well as vivid flowering shrubs.

A pathway led to an old square stone building, originally Somerset Bridge Schoolhouse. It was partially furnished with a large bed, chest, wardrobe, table and chairs. The schoolhouse was where Constantine worked on his second novel when school closed for the summer holidays in June 1947 and we moved in.

Before that was prizegiving and speech day at Saltus, which I had promised to help out with. Con said I should buy a hat to make myself look more the part. Gay Coulter gave me a pretty pink straw with a flower which she said made me look like a Manet painting. I loved it, although it was totally unsuitable for the occasion. I had no idea what my duties would be; most of the masters were unmarried so there was no one to ask.

Bobbie placed me on the stage next to him, other masters on the sides. The large hall was full with shining little boys and their parents. Their names were called out, and they would come up to receive their book prizes. While they were walking up Bobbie would hiss in my ear:

'Damn pretty woman, his mother, wouldn't mind a fling with her,' or 'Face only a mother could love, that one, don't know how she got a husband.'

Each female parent was described according to Bobbie's feelings. Sometimes I feared the other masters would hear, so I would cough or shuffle to mask his comments.

'Now, look at this, fetching little bum isn't it?'

About halfway through I felt the urge to giggle uncontrollably, for it was like a Ben Travers farce acted to perfection. Bobbie's lined, happy-hound face was perfectly in character. I wasn't in the least surprised when some time later I heard he had eloped with one of the prettier mothers.

We had never lived anywhere as pleasant as Graysbank Cottage; it was even nicer than Tranquillity, for we were quite alone, and we pretended it was ours. The sea was our front garden, the water so clear that perforce we became amateur piscologists. We swam several times a day, the hot sun making it unnecessary to towel afterwards; we ate in the little dining room out of doors, lit at night by wall lamps, eating inside only if it rained or a wind was blowing. Then we might light a cedarwood fire, which smelt like 10,000 lead pencils burning, in the Bermudian fireplace which was situated waist-high in the wall, as were all fireplaces there. We had a vast tray ceiling in the sitting room painted cerulean blue with a few rafters across, relics of an earlier age when the house was built.

The kitchen, I must admit, was a bit of a let-down. A two-burner electric stove which gave out massive shocks, and, separate on the other side of the room, the oddest oven, which you opened like a large box – I believe it is called a Dutch oven and I didn't think much of it, often preferring to cook on a grid over the wood fire.

At the road end of the lane was a grocery store run by a very jolly black man called Mr Gilbert, and on the other end of the bridge crossing the Sound was Mrs Skeffington, who ran the post office. Bermudian friends were fairly near, Throck and Julie not too far at Angel Steps, the Wakemans a bicycle ride away, although often Fred and sometimes little Freddie too would sail over in their large boat, often insisting we return with them. One day we did, got a little way out and saw, swimming feverishly, the two little brown heads of Mouche and Flotow who thought we had left them behind. It was quite a business lifting them into the boat. After that they usually came too.

Flotow had some endearing habits. He was perhaps the most amusing dog I have ever owned. He loved collecting; old tins and pretty stones were picked up and arranged in separate piles. If you disarranged them, with the best of goodwill he would set about rearranging them to his liking. He also loved classical music, Mozart and Bach being his favourites; if the wireless was left on, he would sit and listen for hours.

Home-made soup, cold or hot, and cheese with a little free fruit was always our staple lunch. (As yet there were no avocados or melons on Bermuda, although they would have grown profusely.) It was cheap and didn't make us too sleepy afterwards. I must admit that the steaks Father Tom brought were very good for a change.

Everybody loved Graysbank Cottage. The terrace was full of people most evenings and we shared what we had: Throck and Juliet, Father Tom, the Ullmans, the Wakemans, also friends they might bring. On a very hot night we would swim, then resume our drinking and talking. We had a wonderful climbing plant called a night-blooming cereus. This huge white waxy flower with a yellow centre was about twelve inches across, and opened slowly during the night, when it was almost luminous. But it was closed and finished in the morning.

Father Tom arrived one day in a high state of excitement. His face looked more Irish than usual. 'Like a map of Ireland,' Con used to say, 'if you look hard you'll see Bantry Bay.'

'I can get you a couple of fruit machines from the US base,' he said.

'What on earth would we do with them?'

'Theo, you know you can't afford to entertain all these people. If you had these on the terrace you'd make up the cost.'

I felt it would rather spoil the atmosphere, so, to his disappointment, refused them.

'Why don't you fish, then?' he asked, and the next time he came armed with tackle. We all sat on the precarious edge of the fishpond and felt foolish with no catch when a Portuguese fisherman came by in his boat.

'Hey there, I bring you feesh if you want.'

Jimmy, for that was his name, stopped his boat and threw over several large fish, the like of which I had never seen before.

'Good to cook in oven. See you tomorrow,' he said as he chugged away, waving his hand.

I took them up to Mr Gilbert at the grocery shop to ask what they were: one bonito, one yellowtail and several small red snappers.

'What you want is a fish-pot,' Mr Gilbert said, laughing. I didn't know what it was, but agreed. The next day he turned up with a large wire cage with a small round entrance on the side.

'You put some fish-heads in that, then tie string on it and throw it in the sea.'

We did as he told us, and the next morning hauled it up to find two good-sized crawfish in it. The waters were too hot for lobsters.

'How on earth do you get them out?' There was a small door at the side which opened and Con said:

'*You* put your hand in; you're more used to animals than I am.'

A new world was opened up to us so far as free food went. We hardly needed to buy anything except basics. We had found the ground amazingly fertile. If you put fifty lettuce seeds in, fifty lettuce plants came up in an astonishingly short time, yet vegetables in the market were poor and there were no herbs except those grown privately. I found a deserted house with banana-trees in it, and struggled over walls with a huge, heavy stalkful of them. I think I learned more ways to serve bananas than anyone around.

Traditional Bermuda food was restricted to a few rather strange dishes such as cassava pie, an elaborate dish made from cassava root grated, washed, squeezed and then dried in the sun. A mixture of butter, eggs, nutmeg, sugar, salt, salt pork and a whole chicken was put into a huge dish lined with the dried cassava and baked for about eight hours. It took two or three days to make and I must admit although I tasted it I never made it. I don't know what the Dutch oven would have done to it. I did, however, bake a Bermuda sweet potato pudding, which was traditionally served with cedar berry beer on Guy Fawkes's Day. The Bermuda codfish breakfast – salted cod, with potatoes, eggs and banana – gave me another idea of serving sautéed bananas with grilled fish, and delicious it was too. We would make a cedarwood fire on the rocks, sometimes first wrapping the fish in corn husks. I dried bananas in the sun for cakes and puddings; others I preserved in the pale gold rum for Christmas.

Mr Gilbert was a great cook and gave me recipes for the things they ate; I remember his pepperpot soup with great pleasure, as well as many fish dishes cooked with ingredients then unfamiliar to me. I learned the laborious way to prepare and cook shark. Jimmy asked us if we'd like to go out fishing with him sometimes. Coming back, one day, lying on our stomachs in the prow of the boat, looking down through the clear waters, usually so full of colour, we saw nothing but blackness. It was puzzling until, with a tightening of our muscles, we realized we were chugging, but so slowly, over a gigantic manta, or devil fish, as it was called in Bermuda. These triangular-shaped monsters, sometimes over twenty feet across, were frightening; they had a ferocious stingray whip tail, and all through August we used to watch them leaping high out of the sea and coming down with a thunderous splash. Many nights they wakened us with the nerve-chilling noise. As it happened only in the hottest part of the summer, we wondered if it was a mating display. It was always a relief when it was over. Another night I was out with Jimmy and we were anchored. I put my hand over the side to feel the water, but instead I felt something hard like a seaweed-covered rock.

'Jimmy, I think we're on the rocks, come and look.'

He came over with a lantern and looked over the side, said nothing, but quietly started the engine and moved slowly off. When we were some distance away he said:

'Lucky you put your hand over. It was a young whale. One sudden movement by him and the boat would have overturned.'

I never really saw it, but at least I have stroked a whale! When we caught a large sinister-looking moray eel he would cut his line.

'Never bring those things in the boat. My brother got his foot bitten by a decapitated head and was in hospital for four months with poisoning.'

After that I used to scan the water very carefully before diving off from the terrace steps! One of the most superb fish to eat was young barracuda, another man-eater. Steaks cut from it brushed with oil and herbs and grilled over wood tasted like the finest kind of veal.

In theory we were supposed to put the live fish in the fish pond, then hook them out when we wanted to eat them. But they were so beautiful that we just left them to look at: angel fish with long blue-and-orange streaming fins and electric-blue made-up eyelids, parrot fish, and my favourite, cuckold or cow fish, encased in a hard shell, with huge cow-like eyes, little horns and a tiny mouth. They were almost impregnable to predators owing to their casing and would feed from our hands, little rosebud mouths caressing our fingers as they took a tiny piece of bread. They had the ability to change colour at will; most enchanting little creatures.

At one point the weather had been oppressively hot and still for days. At night before going to bed we jumped into the sea, then lay on the bed, damp, with an electric fan going. Yet a little later we would be wet with sweat. The heat was surprising, since usually by the middle of October it was a little cooler. Work of any kind was an effort; all we wanted to do was lie in the shade on the terrace with a cool drink. Halfheartedly, in an attempt to do something ,I lifted up the rope of the fish pot. It was so heavy it wouldn't come out of the water. I called to Con to help and we both tugged away until it was on the side of the fish pond.

'Heavens above, look at all these fish,' we said. 'Whatever's happened?'

We felt some were too large for our little family in the pond, and those we decided to eat: a yellowtail weighing about four to five pounds was detailed for a luncheon with Throck and Julie.

The refrigerator became over-packed so straightaway I set about making a huge fish chowder, which as it turned out was to be a godsend. Fred rang that evening saying he couldn't sail over as there was no wind, but would we bicycle over there? We told him about all the fish and asked them both over for an impromptu dinner from some of it, which we all agreed was the best ever. He talked about his new novel *The Saxon Charm*, about a Broadway producer who was, I suspect, modelled on a real person – as he was saying he would have to be careful to avoid a libel action. They talked about Con's new book, and Fred thought it 'a swell idea'. Fred was musing about a novel of his which Gary Cooper had had for months. That evening he'd called him to find out if at last he had finished it. The reply went like this:

'Well, no, Fred, you see it's kind of difficult.' Cooper was a slow talker and hesitated before going on. 'I want you to know, Fred, I'm giving it a lot of attention. I'm reading it word for word.'

It was an unnaturally still night, very hot and humid as we all sat on the terrace, just the gentle lapping of the sea against steps and in the fish pond. About midnight, Ted the taxi driver came to take them home, we went for our customary quick swim, and found the sea as warm as bath water.

The curiously deadening weather persisted through the next day, as more and more fish came into the sound and were trapped in the fish pot. That evening the announcer on the wireless (Bermuda Radio had just started in a very simple way) told us to 'batten down' as bad weather was expected.

'What on earth does he mean?' said Constantine. We rang up the Misicks to ask if they'd heard the news. They told us to close up the shutters and all the doors, it could mean a bad wind. We did that and it felt quite uncanny being in the house which was never normally closed up. Later that night we listened to the news and heard that a hurricane was approaching. We were warned to make quite sure everything was closed and locked, whilst on no account were we to go out. This was difficult for us, as to get to the bedroom below you had to go down the steps from the sitting room. We decided to get our things up quickly and sleep on a large sofa and divan upstairs.

Lethargy had gone as we sat waiting. It was a little like waiting for a bomb to fall and, as the wind slowly started up, a noticeable feeling of elation rose in us. As the wind determinedly got up, it shook every corner of the room and there were fearful, inexplicable noises outside. Early next morning we peeped through the slats of the bay window to see the most extraordinary sight. It was as though the sea outside had an enormous boiling cauldron under it, for it was almost as high as the window, not washing over the wall, but bubbling, bubbling and bubbling yet more. I had seen a distant typhoon in the Indian Ocean but it was nothing like this hellish brew boiling just outside the window.

'I wish I'd got my camera up here, it's fantastic. No wonder all those poor fish swam into the sound for shelter,' I said.

We were both in a state of high excitement. The dogs felt it too, for they started chasing each other round the room and throwing a ball up in the air.

'I feel full of life,' said Con. 'What on earth can we do all day?'

We played backgammon for hours, in the darkened room, winning and losing vast sums from each other. From time to time ominous cracks came from the front of the house and beyond the closed windows. Through the slats of the shutters we could see tall palm trees almost lying across the road from the force of the wind which was making a continual high whining noise. From time to time the solidly built house shook and shuddered.

'Let's ring up Throck and see how they are.'

The telephone was dead. By lunchtime the electricity was off, which meant no light or cooking, and no radio. How long would it go on for? We had a little wood in the house, so we lit a fire, although it wasn't cold, in order to heat up the soup and some water. Then we had to let it almost go out to conserve the fuel. We also had to go easy with the water, for it had to be pumped daily from the sea; there would be no pumping today. There was but little sleep that night on the improvised beds, and the whining noise continued throughout. In the morning Mouche decided she must go outside. No matter how much paper we put down, she went on making determined efforts with an 'I-went-through-the-war-you-know' look in her eye. We tried to entice her on the floor of the shower; no good. By late afternoon Con agreed the dogs must go out. They'd been shut in for nearly twenty-four hours.

'We want some more logs anyway to cook on, don't we? Which side is the wind noise?'

It appeared to be quieter on the sheltered road side, so slowly he opened the screen and front door and looked out of a crack.

'It's still pretty bad, but maybe for a minute or two.'

They slipped out and I followed to bring in more logs. Flotow was back in seconds but Mouche was determined to see what was going on and jumped up on the sea wall, almost immediately being blown over – luckily for her and us, on to the road side. Indignantly she stalked back to the house and we locked up once more. The hurricane persisted the next night but by the following morning all was quiet. Outside, there was destruction everywhere. Wood and large trees were flung across the road and on to the rocks like matchsticks. Luckily the old house had stood firm. We certainly didn't need firewood for some time and it was fortunate there were no other houses nearby. An unearthly feeling of quiet had followed, and with it came depression. It was also my birthday; as we had nothing but rather high fish in the inactive fridge, the soup finished, no electricity and no phone, Con said he would take me to Hamilton if the ferry was running and give me a birthday lunch.

The ferry was running, but all we got at the hotel was a club sandwich as they had no electricity either. Feeling even more depressed, we wandered along Front Street until we found an open bar called the Ace of Clubs.

'Come on, darling, I'll buy you an Alexander. An uncle of mine always had them instead of tea,' said Constantine.

Now, if you've never had an Alexander, beware, for the innocuous taste of cream disguises its lethal qualities. It consists of cream, brandy and crème de cacao, is perfectly delicious and makes you feel you could go on drinking more for hours – which is what we did, until the ferry went back to Somerset. By the time we got home I was a bit tipsy, at the same time hungover and dejected. I'd had a horrid birthday, I thought, and the dear dogs had been alone all day; there was no electric light, nothing but a pervading smell of rotting fish. We had bought a few tins, to have yet another makeshift meal. I burst into tears and ran into the kitchen to be greeted by Father Tom coming through the screen door. I flung myself at him, still blubbering. We had quite forgotten we had asked him to share my birthday dinner.

'Theo, dear.' He put his arms around me. 'What on earth's the matter?'

From the other room came Con's laconic voice:

'It's all right, Father Tom, she's only drunk.'

He let go of me. 'Oh, thank God,' he said. 'I thought something was the matter.'

CHAPTER THIRTY-TWO

To someone from a northern climate, Christmas in a hot country seems very strange. It needs a fertile imagination to feel the cold winds of winter, or to contemplate frozen fields and leafless trees when one is alternately swimming, then drying off in the sun. I would have found this feat of imagination almost impossible during 1946–47, had it not been for the letters from my family during the hard winter known as the 'ice age' in England, where all major foods, even bread, were still rationed. In restaurants, I read with amazement, bread was considered one of the maximum three dishes allowed at any one meal. It was only slightly better than during the war years, except for cans of a weird fish called snoek. None of this appeared in the Bermuda newspapers. For some time, when we could afford it I had been sending back parcels of food which my grandmother said made her feel like a child at Christmas again. This Christmas I had sent a whole tinned ham. The golden-guinea rum I put into smaller bottles secreted in half-filled giant packets of porridge oats. It was the best packing ever; of about a dozen shipments not a bottle even cracked and the Customs (even if they wondered at the passion for porridge) never rumbled it.

With one of these parcels I had to wait one day at Mrs Skeffington's tiny post office on the bridge while a man produced his own letter scales and carefully weighed his airmail letters. He fussed and peered at the scales for a long time before he was satisfied.

'Are your scales broken then, Mrs Skeffington?' I asked when he had left.

Pushing back a strand of mop-like grey hair, Mrs Skeffington sighed:

'Oh, no, he always does that; says mine aren't accurate. He's very rich, you know, I suppose that's how he's got all that money.'

A week later I was at a party where the same man was as usual talking about his money. Remembering poor, tired, honest Mrs Skeffington I said to him almost involuntarily:

'Just how much money have you got, Mr Mott?'

He turned round, his heavy, rather dull face showing signs of interest. Without having to think, he drawled at me.

'At the last count it was $113,000,000.'

From then on he considered me a friend, always going out of his way to speak some boring platitude by way of conversation.

There were many such parties with many such people in the weeks before the end of the year. Why we went to them I can hardly remember: maybe because Constantine had just finished his novel and, with the subsequent post-birth depression, needed some stimulus. If nothing else we could spend hours afterwards remarking on the oddities of human beings. One elderly man, a director of General Motors in Detroit, appeared fascinated by me, for he always made straight for me and would invariably ask me the same question: had I been to eat at Pink Beach yet? The sand was really pink and the lobsters (there were not in fact any lobsters in Bermuda waters) swell, flown in from the States every day.

Now, Pink Beach was in Smith's Parish, quite an expensive drive away; the price of the food was equally expensive. I grew very tired of thinking up excuses for not going. One evening I had had enough of the question. I told him we didn't have the sort of money to indulge in such extravagance; that we had free crawfish at the bottom of the terrace; that I enjoyed cooking them and asking our own friends to share them. My voice must have been unaccountably sharp and I began to regret my outburst. He looked at me shrewdly, the hard, blue eyes fixed on my face. Putting his head slightly on one side, he said:

'Say, you're not a communist are you?'

Oh! Eugene, I wonder whether they said that to you, too!

———

For Christmas Day we had invited Throck and Juliet, Fred and Margaret, Barney Fawkes (captain of HMS Sheffield, then on a courtesy cruise), his girlfriend Sue Watson, who was also a good friend of ours, Father Tom and two hard-up actors he had discovered would be alone on Christmas evening: a fresh crawfish each, half a ham roasted with guavas, cheese of an unspectacular kind, my bananas preserved in rum, and a rather heavy fruit cake which the Dutch oven had refused to appreciate. It was a beautifully hot day as we prepared the feast in our bathing suits. Our guests were to arrive around three o'clock, we would dine at the eighteenth-century hour of about 4.30 pm.

Making the sauces in the kitchen, I saw one of the huge spiders on the white wall above me apparently carrying a round white Christmas package on its stomach. As I watched, the package, like a huge white pill, the *cachet faivre* of years past, burst open and out ran thousands of tiny spiders, scattering in a thousand directions. So engrossed was I that the opening of the screen door startled me. It was Father Tom, carrying some huge parcels.

'You're early, Father Tom; we've asked the others for three o'clock.'

He was bubbling over with excitement.

'I've got us a turkey from the American base. Come on, let's get going.'

The parcel was enormous, the Dutch oven small, but to complicate matters when the wrapping was undone it was frozen solid. His kind, mobile face lengthened visibly with disappointment. 'What on earth can we do with this lump of rock?'

'Salt,' I said, holding up a half-empty salt drum, 'and sun.' But that would take hours and it was now midday.

'I know, the sea, that's salty – and warm.'

So we tied string to one turkey leg and Father Tom sat on the edge of the slip and dangled it in the sea. There, this improbable dinner bobbed up and down, a curious Christmas captive. After a little while he called me: 'I can't read or do anything, holding this thing.' I tied the string round his ankle and told him to waggle his foot up and down, like the punka-wallahs in India. A turkey-wallah, I called him. Reports on the slow progress were shouted up; one wing was plumper and looked more natural. Then a cry of:

'Theo, Theo, come quickly!'

I ran down to find that a shoal of baby swordfish had arrived. They weren't more than a foot long, but the sharp, pointed snouts were prodding vigorously all over the turkey. Father Tom was hauling the bird up.

'Leave it, it's the best way of thawing it, they'll soften the ice with the constant darts.'

And so they did, the helpful little creatures. After an hour or so squashed in the hopeless oven, we lifted out the whole interior box and cooked it over the cedar fire, liberally basting it with lime butter and endlessly flambéeing it with rum. There never was, or had been, such a magnificent bird, the *pièce de résistance* of a Lucullan feast.

Dawn, with breakfast on the terrace after a swim – everyone agreed it had been the finest Christmas ever, which, as Father Tom pointed out had cost us very little, all the main items being free. While we had all been talking, Throck for once was silent, busily engaged in what appeared to be painting a picture.

'There's the dawn for you to remember this Christmas by,' he squeaked, holding up his work done on a sheet of typing paper.

The rising sun painted with cooked egg yolk was as brilliant as the scene in front of us. Splashes of red tomato sauce streaked across the sky, the shoreline of streaky bacon was most realistic, with houses dotted along it in mustard! The sea showed great ingenuity – ink mixed with a little mint sauce – and it looked like seaweed; boats of coffee, with sails of sugar. As an example of modern art it was striking, but alas by the following evening, after two hot days, the smell was appalling. A pity, since there are many times when I would like to be able to look again at that dawn, Christmas 1947.

The Iron Hoop, for that was the name of Constantine's second novel, was entirely different in subject from *The Arabian Bird*. In the same lucid, simple prose it told of an unnamed ruined city in a defeated country, peopled by the victorious army, and those left of the population surviving in makeshift dwellings. The main character, called The Hero, was a kindly, understanding, poetic man, a victim of misfortune, who looked after two orphaned children, an older girl and a boy. He educated them through elaborate allegories, fairy stories told from memory and his imagination. The Hero's world was one of his own making, exquisitely described. It was a very haunting book, which showed great tenderness, sadness and understanding.

After it was sent to Rinehart, Constantine suffered for a long time the depression which afflicts most writers when a work is completed. He seemed very listless and complained of darts of severe pain at the base of his spine. The doctor diagnosed a fistula (a deep-seated abscess in the anal passage) and he was operated on. Several weeks later it appeared the operation had been a failure, so back he went for another one. It was a debilitating, painful period, and when he came home he couldn't walk far or swim. The dressing had to be changed by a nurse every day. Not only was this very worrying, but the vast expense of two operations, hospitals and nurses was beyond us. Georgette sent us a cheque to cover immediate expenses, but Constantine couldn't concentrate on writing. He had given up Saltus Grammar School, and we were living on a small monthly allowance from Rinehart, so even our frugal purchases of food had to be on credit. Father Tom, friend of everyone in trouble, was a great moral help, as well as bringing us food. His fertile brain kept turning out all kinds of impractical suggestions until one day he said I should get a job and he would give me a reference.

'What on earth could I work at? I've had no experience in anything except acting.'

They both sat and stared at me as though expecting me to produce a hidden talent.

'I know,' he said, 'you can work on a newspaper. I know the owner of the afternoon one very well. He'd be delighted to have you.'

'But, Father Tom, I've never even been in a newspaper office. I did see that film *The Front Page* years ago but I don't think I'd be any good.'

'Nonsense, of course you would, you're very quick at picking things up. I'll come and sit with Con while you go.'

So off I went on the ferry to see Mr Toddings of the *Mid-Ocean News* with my reference in my bag. I was full of alarm and apprehension, and tried to recall less frenetic scenes from the film that I might be able to do.

However, Mr Toddings was not at all frightening and seemed impressed by Father Tom's letter.

'Hm, hm, *Evening Standard*, eh? I think we can fit you in somewhere. Are you married?' I couldn't see what that had to do with it, but said yes, so he promptly said that if I was married I must look after my house for some time in the day, or I wouldn't be concentrating at work, so would I like mornings or afternoons? I chose the afternoons as the nurse usually came in the morning, also I could leave lunch and so on. I was to start on Monday at 2.00 pm. The entire interview was most urbane.

Madeleine, a Portuguese girl working there, was very helpful, also Brock, the editor. I was put on to doing headlines and Madeleine carefully explained what I should do. This I found quite easy and enjoyed selecting the various letters and typefaces. Unfortunately it wasn't as easy as I thought, or I didn't listen properly, because when my first page came out all the words were strung together; nobody had told me to leave two spaces between words. It looked something like this:

NORAINWATERSHORTAGEWORSE

I didn't lose the job, because that evening the paper sold twice as many copies, as people wanted to see the page of startling headlines. I was, however, moved from that job to being society editress, which seemed much more in my line. It meant finding out which celebrities had arrived in Bermuda, then going to interview them. It was in this capacity that I found Romney Brent and his wife Gina Malo had taken a house there for a while.

Romney, despite his name, was Mexican and a very fine actor. He had just finished playing the Dauphin in *Joan of Lorraine* with Ingrid Bergman on Broadway, where he had had exceptional notices. I knew him quite well as he had directed the first play of Anatole de Grunwald in London, in which I had a part, just before the war. Gina Malo was extremely pretty and attractive; she had been the star of the musical *Anything Goes*.

They were just what Constantine needed: new faces, new ideas, full of original improvisation, and nothing to do with literature. Both were fairly small and dark, Gina with huge expressive eyes and a pert manner. Romney's face could assume several different expressions in as many minutes. He had quick graceful movements (I was told his manipulation of the Dauphin's train was a work of art), a puckish sense of humour, a ready wit and a rich granary of theatrical anecdotes which he told with great skill. We thought how well they would get on with the Throckmortons – alas, we were ignorant of an episode which took place during a performance of *The Streets of New York*. At a certain point in the play a hose was brought on stage, which Throck had connected to a water main one night. Romney Brent was drenched to the skin. Not the kind of incident an actor is likely to forgive easily; however, peace was made that evening and they became the best of friends again.

Leaving the office one day on my way to interview Jennifer Jones the actress, I met Father Tom looking very solemn and weary. His large Irish face brightened when he saw me but I could see he was worried so I asked what was the matter. He had found that Shane O'Neill, son of the playwright, was camping in a cave near Eugene's house, Spithead, eating practically nothing and drugging. Would I come with him to see what could be done? This request couldn't have been asked at a worse moment. I was new to the job, we urgently needed the money, Con was still ill, and my appointment already made. What good could I possibly do? Reluctantly I had to refuse, for I felt he needed someone like me to go with him, knowing the rather anticlerical feelings of the O'Neill family.

Jennifer Jones was staying with David Selznick the director near Throck's house, so after the rather exhausting interview I called on him.

'What should I have done, Throck?'

He said I had done the right thing as so many people had tried to help and failed. Shane had always loved that house, for the happiest part of his childhood had been spent there. His mother, Agnes, had lent it to Shane and his wife Cathy after the death of their baby the previous year, but that had been a failure too. They had sold everything in the house right down to the bathroom fittings, even family mementos of James and Ella O'Neill.

I told Father Tom all this, but I still feel that I should have made some effort, even later on. As might have been expected it was Father Tom who took food and arranged for him to get back to the States. Dear Father Tom was constantly in trouble with the bishop, but as Constantine said, he was the best advertisement for the Catholic Church one could ever meet. He helped everyone who needed him, not only spiritually but practically.

————

In early March, *The Arabian Bird* was published in America and received a very good press, which naturally delighted us. Georgette came down to stay with news from New York and told us in how many bookshops it was and showed us more press cuttings we hadn't yet seen. It was a very happy time. Con's health improved more quickly than with any medication. Added to all that he heard that Desmond Flower of Cassell in London had bought the book for publication there. Our spirits revived overnight. Constantine was on the road to success; we were convinced our lives would be different from now on.

Having Georgette to stay made things much easier for me. Not that she was in the least domestic, far from it, but it was a relief to get back in the evening to find odd little jobs done I hadn't even thought of doing, and also to share in her delightful sense of humorous wisdom. On the occasional day I did complain bitterly about the difficulties of our life, she would give that silvery laugh and say:

'Imagine me with a FitzGibbon husband and four FitzGibbon children!'

Just the thought would make me stop. After living alone she enjoyed being with us and meeting the mixture of people who constantly came to the house. How some of them found out about us I will never know; it was as though there was a signpost pointing out a place of interest. Some came once and decided we were not for them, others became good friends. A great surprise was Archie Douglas turning up unexpectedly one day. We had met in London during the war but to see him in Bermuda in the same attire – sports jacket, flannels, beret and bicycle – was startling. Why he had lugged his wife and three children all that way I don't know, but there he was, eyes sparkling behind the spectacles and talking in a kind of bad imitation of his father Norman Douglas.

Archie was endowed with a permanent optimism, so farfetched that it was both amusing and endearing. He behaved as if we were owners of large properties there instead of a small rented cottage, proclaiming it 'not a patch on Provence' which indeed it resembled not at all. He wanted a house and a job and introductions. 'Three children to provide for, you know, and then there's Marion' – as though we could magically provide it instantly. Nevertheless when Con gave him a letter to Bobbie Booker at the school he seemed delighted as if it would solve everything. After a brief swim and a drink he bicycled off, leaving us all a bit stunned. Georgette broke the silence first:

'He's like an enormous St Bernard puppy bouncing all over the place. Not a bit like Norman.'

Nevertheless he did get a job very soon and also a pleasant house right on the beach in Paget which we visited from time to time.

A carriage drove up one evening and out jumped a fair-haired, fresh-complexioned young man, immaculately dressed, unmistakably English. He had a ready smile and a pleasing manner as he came towards us, hand outstretched. After enquiring if we were the FitzGibbons he introduced himself as Emerson Bainbridge.

'Shall I keep the carriage?' he asked, but we replied we could telephone later on for one. Maybe it's just as well he didn't keep it, as he stayed for four days. Emerson was delightful company, giving out good nature and bonhomie extravagantly. Nobody would have thought that he was experiencing frightful marital difficulties, his wife having arrived on the island with their small son and a large, overbearing man she introduced to Bermuda's staid society as her lover.

That, of course, was the reason he was only too delighted to stay with us; he dreaded going home. He was rather rich, so the lady wanted to hold on to both of them. Luckily we lived a distance away, so Emerson often escaped when things got too unbearable, and enjoyed being with us and our friends. When the lady and the lover took trips to America, we were asked over to stay with him which didn't endear her to us at all. The situation got very bad, so I suggested Emer and I write an historical novel together (it was the time of *Forever Amber*) as some sort of therapy. We worked out a very gusty plot. Each of us wrote a number of chapters and each was convinced his or her chapters were better than the others. Eventually the manuscript was packed off to a publisher, only to be lost in the post. Foolishly we only had notes and no second copy. Nevertheless it did Emer a lot of good, taking him over the worst time with his problems, for the lady and the lover departed for another country shortly afterwards. Emer behaved all the way through as a most kind, gentle and generous man.

Georgette said it was too much for me, working and looking after everybody as well, and as she was contributing very generously to the household expenses why didn't I give up the job? With over six hours' work, the cooking, sometimes late hours, I was a bit over-tired, although I had enjoyed my time with the *Mid-Ocean News*.

The news about *The Arabian Bird* was very good, the new novel was with Rinehart, and Cassell's offer had been very heartening. It had been a long time since Christmas when we had last entertained, so with all the change of fortune we decided to celebrate the good news. Giving a party was not expensive with our free fish and fruit; the rum was cheap; I now had time to prepare the food; and the weather was nearly always perfect.

New and old friends came, the food was laid in the outside dining room as a buffet, the night was as soft as sixteenth-century satin. It was nothing like the sometimes frenetic London parties, but leisurely and relaxed. We had all night to eat, drink, swim and talk. Fred had just come back from Hollywood and was glowing with gossipy stories; Father Tom was talking about going to Antigua to build a church there; Emer, who also did a superb imitation of

Queen Victoria after eating a duck dinner, vied with Throck's impersonation of her; Georgette was regaling Sue and Barney with tales of prohibition, and of coming to Bermuda at that time with four cabin trunks and the four children. On their return she had said to each child:

'Now, children, when we get to New York, I want each one of you to sit on a trunk and not to get down until I tell you.' The Customs man had arrived, moving along the trunks, marking them as he went, saying:

'That's a swell bunch of kids you got, lady.'

'You can get down now, children.'

And that's how she got four large steamer trunks full of honest-to-God booze back to New York.

The next day, there was a letter from Rinehart saying their chief editor was coming to Bermuda to see Constantine the following week. We were all overjoyed; imagine sending someone down especially to see him. They obviously thought very highly of him. It seemed that nothing could ever go wrong again. That evening we sat on the terrace, full of love for each other, looking out over the calm, pellucid sea, amid the scent from the luminous pale blue plumbago, and the slender wand-like lilies. We watched the sunset with its explosion of colours like the palettes of myriad celestial painters, and were replete with happiness.

CHAPTER THIRTY-THREE

Walter Pistole, for that was the editor's name, was tall and slender with large dark eyes which looked over your shoulder rather than at your face. He was impeccably polite with a serious manner. After dinner he said he would like to talk to Constantine, so Georgette and I busied ourselves clearing up and speculating on the conversation. Whatever speculations we made we did not foresee the outcome; it was in fact the last thing in our minds.

Briefly, it was that Rinehart thought the book a beautifully written, original story, but it was not for them. It was too different from *The Arabian Bird* and they couldn't see a US market for it. Constantine was very subdued at first when we joined them, then a false, brittle gaiety took over. As long and over-familiar anecdotes were recounted, the bottle got considerably lower. Pistole looked nervous, but said very little. Georgette and I were apprehensive and glad when the evening ended.

Writing seemed to me to be a vocation of unhappiness. Authors, I had discovered, were like Aunt Sallies at a fairground; as soon as someone put them up, a sideswipe knocked them down again. Did it happen to all of them? I wished Fred was here and not in the States. What on earth were we going to do now, eight hundred miles out in the Atlantic? The nearest land port was Jacksonville, Florida, which seemed a very unlikely place for a penniless writer. Why had I given up the *Mid-Ocean News* just when we were likely to need every penny? These unanswered questions chased round my mind during that long, hot night.

The next day I went with Pistole into Hamilton, and over lunch he made apologies which had a depressing effect on me. I would rather he had said nothing. He caught his plane, then I went disconsolately home, not knowing what to expect. Georgette and Con were playing backgammon, at which they were both very good. Con looked up:

'Mummy's been marvellous. She's advanced my birthday and given me this huge cheque.'

A thousand dollars.

'I'm going to write a short story about the visit and send it to the *New Yorker*. Can't think why they had to waste money sending him down. Why couldn't they have written? Better to have sent me the money.'

The wound had been cauterized but it was not to be easily healed.

Throck and Juliet seemed less ebullient too, as there had been no definite news about starting the theatre in over a year. Throck picked up a thriller I had tossed aside – 'Gene (O'Neill) used to love thrillers,' he remarked, 'always read them for relaxation.'

I couldn't help commenting that there was a bit too much relaxation about at present, telling him about Rinehart. Yes, he knew all about it. He'd seen rejection affecting so many brilliant young playwrights. At least Con didn't go on three-day benders, disappearing so nobody could find him. He remembered helping Agnes Boulting, O'Neill's second wife, check all the dives for days at a time.

I caressed Mouche's ears; Flotow was sitting by Juliet.

'He just adored his dogs. Gene, I mean,' said Juliet. 'Liked them better than most people. Do you remember that enormous Irish wolfhound he brought to Bermuda, Throck?'

Throck chuckled.

'I don't think they'd ever seen such a dog here before. It made headlines in the *Royal Gazette*.'

'Do you ever see him now?' I wanted to know, but I was told his health was poor and Carlotta, O'Neill's third wife, didn't approve of his old friends.

———

Constantine was writing another novel about a dominating woman seen from different points of view by the people with whom she had been most closely associated. He no longer read aloud to us every evening, and when he did the old spontaneity and pride were absent. It was a clever book but the humanity shown in the first two had gone. However, criticism was not encouraged, so the readings which we used to enjoy so much became a sad affair which we sat through with solemn faces. I no longer even thought I knew what would sell and what wouldn't. Con became touchy and irritable.

'You want to expose something,' said Father Tom. 'Expose the Catholic Church, I'll give you some pointers. That would sell.'

However, he continued with the novel, now called *Cousin Emily*. Bob Giroux, a New York publisher, arrived one evening, a charming, avuncular man who radiated friendly feelings, read what was written and pronounced it a *tour-de-force*, which secretly I thought was like saying of a painting that the colour was striking.

Most of our friends were leaving the island, or, like the Ullmans and the Wakemans, had gone already. Father Tom said he was going to Antigua to prospect; he would let us know what it was like. Georgette went back to New England and the gap they both left was immeasurable. I was lonely as well as worried. At this time Sue Watson said why didn't she rent the schoolhouse for a month? Barney could come over from HMS *Sheffield* when he was off duty.

This worked out quite well, Sue and I taking turns with the cooking, which made Constantine remark that every man should have two wives to get a good change of menu. She was a charming companion – a quiet and introspective girl of original thought – and I enjoyed her being there. Barney entertained us to dinner on the *Sheffield*, a grand affair where we were piped on and off. He was a marvellous host; his smiling face and kind brown eyes always gave a gentle easiness to occasions.

Father Tom wrote and said he was enjoying Antigua, land was £1 an acre and he had bought seven acres. With the help of three reformed Canadian alcoholics, he was building a church. Why didn't we come down? The money was getting scarce, however, and, although tempted, we thought it was that much more primitive and even further away from the world of publishing. A little money trickled down from *The Arabian Bird*; my grandmother sent me a cheque which I hid for a bit against the day when we had nothing, which came only too soon. By September we realized we must leave. Where to was now the problem.

Georgette now had a small apartment in Irving Place, near Gramercy Park in New York. It was decided that I would go up to New York with Mouche, stay with Georgette and try to get a job. Constantine would follow in a week or so with Flotow when he had cleared up what he could in Bermuda.

Throck gave me a letter to Laurence Langner of the Theater Guild, a very glowing letter, and he was sure Laurence would find me something. An Englishman was anxious to take Graysbank over and pay any back rent. I hated to leave it, for despite all the anxieties we had had during the past two years, it was, and still remains, the most beautiful and *sympathique* house I have ever lived in.

———

Although Georgette's apartment, a first-floor walk-up, was very small, it was a charming quarter with friendly shopkeepers and the delightful green square of Gramercy Park around the corner. Gramercy Park was very dignified, surrounded by elegant nineteenth-century houses, one of which was the famous

Player's Club. At night I would let Mouche run free in the park, and there met a white-haired gentleman with his dog. We got into conversation and I found it was Norman Thomas, the head of the small Socialist Party in America. He was most interested in England (the Labour Party was in power) and we would sit there talking, seeing each other's faces only by the light of a street lamp. I looked forward to those park-bench chats.

The traffic in New York was frightening after our almost car-free island, and getting used to town shoes again was even worse. I had no warm clothes, so had to wear Georgette's, which were far too old for me. However, she did voluntary work for the Quakers, sending parcels of clothes and food to Europe, and sometimes she would see something that would suit me and buy it cheaply.

'After all, you are a sort of war survivor,' she would say.

Jobs: I rang Laurence Langner, a leading figure of the Theater Guild in New York, but he was away. I rang Romney Brent, who said he would let me know if he heard of anything. I scanned the *New York Times* ads; stenographers or secretaries – no good. I rang our Bermuda friends the Ullmans, but the only idea they had was to hire Constantine and myself as butler and cook. Somehow I couldn't see Con as a very good butler. Sue Watson said she would try to get me a job with an eccentric Russian professor who wanted his art objects catalogued. Everyone else said I must go to Columbus Circle and get a work permit. I sat there for two hours one day and didn't see anyone at all. I rang Bob Giroux the publisher, who took me out to dinner but couldn't suggest anything. Constantine would arrive any moment and I'd achieved nothing. We heard of hurricane warnings in the Atlantic and wondered if it would catch Bermuda. It was all unsettling. I spent the days going round museums, for I was starved of good paintings and sculpture. There was a ramshackle cinema at the bottom of Irving Place where they showed old undubbed foreign films. It was a fleapit of sorts and cheap. I remember seeing *Les Enfants du Paradis* twice and Cocteau's *Orphée*, which for a brief time made me think I was back in Paris.

Constantine just appeared early one afternoon, taxi bulging with luggage but no Flotow. Where was he?

The hurricane. The boat wasn't sailing; he had rung some friends, the Ivanovics, and had been staying with them. Vladimir had arranged a seat on the last plane out, but they wouldn't take Flotow, uncrated. So he was with them, and when the hurricane had passed they would have a crate made and put him on the plane. Constantine seemed very bright and cheerful. Pleased to be in New York, he delightedly told us *The Iron Hoop* had been accepted by Cassell in London.

The following week a cable came from Vladimir; Flotow was on such-and-such a plane, so out we went to La Guardia to fetch him. After waiting until everyone was through Customs, we saw there was no dog. Constantine waved the cable about to be answered by shrugs. Somehow we got through to the tarmac, wandered about, and were just leaving, walking past a hangar, when we heard a bark.

'That's Flotow's bark,' I said and we went to the door.

It was quite dark but fortunately the huge door wasn't locked, and there inside, still in his crate, just large enough for standing in, with no food or water, was a dazed little Flotow. There was nobody about, so we just broke the crate open, it was only loosely held by nails, and took him out on his lead saying not a word to anyone. Nobody ever contacted us to find out what had happened to him. I dread to think of the state he would have been in the next day, standing up in the crate on a hot night with no water, but it ended very happily for all of us.

It became obvious that we couldn't all live indefinitely in Georgette's tiny apartment. We went to the Irving Hotel on the corner where they had tiny apartments with kitchenettes. No dogs. I brought Mouche in, the best mannered animal I know, and put her to sit, stand, open the door and close it; so they relented. There were two entrances to the hotel, and for the whole time we were there they never knew we had two dogs, as one of us would go out one door with one dog, and then use the door at the back with the other dog.

The Ullmans asked us to dinner several times in their grand house on 66th Street, always arranging that there was a publisher or someone who might be useful there. We wandered around nearby Greenwich Village, browsing in secondhand bookshops where we were surprised to find several Norman Douglas books we hadn't read. When Norman had escaped from Italy during the war he had been able to bring only a few belongings with him. It was reading *Looking Back* that made Con remember the letter Norman had given him in England to Muriel Draper, with the words:

'Get her to tell you the story of the wood ashes.'

In *Looking Back*, which is based on his going through a large bowl of visiting cards, under the name Muriel Draper he says, 'the story of the wood ashes will have to wait'.

Muriel Draper was an extraordinarily alive woman, very cultured, with a striking head and face like an Aztec sculpture. She was delighted to hear news of Norman and to meet us.

'The old rogue,' she mused. 'Mmm. . . I had to forgive him. Yes, I'll tell you the story of the wood ashes.'

It appears that early in this century she was spending the summer in Berkeley Square, London, with her scholarly husband, enjoying the season, then at its height. She found she was pregnant, and the last thing she wanted was morning sickness and other accompanying *malaises*. All her friends were consulted, but it was Norman who came up with the remedy. It was an old Calabrian folk remedy, he said. You half-filled a hip bath with wood ashes and sat in it while it was topped up with hot water. After a number of hours you were lifted out and the inevitable happened. It was high summer, so the servants were given days off while endless wood fires were burned and the ashes retained. The hip bath, such as Marat was murdered in, she said, was purchased and filled. Friends were asked to attend this levée; Henry James came and read a short story; George Moore came and talked of his newest attachment; Arthur Rubinstein, the leading musician of the time, came and played a piano piece, especially written. The contemporary Rose Bertin designed a hat for her. Meanwhile, she sat in the hip bath, a delicate lace jacket round her shoulders, while Norman saw to the hot water. It was all very *dégagé*. The time was up, she was lifted into the linen sheets (filthy, she said, with ashes), champagne was brought and she waited. The party went on.

The next morning, Norman called.

'Nothing's happened,' she said, and then he laughed and laughed until she thought he would have a paroxysm, tears trickling down his cheeks.

The child born subsequently was to become Paul Draper, the magical dancer who had so entranced us at the Plaza Hotel when we first arrived.

Harold Strauss, then with the publishers Alfred Knopf, was at one of the Ullmans' dinner parties and it was no doubt our preoccupation with Norman Douglas that made Con suggest to him that he go to Italy to write Norman's life. He readily agreed that it was an excellent idea and he would put it up to Alfred Knopf and Blanche, his wife. The idea was just as much a surprise to me as I think it was to Strauss, perhaps even to Constantine. The next thing we knew was about a week later Alfred Knopf asked us out to lunch at his house in the country, at White Plains. It was a fairly large luncheon party, Alfred a charming host, his portly suave figure solicitous to his guests. After lunch he showed me round his large garden, explaining the origin of every plant and tree.

Meanwhile Constantine wrote to Norman in Capri, asking his permission, which was given by return of post. He also wrote putting the idea to Desmond Flower of Cassell in London. We didn't dare to be too hopeful, tried not to talk about it, and we were very close at that time, almost every thought either of us had being anticipated by the other. We did things to take our minds off the subject, explored unknown parts of New York; we went to the cinema. We saw Laurence Olivier's *Hamlet* and were amused to hear the man behind explaining the plot to his girlfriend while the film was running.

'Then she goes nutty, see, and drowns herself; that old guy gets killed,' and so on.

'How marvellous,' said Con, 'to reach that age, and *not* know the plot of Hamlet.'

Both publishers agreed to commission the book almost within days of each other. There were terms to be arranged, and as it came about the Knopf advance was to finance our trip there; the Cassell advance would be sent to Italy to keep us while the book was being written. Alfred Knopf also liked *The Iron Hoop* and bought it for publication the next year. It was all perfect. Thus it was that early in October, Constantine, myself and the two dogs set sail on the SS *Saturnia*, third class, for Naples.

Most of our friends came to the boat to bid farewell. Bob Giroux and his friend Charlie Reilly brought a huge bunch of roses, others brought wine, some a little keepsake. At almost the last minute Emerson Bainbridge, whom we didn't know was in New York, arrived with a massive box and more wine. The little third-class bar was full of our friends, who looked like birds of paradise amongst the many drably dressed emigrants returning to their homeland. It was an emotional send-off. As the hooters sounded for our departure there were tears in our eyes. Turning away as we cast off we saw Emerson had left his brand-new hat and raincoat behind. They were to last Con for years.

———

Our departure had been very simple, no last-minute alarms such as there had been when my father and I left India. Not that our departure then hadn't been simple, but my father had a friend who also wanted to leave India but, unfortunately, owed a lot of money to tinkers, tailors and no doubt candlestick-makers too. Manny, as I will call him, was what used to be known as 'the black sheep' of an extremely rich Middle Eastern family. The name alone gave traders a misplaced confidence; he was often sent things he hadn't ordered, things which somehow or another were absorbed into his household.

'I don't like to hurt their feelings,' he would say to my father, 'and it is very beautiful.'

Nobody could quite understand why Manny and my father were such great friends. To look at together they presented an odd picture: my father, tall, vividly blue-eyed, handsome and always impeccably dressed; Manny, small, dark, untidy, his body seemingly put together from odd pieces, a large head and face on top of a small body with big hands and feet, giving him the appearance of being drawn by a good cartoonist. He walked like a racing duck if such an animal could be imagined. The characteristics they had in common were a love of the outrageous and the desire to explore all the good things of life, preferably together. They seemed to me like a new music-hall team, making me laugh so much sometimes that the tears would pour out of my eyes. They would bicker continuously, always ending up the best of friends. I loved them both.

Two days or so before we were to take ship, Manny came to the house late one night, imploring us somehow to smuggle him aboard.

'All my creditors will be waiting on the dock. You know what happened to young Ernesleigh. I'll be thrown into that dreadful debtors' prison. Do think of something, Adam, you're so resourceful.'

The large black eyes seemed to turn into liquid orbs, as the heavy, sad face looked up. It was such a recognizable face, not easy to camouflage, as my father pointed out. They drank large glasses of beer whilst working out the problem. I went out to bring in another jug from the huge barrel we ordered every week, to find that was the last of it.

'The barrel's empty now; shall I get Hari to tap another?'

'My God!' My father slapped his knee hard. 'That's it. You're only a little fellow and you're always boasting about being double-jointed. Come on, let's go out and measure up. Everyone knows I always have a barrel of beer.'

Manny looked a little apprehensive as we stood him beside the large barrel.

'My head's outside,' he complained.

'Oh, that's easy, you can sit down.'

'Won't it smell terribly of beer? I'll get all wet, won't I?'

My father pointed out it was that or face the creditors. The top would be lifted, the barrel well washed, and air holes punched in concealed places. It would only be for the most about an hour. It seemed the only way, so for the next two days Manny practised sitting in the barrel, the top being left on for longer and longer periods.

'I might be starting you in a new career,' my father said delightedly, 'if you get in this situation again you can do it at fairs, and then, when you're more proficient, there's Niagara Falls.'

I was detailed to take care of the luggage and the animals, including my tiny monkey and the barrel. Hari was the only member of the household to be taken into the secret and would be with me. Since our journey across India we had become firm friends, and many was the time he had covered up for me if I was out too late, or where I shouldn't have been.

Sure enough the weasel-eyed creditors lined the dock. My father swept majestically on board with an imperceptible greeting, to be followed by his numerous friends for the leave-taking. Hari and I saw to the luggage with special instructions; the barrel, for the time being, was to be put in my father's stateroom. I accompanied it and was alarmed when I saw it being rolled, very roughly, up the gangway. When we were alone, I prised out some of the bungs and whispered through them.

'Are you all right? You're on board now. I'll try to get Hari to take off the lid. Wait a minute.'

Try as I did, I couldn't find Hari, so I went to my father, who was in the middle of a circle of admiring – mostly women – friends.

'The beer's getting very hot,' I said. 'I can't find Hari to settle it.'

He waved his arm, and cheerfully said it would be all right for a while. I hoped so for it was airless in the stateroom. I didn't know what to do, for I couldn't ask a steward to release a stowaway. Poor Manny, would he survive? I wandered about for some time; it seemed as if the ship would never sail. I looked over the rails feeling as though I were taking part in a murder. After a while, someone touched my arm; it was Hari, who walked as silently as a cat.

'Barrel-Sahib whistling,' he said.

'Whistling? Whatever for? He'll be discovered.'

'Wanted to get air, missy. I lifted off top and put him in bathroom. Now top is back so beer is all right.' He looked sad. 'Will you come back to India?'

I hoped I would. Taking off a small turquoise ring I had, I gave it to him for his bride. I watched him go down the gangplank, and as the engines started up and the ship pulled away, I waved at the thin figure with the purple shirt until it was just a speck.

———

On the *Saturnia* we had a four-berth cabin, somewhere down below, to ourselves. The dogs were to travel on the top deck in large separate kennels. This was in the first class. They both looked horrified at being put into a kennel and took no comfort at the fact that other dogs were travelling too. I didn't feel at all happy about it, for Flotow was prehensile and could open almost any door, a talent which had much impressed the poodle-clipping shop in New York.

Down in our cabin we opened our cases and the presents. Emerson's massive box contained twenty cartons of Chesterfield cigarettes, about 4,000. The Italian steward came in as we had them open. His eyes glistened at the sight, so I gave him a carton, which proved a very good investment, for later on he let us bring the dogs down with us; we had the top bunks and they the bottom ones. Their exercise deck was the one adjoining the first-class deck so it was through the dogs that we met Sinclair Lewis, the first American writer to get the Nobel Prize in 1930 for his novel *Main Street*.

Sinclair Lewis was at that time in his early sixties, a tall thin man with scant, greying red hair and a skull-like face which was mottled in colour, as if he had at one time a skin ailment. He was travelling with his ex-mistress's mother, an ingenuous American lady called Mrs Power. Her daughter, Marcella, had apparently, in Lewis's words, 'Gone off with that son-of-a-bitch Mike'. Also in first class was an American doctor, Dr Camp, a party of young American girls who were the first contingent to go to Myron Taylor's newly opened Academy of Arts in Florence, and a dashing Brazilian called Prince Oliviera. Every morning I would sit on deck with Mrs Power and the dogs, Constantine and Sinclair Lewis usually having drinks in the bar with Dr Camp. Later we would join them; it was all very enjoyable.

After a while, I asked if I could call him Sinclair, he having called me Theodora from the first.

'You can if you like, but you'll be the first person since I left second grade school who has. Why don't you call me Red like everyone else?' So Red he became.

He was loving the journey and longing to get to Italy. Mrs Power was an ideal travelling companion, interested in everything.

'Different from my first wife, Dorothy Thompson. When I travelled Italy with her and would admire a view, she would answer: "Yes, and you see that factory? All the workers are getting a slave wage. No proper trade unions!"'

He enquired who Constantine's publisher was, and on being told Alfred Knopf, he screwed up his mouth and mused:

'Hm, Alfred, hm . . . when I was a young man we always had to have the *mot juste* for everything. Alfred, yes, we decided he wasn't a personality, or even really a person, so we called him a *personage*. Hm. Alfred. I hope you're getting good terms.'

The young American girls were picked, I think, more for their piety than their talent, a noisy, chattering, pretty little crew, who were asked occasionally to sing or play the piano in the evenings. We all grew very fond of them, none more so than Prince Oliviera. This infuriated Red Lewis, whose face would scowl when he saw the prince dancing with first one then another. He also had his eye on me, which is what brought Red to boiling point. I must say Oliviera's line was pretty good. I was the fulfilled young woman, which is attractive to any man, he said; '*Les pucelles* are charming, but . . . in a few years maybe. They have money, no?'

I reported this to Red during one of the evening dances and his face swelled up like a bull-frog.

'Son-of-a-bitch! I tell you what I want you to do, Theodora. When those girls go to the powder room you go in and say I want them, *all of them*, to come and see me, at once.'

This I did, and we all agreed to meet back there afterwards. He got them grouped around in a circle. Ten youthful, expectant faces turned to his.

'Now, listen to me, girls. You're all coming to Europe for the first time, and a lot of princes and other so-called nobility will pay court to you. Sooner or later you're going to go to bed with one of them and in the morning you'll find you have nothing in common. This won't hurt you, but by God, it'll hurt me. I'm not proposing you don't go to bed with anyone, but for God's sake make it someone you can talk to, and laugh with in the morning. Now you can continue your dancing.'

'But we all knew that,' they said, giggling with me afterwards. 'Still, it was nice of him, wasn't it?' One, rather more advanced than the rest, said thoughtfully:

'I hope I don't remember it all my life.'

On October 21st it was my birthday, so Red invited us up to a posh dinner in first class. He was very funny about certain New York characters, particularly Alexander Woolcott the writer and critic whom, he maintained, went out for a drink after the first act of a particular New York play (all theatres were dry at that time) and went back to the wrong theatre for the second and third acts. It was quite a stimulating if mystifying review, he said; nevertheless the first play ran for a long time.

'Never took any notice of my reviews after that,' he said. 'In those days, just to be noticed by Woolcott meant a success.'

I always felt it was a bit hard on the second play.

After dinner Con and I took the dogs for a turn around the deck, and looking out to sea thought there were lights in the distance, Sardinia maybe. We sat down enjoying the balmy night air, sitting close to each other in silence. There was no need for words; we were completely in harmony, our hearts full of hope and love for each other.

Downstairs in the third-class bar the Italians were singing their local songs; the air was thick with smoke and wine fumes. The barman on hearing it was my *festa* gave us a bottle of Asti Spumante, which we shared with a young Italian couple about the same age as us who had been working in America.

Now they had enough money to get married. We, too, were starting a new life; the past was behind us.

Packing up I realized we still had far too many cigarettes to get past Customs, despite the packets we had handed out as tips. So I unpacked the large canvas sack of books and put a lot on the bottom, then systematically went through our luggage tucking them into suit pockets, sponge bags and so on, until I had a reasonable amount left. I put two cartons in the bottom of my hand luggage and two on top.

'You're optimistic,' Constantine remarked. 'Don't expect me to stand by you. I'll look after the dogs while you deal with the Customs man.'

My Italian was very limited and as we got there I gave the Customs man the top two cartons. Con was some distance away, holding the dogs. We chatted as he marked our cases; suddenly he pulled my bag towards him. I pointed out his mark on it, yet still he persisted. All was up, I realized. But to my surprise he brought one of the cartons I had given him out and popped it back on top.

'For you, *signora.*'

'*Grazie, grazie molto.*'

Red Lewis and Mrs Power were staying at the Excelsior, and asked us to dine with them. We were in a smaller hotel a little distance away. Looking out of our bedroom window I was amazed at the vast destruction all over this area from the war, even two and a half years later. Whole blocks of buildings had been blown up and there was nothing but large empty spaces. I took a photograph from the window.

'Let's take the dogs for a walk and look around; it's good to be back in Europe again. We are, after all, Europeans,' Constantine said.

Which was exactly what my father had remarked when we landed at Naples over thirty years ago from India, prior to he, Manny and I starting our Grand Tour of Europe.

PART FOUR

Capri and Rome

CHAPTER THIRTY-FOUR

The *vaporetto* to Capri was small and battered. It badly needed painting and smelt of grease and oil. Downstairs there was a small bar set in a tiny cabin with slatted wooden seats around the walls. It was a fine day with a brisk wind, so I took the dogs up and we walked round the deck. Over the rails on the port side a priest was hanging his head over, so I asked if he was all right. He answered me in a heavy Limerick accent:

''Tis terrible I feel,' he said. 'Would there be a drop of whisky anywhere?'

I went down and got him an Italian brandy, the nearest drink to his request, which he swallowed gratefully, without apparently noticing the difference. What was he doing in Italy? I wondered, for he didn't seem to be a very good traveller. He told me he had come over for his niece's wedding in Rome, and was seeing a bit of the country before he went back.

I said how much he must have enjoyed it, what a good idea of his.

He shook his head sadly, before continuing:

'Ah,' he said, 'it t'was all very strange. Not a bit like an Irish wedding.' He hadn't enjoyed it very much at all. He would be glad to get back home where he understood the life. I left him sadly shaking his head.

From the harbour the island looked much larger than I had expected. Unlike the flatness of Bermuda, the mountains were quite astonishingly high, and everywhere, sometimes in the remotest places, villas were precariously perched, dotted over steep slopes. There were a few men at the port, and some small cafés set back against the rock walls, in which was situated the little red funicular to take us up. Norman Douglas was waiting at the top when we arrived, looking much happier and about ten years younger than he had when we had last seen him in London at the end of the war.

'Hello, duckums,' he chuckled as we came out with the dogs and three young men struggling with our luggage.

'Come on, we'll all have a nice drink.' He spoke fluently to the porters and they disappeared with the luggage around the corner.

'They'll take the stuff down to the *pensione*, then we'll join them.'

As we sat down at the funicular café, the familiar voice rapped out:

'Giorgio, *subito*,' but Giorgio was already at his elbow.

'Norman, I do hope it's absolutely all right my writing your life,' Constantine said almost at once.

'I don't mind what you write so long as you tell the truth.' He hesitated for a moment. 'But I don't know how you're going to get over Eric.' It was to prove a prophetic remark. Our seats had been carefully chosen at the café, not immediately opposite the railings where tourists took photographs of each other with their backs to the sea, but where we could look down on the last traces of megalithic walls built to protect the upper town from invasion. Norman recalled having seen other remains on his first visit to the island in 1888. On our right was the higher part of the old town, studded with ancient houses. With Norman was all the paraphernalia I remembered as always being with him: his pipe, the old tobacco tin, the snuffbox and his stick, but on his head, instead of the out-of-shape hat, a beret.

'Are those American cigarettes?' he asked. 'I'd like to try one, please.' After a few puffs he put it out with the solitary words: 'Muck, dearie, M-U-C-K.'

After several drinks we wandered across the piazza and down tortuous lanes lined with stone walls.

'They were built twisty like this to confuse the Saracen invaders,' he said.

Stopping outside a modest establishment called the Pensione Floridiana, we saw the porters patiently waiting.

'Here we are, dearie, you'll be all right here for a bit. We'll all have dinner in a little while when you've settled in.'

We walked into the small hall where the first person we saw was Emlyn Williams, the actor, talking fluently to the proprietor. It seemed as if we had come home. The dogs were delighted to be in a house with a garden once more. Mouche, with her proprietorial sense, greeted visitors in the hall.

Every day we would meet Norman at the Café Vittorio, which we called Giorgio's, about noon, when the campanile bell would boom its chimes and the church bell opposite would ring for the angelus.

At 1.00 pm precisely Norman would say:

'I must toddle off now, dearies. I'll call for you at four o'clock.'

Then there would be a planned expedition, so that before long we'd seen all over the island. At eighty years old Norman was still an amazing walker, thinking nothing of walking several miles up to a cave-like tavern above, the Arco Naturale, drinking one or two bottles of wine, and coming back to the piazza before yet another long uphill walk home. Of all the places he took us to I think Peppinella's cave was his favourite spot on Capri. It was literally an inhabited cave, the earth floor scrupulously swept, wooden tables and chairs, with fresh, cold wine made by Peppinella and her husband. Or sometimes we would go on the stiff walk up to the Villa Jovis, the ruined pharos nearby, where we drank with Carmolina, then nearly ninety, in her youth the island's most famous tarantella dancer, whom Norman had known for over fifty years. Her old tarantella costume was always to hand and, when she got bored with talking to us, she would dress us up in it. Then there was the old ruined Bishop's Palace in the middle of a huge vineyard where Norman would chat volubly to the inhabitants. Or perhaps it was the Piccola Marina, the small café there closed up for the winter, but always opened for the *signor Inglese*.

Sometimes while walking we were companionably silent; at other times he would tell of the history of the place, or some personal reminiscence, always in his erudite, crisp style. He peopled the places with ancient characters. On the occasions I didn't accompany them, Constantine would ask Norman about his early life, and as soon as he came back to the *pensione* he would make copious notes.

On one of our walks I remarked I hadn't seen any birds, which was strange.

'They shoot them all,' he said. 'The quails used to fly over here on their migration, but so many were slaughtered, they learned sense and now take a different route.'

We were sitting at Peppinella's one day when a young boy with a gun and a small haversack approached. Norman asked him in Capresi dialect what he had in the bag. He brought out a beautiful hoopoe.

'Surely he's not going to eat that?' I asked.

'They'll eat anything that flies,' Norman answered. 'Pity about that hoopoe, though, it's a rare bird here.'

Capri seemed inexpressibly beautiful: a livelier more colourful beauty than Bermuda, the limestone hills and mountains with their ever-changing colours, the Faraglione Rocks where Norman had found the first blue lizards in 1888; the sea shimmering, sometimes blue and often when the hot sun blazed down on it silver-gold, as if lit from underneath; the multi-coloured old and new houses, the peaceful symmetry of the Certosa; the Punta Tragara, and, out to sea, the large island of Ischia would appear as if floating on the water. It was all breathtaking, spiced with Norman's sparkling conversation, 'a sun of laughter'.

We met Norman's friends, too – the dear gentle lawyer Arthur Johnson and his beautiful wife Viola. He had been a great friend of Guillaume Appollinaire in Paris in the 1920s. The Johnsons lived in Rome but also had a gracious house, Molino a Vento, in Anacapri. Arthur Johnson was extremely well read, a good foil for Norman's pungent wit, and could be relied on to intervene with a quiet, amusing comment, always well taken by Norman. There was the musicologist Cecil Woolf who was to write a good bibliography of Norman's books for Nancy Cunard's book *Grand Man*. We were to see a lot of Cecil later on. Edwin Cerio, an impressive-looking man, who always appeared deep in thought as he walked about the island, wrote an excellent book about Capri

(*L'ora di Capri*) and wrote also with great perceptive finesse about Norman's own work. Then there were the two Prince Caracciolos; one tubby and gossipy who knew everybody's life story, or if he didn't, invented one; he was known as the 'day Caracciolo'. His brother, Prince Stefano Caracciolo, only appeared in the evening and was known as the 'night Caracciolo'. He was small and frail-looking, always dressed in a black cloak, which went well with his silver hair and fine features. Gracie Fields, just about to marry her Boris and long before she built her Lido, always used to call him 'Uncle', and was as cheerful and outgoing a person as you would wish to meet, sometimes breaking spontaneously into song as she walked up from the Piccolo Marina.

Baron Schack, the incredibly tall German who had lived in Capri for many years, looked the epitome of the German cavalry officer (he had been an Uhlan) with a sabre scar on his face, but was the gentlest of souls, whose principal occupation was searching for rare wild flowers which he would bring to Norman. When Goering had come to Capri during the war, Schack, being the senior German resident, was asked to lead a deputation to greet him. This he refused to do, saying he didn't see how Herr Goering had been promoted from Captain to Air Marshal in peacetime. On the Kaiser's birthday he would put on his helmet and what was left of his uniform and drink a toast to a photograph of the Kaiser. After knowing him for many months, I still called him *Herr Baron*, and as he called me by my first name I suggested maybe there was something less formal I could call him. He thought for a moment, then said:

'Yes, you can call me Schack.'

Then there was perhaps the most important of all Norman's friends, Kenneth Macpherson. Tall, with fine brown curly hair, a kind, sensitive, smiling face, Kenneth was the staunchest and truest of people. In an unobtrusive way he saw that Norman's last years were comfortable and agreeable, giving him every attention and consideration. In 1947 Kenneth bought the Villa Tuoro, high up on Tuoro or Telegrafo Hill overlooking the serene Certosa, a charming villa which he divided into two. The larger top floor with a large terrace he shared with his friend Islay de Courcy Lyons, an extremely good photographer. Below was a bedroom, sitting room and bathroom in perpetuity for Norman. Nancy Cunard has described the Villa Tuoro thus:

> . . . elaborately beautiful as the result of perfect taste and lavish development of natural resources, its terraces embowered, its rooms ideally coloured and furnished, spacious and comfortable . . . the enchanting company of Kenneth . . . when so disposed. Long, low rooms, shaded or light at will. Book-filled, everything in perfect order.

To begin with, Ettore, a little Naples urchin Norman had befriended, came as cook and to run Norman's messages. By the time we arrived late the following year Ettore had gone back to his parents; installed in his place was Antonino, or Tonino, a major-domo of a man, who according to Norman 'got a cabinet minister's salary'. There was also the maid Rita, and Peppino the odd-job boy.

Many were the perfect meals we had on that terrace, enjoying Tonino's home-made ravioli Caprese followed by exquisite veal, or Norman's favourite dish, tongue.

'Afraid I'm going to punish your tongue, my pet. I'm rather heavy-handed when it comes to tongue,' said Norman, always sitting with his back to 'all that ridiculous water'.

Those lunches particularly are like etchings done in pure shimmering crystal in my memory: the sun, the silver glinting waves far below us, the profundity of the many-coloured flowers, the good food, wine and charm of the witty, carefree company.

Then the cool, nectar-like drinks in the evening. Shall we dine here, or in the town? In the town tonight, duckums. Where shall it be? Gemma's in the cloister-like passages by the church? No, too hot. What about the Sett'Anni or the Savoia? We decide on the Savoia because it has a large door open on to the street and tables outside.

'Might be a bit nippy for that, later on,' says Norman. 'Don't forget, I'm beginning to break up.'

After three weeks at the *pensione* we decided to rent a villa, as we would be there for some time. The 'day' Prince Caracciolo, of course, was the person to ask and he put us in touch with Contessa Delafeld, who lived in Rome, and who owned the Casa Solatia on the via Mulo, once a twisty mule track, which led down to the Piccola Marina. It was a lovely house, large and well appointed with a huge terrace looking over the sea. A green patch of rough ground was in front opposite and it nestled below Monte Solaro. Behind the house lived Concetta, the permanent caretaker and housekeeper employed by the contessa, and her fisherman husband, her son and her daughter Rosetta. There were five bedrooms, two bathrooms, also a large *salone* opening on to the terrace. We paid the first month's rent and found that it was just about all we had left. The money from Cassell had not arrived despite constant enquiries. It began to get worrying, only too familiar. I was taking Italian lessons, so I was left to deal with the shops.

'Prego, vorrei aprire uno conto, per favore?' ('Please may I open an account?') was repeated in many places, at first to ready agreement, later to 'Non e possible, signora.'

I wrote to my family and asked them to go to Cassell to find out what had happened. It was simple: the Treasury were taking their time deciding to send sterling out of the country. An impossible situation: the money was there and we were unable to use it. My mother sent us small cheques, some of which never reached us; Kenneth lent us a little; and fortunately the very handsome butcher in the piazza fell in love with me. We could have any amount of the choicest meat, and when I said plaintively that our money still hadn't arrived he would wave his hand nonchalantly and say it didn't matter.

However, you get very tired of eating nothing but meat, with nothing except the occasional slice of bread to accompany it. I suggested Constantine might try his charms on the girl at the wine shop. He did get a few bottles, but nothing like the continuous amount of meat I got. The butcher was apparently a cousin of Concetta's, so when he asked if he could call one afternoon, Concetta produced a bottle of wine and entertained us very grandly with little cakes too, as though it was her house. She also found some wood for a fire.

Everything was made much worse by the weather – the coldest winter for thirty years. There was even snow, and all we had were light Bermuda clothes and few blankets. Stepping on the ceramic tiles when we got out of bed in the morning was like putting our feet in an ice bucket. We couldn't afford wood, only a little charcoal for the cooker, so we made do with some of those tiny charcoal braziers that you have to huddle over.

Fortunately, at a very critical moment we ran into two old friends, David Tennant (a cousin of the owner of the Gargoyle) and Peter Elder, a classics don whom we had met in London when he was in the American Army during the war. Both lent us what money they could spare, without any hesitation. It was a godsend. Peter Elder was an optimistic, outgoing man, whose learning sat lightly on him. Sometimes he was very boyish, always adventurous; his enthusiasm would often envelop me as well.

'Come on, Theodora, let's explore. I'm tired of passing that enormous hill on the way to the piazza and not knowing what's at the top of it.'

Never a mountain climber, I was apprehensive, but he persuaded me it would be easy. In fact it wasn't too bad, but it took all one's concentration, the small stones wretchedly and treacherously slipping when you thought you had a firm foothold. We made for a house at the top.

'They'll probably be delighted to see us,' he said. 'Must be almost shut off from all Capri life up here. Might give us a glass of wine.'

Eventually we reached the top, steadying ourselves on a sturdy stone wall before we looked over. A strange sight greeted us: a tall, very white-faced woman dressed in the style of about 1912 with a long black skirt, high collared blouse and a large straw hat. She walked up and down continuously, her hands clasped in front of her, apparently talking to herself on a long bare terrace. Behind her, at what seemed like a respectful distance, was a man also dressed in old-fashioned clothes. On a bench outside the villa sat a female servant in cap and apron and a male servant wearing a green apron. We watched, fascinated, for some minutes, the walking up and down never ceasing for a second. The house behind was grey in colour; there were no plants of any kind. It was like looking at an eerie black-and-white film.

'They look like crazy people,' said Peter, and I agreed. After a minute or two, he gasped:

'My God, they are. I've just remembered hearing some sort of story. Nearly forty years ago they murdered a close member of the family, I can't think who right now, and were shut away up here for life, with their keepers. There's no prison on Capri, you know.'

We stared at each other, wide-eyed, turned and went down the hill considerably faster than we had come up. Norman was at a café in the piazza when we got breathlessly down.

'That's right,' Norman replied when we told him of our adventure. 'They poisoned their father to get hold of his money. Very *cinquecento*, my deeaws. You should go up to Barbarossa's castle next. It's safer if you don't go too near the edge.'

Talking to Norman was like being in a magic circle of his creation. For brief moments you were allowed into his treasure house of past enjoyments. 'The pleasure of memory and reconstruction at a distance,' as he wrote in one of his books. Everything he saw or heard which interested him was carefully filed away in his mental storehouse. Sometimes he would shoot very unexpected questions at me.

'You were in India, weren't you? Did you ever go to Rawalpindi?'

'Many times, Norman. I loved all that part and Kashmir.'

'Is the regimental library still there?' he asked, and I replied it had been there in 1933, as my father was fond of using it. He was very interested in that.

'I spent three weeks in that library in 1898. I think the reading I did there gave me the idea of becoming a writer; I felt I gained a true understanding of literature in that library.'

I tried to learn more but the sudden flash of revelation was over. As he wrote himself in the Maurice Magnus pamphlet (or *A Plea for Better Manners*, a pungent essay Norman wrote to D. H. Lawrence), he liked 'to taste his friends and not to eat them'.

By February, over three months since we had arrived, the money had still not been released by the Treasury and we were desperate. The once-kindly

Throck and Constantine on Somerset Beach.

Graysbank Cottage viewed from the sea.

Father Tom and Constantine in 1947 at Graysbank.

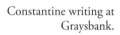

Constantine writing at Graysbank.

Casa Solatia, Capri, 1948.

Constantine and Norman Douglas at Giorgio's, Capri, 1948.

Baron Schack in his old uniform on the Kaiser's birthday.

Studio portrait of Theodora, Rome, 1949,
photographed by Superbi.

Gerald Kersh in the Hotel
Inghilterra, 1949.

Theodora in rehearsal for *Her Favourite
Husband*, 1949, with Margaret Rutherford
and Gordon Harker.

Theodora with Constantine and Flotow on the terrace of her apartment in the Piazza di
Spagna, 1950.

Sacomb's Ash, 1950.

Constantine with Giles Playfair on board MV *Grebe* on the way to Bordeaux in April 1953.

On the *chaise-longue* at Sacomb's Ash, 1954.

Constantine, Diana Graves and Minka in the garden of Sacomb's Ash, 1954.

Mimi Mounsey three months before her death in London, 1956.

Theodora on a lonely walk with Minka and the cat along the 'engine path' in Allen's Green, Hertfordshire, 1958.

Arland Ussher in Wicklow, 1958.

George Morrison in his cutting room in
Dublin, 1959.

shopkeepers were very demanding, all except the butcher. Concetta, too, had been very kind, often leaving us little cakes and sometimes small fish from her husband's catch. At Christmas we had been asked to the Villa Tuoro and when we came home a tiny little tree had been put in the *salone* – little branches of fir to resemble a tree – and underneath little fritters of apple rings. She was such a dear little woman, round and short with fat little legs which moved at an amazing pace.

Then I remembered my father's advice: 'If you're broke always go to the best hotel. Not only do they never ask for money until you leave, but you might see someone you know.' Constantine thought it an excellent idea – we could sleep there until the money came – it couldn't be long now, surely – and come home during the day. Concetta would look after the dogs at night. So we packed our best suitcase with a minimum of things, night clothes and toilet articles, and set off for La Palma Hotel, the larger Quisisana being closed for the winter. They were delighted to see us.

What a night we had: expensive cocktails, something we usually avoided, in the bar, then we ordered a soufflé, followed by a whole fish grilled with herbs and excellent wine. We sat on our little balcony with a night cap, saying what a capital idea it had been, before having a most comfortable night with plenty of blankets on the bed. The next day we went home and towards evening looked forward to a repeat performance. The following evening when we ordered our drinks at the bar, we were asked to pay for the previous two days, as the bar did not belong to the hotel, but was a *concessione*. This was certainly something that never arose in my father's time. Constantine explained, but it made no difference – no more drinks until the bill was paid. By the next morning, after an uneasy night, the news had percolated to the hotel manager who greeted us sternly.

He was sorry, but we would have to leave and we must leave our luggage as surety.

In melancholy manner we trudged home, picking up yet another parcel of meat on the way and telephoning the American Express at Naples to see if by any chance . . .?

'Niente, signor.'

The next few weeks were very hard. I was beginning to think we had starved in some of the most beautiful places in the world. True, we were invited out a few times, but there was no coffee for breakfast, and only an occasional loaf of bread which got stale very quickly, so sometimes I would fry it in dripping which we would sprinkle with salt. It was better than nothing at all. I pawned my ring, the last thing of value I had left, but got very little for it. By now the whole of Capri must have known we were penniless; news travels as quickly there as in Ireland. I did hide enough money for the ferry to Naples, just in case. Towards the end of February, the note came from the American Express to say money was there. Over went Constantine jubilantly on the early morning ferry. I went to Giorgio's to wait with Norman for his return that evening, a new lightness in my step as I walked up. No Constantine. I waited for several hours, then trudged miserably home in the dark. The next morning early, a telephone call, and a sad small voice saying:

'Can you come over? I've been drugged and I'm frightened. What shall I do?'

I said I had no money left and whatever had happened?

Slowly, and in a voice very unlike his own, he told me it wasn't Cassell's money at all, but $50 in royalties. He had gone to a bar, had a beer and got talking to some Italians at another table. He remembered having another drink with them, which must have been drugged, and much later, early this morning, waking up in an unfamiliar quarter of Naples in a bed in a huge room with a painted ceiling and a muddle of women's clothes about. Nobody else was there, but almost all the $50 was gone. He felt dreadful. I advised him to go to the American hospital in Naples to have a check-up, then if he had enough left to come home.

While he was talking there was a knock at the door. Telling him to count what he had I turned round and opened it. The postman. Quickly I ripped open the envelope and turned back to the hall phone.

'It's here darling, Cassell's money – it must be that. Go quickly and get it, then go to the hospital, just in case. Darling, darling, don't worry, I'll meet you this evening at Giorgio's. Oh! Thank God!'

CHAPTER THIRTY-FIVE

After all our debts had been paid there was still enough money left for us to live comfortably for several months, so we had a certain peace of mind. Various friends had written saying how much they would like to visit. Mimi, Constantine's sister, had also suggested coming to stay. It was a warm and sunny spring, the hillsides glowing with the golden glory of *ginestra*, the prolific broom, and a mass of fragile early flowers on the mountain, plants of which Baron Schack liked to bring me little bunches. We had closed some of the bedrooms up in the winter; now, with the huge vines of bougainvillaea starting to bloom, the windows were flung open, the rooms prepared for guests. It was while going through an old handsome chest of drawers, removing bits of fluff and lining them with paper, that my eye caught a glint of metal stuck down one side. It took me some time to extricate; then I saw it was a small holy medal of the Virgin Mary. Examining it more closely, I thought the writing round it was in Greek for they were not Roman characters.

Norman's customary knock on the hall window with his walking stick disturbed me. I went to answer it; I still had the medal in my hand as I opened the door.

'Look what I've just found in one of the drawers, Norman. I think it's Greek.'

He examined it closely in the bright light of the terrace.

'Not Greek, duckums, it's Russian. Probably belonged to Gorki's summer wife. They lived in this house for a time, you know.'

'Gorki? Maxim Gorki the writer lived here? When, for heaven's sake?'

Norman was chuckling, then he stopped to take some snuff before replying.

'He settled in Capri about 1907, I think it was. He had a summer wife here, and a winter wife somewhere else. I only met the summer wife. Hm, hm, that would be hers; very holy she was, living in sin and feeling guilty about it. All humbug.'

I wanted to know much more, but Norman was always a bit miserly about revealing scandal, telling you only so much. He took a swallow of his wine before continuing.

'I remember calling one morning in the 1920s, the maid took me upstairs and he called to me to come in. He was standing naked in front of a cheval looking-glass, admiring himself. I heard him say:

'"Ten books, one play, twenty-seven women, fifty-five years old today. Not bad, not bad."

'Then he turned round and we had a birthday drink. Polished off a good bottle, duckums!'

Try as I would nothing more could be gleaned about Maxim Gorki, except that I gathered Norman must have liked him very much.

Constantine took his daily stroll with Norman and would go through his notes most evenings in his charming work room which opened out on to a small balcony. In the mornings he would write until a little after noon, when he would join me if I had been shopping, in the piazza, and also Norman and any of our friends who were there. Always at Giorgio's Café in the morning, but the piazza in the evenings. Everyone always bought their own drinks unless it was a particular celebration. Few houses had telephones, so messages were carried by young boys glad to earn a few lire. Grubby little notes would be pressed into one's hand: 'Can you come up this evening at 6.30 pm?' Which would be answered by the same method. Norman produced a very sickly-looking child to run my messages, called Eduardo. He was suffering from severe undernourishment with consequent ailments. I must look after him, Norman said.

My first step was to entice him into a bath, firmly resisted to begin with, but once in he refused to get out for some hours; then good, regular meals and a new suit of clothes which a tailor made from an old suit of Constantine's. He looked a different child in a few weeks, becoming very devoted to me and the dogs. Norman walked me for miles, past Peppinella's cave, to where Eduardo's mother and a younger child about three, called Carmine, lived. This, too, was a cave but so clean and homely-looking, with one huge double bed covered with snow-white sheets, a table, a few rickety chairs and a cupboard.

'Never give her money,' said Norman. 'We'll take food for them. Otherwise she'll spend money on a bedspread or some damn-fool thing.'

So often we would walk up with pasta, flour, cheese and perhaps some fruit. They all spoke only Capresi dialect, difficult for me to understand, but through Eduardo I learned a little. I grew fond of the family and wondered what would happen when the baby she was carrying was born. Concetta didn't approve of Eduardo at all. *Cattivo*, naughty, she called him, but when pressed could give me no details. Also the family were *straniero*, foreign, which I found difficult to believe as the mother was obviously a native of Capri. I found out later that their name was *Albanese*, which is of course 'Albanian' in English, but that must have been a very long while ago. In any event he stayed as 'my boy' all the time

I was on Capri. One morning he arrived handsomely dressed in a new suit and handed me a packet of sugared almonds. But where had he got the new suit and everything?

'From my uncle in America for my first communion.'

Oh dear, I thought, how much better to have sent small amounts regularly to help them. I realized how right Norman had been about giving money.

Our first guests were Roy and Lotte Sworn. He was a surgeon from Stafford, his wife an amusing Austrian girl. Both were our good friends and had been very kind to us before we left England. Almost immediately Con's sister Mimi arrived with plans for an indefinite stay. The Treasury allowed tourists only £50 at that time; however, her allowance from Georgette came from America – not that, as long as I knew her, she was ever able to manage on it. They all revelled in the beauty and interest of Capri and felt very relaxed after the rigours of England. Apart from the long and fascinating walks with Norman, we all went with Concetta's husband in his boat to the Blue Grotto which Norman had written a monograph about in 1904.

Lotte wanted to go to the Swedish writer Axel Munthe's house, then not at all like the industry it is today.

'Oh, don't be so German, Lotte,' Roy said in his sad voice.

But to Munthe's house, Materita, we went, a rather boring little villa with brown paintwork inside, most of the cramped rooms in disarray, but not much to display in any event. The garden had a few rather poor pieces of statuary, and all in all I found it very disappointing. Even Lotte found it difficult to enthuse about it, so when talking to Norman she also talked about 'the wonderful book *San Michele*'.

'Hah! Wonderful book,' said Norman. 'It was written by Rennell Rodd, you know. Munthe was very good at getting people to do things for him. Especially rich and titled women; even persuaded the Queen of Sweden he was related to her husband.' Here he paused and mimicked an adoring woman:

'"Poor Doctor Munthe, his sight is going, you know, we must raise a subscription for him." Funny thing, I was lunching with him just about then and he was able to pick a minute fly out of his pasta which I could hardly see.'

His dislike of 'the dear doctor' was apparent in every word.

'Those statues he dug up in his garden, quite true, dearies, but he forgot to mention he bought them in Naples and had them buried there first. Well, I must evaporate now.'

I often thought Capri resembled a great big beautiful railway station, people coming and going all the time. However, there were also colourful characters who paid longer visits. Mimi stayed on and decided to settle in Italy. David

Jeffreys, a great friend of Norman's, was vice consul in Naples. He had a small place in Positano called La Brescia, which he used for some weekends and offered to lend her. Mimi and I took the ferry to Sorrento, then a very rickety bus to Positano along that fearsome coast road with its low, then very much decayed walls at the top of the cliffs. The long drop down was only too evident. We soon found the top of the hundreds of steps which lead down to the beach, to the then only café there, the Buca di Baco, where we had been told to go. Positano is like a giant amphitheatre, the beach the stage, with a permanent backdrop of the ever-changing sea. Villas were dotted about the curved cliffs, not very many then, with just a few hotels mixed amongst them. The beach of grey-brown volcanic sand was the focal point on which many dramas were enacted.

The scene which greeted our eyes at the Buca could have been from a Buñuel film: tables set out on a small terrace with, as we found, a very cosmopolitan group of characters drinking and talking on a variety of subjects. Mimi was extremely attractive to look at and we were the object of much attention. We, too, were quite interested in them, for like many parties at another table, everyone appears to be wittier and more amusing than oneself. After lunch we decided to look for La Brescia, so we asked the attentive waiter where it was. A rather languid English voice coming from the next table was accompanied by an arm waving to his right.

'It's quite near, along there. Isabella will show you.'

A very beautiful Italian girl with long, glossy dark hair stood up and we followed her along the beach, past many paint-flaked houses with small terraces. At the end was La Brescia, a charming little house with a few rooms, simply furnished. It was just right.

'Come back and join us,' said Isabella. 'I hope you are coming to stay here.'

We were introduced to the rest of the party. The possessor of the languid voice was an Englishman called Alex Smith who lived in Positano with Isabella. A very jolly, rotund American with a laughing face was Reynolds Packard, a journalist who lived in Rome with his equally large wife, Pibe. There was an elderly English couple, whose names I never discovered over the months; also an attractive young man, very blond, called Pinky, sitting next to a woman addressed as Franca. It was all very easy and pleasant. The thought of the long walk up the steps to catch the bus became daunting. A swim, maybe, would freshen us up. Coming back from the sea, we saw that a tall, dark, bearded man had joined the table and was standing by Packard's chair. He had an extremely arresting face.

'Wow,' said Mimi, 'look at that.'

I looked up to see an amused yet slightly arrogant expression on the handsome face as he said 'Hello' and vanished around the corner. On the bus he was sitting in the seat in front of us. The damp bathing suits we had hung out of the window were flapping about his head, so we took them down, exchanging a few words only.

At Giorgio's, Constantine and Norman were having their evening drink while we enthused about Positano.

'Positano. I was staying there last year with David Jeffreys when I was homeless. People used to go there when they got turned out of Capri. Nobody's ever been turned out of Positano. Well, dearies, I must evaporate – I've had a tiring time with Graham Greene – ruins my whole morning,' Norman said as he toddled off.

Graham Greene had arrived in Capri early in the month, accompanied by a blonde woman and three or four of her blonde children. He had bought a charming villa, called Rosaio, in Anacapri, where Compton Mackenzie and Francis Brett-Young had also lived and worked. I think he had been instrumental in getting the Italian Lux Films to sign a preliminary contract with Norman for the rights to his book *South Wind*, which was to be filmed on Capri. Graham was to write the script, hence Norman being with him for consultations. However, as with many films, difficulties arose before filming started.

'I just want to see Norman gets his money,' Graham confessed to me one evening.

The film proceedings fluctuated throughout the summer. There were about three film companies already working on Capri, and it was, as Norman pointed out, 'in danger of developing into a second Hollywood, and that, it seems, is precisely what it aspires to become'. It was due to these film companies being there that I first met Vernon Jarratt, then working with the film lighting company Moles Richardson, having been film attaché in Rome after the war. Vernon was a very professional, painstaking person at whatever he did. Jovial and pink-faced, he appeared a typical Major Thompson type of Englishman, but underneath he was far from blimpish, being outspoken and amusing, with a sense of fun. He lived just outside Rome on the via Appia.

Vernon Jarratt was at the house one evening with Mimi, Peter Elder and Norman. Norman kept on about some poor people from Trani he had asked here to meet him. A knock came at the door, which, when I opened it, revealed a small Italian man standing there in an odd assortment of mixed clothes, a beret and a pair of sneakers. I didn't catch the name, so I assumed he was part of the poor family from Trani when he asked for Norman. I asked him to wait in the hall while I fetched Signor Douglas. A burst of laughter came from the hall as I was going back into the drawing room. After a moment they both came in and Norman introduced the quaint little man as Mario Soldati, the well-known Italian film director who was to direct *South Wind*. Mario never allowed me to forget it, but it was a fortunate meeting for me as time went on.

My mother wrote that she was coming for a visit in April, so Mimi and I decided to go to Rome to meet her.

——

It was not the first time I had been to Rome; that was almost ten years earlier. On the journey back from India with my father and Manny, the ship called in at Naples and we went ashore. There were large notices up indicating that Mussolini was offering very reduced fares for those travelling to Rome.

'What a capital idea,' said my father. 'I've done this journey so many times before. I'm weary of the ship; let's get off and go to Rome.'

After our luggage was brought up from the hold, we set off on a long, extraordinary expedition. At once I felt Rome to be familiar, for brightly coloured prints of St Peter's had decorated the walls of several convents; at home, long-dead relations had left water-colours of the Colosseum and other buildings as mementos of their visits. However, in reality the sights were breathtaking. Even all those endless books about the Gallic wars which had bored me so much at school came to life amidst the ancient dust and stones of the Roman Forum. What impressed me most as a young girl was that it all mingled so well with modern Rome. On every street corner or in some alleyway were traces of earlier civilizations. I had seen some very beautiful buildings in India of different religions and culture; here, walking along the via Sacra under the Arch of Titus, I could share in the glories of Roman triumphs. Who was it who said, 'Go to Rome first and let all the rest follow'?

Every day we visited a new wonder and marvelled. We would sip coffee or a *granita* at the eighteenth-century Café Greco, shop in the via Condotti, perhaps dine at Casina Valadier (built by Napoleon's architect, Valadier), gazing out over the magnificent panorama of the Eternal City. My father and Manny visited monasteries, more for tasting the wines than any religious experience, or so it seemed from their condition when they returned.

Arrangements were made for a papal audience, with all the excitement of buying new clothes and, for me, a veil. This was one time when my father was adamant: Manny was not to accompany us. He was of another religion; this was to be a personal and private visit for him with his daughter. However,

Manny displayed as much excitement as I did, taking the greatest interest in the preliminary proceedings, buying new clothes, too, when we shopped. The day arrived, the maid at the hotel helping me to dress and to arrange my veil; it was a fine, fair Roman morning. On the way Manny was left at a nearby café and told very firmly to wait for us there.

The Swiss Guards in their colourful costumes, the crowded, ornate anteroom, the atmosphere one of expectation and solemnity – after a little while we were ushered into the presence and told to kneel on a cushion which was provided. There were other people behind us, but not too many. I tried to compose my thoughts, think of holy things and not let my gaze wander about the room. I looked to the ground. Then behind me I heard a slight clearing of the throat, a little cough, which was only too familiar. I half-turned, my father frowned at me, but in that second I caught a glimpse of Manny's swarthy face and black hair. A voice was talking and I could see white vestments in front of me. In a mysterious way Manny was back at the café before us, looking as angelic as he could.

'This is the end between us, Manny. I particularly asked you not to come with us, to leave us alone for once, not always to be padding behind. I'm very annoyed indeed; this is the last straw and I'm finished with you.' My father stopped suddenly in the middle of his tirade, saying:

'But how on earth did you get in without an invitation?'

Manny beamed, for he knew my father's lightning moods.

'I said I was with you, that *you* had it.'

'I think it was very clever of Manny; and what harm has it done?' I asked.

There was very nearly a rift in their friendship, but humour prevailed in the end. From then on Manny came everywhere with us, kissing St Peter's toe in the basilica like the most pious of Catholics.

––––

Mimi and I were advised to stay at the Hotel Inghilterra in the Bocca di Leone just behind the beautiful and historic Piazza di Spagna. It was the most perfect old rabbit-warren of a hotel which in the past had housed a good many writers, painters and musicians. It was very cheap with an old-fashioned comfort and few amenities such as private baths and so on. To me it was not unlike the Cavendish in London, and I loved it. There was little service, no food, and only a small bar to the left as you entered where you could also get coffee and sometimes a roll or a packet of biscuits. That bar, small as it was, catered for a most interesting selection of people of all nationalities. If you wanted to meet someone in Rome you went to the Hotel Inghilterra, for the bar had the atmosphere of a club. It transpired that Reynolds and Pibe Packard lived at the Inghilterra, although they usually drank at the press club, the Stampa Estera in the via della Mercede, a few streets away.

In a matter of hours we were talking to Tennessee Williams, looking a bit dazed, with a young golden-haired, boyish Truman Capote; Eugene Deckers, an English actor who was acting in a film there; an American photographer called Carl Perutz; sad-looking Gerald Osborne, a young, slightly mysterious Englishman who lived in the via Babuino; and a handsome, rather shy German called Reinhard Woolf, whom I had met briefly before, with his ebullient friend Count Bendi Esterhazy. Reinhard was a tall, slender young man with kind brown eyes and straight black hair brushed back. He had been studying law before the war, and had been in the north of Italy in 1945. They usually ate at a nearby trattoria called Toto's, now alas no more, which served excellent, cheap and good food.

Something unexpected always happened when you were with Mimi, for she was irrepressibly full of fun and high spirits. This time was no exception. Our new friends seemed delighted to take us around Rome, Gerald Osborne appointing himself as my guide, while Eugene Deckers appeared taken with Mimi. Gerald took us to the Flora Hotel, where the airport bus arrived, to meet my mother, who looked very pale and not at all her exuberant self. The next day we showed her a little of Rome, Gerry bringing us to St Peter's, and the little-known coffee bar in the basilica, then taking her to Toto's for lunch; there we saw the handsome, dark stranger of Positano sitting with a very slim young woman, not pretty but extremely striking, her large sad brown eyes seeming to dominate her small pointed face. As I looked over, smiling, he nodded, his companion's face showing an expression of surprise.

'Who's that man?' I queried. Gerry looked in my direction.

'Oh, that's Peter Tompkins and his wife. He's supposed to be an illegitimate son of Bernard Shaw. He did something frightfully brave during the war. Don't know what he does now.'

The small restaurant was full of people who all knew each other, and who I was to know well later, such as the writer Sybille Bedford and her friend Esther Arthur; Reinhard and Bendi; and an American painter called Gabriel Cohn. It was very like the atmosphere in a Paris café before the war.

My mother went to bed early to prepare for the long journey the next day. So when Mimi and I went down to the bar, Reinhard and Bendi suggested we should see some of Rome's night life. Eugene Deckers came as well, as he wasn't working the next day. I have only the vaguest memories of that long night, but I do remember a very sparkling dinner at the exclusive Whip Club, late drinks in the rather squalid all-night Café Notturno, frequented by journalists and many others, also Mimi driving a *carozza* down the via Veneto, a wildly protesting driver sitting beside her. It was about 4.00 am when we got back, the bus to Naples leaving at 8.30 am. Three hours' sleep, then a quick bath and the packing. The porter knocked at 8.00 am to collect our bags for the bus. We sat on the bed feeling pleased with ourselves while the luggage was all whisked away. Everything was ready. Then we looked at each other, both in open kimono-like dressing gowns.

'My God! We've packed our clothes!'

My mother appeared, saying 'not dressed yet', and we told her. Heavens knew where our bags were, as the bus first made a tour of the hotels for the luggage. Another knock on the door:

'L'autobus e qui, signore.'

What on earth could we do? I thought of Reinhard who lived at the Inghilterra and whose room was just along the balcony on our floor.

'I'll go along the balcony and wake Reinhard, he'll know what to do.'

Roused from deep sleep, he took over immediately.

'Don't worry, Theodora, we'll manage. I'll put on some clothes and come along to your room.' In minutes he was there, then downstairs on the telephone, and he traced the bags to the bus station, where they would be left. Within half an hour he was back with them, looking as imperturbable as ever.

'You can take a later bus, I've arranged it. Get some clothes on and we'll all go and have breakfast.'

When we were ready he called a taxi and we all went off to the bus terminus, where he checked us in. The bus would go in a few hours. Then he took us to a small café within an easy walk, which was nothing more than a room in a house with a large wooden table in the centre. There we had freshly baked bread, hot from the oven, farm-fresh butter and boiled eggs with the most delicious very slightly sparkling white wine. The most exquisite meal ever, and we too were all sparkling by the time it was over.

We caught the ferry to Capri easily; there was nobody to meet us, so we had a drink while we found some boys to bring our luggage to the house. Nobody there either, except the dogs.

About nine o'clock Constantine came home rather drunk and aggressive. He hardly addressed my mother at all, only saying to us before he left the room:

'Have a good time?'

We had been away for four days but it was obvious that something had happened during that time to bring about the change.

CHAPTER THIRTY-SIX

My mother's visit was not a success, for Constantine's aggressive mood lasted almost all the time she was there and was extended to me when he saw that I was spending time with her which he felt should be given to him. I hadn't seen her since I had left England in 1946 and it was her first holiday abroad since we had both been in France in 1939. I was determined that she would enjoy at least part of her time with us. She had known and liked Norman in London, Baron Schack amused her, but she grew very fond of Reinhard, who had come down to stay in Capri. He was always charming, and I came to rely on him as a calm, civilized person who was helpful and easy to talk to.

Constantine seemed reluctant to talk to me, which had never happened before; he showed only hostility if I tried to find out what was wrong. Even the good news that *The Arabian Bird* had been sold to Denmark didn't change him, except to make him spend more on drink, and more and more nights in a newly opened club called Tabu, with Mimi, an American girl and her friend, a young sculptor. The house was divided in a way, as we only met for occasional meals and drinks. Through Reinhard we met a Swedish painter called Harald Klinckowström, a very engaging personality, with a fierce Saxon wife called Blanca who first thing took me aside and said Harald mustn't drink as he was ill. He seemed very lively without it and we all enjoyed his company.

My mother and I were sitting one morning in the piazza – Constantine had gone to Naples – when we were joined by Reinhard and Harald, who said Blanca had gone to Naples for the day too. It was late when we all decided to have lunch at Sett' Anni, which had a tiny balcony overlooking the terraces down to the Marina Grande and the funicular. During lunch I asked Harald what was the matter with him that he couldn't drink, and he replied:

'Nothing at all. Blanca just says that to stop me drinking.'

'Right,' said Reinhard. 'You had better start now. You have to catch up with us.'

Another bottle of wine was ordered as we all grew happier every moment, then yet another and maybe another too.

'Siesta time,' we said, looking at the late hour on our watches. 'Leave that bottle, we can drink it tomorrow.'

Reinhard got up to go and settle the bill. The door to the main restaurant was locked. We shouted, banged and rattled, but it was obvious the owners had shut up and gone for their siesta. Our table had been against the main wall, and, looking out, we realised we wouldn't have been seen by them.

'They'll be back soon,' said Reinhard.

'I don't care if they never come back,' cried Harald.

'It's the nicest day I've had here,' exclaimed my mother.

I said nothing just then, hoping they would return before the ferry.

But they didn't: we saw the ferry come in, the funicular disgorge, Constantine and Blanca on the terrace outside. They were talking and looking around, even up. It was a little nerve-racking.

'My God! Blanca, and I'm drunk,' said Harald.

'Constantine! Whatever can we say?'

'We were only having lunch,' said my mother. 'It's not our fault.'

Reinhard was calmer than usual. We heard the door of the restaurant unlocking, saw the owners' amazement when they saw our faces pressed to the glass. They started to laugh and laugh and laugh, and approached our doors with another bottle of wine.

'Just one glass,' said Harald.

'I need something,' echoed my mother.

I took just one. Reinhard swallowed his quickly.

'I'll go out and find out where they are. Then you follow when I come back.' The owners were quite hilarious and begged us to stay for dinner. Reinhard returned.

'Constantine's drinking with Norman. There's no sign of Blanca. I think it's quite safe to come out.'

We were all halfway across the piazza when we saw a *carabinieri* approaching; he stopped in front of us and, addressing me, said:

'The Countess Klincköwstrom wishes to see you at the station.'

Bewildered, we followed him, having sent Harald back to his hotel. It appeared Blanca had caught sight of us on the balcony, the table covered with bottles, and had at once gone to the *carabinieri* and reported that I was trying to poison her husband. What had I to say?

Reinhard, with his most urbane manner, took over in fluent Italian. There seemed to be a certain amount of argument; then, quite suddenly, the *carabiniere* were apologizing, Blanca was ushered out firmly, and they shook hands with us, smiling broadly.

Harald was kept in close confinement for a few days after that, then managed somehow to escape. My mother and I walked home and looked the picture of domesticity when Constantine returned.

The time came for my mother to go home. In an impulsive moment she had given Constantine most of her travel allowance soon after she arrived and was now left with very little. He disappeared after dinner before I had time to ask him for some money to get to Rome. Mimi had finally gone to Positano, so there was no appealing to her. Late that night we found him at the night club, Tabu, looking very annoyed at our appearance. On being asked for some money, his reply was:

'I have very little money and what I have I need for myself.' It was very uncharacteristic.

Could we appeal to Reinhard yet again? It was almost one o'clock in the morning and vital my mother returned in a few days. When I woke him yet again he said he too was going on the *rapido* to Rome in the morning and would meet us at the boat. It wasn't easy at 7.30 am struggling up the via Mulo with our luggage, as the boy hadn't turned up. We had a little over a thousand lire left. There was no sign of Reinhard at the boat, but over a cup of coffee we decided we were better in Capri with no money than in Naples. Later I plodded up the steps, saving the lire on the funicular, to look for Reinhard to see what had happened. He too was distraught, having had most of his money stolen the previous evening. He would get more when the only bank opened, and meet us at 5.30 pm. Did I need a little now? It seemed a very long day; we were reluctant to go up to the piazza, and spent it at the Marina Grande, wandering about, eating very little and waiting, waiting.

When we finally got to the Inghilterra in Rome very late, we found it was booked out owing to the Rome Horse Show. Reinhard offered us his room there, saying he would find somewhere else. It was only a single room, however, so it meant more telephoning, another taxi, until well after midnight when we got a hotel and gratefully got to bed.

At a tearful farewell the next day, my mother pressed a cheque into my hand.

'Try to find someone to cash it and keep part of it for an emergency like this. I wish you would come back with me for a little while. You have to pay Reinhard back, too.'

I looked at the fifty-pound cheque, wondering what to do with it, for it was quite impossible to cash it in the normal way. Wandering about the nearby streets, I passed the Ambasciatori Hotel, where my father, Manny and I had stayed when we departed from that eventful passage from India.

For old time's sake I went into the crowded bar and ordered the cheapest drink, mineral water with lemon. Again I remembered my father saying:

'Always go to the best hotel, you're bound to see someone you know.'

The bar itself was packed with men in uniform. I looked closer; yes, it was some of the teams riding at the horse show. The uniform at the end was familiar, and wasn't that . . .? I moved over to see more clearly – the Irish team. The laughing face of my father's old friend Captain Dan Corry turned slightly towards me.

'I suppose you don't remember me?' For an instant the weathered face looked at mine.

'Begod, I do,' he said. 'You're Adam's daughter. A great little girl on a horse. Not so little now, though. What'll you have? Coming to the show? Tomorrow's our big day.'

As drink after drink was put in front of me, I thought more and more about the cheque in my bag. Could I, would he, be able to cash it? I must do something quickly, now.

'Could you ever cash me a cheque? I've run out of money. It's my mother's, so it's all right,' was gabbled very quickly. Within minutes my bag was stuffed with pound notes.

'Sure that's enough, now? Here, take this too. Many's the time Adam's helped me out.'

I left to find a *cambio*, the banks being closed by that time. I changed it, luxuriously took a taxi to the Inghilterra, repaid Reinhard and went back to my hotel. I rang Vernon Jarratt, who asked me to dinner, and I told him briefly a little of what had happened.

'Give me half, Theodora, I'll keep it as a safety valve for you. You know if you take it all back you'll give it to Con.'

I gave him the half I had left. I also wrote a cheerful letter to my mother.

Travelling back to Capri, I was in an optimistic mood. Now, with the house to ourselves at last we would get back to the old comradeship. No more of this exhausting hostility. Concetta was the only person in the house when I got back. She burst out of the kitchen with a voluble flow of Italian which seemed to be about the dogs. Where were they? La Signora Mimi had taken Flotow to Positano and the old dog was ill. She had made a bed for her in the *salone*. Mouche, who had never had a thing wrong with her, was certainly ill, but with what? She looked sad and dejected and was unable to stand up. Her back legs seemed paralysed. I rubbed them and lifted her on to her feet and she wagged her tail feebly. Where did the vet live? Another flow of Italian, from which I gathered there wasn't one on Capri, but a Neapolitan vet came over once a week. There was a German woman who looked after sick dogs; Concetta would find her tomorrow. No, she did not think Il Signor would be here for dinner. Perhaps he was with Signor Douglas? I stayed with Mouche a little while, giving her something to eat and helping her out to the terrace. She seemed a little better.

Norman was dining alone at the Savoia, so I asked if I could join him. Constantine might look in later. He looked at me quizzically:

'Mummy gone home? I like her, not always fussing. Didn't seem to think the pins and needles in my hand was much to worry about. I'm just breaking up I suppose, my dear. Enjoy Rome? Archie said he couldn't find any pretty girls when I found him that job in Rome. Bah! Rome's *full* of pretty girls. Damn fool.'

It was the night for settling his monthly *conto* at the trattoria. I always dreaded this, being very bad at arithmetic. He would make everyone add it up, to make sure they 'hadn't cocked it on, dearie'. He himself was equally bad at addition – 'those infernal mathematics', he called it. When he took his examination for the Diplomatic Service in 1893 he had been top in everything and next to bottom in mathematics. Both our totals would end up differently, but always in Norman's favour. I got to believe the restaurant did it deliberately, for they seemed to enjoy it thoroughly. Telling him about Mouche, I said I would go back now, but not before he had promised to come to dinner the following evening. He would never dine with us more than about once a week, as he said, 'I know what an infernal nuisance entertaining is, my dear.'

About midnight I went to bed; much later I heard Constantine come in, and feigned sleep when he came to bed. He came down to breakfast just as I was finishing, with what looked like a hangover; I said I was going up early to try to find the animal woman, also to do some shopping as Norman was coming to dinner. Would he join me at Giorgio's? A quiet affirmative was given.

Having our lunchtime drinks with Norman, the American girl and a tall, blonde Englishwoman greeted Constantine affectionately. I was introduced to the English girl; her name was Gavrelle Verschoyle, her husband being at the British Embassy in Rome. I mentioned I was in Rome for a few days and that I had been to the horse show, a great mistake on my part for it led to endless questioning and acrimony later that evening because of Constantine's mistrust and jealousy.

Several days later he said he wanted to talk to me, which I was glad about, for we had discussed many things in the past and he was obviously worried about something. We sat on the terrace after breakfast, the early, yet hot, May sun warming our shoulders. He didn't see how he was going to finish the book about Norman, honestly discussing his sex life and its great influence on his writing. What on earth could he do? He'd written about four chapters and was now irrevocably stuck. In the 1940s society's attitude to sexual misdemeanours was not as liberal as today. It would have been impossible to persuade English-speaking countries that it was quite common practice for poor Italian families to 'loan' their older children, girls and boys, to rich (as they thought) foreigners, in exchange for money which went towards their dowries, or their education. Alas, too, he couldn't 'get round Eric', now a happily married chief superintendent in East Africa. Did he have to be explicit about it? Couldn't he write round it? To which the answer always was, not if he was to tell the truth, as Norman had insisted. I suggested he talk to Norman to see if he couldn't think of a way. But all his life Norman had defied authority, both in lifestyle and in some of his books. It wasn't the sort of idea to appeal to him.

Indeed it would be easier to persuade many that there was in Norman an affiliation with the wise old centaur Chiron who spent much time advising and instructing the young. It was not difficult, either, to be certain he would have infinitely preferred to renounce immortality for some modern-day Prometheus rather than suffer long drawn out, incurable pain.

We were in a strange country, with very little money, unable to work, with the awful prospect of being penniless once more.

'Why don't you finish *Cousin Emily*, the novel you started in Bermuda? You can still go on with your walks and talks with Norman just in case you think of a way, yet you would have another book ready to sell.'

He nodded, looking glum, showing no enthusiasm at all for my idea, and wandered off, saying he was going up to the piazza.

The German woman, to whom Mouche took an instant dislike, arrived with the vet, who didn't seem to know what was wrong with the dog, but gave me some pills for her and a prescription. She seemed a little better but still could only take a few tottering steps. It was an added worry. I sat on the terrace for some time. Was it true, then, what Goethe said: 'Beginnings are always delightful; the threshold is the place to pause'? I paused to remember how many knife-pangs of hunger I had known, in Paris, London, Bermuda, and in this beautiful, sun-filled villa where we had searched in vain sometimes for even an edible crust of bread. There was not even a scrubby tree or bush to bear fruit in this planned, pretty garden. I walked up to get the prescription filled, later joining Constantine and Norman at Giorgio's. A tall man was leaving as I arrived, apparently someone attached to the British Council in Naples.

'British Council twaddle,' said Norman; 'coming over here to teach the Italians how to build houses. They were building magnificent houses when the English were still painting themselves blue and living in caves, bah!'

I enquired how he was after our late night, as I hadn't seen him since.

'Decidedly squimpy, my dear.'

'We did consume eleven bottle of wine, Norman. I didn't feel all that good either.'

He affected not to hear what I had said.

'The doctoressa was there this morning. Insists I have to drink a lot of liquid and do the goosestep. Goosestep, duckums, whatever next? Get up my circulation, she says. Ever hear such rubbish? Takes me off whisky to wine, didn't dare suggest water, anyway it can't be good for arterio-sclerosis, can it? Most of this wine is water, hah! Goosestep indeed, as well as walking about five miles a day.' He slapped the empty glass down on the table.

'If that muck's able to check arterio-sclerosis, dearie, it's time to put your trust in God! How's that dog of yours? Vet come yet?'

I told him what had occurred and he made that loud 'hah' noise which sounded like a cross between a growl and a muffled bark.

In the two weeks that followed, Mouche made no improvement; neither could Constantine think of any solution to his book. The only cheering news was that an Italian publisher had bought *The Arabian Bird*, a welcome and unexpected bonus, but as Constantine now had no agent, it would be up to him to get the money here. He did very little writing, mainly going through his notes, sometimes lengthening them.

One day a very handsome young German arrived saying Norman had asked him to call to look at the dog. He examined her, injected her, and the treatment seemed to do some good. I told the little German woman about it; she seemed mystified, making me describe him in detail, asking where he was staying. When I told her, she started to laugh, then speaking rapid German, which I asked her to repeat more slowly, she told me he wasn't a vet at all, but the Shah of Persia's psychiatrist. Could it be true or was it just Capri gossip? I begged her to find me a better vet, but she shook her head, and said the only good place was an animal hospital in Naples run by the old blind Princess Pignatelli, who used all her money and her house for sick dogs mainly, but also some cats. Would I let Mouche go there? Con and I talked it over, and after a week of no improvement I said I would take her over and spend a night to see how she liked it. I rang David Jeffreys, the vice consul, to book me into a hotel. It is not difficult to imagine the nightmare of a journey with a sick, heavy dog, on the ferry, then a taxi out to the Posilipo, where Norman had built a house in 1896 and lived with his wife.

The animal hospital was in a large *palazzo*; it had a pleasant atmosphere, a resident vet, the dogs housed in the large rooms with covered mattresses on the floor. The old blind princess was kind and gentle, grey hair framing her serene face as she sat in an elaborately carved chair. She caressed Mouche and asked what she looked like, her colour and so on, the sightless eyes looking ahead, not down at the dog. I went back to the large Londra Hotel, having said I would go out again in the evening. It seemed an endless tram journey, looking out all the time so as not to miss the house. Mouche seemed quite at home, comfortable on her linen-covered soft mattress, somehow pleased to be in a place which might make her better. I stayed until it was quite dark, talking quietly in my limited Italian to the princess, still sitting in the chair. I felt quite relieved.

On the way back I got off the tram a stop too soon, so walked along the quays in the warm night air. Then I saw three men advancing, a black American sailor being held up by a man on either side. He appeared very drunk. Not wishing to tangle with drunks, I hid in a gateway while they passed. As I came out I turned to see how far up they had gone and saw the sailor collapsed on the ground, the other two men bending over him. Quickly I slipped away, almost running until I reached the hotel. The next morning when the maid brought in my breakfast, she moved over to the window and stood looking out for some time. What was she looking at?

'Omicidio, signora.'

'*Omicidio?* Homicide? Where?'

It was difficult to follow her rapid Neapolitan accent with all the ends of the words chopped off. Murder? It seemed unlikely on that May morning. An American sailor had been knifed and robbed. This was accompanied by dramatic gestures. Along the quay, last night. It didn't take long to connect what I had seen with the murder. What should I do? I couldn't identify anyone. I telephoned David Jeffreys and he invited me to lunch. Upset as I was, I still remember the exquisite pasta with fresh basil and his cheerful attitude.

'Don't say a word, Theodora. As you say, you can't identify anyone and you'd be kept here for weeks of questioning. What good would it do? Come on, have some more wine and take the evening ferry back. It's happening all the time in Naples.'

Back in Capri that evening telling Con and Norman about it, Norman said:

'Hum, don't forget Naples is halfway to Baghdad.' A somewhat cryptic remark, nevertheless somehow applicable.

Towards the end of the month, yet another problem occurred. The Contessa Delafeld called and very politely, so delicately, said she must raise the rent to double for the summer months. She hoped that would be in order.

It was of course impossible.

More and more, one's tired brain thought in clichés or adages, words which over the centuries had been well used for similarly repetitive events. 'The more things change, the more they are the same.' Was it La Rochefoucauld who said that? Did it matter? We went to Positano, where Mimi had settled, now with a young Italian lover, and explored the possibilities of living there, as it was much cheaper, though at that time much more primitive. We had no furniture, no pots and pans, nothing but books, and there would be no chance of doing any more research into Norman's life. Mimi was delighted to see us, Flotow overjoyed by our visit. Mimi said could we take him back with us, as he had been asked to leave.

'Asked to leave? By whom and what on earth for?' we queried. 'He's the gentlest dog ever.'

'For chasing boys on the beach; the mayor has requested he leave,' Mimi answered. 'I told him straight. You can't blame the dog, he's only copying everyone else in Positano!'

Constantine was rather pleased: no person had ever been asked to leave, and it was rather a distinction when one's dog was.

During most of May we searched Capri for a suitable house at the right rent, but many places which had been empty all winter were filling up with families or lovers from all over Europe and America. We could not help but resent most of them, for what they engendered – as Norman wrote in a postscript to *Footnote on Capri*, published in 1952, four months after his death:

> The island is too small to endure all these outrages without loss of dignity – the pest of so-called musicians who deafen one's ears in every restaurant, roads blocked up by lorries and cars, steamers and motor boats disgorging a rabble of flashy trippers at every hour of the day.

However, it is probably true that everyone who has known Capri when it has been quiet and almost peopleless has felt the same and has complained, from the days of the Roman Emperors onwards. Eventually we took a house in a remote part of Anacapri. We were sad to leave Solatia; Concetta was almost in tears, insisting her daughter Rosetta accompany us, to see we were *comodo*.

The large, old, open taxi couldn't come down the via Mulo, which had many wide steps; it was waiting outside Concetta's small house on the road. Constantine, Flotow and I sat in the back, Rosetta in front with the driver. A sad leave-taking, Concetta's face unaccustomedly downcast. At the last moment little Eduardo came running up, begging to be brought with us. Alas no, but we would see him tomorrow. It was as though we were going to another country.

CHAPTER THIRTY-SEVEN

In 1949 Anacapri was very rural with a few old houses, and lanes rather than roads, which converged on to a road leading to a small piazza dominated by a church. The church was not large but had an extremely attractive ceramic floor. Around the piazza were some little houses, joined together, and some shops, the largest being a grocery on the corner; it was pleasant inside, with old wooden counters, wooden shelves and drawers. For such a village-like community it was remarkably well stocked. There was also a small café. A bus to Capri and back ran several times a day but stopped running quite early in the evening. There were few *pensione*, no hotels, except, about halfway up from Capri, the Cesar Augustus, then in the course of being completed. The only restaurant, I remember with pleasure, was called Mingetti's, small with a garden; it was cool and shady in the summer when tables and chairs were set outside.

Mingetti was squat and square, remarkably like the actor Edward G. Robinson to look at, which no doubt gave rise to the story that he had been a gangster in America. If he was, he was also one of the kindest men I have ever met, capable, always helpful, and most interesting to talk to. He loved to speak what passed for English, words like 'boids', 'goils', and 'dames' peppering most of his anecdotes.

He was very pro-American, especially with regard to Marshall Aid, but said quite firmly: 'Every guy oughta end up in his homeland.' He did all the cooking himself with only a girl to help him; it is with great pleasure I remember his superb *pizza rusticana*, the size of a small wheel, filled with ricotta cheese, eggs, herbs, and just the suspicion of nutmeg it needed. Anything you wanted to know, or have done, you asked Mingetti, and that was enough. The Anacapresi were a superstitious people: the postmistress was reported to have the evil eye, so nobody dared to complain when her five-year-old grandson, who couldn't read, was made the delivery boy for telegrams.

Our house was quite a long way down one of the lanes, past small houses owned by peasant farmers, who kept the cow or the bull on the ground floor (the poor bull was led all over Capri to serve the cows), and had a vineyard at the side or back, some chickens and maybe a pig or two. Graham Greene's house, Rosaio, was down the lane and at the end was Arthur and Viola Johnson's beautiful villa, Molino a Vento. Baron Schack had two rooms in a *pensione* on the other side of Anacapri. He would walk down to Capri and back every day: quite a few miles. Sometimes if he was tired coming back, or after a lot of wine, he would go to sleep on the stone shelf under the statue of the Madonna about halfway up the long, winding hill.

After the Casa Solatia we felt as if we had been imprisoned, for the house, Casa Carracciolo, was in two parts; the ground floor had two not very large rooms, downstairs a primitive kitchen and small dining room. Outside the ground floor were white-painted steps winding around the house to another floor of two rooms with a bathroom and a terrace. In effect, it was two flats, one on top of the other. To begin with we thought it rather amusing to withdraw to the drawing room above, for it had wonderful views of the surrounding country, with Ischia in the distance. This novelty soon palled, especially as it meant carrying up books, glasses and bottles. Another irritating thing was three twittering little girls with a much older woman in charge, who were sent by the owner to clean the house. It was all impossible in a small house, four extra people scurrying about, moving everything daily, even Constantine's writing paper. If we went out while they were there, things were successfully hidden. For instance the bedcovers were removed, nowhere to be found, and when we asked where they were it turned out they had all been put under the mattresses. Either they went or we did, was our ultimatum to Mingetti, who understood completely and sent down a sad, sweet, madonna-faced girl called Ilda instead. After two days she didn't come; apparently the three girls and the woman had waited for her on the road and intimidated her. Mingetti again soon put a stop to that, but we had provoked almost a vendetta and Ilda was sometimes nervous.

Between Graham Greene's house and ours, a plump, pop-eyed Dutchman called Tony Paanaker was building a house to be called Casa della Madonna. He strutted about Capri, always with a silver-topped stick which he twirled when he stopped to talk to you, joining your party unasked. He was certain that Graham, also Constantine and myself, would be interested to see the magnificent place he was erecting – we must all come *now* to see it. The building was certainly extensive with Madonnas everywhere – outside, in niches up the stairs, over the doors, in the rooms. It was more like a temple than a house. Halfway up, Graham and I got the giggles and had to sit on a stone bench underneath one of these appallingly modelled statues. We were almost helpless with laughter. Paanaker appeared round the corner twirling his stick, Constantine with an expression of exhausted helplessness behind him.

'Ah, I see the beauty has overcome you both. Rest awhile, then we will see the top floor.'

'But I couldn't, Tony, it's all so overwhelming. Another time, don't you think so, Graham?'

Graham was mopping his eyes with his handkerchief, gratefully agreeing with me. Constantine, quick to latch on, said:

'Theo will tell you, I can only look at a few pictures in a museum. Too many makes me dizzy.'

'What an extraordinary man,' Graham said afterwards. 'Is he very religious?'

I replied that I didn't think he was, and certainly he was not a Catholic, as he was never in church.

Although Graham lived nearby, we didn't see very much of him. He was writing a lot I think. He came to lunch and sometimes we had a drink together. I was a little in awe of him, and those pale blue eyes with a slightly tortured expression worried me a little. I wondered if since becoming a Catholic he was finding it too difficult. Born Catholics have had longer to get accustomed to the rigidity. Did he have feelings of guilt? At this time the only books of his I had read were *Brighton Rock* and *Ministry of Fear*, for *The Heart of the Matter* and *The End of the Affair* had yet to be written. If he did have feelings of guilt, it was something I didn't understand, for I firmly believe that every thinking person knows, maybe even for only a few seconds, they are about to do wrong before they do it, and therefore they have a choice. If the doubtful one is taken, it is permissible, even essential, to have a conscience, but never guilt. My father was a good example of this principle, and to a lesser extent my mother and grandmother.

We talked on many subjects; he told me he always tried to write a thousand words a day.

'It's amazing how much you get done if you do.'

Of Norman we talked frequently; he was beginning to think *South Wind* wouldn't be made into a film now, but he was determined Norman should get some money from it. He seemed a very concerned person. We spent one curious evening at Rosaio with Graham and a very small dark woman with a masculine, Scottish-sounding name. I think she wrote plays. The blonde and her blond children had left some time past. It was a very hot night, the drinks much stronger than the wine we were accustomed to; I don't remember having anything to eat either. At some time, fairly late, Constantine said he was so hot he would take a walk in the garden. Graham and I were talking in his work-room when I realized we must go home. The time had passed very quickly, none of us thought it was so late.

Graham and I picked our way through the garden looking for Constantine. Then we heard a faint voice calling, 'Theo, Theo.'

We intensified our search, the voice, sometimes fainter than others, still calling from time to time.

'Where on earth is he?' said Graham.

'He can't have gone home, for we can hear him,' I replied.

We went on looking, stumbling and holding on to each other through rockeries, prickly cacti and small bushes. The moon 'was having one of her fits' as Norman used to say, capriciously there one moment and gone the next. The leaves whispered as we brushed past them.

'My God, there's a well in the garden. I hope he hasn't fallen down that,' Graham cried. He ran off to look. I stood, completely perplexed, straightening myself for I was cramped from bending over, looking where I was going; then I looked up at the sky.

'Theo, Theo.'

I called back: 'Where are you?'

As I looked up I thought I saw something moving in the sky. Impossible. Graham came back saying, thankfully, he wasn't in the well.

'Look up, there, Graham. Isn't something moving, or am I going mad?'

For some minutes we stared. Yes, there was something briefly, then it would disappear.

'He's on . . . no, he can't be, he is . . . he's on the roof. How in God's name did he get there?'

We hurried over and found a small but convenient tree, which Graham said wouldn't hold him. I scrambled up a little way.

'Here I am, darling. Come on, I'll help you down.'

He came over, bent down, then stood up again.

'No, I don't trust you. You'll let me fall.'

We tried to persuade him; no good. Like a frightened horse he would veer away as we got closer.

'It's no good, Graham, he won't come down for me. What about your friend? She's small and we could be behind her.'

Constantine was more against her then me, refusing even to stay that end of the roof. We were getting annoyed with him.

'Who will you come down for, then?' I called up. A faint voice answered: 'Graham wouldn't let me fall.'

'You'll have to try, we'll hold you, Graham. He can't stay up there all night.'

So Graham crawled up the very flexible tree, supported by the two of us. Very slowly Constantine lowered himself on to Graham's shoulders. Together they were very heavy; we had to hold on very tightly to keep steady. With much crackling and snapping of twigs he was down in the garden. We all reeled back with exhaustion. The first thing he said was:

'How did I get up there?'

Every time we passed Graham's house we looked, first at the roof, then at the slender tree.

'I couldn't possibly have gone up that, could I?'

I asked him where he'd thought he was going when he left the garden.

'I thought I was going home,' he replied instantly. 'It was a funny way to choose, wasn't it?'

As long as we lived in Anacapri the riddle was never solved and we were never asked again to Rosaio, although we did meet occasionally in the piazza.

———

From time to time we had a few friends to lunch, for if they lived in Capri it meant they could get back by bus. Sometimes we met at Mingetti's, where we could eat very cheaply. The kitchen at the house only had a small charcoal brazier, difficult for cooking any but the simplest food.

The Johnsons entertained us a few times, the elegance of their villa contrasting greatly with our rather unpleasant one. Occasionally, if Kenneth or someone asked us to lunch we would go down to Capri, sometimes walking one way. It was a very different existence in Anacapri, perfect for those who came from a city for a few months' peace and relaxation; or if you wanted to get away to write. However, writing was one thing Constantine was quite unable to do at this time, so he became more and more disconsolate and restless. He started to go down to Capri on his own, quite early, and spend all day there, catching the last bus back. Gradually the last bus was missed, so an expensive taxi was taken. He would sometimes arrive early in the morning, go to the upper part of the house and stay there until the following evening. Money was getting perilously short again; the Italian publishers of *The Arabian Bird* hadn't paid their advance despite repeated letters. I asked Mingetti if there was any job I could do for him. When he saw I was worried he would wave his hand and say:

'Sit down.'

Then a bottle of wine and a plate of food would be put in front of me, with always a dish of pasta for Flotow.

'Everyboda feela better on a full stomacho.'

I tried not to harass Constantine but our life together had to be discussed, for I began to dread being hungry again, apart from worrying about his writing. It was Mingetti who said one day:

'You live in all that house down there?'

I said, no, not really, for we only occasionally bothered to go upstairs.

'Why notta get good rent for that part? You know people.'

But we didn't know anyone who wasn't already living in either their own villa or a *pensione*. Yet the very next day when I was down on Capri in the morning I met the Swedish woman who lived with Norman's great friend Cecil Woolf. Usually very placid, she looked flustered, and without my asking she volunteered the reason. The owner of their apartment wanted it for his nephew who was getting married. Where could they find something reasonable in summer? Timorously I suggested that we had the very small apartment in our house. Would she like to look at it? We took the next bus back and she thought it was just right. Quiet, and far enough away from the fatal piazza with its teasing charms to get Cecil working on his book. She would talk to him and I to Constantine.

It turned out very well, Cecil and his friend being perfect tenants, quiet, yet amusing and interesting to talk to. He told us Norman had at one time been an accomplished pianist, having studied years before under Rubinstein; this surprised us, as he had appeared to dislike some German music, but maybe it was only Wagner, of whom he said he had had a surfeit when young. I should have remembered his words at the end of *Alone* as he is walking in Italy near Ferento, not far from Viterbo, and 'a wistful intermezzo of Brahms' comes into his head: '*It seemed to spring out of the hot earth. Such a natural song, elvishly coaxing! Would I ever play it again? Neither that, nor any other.*'

However, I was not to enjoy Cecil's conversation for very long. Alone most days, with money getting very low, I suggested I go to Rome, try to get the advance from the Italian publishers, and look about for work. Acting was about the only profession I had any real experience in and there were many films being made in Rome then, not only good Italian ones but British and American ones too, using blocked sterling and dollars. Rather to my surprise this idea was accepted immediately. If I had a suspicious mind, I might have realized why. I suppose I was preoccupied with the immediate problems.

Friends gave me telephone numbers to ring in Rome, including that of Gavrelle Verschoyle, who was leaving that week. I arranged for a German girl, who also had very little money, to cook Constantine one meal a day. Mouche was still with the Princess Pignatelli in Naples.

Would I take Flotow with me? Constantine asked, as he might be out a lot.

I took only the minimum amount of money, for I thought of my 'safety valve' I had left with Vernon Jarratt. So early one morning Flotow and I, with a little luggage, took the bus down for the ferry, then on to the bus for Rome. I was glad to have my loving little travelling companion snuggled under the seat.

CHAPTER THIRTY-EIGHT

Arriving at the Hotel Inghilterra, I found that the usual hall porter, Cipriani, who knew me, was off duty. A strange man was there who asked for money in advance which I hadn't got. Reinhard was out and Vernon Jarratt didn't answer his phone. After waiting for some time, I left the luggage there, deciding to take Flotow for a walk in the Pincio Gardens. It was late afternoon on the hot July day. We walked up the elegant eighteenth-century Spanish Steps, by the house where Keats died, along the path so many people of note have walked. As we passed the Trinità dei Monti church, I wondered if the nuns were still singing vespers as they had in Mendelssohn's time. I thought of Lucullus, who had lived on these slopes, and on the platform of the Pincio Terrace, once the favourite promenade of Roman aristocracy, looking out over the superb panorama of Rome, I thought too of Nathaniel Hawthorne's *Notebooks in France and Italy* which I had read at Aunt Maud's house in Bermuda, what seemed so many worlds ago:

> Here are beautiful sunsets; and here whichever way you turn your eyes, are scenes as well worth gazing at, both in themselves, and for their historical interest, as any that the sun ever rose and set upon.

As I gazed at the view there came over me a love of Rome which would last for ever. I walked through the gardens under the shade of noble trees; there was a small hut-like café where my money was just enough for two large sandwiches, which I would share with Flotow, and a fresh lemon drink. I sat under a tree with the picnic and read my book for some time, feeling more peaceful than I had for ages, although little twinges of apprehension would dart through my mind, then disappear, as I went on reading some Turgenev. It had been a long, emotional day; the food, the quiet and the warmth combined to make me feel sleepy. I dozed, woke up, then putting my bag under my head thought a little sleep would be a good idea. Alas, when I woke it was pitch dark, Flotow lying beside me, fast asleep too. I wandered about a little but was completely lost, so I returned to my tree and slept the night through. My watch had stopped in the morning so I had no idea of the time, but it was gloriously sunny and I felt refreshed and full of energy.

We walked through the leafy groves towards the Spanish Steps.

'Buon giorno, signorina,' a voice said.

Turning, I saw a small, undernourished man with a camera, one of the many who earned a precarious living photographing tourists. He snapped his camera. I explained I had no money. He said he had none either but was hoping to get enough for breakfast. Putting into my hand a grubby piece of cardboard with his name and address on it he walked along with me. He looked even hungrier than I was; it was nearly 8.00 am. I said to him:

'Stay with me, we'll have breakfast together.'

At the Inghilterra, he waited outside, sometimes taking a photograph, while I rang Vernon. Yes, he would meet me at the café in the via Frattina. I was to have breakfast and he would bring me the money as soon as the banks opened. So my new friend, Luigi, and I went and had the most delicious *caffe latte* and fried eggs with crusty, fresh bread. Flotow had a bowl of milk with some rusks. Even with my limited Italian I was able to follow the conversation about Luigi's family. My troubles seemed minimal compared with his. By the time Vernon came we were in a replete stupor. Luigi said he would leave the photographs at the Inghilterra – no, I was not to pay for them. Vernon said he would telephone me that evening. I retrieved my luggage, and Cipriani, full of apologies for the previous evening, gave me a far better room than I would have taken myself, with a balcony.

I rang the publisher, but he wasn't in. Reinhard seemed pleased to see me, and when I told him about getting the money he said:

'There's only one way. You must go and sit there, all day if necessary. That way you will catch him. It's no use telephoning. I'll come with you tomorrow.'

However, it took about three days of camping in the office, with sandwiches, before I got the cheque. But I felt an enormous sense of achievement. What would I have done without Reinhard? Once again I was reliant on him, that kind, gentle man whom it was difficult to believe had ever been the enemy. Vernon too seemed concerned about me; what sort of job did I want? And why did I go on staying at the Inghilterra which was depleting my little store of money? Why didn't I come out and stay with him? He had a house on the via di Porto San Sebastiano. It was a bit far out, but he could bring me into Rome when he went in the morning and I could get a bus back.

'I've got a permanent girlfriend,' Vernon went on, 'so I haven't got designs on you. You'll meet her later.'

It was very rural at Vernon's house, for it was set far back from the road and had a lot of land in front where he grew globe artichokes and sweetcorn. Flotow loved it, for he had plenty of freedom, and he became a good guard dog. To begin with I didn't know how or to whom to go for a job, so I helped Vernon by working in the garden – setting up sort of sunshades for the artichokes against the strong heat. I got tanned and felt very healthy. Enrica, his Italian girl, would come out at weekends. Later they were married and together started the well-known George's restaurant in the via Marché. She was an excellent cook then, subsequently becoming highly qualified professionally. Some days I would go in early with Vernon, wander about Rome exhausting myself with its beauty, then go to Toto's for a bowl of soup, where I was sure to see someone I had met on earlier visits and find out what was going on. Everyone, even the waiter, knew I was looking for work. Peter Tompkins and his wife Jerree became very good friends and were always asking me to meals.

Vernon's house was near the Terme di Caracalla, where they were staging spectacular open-air opera in the ruins. I went along there one evening but couldn't get a seat, so I wandered around the back hoping to see something, or at least hear it. A young mounted *carabinieri* saw me, offered me a seat on his horse and lifted me up. So that is how I saw *Aida*, elephants and all, sitting on the front of the *carabinieri*'s horse. Vernon thought it was very brave of me.

'I'm not frightened of horses,' I replied.

'I wasn't thinking of the horse, just that you might have been in too close contact with the carabinieri,' he said, laughing.

One evening quite soon after I went to stay there, Vernon came back, his blue eyes dancing with pleasure.

'I think I've got you a part in an English film being made here. We're doing the lighting. Soldati's directing. You've met him, haven't you? I'll give you a letter to him.'

In the old wartime jeep he had been given, Peter drove me out to the studios to see Soldati. But at the last minute I got cold feet. I hadn't acted for years. Would I, could I, do it? He more or less frog-marched me into the studios, almost into Soldati's arms. He looked up, his face not unlike Groucho Marx's, smiled and said:

'You want the part? Go and see Mario right away.'

Bewildered, I asked where Mario was, found him and was told to be there for rehearsals in a week's time. No money was mentioned and I was too scared to ask. It seemed unbelievable. Peter was waiting in the hall, talking earnestly in Italian to an official-looking man. He had found out much more than I had. He told me it was a splendid cast: Margaret Rutherford, Gordon Harker, Jean Kent, Robert Beatty, Walter Crisham, on and on he went. I couldn't take it all in.

'But why me, then?'

Apparently the actress they had engaged had fallen ill.

I felt in my handbag for a cigarette. Vernon's letter was still there; I had forgotten all about it. With excitement I cabled Constantine, as well as telling my friends.

It was a long journey from Vernon's house to rehearsals and often I would be too late for the bus. Later they would be filming at a variety of locations around Rome and I had to be living somewhere central. Without hesitation, Peter and Jerree asked me to stay in their apartment in the via Gregoriana, although they had little room for guests. Jerree too was working all day as a sort of custodian of the Palazzo Antici Mattei, one of the places in Rome where Peter had lived as a child. Peter did all the cooking and was extremely good at it. Jerree was the daughter of an American diplomat, so had travelled widely since early childhood. She spoke several languages and had been a very gifted pianist as a young girl, but unfortunately had had a breakdown in Milan just before a concert. She had never played again. She did, however, do exquisitely fine ink drawings, as delicate as her sensitive and original nature. She had eloped with Peter during the war, in East Africa when he was a war correspondent, but that is their story, and not for me to mis-write.

Peter was tall, with a fine-shaped head and a handsome face, yet with a touch of devilry about it. Jerree had told me he was Bernard Shaw's son. Peter neither denied or confirmed this; yet once when I was talking about Ireland, he said quickly:

'I suppose I'm half-Irish.'

Whatever the true story, Shaw certainly felt great affection for Molly Tompkins, wrote her numerous and interesting letters proclaiming it, and paid for Peter to be educated at Stowe, in England. Peter found the letters in a trunk hidden in a Roman *palazzo* during the war and published them in 1960. To Peter nothing was impossible; he reminded me of a late eighteenth- or nineteenth-century adventurer or an aristocratic traveller. His quick-thinking mind was at ease with many subjects and some of his abilities were very practical, for instance breaking down one wall of the via Gregoriana flat to make a large room with an archway. He was to a certain extent mysterious, and although I learnt a little from Jerree, nothing but occasional hints emerged from Peter. There were trunks everywhere; Jerree said they were full of diaries and notebooks.

'Get him to show you them,' she urged, but he never did.

Yet when those trunks were opened he wrote his book, *A Spy in Rome*, and I realized that I wasn't wrong in thinking I had been in contact with an extraordinary person.

Peter had arrived (in his early twenties) in Salerno while it was still under German fire. He then recruited and trained democratic Italians to carry out espionage behind German lines. By the time Naples was captured he had a sizeable and enthusiastic, almost personal espionage service. It was from here with a few trusted friends that he made the perilous journey to Rome, where he remained until it was liberated on June 5th. He managed to keep a remarkable diary of these events, which was smuggled in parts every week or so into the Vatican, where it was hidden in the room of an ageing cardinal.

Donald Downes of American Special Intelligence, whom I met in Rome then, wrote in the preface to Peter's book:

> To land on a hostile coast and go into Rome, with no one prearranged to receive or hide him, required of Peter Tompkins a courage beyond that of charging up San Juan Hill or planting the flag atop Iwo Jima. To live for months on end as a fugitive from justice (or injustice) believing, rightly or wrongly, that your own side are betraying you, to hide in the uniform of the political police who are hunting you, to be in terror of meeting your boyhood friends on the street lest they turn you in, to have your agents caught, tortured and killed – that takes something beyond mere courage; it requires foolhardiness, determination, bravado, and a lusty appetite for adventure and danger, all sharpened by a taste for the cold sensation of fear.

This was 1949, however, and acts of bravery had been soon forgotten. Now we were all more or less penniless, but no two people could have been both kinder to me and more fun. Our problems and our money were often shared. I loved them both deeply for themselves; also because they, as much as anything, gave me back a feeling of warmth and belonging.

Constantine and I exchanged many letters; his took some time to reach me. Telegrams got hopelessly muddled and became incomprehensible, sometimes amusingly so. I still have one, of which part says: 'stop fianning'; neither of us ever knew what he had said originally. He wrote that he had been writing a film script of the July 20th plot to kill Hitler, as well as going to a lot of parties, and he generally seemed to be having not too bad a time. He was, however, beginning to show signs of jealousy. There was an English newspaper then, called the *Rome Daily American*, which had a gossip column about who was seen where and with whom. I was often reported as having been with a party of people, when perhaps I had been at the next table, or maybe just saying a few words to them in a hotel foyer. This was read avidly by Constantine, who commented that I seemed 'to be spending a lot of time in the company of some very unsavoury people'. As he knew none of them, I wondered how he reached that conclusion. I decided to go down for the weekend before I started filming. I also realized it would be difficult leaving Flotow all day, and maybe Constantine would take him for a few weeks. Full of hope, I sent a telegram saying I was coming.

I arrived in Capri on the afternoon ferry, to be greeted by the 'day' Prince Carracciolo, who of course wanted to know how long I was going to stay, his round inquisitive eyes searching my face. When I told him, he said Constantine wasn't there but in Positano, as Mimi had been ill. I wondered if it was true; if so I had wasted a day. I saw a friend who confirmed it.

When I arrived in Positano about lunchtime the next day, everyone was in festive mood; Mimi had completely recovered, Constantine was sparkling and delighted to see me (no telegram had arrived), and there was a very jolly pre-luncheon drinks party going on at the Buca. Some of the Sadler's Wells Ballet Company were there: Robert Helpman, Margot Fonteyn, Freddy Ashton and Brian Shaw, all bubbling and delightful. Their conversation and company made it easy to forget things, which I did for the rest of the day. That night Robert Helpman and Margot Fonteyn did a superb dance on the beach, by the light of a full and sparkling moon. Then, the water shimmering and enticing, everyone went swimming without their clothes. Our laughter must have been heard all over Positano, for when we came out, there was a semi-circle of armed *carabiniere*, waiting to make arrests. Unfortunately our clothes were behind them so there was no chance of getting to them. I felt very defenceless trying to argue with no clothes on, and trying not to laugh, for all this time Bobby Helpman was making very funny quips. I was glad Flotow was with me; otherwise he would undoubtedly have been growling at them, and he wasn't popular in Positano anyway. However, help was at hand, as they used to say in early films, once the Mayor and the tourist chief arrived and bailed us all out. Nothing more was heard of the incident.

As I had to get back for rehearsals, there was only time for a hurried conversation with Constantine before I climbed all those steps for the bus back to Sorrento, and then Rome. He would keep Flotow for a couple of weeks before bringing him up to Rome. Mouche apparently was a little better but still not well.

Rehearsing, rehearsing, rehearsing. My small part was with Margaret Rutherford, Gordon Harker and Robert Beatty, and I found it very enlightening to be working with such fine professional actors. To begin with I felt awkward, for they had been filming for several weeks; it was like being the new girl at school. Soldati put me at my ease, as did the Italian work crew. In a day or two I was one of them. There was, however, a problem. The actress originally engaged for my part was considerably shorter than me, and the budget didn't run to more clothes being made. It was evening dress. Surely I had one I liked particularly? The trouble was I hadn't. We'd been so poor in Bermuda that only the minimum wardrobe was possible, and formal evening dress never played any part in our entertaining. Esther Arthur, a friend of Sybille Bedford, said she had a trunkful of evening clothes; I must come to their rooms at the Inghilterra and select one. Sybille was making grimaces at me, but I didn't know why and so a time was fixed.

Yes, certainly Esther did have several trunkfuls of evening clothes, but she was about six feet tall – 'they can be taken up' – and all the clothes were Chanel models of the early 1920s. Nevertheless I had to try them on. It was very comical, for I looked like something out of a Twenties magazine, except all the dresses were looped about my feet. Sybille and I got the giggles, but Esther remained unperturbed, picking out one, in violent yellow and mauve with a waist around my hips, as being particularly suitable. She remained adamant I must wear it. I took it, hoping to think of some excuse for never appearing in it, except as a fancy dress. I returned it later, saying the director thought it too similar to the leading actress's dress. I hoped she would never see the film, and I'm sure she didn't. The problem was solved very unexpectedly by some friends we had met in New York, a sculptor called Harold Ambellan and his wife, Elizabeth, turning up. She lent me a very suitable dress, which I promised to send back but couldn't as it turned out.

It was the happiest production I have ever worked on; everybody seemed to be *en fête*. Soldati was a tireless director, kind but very certain of what he wanted. He lived in the via Gregoriana too, so we became friends. At one point in the script of the film, a large party was given; extras were wanted, so I immediately went to see Mario the production manager and said I could find several very suitable people. As the film was British they were looking for non-Italian actors. He was therefore delighted when I turned up with the distinguished trio of Peter, Jerree and a friend called Richard Brookbank. By this time we were filming in a large house just outside the city; it was a night party scene so we worked all night from 6.00 pm on to eight o'clock in the morning. Peter produced a small bottle of spirits which, judiciously poured into the coloured water, kept our morale up. It was all great fun, acting and dancing all night for about four days. One mystery for me was never solved: how Peter had lived in Rome all those months, even in the enemy's ranks without being discovered – for he was, without any doubt, the worst actor I have ever seen. A very small scene had to be rehearsed and shot endless times. He would be the first to admit it. Then Jerree, too, had to have an evening dress, but that was easy. Peter disappeared to one of his resistance friends, now an *haute couturier*, and arrived with a most beautiful filmy model dress. Unfortunately it was almost exactly the same as the dress Jean Kent, the star, was wearing, so of necessity all Jerree's scenes were very distanced.

After filming ended, Peter and Jerree gave a real party for our friends in the cast. All those people remain in my memory very affectionately. Coming back through the busy, sunny streets to the via Gregoriana at about eight-thirty in the morning, having a large breakfast, then closing the shutters against both the sun and Roman street noises, and sleeping until about three-thirty was the pattern of those lovely working nights and days. When the film was finished, other offers came in, some of which I accepted. Through Vernon I met many of the well-known Italian directors, such as Alberto Lattuada, who made *Il Molino del Po*; Vittoria de Sica, director of *Ladro di Bicicletta* (*The Bicycle Thief*) and *Sciuscià*, the superb film about the shoeshine boys.

I played a small part in an Italian film, a comedy with Mischa Auer, which to my relief I found would be dubbed afterwards by someone else, so my accent didn't matter. I did a fair amount of dubbing work myself – Italian films into English. Here I found that if you were a pretty girl you got paid more than a plain one, or a man. I mentioned this to Peter, who immediately started to organize a dubber's union.

I had also been lent a large apartment in the via di San 'Costanza off the long via Nomentana. The apartment belonged to a girl in the British Council who was going back to England for a month and wanted someone reliable to look after her cat, Figaro. This came about through Derek Verschoyle, Gavrelle's husband, who was at the British Embassy. I had been to several dinners at their house. Derek was in fact an Irishman from County Sligo, which is no doubt why we got on so well together. He was very mondaine and charming, with an unusual face of regular features, and a very attractive mouth and smile. His manners were impeccable, putting people at ease immediately. He talked in a slightly muffled voice on a variety of subjects – sometimes, as I was to find out later, Irish-fashion; that is, he tended to please rather than be factually correct. His walk was quick, but with a gliding motion; one almost felt he could disappear at will. His manner too was sometimes guarded, to cause one to think his life held many secrets, but this was undoubtedly part of his attraction to women. I had known several Irishmen of similar secretive attitude, so I was never in any danger of falling under his spell, although I was extremely fond of him.

Derek was chivalrous towards me at that time, doing what he could to help.

He would call from time to time, always with some wine or a bottle of Saccone and Speed gin, the old firm of wine and spirit merchants that usually supplied embassies. We would talk about Ireland, books and many other things, as if we had been lifelong friends. I had no work at that time so I spent my day telephoning likely people, going into the city to the Inghilterra, or to Toto's to see what was going on.

One day Derek said in his muffled voice, scarcely opening his lips, that he might have a job for me. I was to meet a man at a café one evening, carrying a walking stick. Because of the stick he would know me. After that I would report to Derek all that took place when he called at the end of the week. I duly did this, feeling a little stupid sitting at the café for several hours alone, for nobody ever arrived. However, Derek seemed quite satisfied, nodding knowledgeably, and paid me quite handsomely for the service. Several other little missions were entrusted to me, but never once did I ever make contact with anyone. I felt like a spy without a cause. Each time I got paid very well, so I didn't complain. In retrospect, I think he had made the whole idea up, and it was just a way of helping me out without embarrassing me. I rather enjoyed it and will now never know the truth of the matter.

I had a number of other jobs at this time, so with my new-found wealth I gave dinner parties in my large apartment for the friends who had helped me, such as Vernon and Reinhard, also Bendi Esterhazy. Bendi lived in a *pensione* somewhere in Rome on a very small allowance, difficult to manage on. He had had a hard time since leaving Hungary. He had been in prison there and he told me that what really kept him going was the amazing fortitude of the elderly, aristocratic ladies who were in prison with him. He had never been trained for earning his living, so his life was hard. Yet he showed amazing resilience, never complaining about his present life, often imparting a wonderful middle-European gaiety to the evening. He was very dark with a slightly pointed nose, large eyes with a quizzical expression, and wavy black hair which seemed to grow almost straight up from his head, having to be tamed to make it lie flat. He always walked very quickly and his voice was inclined to be high, as though coming from the top of his throat rather than his chest. His well-shaped hands were used expressively. As we walked around my apartment with its many bedrooms, Bendi exclaimed that we could all live there comfortably. Impulsively I said:

'Why don't you stay for a few days, Bendi?'

He readily agreed, as he was weary of his small, cheap room. The days lengthened to weeks, but I have seldom ever been so well looked after by anyone. The place was kept immaculately, accounts made of what was spent on food, my appointments arranged in perfect order. He was also interesting to talk to, for he told me of his early childhood, with an English nanny – all European aristocratic families had them – which explained why his English was so good. He'd had early attachments to young women, but none for many years. That was as far as he would go.

One day I was summoned to Scalera Studios. Bendi was as thrilled as I was, pressing my clothes and being very emphatic as to what I should wear. For if I ever disagreed or did something unusual, which seemed very often, he would raise his thick eyebrows and say:

'Theodora, I find you very extraordinary.'

One film I was in was called *La Strada Buio* (*The Dark Street*); I never found out the entire plot, but there were a lot of scenes with hands going into medicine cupboards, and taking out of bottles. One leading part was played by Eduardo Ciannelli, an Italo-American actor who usually played 'baddies' in Hollywood, so I assumed the hands were up to no good. I didn't have much of a part; there was nothing like the cohesion and pleasure of working with Soldati, although Sidney Salkow the director was a pleasant if uninspiring man.

The English actress Binnie Barnes (her husband was producing) was in the cast; we got on very well together, for I think she was a bit homesick for England and English voices, as she asked if I would like to be her stand-in, with the promise of a part later on. I accepted. As a young woman I had seen her in various stage plays, also in Korda's *Private Life of Henry VIII*, and I had quite admired her forthright style of acting. I didn't know many women in Rome, and Binnie seemed a congenial person. She and I became quite friendly and often she took me to their apartment for tea, or drinks when she wasn't working.

The late August weather was stiflingly hot. When filming, we had to sit with moistened chamois leather around our necks and sometimes on our foreheads to stop the make-up running. Binnie had the first fixative aerosol hair spray from America, which she sprayed over her hair to keep it in shape, and she lent me some too. It seemed very ingenious then. We all suffered tremendously from the heat, none more so than Bendi who was forever dabbing his forehead with a spotless white handkerchief. I told him about the chamois leather.

'But, Theodora, I suffer from the Esterhazy complaint, heat about the head, we all have it. Some years ago my uncle, the cardinal, was in conclave to elect a new pope. He had it so badly his handkerchief soon became very wet. So he opened the window, to shake it out to dry.' He dabbed away more furiously as if even the memory made him hotter. 'People watching in the piazza saw something white, and immediately jumped to the conclusion it was the puff of white smoke.' He smiled wistfully. 'It was very embarrassing for my uncle.'

When I came home early one day he was coming out of the bathroom after a shower wearing my black velvet dressing gown, his hair standing on end, the long bell sleeves trailing at his side. I collapsed with laughter, saying:

'Bendi, you look just like the Widow Twankey!'

'And what, Theodora, is the Widow Twankey?' He glared at me.

One of these days when you have nothing better to do, try explaining the Widow Twankey to an Hungarian count.

'You see, it's a character in English pantomime, you know like *commedia del arte*. She's a washerwoman, always played by a leading male comedian, the principal boy's part is played by a girl. The Widow Twankey's son is . . .'

I couldn't go further; his expression ranged between annoyance and mystification. Sweeping my négligée around him, he said: 'Really, Theodora, I find you very extraordinary.'

The best thing about the film was that they shot it on location all over Rome, both inside buildings and out of doors, so I was able to really savour Rome as never before. They even filmed at Castelgandolfo, the pope's summer residence, one night.

Bendi was invaluable; he knew Rome far better than I did, so he always directed me the best way to get to the locations, often coming to the bus or train with me when they didn't send a car. Food would be ready for me when I returned, and if I had a late morning call, he might have asked a few friends for a simple meal. However, certain friends were not approved of and were *never* asked. He was very correct most of the time and expected me to behave accordingly.

Films and filming were the rage in Rome in those days. Even Bendi was delighted when I suggested to him he become an extra (in a rather grand scene), and Sidney Salkow, who had Hungarian connections, seemed thrilled at having a Count Esterhazy on the set. Most of the extras were just called *generica*, and they were led about together, but with Bendi it was a case of, 'Count Esterhazy, would you please come this way?'

Constantine wrote frequently. He had finished the film script and wanted to come up to Rome. Having the large apartment made it simple, so we made arrangements. Bendi took the whole matter in hand at once.

'Should I stay here, or leave, do you think? Will he be jealous?'

I had told Constantine of Bendi's stay with me and of his great help. No, he wasn't at all jealous; he had made enquiries about Bendi, everything pointing to the fact that we were not, and never would be, having an affair.

'There's no need to strip my bed, Bendi, it was only changed two days ago.'

'Theodora, of course it must be changed. What are you thinking of? I will also make up the bed in the other small room.'

'Whatever for? We always share the same bed,' I replied.

'Theodora, I find you extraordinary; of course Constantine must have a dressing room!'

It would have been much better if Constantine had waited a week until I had finished filming, for my hours were irregular, but I didn't want to appear to be putting him off. Fortunately he arrived on a free evening, but with Flotow. I had forgotten to mention the cat. It was all right for a few hours or a night, as there were so many rooms, but not for a week, for Flotow had never been close to a cat and would surely want to investigate the frightened Figaro. The Tompkinses said they would take him, providing one of us exercised him.

In other ways the week was a disaster: my part came up, which meant learning lines, as well as rehearsing, so Constantine was left alone most of the day. He apparently went in to get Flotow, then spent most of the day in bars with Gerry Osborne, who also had nothing much to do. By the time I had finished working, sometimes very late, he was quarrelsome with drink. Being tired, I was not always tactful when we met. The climax was one night when Rome had had one of its violent thunderstorms, always guaranteed to make me hyperexcited and rather headachy. We were going up the Spanish Steps with the Tompkinses, back to the via Gregoriana, Constantine berating me for leaving him alone all day. To avoid answering, I hurried a little ahead, not easy on those steps; he leant forward and pulled me back by the dress, which ripped right down the back. I had hurried from the set, not changing, so it was a serious problem for me, as for continuity I had to wear the same clothes throughout the filming. Jerree, fearing I would be pulled backwards, and be hurt, quickly whipped round and hit Constantine sharply over the head with her umbrella to make him let go of me. Nobody said a word. He wasn't hurt, but sobered, and he stopped the verbal assault. Jerree also sat up until nearly three o'clock mending the dress, painstakingly, so I could wear it that day. We were filming at the Teatro Argentina then, and wearing a jacket over the top it passed unnoticed. But that was the reason Elizabeth Ambellan never received back her dress.

Two days later, at about ten at night, one of the grips came to me and said there was a man in the foyer who was demanding to see me. I hurried out after the scene ended. As I rounded the corner I saw Constantine arguing with the producer; never a good idea, particularly not for an unasked visitor. I was deadly tired, and somehow feeling I should support him, I too got into the argument in a very hot-headed fashion. It was a very bad mistake on my part. There was never another call from that company. I wrote to Binnie Barnes apologizing but there was no answer. Scalera Studios became wary of engaging me, as they said I had 'a difficult husband'.

It was very depressing on every count; we were both dejected. But for Bendi giving us both moral and practical support, I think I too would have been inclined to drink rather too much. These violent scenes were occurring frequently, but only when Constantine had been drinking. They exhausted both of us, but for me they were tinged not with anger but with sorrow. I could feel the helplessness of his rage which particularly thundered against anyone or anything that gave me work and money, and thus made him to a certain extent reliant on me. I was in the impossible position of starving with him or trying to make my own way. Many times I wavered but my sense of survival proved too strong. Ultimately, I felt, he must find the strength of will to moderate his drinking and write. I had known several painters and writers in Paris as a girl and knew that in order to survive they had had to be single-minded in purpose. He knew I loved him with the same certainty that I knew he loved me.

I would have gone back to Anacapri with Constantine for a few days, but I had a dubbing session and a photographic job coming up. After that there would be nothing, and the month's stay at the apartment was coming to an end.

CHAPTER THIRTY-NINE

It was Bendi who solved the problem of where I was to live. A young friend of his, wanting, I think, to escape the close proximity of his stern mother, decided to rent out his Rome apartment. 'Apartment' is rather a grand word for the place in the Piazza di Spagna. It was on the roof of a tall building, about five storeys up, at the end of a large terrace, the front of which looked over the American Express, Keats's house and the Spanish Steps, and had a view of the Trinità dei Monti; a stone and brick bungalow with a flat roof (on which Rossellini had set the opening shots of his film *An Open City*), with pottery vases, pretty creeping and climbing plants around it, and a vine trained over a section as a shelter from the sun. There was a large L-shaped room with two divans, a bookcase separating a dining area, a pleasant little fireplace, a small hall with cupboards, a kitchen and a bathroom. It was most agreeable and cosy. French windows led out to the flower-decked terrace, which also had a table and chairs. The Inghilterra and Toto's were just round the corner, the Tompkinses just up the steps. I took to it at once.

Constantine worried me, especially as he had written that Mouche had been sent back from the old Princess Pignatelli's, so I wondered how he could cope with her. I decided to go for a week to Anacapri. As I was leaving, my agent rang to say Pabst, the German film director, was in Rome, contemplating making a film of Homer's *Odyssey*, with Greta Garbo playing Circe. He had suggested to Pabst that I be tested to play Penelope, therefore I must return at once if I was called. It was an exciting project which helped to take my mind off more pressing problems.

The house was sad – Mouche really not much better, although delighted to see me; Constantine jittery, alternately depressed and elated. He had heard nothing from any of the people he had sent the July 20th filmscript to, was writing very little, just occasionally rewriting parts of the novel *Cousin Emily*. His money had mostly been spent. But for Mingetti feeding him from time to time I don't think he would have been eating at all. I had very little money to spare but he said he had written to his mother in New York; he was sure she would send something. When he heard about my little place in the Piazza di Spagna he became determined to pay all the bills here, give up 'this horrible villa' and join me. I made it very clear that, if he did come up, he must work regularly, and also respect my working hours, no matter how trivial he thought the work was. I was surprised, as he didn't really like Rome, saying it was too noisy; somehow I felt there were other reasons for leaving Capri, that he was withholding something. We had always been very close to each other, sensitive of each other's emotions. We both agreed that he must, from now on, drink only wine or beer and not too much of either.

'But you know, darling, I want to work. If only something would be accepted to give me a bit of encouragement.'

The Iron Hoop had come out in New York, and he showed me some very good notices, one particularly by the Irish writer James Stern in the *Saturday Review*.

'Didn't you get the publication advance money?' I asked.

Yes he did, but that too had been spent. There was a little money to come from Cassell but that was all. We also came to the reluctant conclusion that Mouche wasn't going to get any better. Since there was no vet on Capri, it meant taking her back to the best vet in Naples. The sadness at parting with my old friend from the war years was great, but I saw the cruelty and futility of keeping her alive. While down in Capri we had dinner with friends who introduced us to Admiral Manfredi of the Italian navy, who gallantly said he was driving to Rome in two days' time and would be happy to have me as his passenger. My agent had said I was wanted back there shortly.

At Kenneth Macpherson's we met Harold Acton, the aesthete and writer, who lived with his many beautiful treasures in Florence. He had been much influenced by Norman Douglas in his younger days, and was in good form that evening, reminiscing about things Norman had said to him in the past. One subject was D. H. Lawrence, and how Norman had considered that Lawrence was a sexual adolescent who never recovered from the shock of puberty, never outgrew it, remaining a frustrated schoolboy, who persuaded himself, and many others, that he was a pioneering genius in a *terra incognito*. Norman, however, always maintained to me that Lawrence was a superb travel writer; he particularly admired *Etruscan Places*. Harold Acton not only invited me to Florence but also gave me a letter to his friend Baron Paolo Langheim in Rome.

Everything about Mouche's last journey was distressing, from carrying her to the bus, the ferry, and the journey with Manfredi to the vet. Both Con and I were in tears, but Admiral Manfredi was very helpful, interviewing the vet for us as we sat in the crowded waiting room, then seeing that everything was carried out properly. Afterwards we went to the Hotel Excelsior for coffee and a drink, before starting on the long drive to Rome. In the bar, Lucky Luciano (the American gangster who had returned home after he was freed from prison in America) sat in his usual corner, alone. Then we heard our names called and turned round to see Vladimir and Scarlet Ivanovič, our friends from Bermuda who had looked after Flotow during the hurricane. They were on a tour of Italy, so I was pleased to be able to leave Constantine in such congenial company.

The Piazza di Spagna apartment was perfect for me; also for Flotow, as it had the terrace. It was just right, not unlike Graysbank Cottage in charm, central for my friends as well as being near some of the most beautiful places and parks in Rome. If only I could make enough money to live there without too much worry. Physically I was exhausted after the last weeks; so much so, my tired body seemed relaxed. Now I had to go through the slow process of unwinding while the brain still worked double time. Being alone for a little while helped me to do this, sitting on the terrace in the lazy September sun. Georgette, Constantine's mother, in her generous fashion sent me a hundred dollars, which meant I had another month's rent in hand and a certain respite from worry. One weekend Peter drove Jerree, Reynolds Packard (always known as Pack) and me in the jeep to the island of Guilia, some miles north of Rome, once the watering-place of rich Romans until malaria made it unsuitable.

'Let's get away from tourists,' Peter had said. 'I know a very remote island.'

It did seem remote – a dark, forbidding mountain in the centre, with what seemed to be a collection of houses on the top. There was a primitive *albergo* near to where the ferry got in, where we booked large bare rooms furnished with enormous country-style wooden beds, a chair and a washbasin. We had certainly got away from the tourists, I thought. Old black ovens stoked with wood cooked home-made bread; and there was always a pot of coarse salt on the table to eat with it. Vast saucepans bubbled with home-made pasta, and fishermen and boys would come into the kitchen with small fish of the kind Norman Douglas used to call 'floating pincushions, duckums'. We wandered along the rocky shore, occasionally finding little sandy bays, and towards the end of the path we came across a large hall advertising a dance on Saturday night. There was also a small, simple *trattoria* we decided to try later. We gazed up at the seemingly unscalable mountain.

'I wonder how you get up there?' I asked. 'They must need food. How would they get it?'

'Probably from the other side,' Peter replied. 'We could no doubt go round by boat.'

But neither Jerree nor Pack felt like an expedition, so Peter and I wandered off behind the sea-front habitation. It was very overgrown once we had left the few houses, but a path winding up the mountain was just visible. Finally we came to some crumbling steps up which we started.

'They have been here since Roman times, I would think,' said Peter. 'I hope they don't get any worse.'

They did get much worse before we reached the top. Many times I thought I couldn't make it, but Peter would then hold my hand and pull me up. I didn't dare think about the return. Once there, the atmosphere was extraordinary. There was quite a large town with shops, larger houses, quite good roads, even a few vans or rickety motorcars. However, it wasn't like an Italian village, where everyone nodded, smiled or said 'Giorno'; the inhabitants left their shops and stared at us without a word.

'Go and talk to them, Peter. I don't like being stared at like this. It's almost hostile.'

He went over and with his usual fluent Italian talked to one of them, but I saw the man just shrug a reply.

'I don't like it either,' he said. 'They're obviously not anxious to have visitors. I wonder why. Come on, let's go back.'

It was one of the worst journeys I have ever made. The crumbling steps crumbled even more as we went down. It would soon be dark, which isn't the gradual process it is in colder countries. My sandals were far from good walking gear. At one point I decided I'd be better without them.

'You can't go down in bare feet. The sharp edges will cut into you.'

'My soles are quite hard after running over rocks in Bermuda. I think I'd be better off, for I'm frightened of turning my ankle in these sandals.'

'No. Here, put my socks on over the sandals, they'll give you some protection.'

So that is how, some hours later, we arrived back at the *albergo*, to find no Jerree and no Pack. We wandered along, it was now quite dark, to find them comfortably seated outside the *trattoria* drinking wine. Pack laughed his infectious fat person's laugh; Jerree glared, her dark eyes brooding. I knew at once what had happened, for had I not known so many heart-clawing tentacles of jealousy in those months with Constantine in Capri? The still, hot nights lying almost rigid, with torturing thoughts, actual pain around the area of the heart like a cold hand squeezing it hard; listening, holding one's breath, waiting for the sound of footsteps or the steady throb of a motorcar engine; then an exhausted sleep, the bedclothes knotted like string underneath – no, never would I want to be the cause of anyone feeling like that. Not that there was the slightest reason. Peter told them of our adventures; I said nothing for there was nothing to say. He started to dress the salad.

'Don't put too much salt on mine, Peter, please.'

Quickly, like a chameleon's tongue darting out, Jerree picked up the salt cellar and poured a pyramid of salt over the top. I burst out laughing.

'Oh, Jerree, how wonderful! There have been so many times when I wanted to do just that.'

It broke the tension; we all felt better after that contretemps. It was far better than any wordy recrimination.

'I'm going to that dance,' Pack stated firmly. 'Just as soon as we've eaten. Coming, anyone?'

———

It's a mystery how any film ever gets made with all the variables: not only the cast, but an army of technicians, then perhaps the biggest hazard, finding all the money. The director, his head full of ideas, must each time be like a conductor with an entirely new orchestra and a new sponsor. However, music can be played, whereas a film often starts in somebody's head, the script having no significance on its own. Pabst's idea for *Ulysses* seemed to me wonderful. How sublime Garbo would be as Circe; could I sustain Penelope against such magnetism? It was better not to think about it, but that was difficult too.

I telephoned Baron Langheim, who appeared pleased I had called, asking me for dinner in two days' time. His house was near the Villa Doria Pamphili, a part of Rome I didn't know, but a sleek, long, low car was sent to bring me there. Paolo Langheim greeted me, a fairly tall, suave man, with a smooth skin, almost like a child's, bright enquiring eyes behind his spectacles, and brown hair receding on a domed head. He walked silently through a sumptuously furnished hall bringing me to the *salone*. It was with the greatest difficulty I kept my eyes from looking around the room, which had many beautiful sculptures and paintings. It was a loved and comfortable room with luxurious sofas, chairs and a *chaise-longue* which was so beautiful I involuntarily stroked it with my hand.

'You like beautiful furniture, I see.'

I withdrew my hand quickly.

'There is something upstairs I think you would appreciate,' he purred, 'if you'd like to accompany me?'

It was a bedroom of unbelievable opulence, the magnificent bed taking pride of place, glowing in gold and clear azure blue colours to take my breath away.

'It was the bed of Pauline Buonaparte . . .' He lingered over the words. 'A fitting monument for a beautiful woman, is it not? But, come, I must see if my other guests are ready. It is a small, very private dinner, as you will see.'

I followed, not knowing what to expect, still enfolded in a maze of colour and richness. It was to contrast sharply with the clothes of the woman sitting on the sofa, who was dressed in a dark grey suit with a large-brimmed hat, her head turned away. Then she moved to smile a greeting: I almost gasped out loud, for it was Greta Garbo. She took off the hat, shaking out her hair, then smiled up at us. It was breathtaking to see such cool calm eyes above perfect features. A very blond young man, like an Adonis, came into the room and leant on the back of the sofa. He was introduced as Lord Montague. I thought as I looked at them both how right they were for the surroundings. Each in their way magnificent jewels in a superb setting. Garbo ate very little, using her large spatula-topped fingers elegantly. I found no difficulty in talking to her and was longing to ask her about the Pabst film but couldn't think how to phrase it. We talked about Rome, remarking our surprise that there were no theatres open in a city where so much drama had been enacted.

'They are all actors here,' she said in her inimitable voice. 'I've never seen such beautiful gestures.'

I enquired how long she was staying, thinking that might lead to my finding out more, but alas she was leaving in two days' time.

'For good?' I enquired; maybe she would be returning?

'Alas, no.' I couldn't help thinking it didn't augur well for the film.

The time went all too quickly; I could have spent hours just looking at her. Garbo was staying at the Hassler Hotel at the top of the Spanish Steps, so we went in the same car. It had been a fascinating evening for me even if it was tinged with apprehension.

Instead of hanging around Rome doing odd dubbing sessions, I decided I would go down for a few days to Mimi in Positano, where it was much cheaper, and maybe Constantine would join me there. I didn't want to go to Anacapri, for if I was wanted it always meant at least a day's extra delay getting the ferry to Naples.

Arriving in Positano to Mimi's rooms in the early afternoon I saw only Assunta, the large motherly woman who used to get the very odd stove working, make huge pots of soup and tidy up. The signora, her brother and the other signora had gone to Amalfi for the day, she told me, offering to make some coffee.

I went upstairs with my bag to find the room Constantine and I usually had littered with a woman's clothes and make-up, as well as various things of his I recognized. Envelopes were scattered here and there so it was easy to see with whom he was sharing the room.

I felt quite numb, particularly so as that morning I had had a letter from him assuring me of his love, also saying he was coming to Rome shortly. Supposing they all came back and found me here? In panic I picked up my bag, muttered to Assunta I was sorry to have missed them, then made my way up to a small hotel near the bus-stop. The bus had just left but there was one more in a few hours.

I had seldom felt so dejected, almost hiding lest they should return by bus and see me there. What was the point of my trying to earn money for us to be together again? I kept Flotow closely by my side so he wouldn't give away my presence. I ached to be comforted.

The journey back seemed interminable; I had no appetite, and no doubt drank too much. The thought of being alone terrified me so much that I was alternately stiflingly hot, then cold. From the station I made a telephone call; it was late at night but I was welcomed. I did not spend the night alone; the anxieties and humiliations were washed away for the time being, in a warm embracing sexual ocean.

CHAPTER FORTY

It was a bleak period made tolerable by my friends. There was no news about Pabst and in my bones I knew there wouldn't be. Meeting Garbo had been a dream; reality was a future of little hope. The Tompkinses too, had financial troubles, yet their apartment was a haven. It reminded me of Bermuda, when so many people came to our house. Martha Gelhorn, Hemingway's wife, was sometimes there; Janet Flanner of the *New Yorker* called, as well as many other congenial visitors from all over. There was wine and often one of Peter's prodigious, inventive pasta dishes, a big salad and fruit. To add to everything they had heard rumours they might have to move, but somehow one never doubted Peter's ability to find something else.

Constantine wrote several letters to me, apparently unaware I had visited Positano. He was unable to settle down to writing any kind of book and had no good news of the film script. His letters touched me, for I knew that although he had a fiercely possessive love for me, his first love was writing. Had I done any good in coming to Rome, apart from being able to support myself and occasionally help him out? Mimi sent a telegram that she was coming to Rome and would I meet her at the Inghilterra? As I sat alone in the tiny bar waiting for her I turned over these questions in my mind. Tennessee Williams came in and I thought, as I had when I met him briefly before, what very tortured eyes he had, set in the determined face of a businessman. He had a curiously set facial expression, yet the eyes betrayed the agonies of a different person. He put his coffee on the small table next to mine and nodded. We sat in silence for some minutes, then abruptly he said:

'Why don't you go home, honey?'

'Do I look as gloomy as that?' I replied quickly.

Then I thought, home – where was home? I couldn't go back to my mother at almost thirty years old, or to Ireland. Both were unthinkable. My home was with Constantine, no matter what. I had been behaving like a tragedy queen about very little. Of course if I left him alone he was bound to go to bed with another woman. What on earth was I making all the fuss about? It happened all the time: look at my father, whom I adored. He did cause a certain furore from time to time but it settled down eventually. It was the shock of seeing that squalid little room with the unmade, rumpled bed that had so disturbed me

and turned my thoughts inwards so they focused entirely on myself. Georgette's
words came back:

'Imagine me with a FitzGibbon husband and four FitzGibbon children!'

Yes, indeed, she must have known several similar situations. I smiled across
the table.

'Maybe you've got a good idea,' I said.

Forthwith I wrote to Constantine asking him to come up, to leave Capri
altogether, if he thought it was a good idea. The bar was filling up; Carl Perutz,
a young American photographer who worked in Paris, came in, possibly to
photograph Tennessee Williams. Behind him was a man of most impressive
mien, who had a young dark girl by his side. He was in his late forties, of sturdy
build, just above average height, with strong almost Middle Eastern features,
black hair, a small, trimmed black beard, and the most compelling dark brown
eyes, which seemed to flash sparks. His voice was surprisingly very English,
deep-throated, almost booming yet muted. Everyone looked up, for he was
impossible to ignore. Carl seemed to know him and introduced me. He was an
English writer called Gerald Kersh, with his stepdaughter Ann.

Today when people meet someone they have seen on television they feel
they know them. In pre-television days, if you had read an author's book, you
too assumed that knowledge. As a girl I had greatly enjoyed his book *The Night
and the City* about London with its Soho prostitutes and their pimps – what
used to be called the 'seamy side' of London. Kersh wrote about it with great
understanding, tenderness and humour. They were sad human beings to be
looked after, not hounded. The book stayed in my memory long after it had
been confiscated by a pertinacious schoolteacher. To me, Kersh looked just as
the creator of such books ought to be, for one could believe that, behind the
extraordinary face with the penetrating eyes, an amazing imagination explored
many depths.

Despite his looks, Kersh's manner was extremely English, rather guarded
and polite. He asked Carl and me to lunch with them, saying he was tired
of veal; where could they get a good hearty beef dish? I mentioned Carlo's in
Trastevere, where writers like Moravia and Carlo Levi often went, famous for
its Roman speciality of *coda di bue alla vaccinara* – oxtail simmered in wine. He
almost jumped from the chair.

'My God, let's go. It's my favourite meal.'

I explained about Mimi, but he said couldn't we leave a message asking
her to follow? She was just arriving as I went into the hall, and she looked
somewhat hungover. No, she must have a drink, then she had to go and see
Pibe Packard who was ill at the Anglo-American Clinic. I told Kersh to go on

and start eating; I would try to follow, but it seemed unlikely. Mimi swallowed several brandies one after the other but repeatedly refused lunch, saying she had had something on the train, which I doubted. Would I come and see Pibe with her later on? Apropos of nothing, she said:

'Con should have come up with me. Have you heard from him?'

I said I had just written asking him to join me.

'He's in a bad way, drinking far too much, you know.'

I nodded and thought it must be too much if Mimi said so. She seemed to be unaware I had visited Positano. Assunta must have been very discreet, or more probably simply said a signora called, for she could never pronounce foreign names.

———

Constantine arrived unannounced, about three days later, in his most charming mood. He repeatedly said how glad he was to be there, particularly to see me again; he had missed me more than he ever thought possible. He'd borrowed money from Vladimir, paid all his debts and 'was heartily glad to be off that confounded island'. Looking around, he said:

'What a nice place you've got.' Then: 'Is Mimi still in Rome? She's drinking far too much. You don't know the trouble I've had with her.'

I nodded thoughtfully, waiting tactfully to approach him with an idea I had. We talked about his work and how we were going to live. I told him I had only a small reserve left until I got more work of some kind. He had next to nothing apparently, but thought he could soon finish the novel if he was in a tranquil atmosphere. I asked him who was still on Capri. He mentioned several friends, telling amusing stories about them. Then he said:

'A lot of Americans too. I can't think where they all get enough money to live on. Some are quite interesting, ex GIs mostly.'

This gave me my opportunity to broach the topic I was bursting to put forward.

'If they're ex GIs I know what they live on,' I replied quickly. 'They're all here on the GI Bill of Rights studying something or other. Why don't you get on it? It would give you a small regular income to write on.'

He said nothing for a few minutes, then: 'What on earth would I study that wouldn't take all my time?'

'Your Italian's still very limited but you have the groundwork, and what about French, which you speak so excellently?'

'Mmm, mmm . . . I might, at that. It's not a bad idea. But how do I apply?'

I had made enquiries. It was all remarkably easy to arrange and within a week he was off for a few hours a day for his lessons, for which he was allowed about $120 a month, paid weekly, quite enough to live quietly on. The Italian teacher he loved. She was an elderly contessa who passed on most interesting Roman gossip. The French instructor bored him as he constantly had to keep pretending he didn't know what he was being taught. Nevertheless the regular money was a great attraction, for he could work for several hours a day on his novel. *The Iron Hoop* was coming out in England in a few months' time, there would be a little to come on that. I was working very little so for a brief period we shared a tenuous happiness.

As the place was small I tried to leave him alone when he was writing. I had many friends, so it wasn't difficult. Some Constantine liked very much and he enjoyed talking to Kersh about books. Carl Perutz took many photographs of us, Kersh and others. I think Carl was attracted to Ann Allward, Kersh's stepdaughter, an extremely bright and attractive young girl of about twenty.

As there was only one large old key to the heavy wooden outer door, I tied it to a piece of wood, so when the top bell was rung we always went out to the terrace and threw it over, for five floors down and up was too much at one go. Luckily there was good street lighting in the piazza, particularly outside the house. If either of us went out separately we would either arrange a time to return, telephone each other to make arrangements or, failing that, leave the key at the Inghilterra. One evening, over dinner, Constantine said the novel was going well and he would work again afterwards. I decided to go to the cinema to see Visconti's film *La Terra Trema* which I had missed earlier on. It sounded fascinating, an impressionist film about a community of Italian fishermen, made on location with a mainly non-professional cast. The cinema was on the outskirts of Rome, therefore I told him I would be home later than usual. It was nearing midnight when I got back and rang the bell. No answer. Maybe he'd gone to bed, I thought, so I rang again and waited. No answer. This went on for about twenty minutes before I went round to the Inghilterra, to find no key there and no message left. I went into the bar and ordered a coffee. After about half an hour Carl looked in and seemed very surprised to see me there. I told him I was locked out, what could I do? We had a drink together, he assuring me Con would be there soon.

'He probably got sick of writing and went out for a nightcap. But I've a big double room upstairs – why don't we go up and sit comfortably? We can telephone from time to time.'

It was a large room with two beds. I noticed on the central bedside table a copy of *The Iron Hoop* Con had lent him. We discussed it, and also a book of Kersh's he had borrowed.

'I know,' he said. 'Before it gets too late I'll go along to Kersh's room, ask him to share it with me, and you can sleep here.'

Alas Kersh wasn't there. It was getting very late; we were both tired. The ring of the phone broke the drowsy silence. Carl went to answer it; quickly I said:

'Don't say I'm here. Say you saw me and you'll leave a message with the night porter for when I come back.'

When he put down the phone I asked how Con sounded.

'Rather high and very annoyed.'

I decided to leave the room and either go back to the bar if it was still open, or maybe walk round to the piazza. The phone rang again, and I could hear Con being abusive to Carl. He was coming round.

'I'll go along to the bathroom and wait,' I said. 'Then you let me know when he's gone and I'll go back. I rather dread it if he's drunk.'

It seemed like an hour, sitting on the hard bathroom chair in the dim light. I had started to shake when Carl knocked on the door.

'He's gone. I said you'd be back soon, you'd gone to buy some cigarettes. For God's sake come and have a quick slug before you go, I've got a bottle in the room. You're shaking.'

We were just sipping a brandy when the door was flung open and Constantine stalked in, eyes blazing.

'If you want to have an affair with this, this specimen, I can't think why you don't say so, instead of pretending you're going to the cinema.'

We were both speechless; I was frightened for I knew Con in these moods. He would lash out. I felt trapped and sorry I had got Carl to lie about where I was; but would the truth have been any better? He strode about the room, pulling down the beds which we had only sat on, flung Carl's toilet articles about, then pounced on *The Iron Hoop* I had left open on the bed.

'Ah!' he said. 'Reading aloud to each other no doubt. I *hope* you enjoyed it.' Whereupon he turned to the dedication page and read aloud:

This book is dedicated to my wife
Theodora
With love and gratitude

He ripped the page out, tearing it into little pieces, saying:

'This is all the thanks I get for dedicating my book to you. Gratitude, love: from now on it doesn't exist.'

'You're making a scene about nothing,' I remonstrated. 'You locked me out and Carl was kind enough to give me shelter and friendship.'

I moved forward between him and Carl.

'You know quite well you are making all this up because you feel guilty yourself,' I said. 'For heaven's sake, try to be reasonable.'

He flung the book at me so that it glanced my temple. Carl moved protectively, which only inflamed Constantine further.

I turned to look at Con and realized I wasn't brave enough or masochistic enough to go back with him that night.

'I'll go and get a room here,' I told him. 'Maybe in the morning you will be more amenable.'

Carl said immediately: 'No, you stay here; I'll get another room.'

He went out. Constantine stayed glaring at me, saying nothing. I tried to be as gentle as I could for I could see he was going through an agony. It was as though another vile person coexisted in the same body.

'Couldn't we please talk about this, if there's anything to say, in the morning?' I pleaded. 'I'm deadly tired.'

He left abruptly without a word. I lay on the bed for a few minutes, then got up and pushed the small bolt on the door. Lying on the bed I realized sleep was not going to come easily. My mind raced like a piece of eccentric clockwork. What on earth had provoked all this? When I left to go to the cinema he had appeared quite normal, looking forward to an evening's work. There was wine left over from dinner and some beer in the kitchen. I closed my eyes, wanting to shut out thoughts of seeing him in the morning. I must rest at least, for if I was edgy and lost my temper I feared for the consequences. He could be very violent sometimes. I turned out the bedside light and went into a light troubled sleep. I was woken by a splintering crash, and the main lights were switched on. Constantine had kicked in the door and was standing over me, a look of fury on his face.

'What have you done with your lover?' he screamed, then went round opening the cupboard doors as though he expected Carl to be hiding in one of them. It gave me a chance to get up and pull on my dress, for I hadn't undressed completely.

'Constantine, please, oh please stop. There's nobody here but me. What on earth's the matter with you? Sit down and be reasonable.'

I went over and pushed the broken door to, not wanting to awaken the whole hotel.

'Have a drink or something, but for God's sake stop all this. We've had enough for one night.'

I think he would have done this but the night manager and the night porter had arrived and were surveying the broken door. Quite politely but firmly he was requested to leave. Whereupon he went over, took the manager, who was a small man, by the shoulders and shook him very hard, shouting at him all the time. The porter came to the manager's assistance and between them they got Con out and downstairs. I hadn't the energy to follow; it was four in the morning and I couldn't see what good I could do. The sight of me seemed to inflame him.

I left about eight o'clock, found the *portiere* up and the door open, so with a heavy heart I went up the flights of stairs. On the way up I realized I hadn't got the apartment key either, but fortunately Con hadn't locked the door, only shut it. He was sleeping peacefully on the divan at the far end of the L-shape. Flotow greeted me effusively. I went into the kitchen, made some strong coffee and took it out to the terrace by the other door. About ten o'clock he got up, came out to the terrace and said quite normally:

'Is there any coffee? I'll just have a shower and join you.'

To a stranger it would have seemed like any ordinary household enjoying breakfast on the terrace, but I knew better. His ultra-quiet manner betrayed remorse, but apart from saying he felt like hell and he hoped he hadn't been a nuisance, nothing else was mentioned. It was as though he had managed to erase any of the night's actions from his mind, like rubbing a damp sponge over a blackboard. I saw no point in bringing up the sordid business to be argued back and forth, with no sensible agreement ever reached. It was as if he had had a brainstorm which had left him with no memory of his actions. I said I was going to see my agent, then get some food, and I would be back by lunchtime. What were his plans? He replied he was going to see someone about his film script and would telephone me later. I didn't believe it, for he knew only my friends, and he would surely have mentioned it earlier. However, I was glad he wasn't going to be hanging about the apartment.

Carl accepted my apologies with a laconic smile.

'Is he often like that?' he asked. 'He seemed so friendly and easy the other times we've met. Why, I've never even made a pass at you, have I?'

'It wouldn't make any difference if you'd made dozens of passes, Carl. When Con's been drinking and he gets an idea, that's that. What worries me is, why did he suddenly go out and deliberately get so drunk when everything's been comparatively tranquil? I left him looking forward to an evening's work – I wonder did somebody telephone?'

Carl asked me to lunch, but I refused saying I was going to have a quiet day if possible. In fact I had several quiet days. Constantine was a model husband; nothing more was ever said about that night. However, we were reminded of it when we were meeting friends for drinks in the Inghilterra Hotel. The manager called Constantine out and requested he didn't use the hotel any more. This he accepted with a shrug of the shoulders. About a week later (having before that insisted on being with me the entire day, even when I had business appointments), he started going out for long periods at odd hours, once staying out all night, arriving home in various moods and having drunk quite a lot. Sometimes he would be extremely amorous, at other times treat me with hostility. There was no pattern to it, which was very unsettling.

Then I got flu quite badly, which made him absent himself as much as possible. This was not unusual; he hated any illness. It took me longer than it would normally to recover from this flu and I had horrible depression afterwards. I'd had to forgo a job because I simply didn't feel strong enough. My money was running out again; Constantine seemed to spend an awful lot. At the beginning of November he came in late one night, looking very thoughtful, and for once quite sober, but he seemed restless, walking up and down the room incessantly. At last he said:

'I can't work here. I think I'll go back to Capri; it'll be quiet there in the winter.'

'But you hate Capri, you've said so over and over. You came up here because you couldn't work there.'

'No, I came up here because I love you and wanted to be with you. Anyway it's Anacapri I hated, especially that horrid little house. Since Riette [Gerald Osborne's wife] left him with the baby, he wants me to go too. He's willing to pay the rent of a villa, and I've got my GI Bill money as well. I must get that book finished.'

'I've got practically nothing left and I don't feel well enough to work at the moment,' I answered. 'Can't I come too?'

'He's only asked me. He obviously can't support both of us. You'll be all right. I'll ask him for some money before we go and let you have some to tide you over.'

I could hardly believe what I was hearing. He was prepared to be bought by Gerry Osborne to live a comfortable life on Capri whilst I half-starved in Rome. Was this a sign of love? Surely not. I honestly didn't feel I had any strength left to argue with him: I just felt utterly depressed. In any case I knew that whatever I said would make little difference, if he had made up his mind to go. He, on the other hand, became remarkably cheerful, saying it would be wonderful to be in a quiet place again, with good air, a nice large comfortable villa and so on. I wished he would go at once although my heart was breaking. It had all been an utter failure my coming to Rome. Instead of mending the rift between us, it seemed to have widened it. Now we were to be separated yet again and there seemed no chance of our living together for some time. My friendship with Gerry Osborne, too, had been strained since I had heard from Constantine some very untrue gossip he had passed on about me, well knowing Constantine's violently jealous nature.

Thankfully Con spent a large part of the day away from the apartment, presumably making arrangements with Gerry. Every day dragged interminably and I dragged with it, feeling heavy, sleepy, and unlike myself. Constantine by contrast was lively, drinking fairly moderately, quite pleasant to me, although I felt boring and I'm sure I was. It hurt me rather, until I remembered how much he loved change, having almost a child's expectation of a journey. Several days later he came home and, sitting at the table, started to count what seemed to me like a lot of money. He gave me the equivalent of about twenty pounds, shovelling the rest into his pocket.

'That should keep you going until you get some work,' he said. 'We're leaving the day after tomorrow. Can I take your big suitcase? I'll send it back by someone who's coming to Rome.'

The day he left I told him I didn't care to see him leave, so I took Flotow for a long walk in the Pincio Gardens. It was far colder than when we had arrived that day half a world ago, full of hope and love. When I got home I walked out on the terrace; even Rome seemed silent, as silent as the beats of my heart. I shivered, turned and went indoors, shutting the doors, then lighting a fire. I was cold even so, and restless. Pictures of the rumpled bed and the torn-open air-mail letters flashed through my mind. Quickly I drank the half-bottle of wine on the table – a *fiasco*, wasn't that what I was drinking to? I found an almost empty bottle of strega, the herby, strong, sweet liqueur of the north, reputedly an aphrodisiac. Then, still restless, I went round to the café in the via Frattina; thankfully, nobody I knew was there. I don't know how much brandy I drank, the strong vanilla-tasting Italian brandy with the horse's head on the bottle. My mind was almost a blank. I felt nothing except a vague feeling of warmth and confusion. I suppose I was drunk, but it wasn't like any sort of drunkenness I had had before. The night air made me feel dizzy when I walked home. I went into my once much-loved apartment, which looked strangely unlived-in. I was violently sick; Flotow seemed worried about me and tried to amuse me by bringing a shoe. Later he came up on the divan and curled down the long curve of my back. Thus we slept dreamlessly for ten hours or more.

Surprisingly I felt much better in the morning and I went to shop in the via della Croce. On the way I met Ann Allward, who said she was on her way round to me as Kersh had asked us to lunch; he was leaving in two days' time. As she accompanied me I told her Constantine had left for Capri and I didn't know if I'd be able to keep the apartment on. Immediately she asked if she could share it with me. Her mother was in America, Kersh was going to London and she wanted to stay in Rome. She had an allowance, so could easily pay her way. I said I must think about it, and she must get Kersh's approval. Kersh was in fact against the idea, fearing Constantine might suddenly turn up and make scenes, but I assured him I wouldn't let it happen. It was fortunate for both of us as it turned out, for we got on extremely well together. We both had things to learn from each other.

Sometime later when she woke me up in the middle of the night complaining of violent pains and sickness, I was able to get her to hospital for an appendix operation. When I went to see her the next day she looked very well, but said she was extremely hungry. In the same ward other visitors were giving their relatives hampers of food, which made us both hungry.

'Maybe you're not supposed to have anything yet,' I ventured. 'I'll find a nun and see if I can get you something.'

The nun said yes, she could have food, and went to move on.

'Will you bring her something, then?'

'Oh no, signora, we don't provide food here. You must get it from the café opposite!'

I got her a sandwich consisting of a loaf split in half with ham and cheese, some fruit and milk. It wasn't exactly invalid fare but was better than nothing. Later that day I told Peter and Jerree, Peter saying at once it was a charity hospital and she must be got out of there and put in the Anglo-American Clinic; Kersh would send some money. A young American there said if Peter lent him the jeep he would get her out the next day. Chuck, the American, and I went in the jeep to fetch her. Nobody said anything as I put a coat around her, took a wheelchair from the hall and wheeled her down to the jeep. If they wondered where their patient was they certainly never contacted me to ask. Chuck drove his strange cargo across Rome, leaving me in the hall of the clinic while he went on with Ann, saying he would pick me up later. She was bubbling with laughter when I visited her in the comfortable clinic the next day.

'Did you hear what happened to me?' she burst out immediately. 'Chuck handed me over, and I was put on a table for some time,' she went on, 'then a young doctor came in and examined me. "Are you sure you should be here?" he asked, and I said of course, I only left the hospital today. "I can't make it out," he replied.' She started to laugh again before continuing. 'Chuck had asked for the delivery room, so there I was in the maternity section. The doctor and I started to giggle so much I broke open my stitches. But I'm OK now.'

Pibe Packard was just along the corridor in the same hospital, so when Ann was walking I used to find her in Pibe's room sometimes. We spent several very pleasant weeks together, her fresh outlook and straightforward personality being just what I needed to face up to everything again. Together we looked for work and made plans.

Constantine wrote affectionate letters mainly about himself and Capri. To begin with he stayed at the Quisisana, Capri's most expensive hotel, and had 'a total rest'. He had seen Paolo Langheim, who had asked after me 'rather warmly'. He wasn't going to indulge in any two-day drinking and was longing to get to work again. It was much better this way, he was sure. Then an astonishing letter came saying they had all moved into the Casa Solatia, could I lend them some linen and blankets? It was very annoying, he also wrote, of Concetta to keep asking after me every twenty minutes. Somehow, to me, it seemed like betrayal going back to our house, which we had shared with so much hope and love despite all the worries.

There was another problem ahead I was reluctant to face. It was no use pretending to myself day after day that it wasn't so, and as another month passed, I knew for certain I was pregnant. Ann was the first person I told when the *malaise* and sickness began to get worse, and she was concerned for me. I must tell Constantine, she insisted. This I was hesitant to do. However, when I found some days I was too sick to work, I did write. He replied very coolly that I must go to an American doctor, this was stressed, and get him 'to inform me by letter of the state of your health'. Also why didn't I go to Positano? He could come over for a bit. He had a continual headache after flu; he had been drinking with Graham Greene and Rex Warner; Peggy Guggenheim was expected for the winter; the mayor and the entire *municipio* had been sacked owing to a matter of 130,000,000 lire being missing from municipal funds. It was an oddly impersonal letter, as if written to a distant friend. There was no word of comfort or concern.

Ann was extremely kind, always helpful. I loved her fresh, young approach to everything. It made me remember myself ten years back, determinedly facing up to reality, not knowing or even caring about the future. Ten years back I had been even younger than Ann, living in Paris on the small amount of money I had saved, contemplating, as I sat in the Café Flore, that Paris was where I wanted to be. There was so much I wanted to learn about that wonderful city, and I was confident that I could become a good actress if I worked hard enough, and really studied actresses like Edwige Feuillère or Françoise Rosay and absorbed the timing of their words and actions. Night after night I sat in cheap seats in the theatre, watching Madeleine Ozeray in Cocteau's *Ondine* until I could have played the part, so word perfect was I. Whereas now I was apprehensive, wondering how I was going to manage, and pondering much of the time what Constantine's reaction would be.

Ann urged me to write to Mimi and to go down to Positano for a rest. She could easily pay the rent, I mustn't worry. Then when I had sorted something out I could come back, for she would always welcome me. She even gave me the fare, so I would have a bit extra to spend there.

Mimi wrote a welcoming letter back saying there was hardly anyone there and it would be 'fun to see me'. It was beastly cold so I should bring warm clothes. She was off with Con and expressed her feelings about him vividly and somewhat coarsely. Once more I packed up a few clothes and possessions, and one raw November day Flotow and I took the bus to Positano. I was not looking forward to it as I left the snug room at the Piazza di Spagna.

CHAPTER FORTY-ONE

The old bus had no heating, the only warmth emanating from the *esprit de corps* of the other passengers. As they left, the temperature dropped considerably, but when we made a convenience stop, and I walked Flotow for a minute in the chill air, I was glad to get back to the bus, empty save for the driver. Dim lights glowed feebly and I thought for a minute I was going to be the only passenger. Then a light, quick step sounded; I looked up and saw a man talking to the driver. He turned and came towards me.

'Aren't you . . .? Didn't we . . .?' We both said together.

Then he said: 'I'm Mario Prodan. Didn't we meet visiting Pibe Packard once?' He smiled, an attractive smile, white teeth shining in the dim light. 'May I sit next to you? It's cold, isn't it?' He folded his lapels over and pulled down his hat.

'Wait a minute. I must get Flotow out first. You might tread on him.' Flotow's brown curly head loomed up from under the seat; he looked pleased to be out.

'What a well-behaved dog. I didn't dream he was even on the bus. Here boy, come right out.' Mario sat beside me, Flotow awkwardly in the aisle.

'Why don't we have him on our laps?' he said. 'He'd keep us beautifully warm.'

So that is how we travelled on to Positano, Flotow spread across us like a excellent fur rug, his dear head resting on my arm.

A stranger on a bus driving into the dark encourages confidences. You learn more about a person in an hour than you would over many weeks of meeting in company. I had had similar experiences on long-distance trains; somehow the movement made you feel it was important to say things before you parted. I learned he was a sinologist, had lived in China for many years, spoke good Chinese, had studied Chinese art, at which he was an expert, and while there had married a girl of Scottish ancestry whose name was Cissie. They had two daughters and now lived in Rome, but he made many Far Eastern trips, on one of which he had met the Packards, both journalists for *Time* magazine. He was like many in Italy in those days, film crazy. His ambition was to write and make his own film, which is why he was coming to Positano to a quiet house, up in the hills, to write his script.

'And you?' he enquired.

I mentioned acting, which interested him. I said Constantine was a writer with two accepted novels and other books commissioned, which interested him even more. I found myself describing Constantine as he once was: amusing, clever, full of ideas, altogether charming – all of which he could be still when he chose. It must have sounded an ideal marriage in many ways. The curious thing is, that while I was saying it I thought of Con just like that. I had almost forgotten the humiliations and scenes, so much so I almost looked forward to seeing him when we arrived.

However, there was nobody to meet me when we stopped at the piazza in front of the church. Inwardly I began to quake; supposing he was in the Buca with—? Could I trust myself to behave properly? Mario stamped his feet, turned to me and said:

'Where are you going, then?'

I replied I would walk down to the Buca to look for Mimi.

He said graciously that he would accompany me. The Buca seemed very gay, lively and, most of all, warm. There were quite a few people there I knew: Pinky Hartman, Alex, Isabella, Mimi and a tall arresting-looking woman dressed in a very beautiful velvet trouser suit, with dark hair, large expressive brown eyes and a deep Italian voice, whom I had seen before. She was introduced as Fiore de Henriques, a sculptor. Even while I was admiring her *tenue*, I couldn't help noting to myself that 'flower' was a remarkably unsuitable name. There was no sign of Constantine. Mimi looked up from her seat by the bar, seemingly delighted at a new injection of life into the party. She took charge of Mario and ordered drinks. Everyone ordered drinks in fact, and on an empty stomach they worked faster than usual.

'Is Constantine here, or where?'

'Don't talk to me about that shit of a brother of mine,' she said. 'I suppose he's still in Capri enjoying Gerry's hospitality. There are quite a few people there now, all lapping it up.'

I gathered from subsequent remarks that the main cause for the resentment was because she had been left out. I went over to speak to Luca, the waiter who had been Mimi's lover for some time. I was feeling quite muzzy.

'Can you get me a room somewhere, Luca? I don't want to stay in Mimi's spare room.'

'She's not in Pack's apartment any more. Come, I'll show you where she is now.'

He carried my case as we walked along the narrow street of crumbling houses, all now either restaurants or boutiques, and led me upstairs.

'You can have this room, there's nobody staying here. Mimi's downstairs. I must get back. *Ciao.*'

I sat on the bed and looked around. No, it wasn't the same room, but it was very cold and cheerless without even one of the little brass charcoal braziers going, over which we huddled in the winter. I did the old trick I had been taught during my early theatrical touring days, of putting the electric lamp with shade inside the bed to produce a bit of heat. I remembered an old pro saying to me, 'The real ones like this are called a "priest". Funny name, isn't it?' I giggled to myself at the thought. I didn't remember anything of the last half-hour at the Buca, but consoled myself with the thought that probably no one else did either. Piling my coat and Flotow on the bed, I put on a sweater and went to bed after taking the lamp out. It had produced a faint warmth.

In the morning I was woken up by Mimi coming in waving a brandy bottle.

'If you feel anything like me you'll need a shot,' she said.

'But I haven't had coffee yet. What's the time? No, Mimi, I couldn't face it. I'd be sick.'

She glugged away, making a face each time she swallowed. As the days went by, the same pattern was followed. I had somehow to get her to cut it down. Luca agreed, but how to do it was what we both wanted to know. There was a very charming Hungarian woman living quietly in Positano who was writing a book about her experiences during the war, then her escape. She needed typing done, and general help. Although a slow two-finger typist, I offered to help and roped Mimi in. She didn't do very much but it gave her an interest and kept her off the bottle until the evenings. Then I asked people to meals, anything to prevent her getting bored again. She loved thinking up recipes, 'a change from that bloody pasta all the time', and became both inventive and active. They were simple meals because we hadn't much money, but Luca would get us chickens and meat cheaply, which we transformed into many different dishes.

'How d'you make a curry?' she asked one day. 'I'm dying for a curry.'

Carefully I made out a list of spices for the next person who was going to Naples to bring back. It was very exciting the day they came; just the aroma of them took me back to Paris and the meal Peter Rose Pulham and I had made the day after some money arrived, and we had been living for a week on bread rubbed with garlic. The day came; a few friends had been asked; we chopped and ground spices all morning. We peeled and sliced, had to send out for more charcoal to feed the ugly old stove, but then it was nearing completion, the rich juices tasted endlessly, the warm strong wild smell wafting out on to the street.

'I don't think I can wait until they all come,' said Mimi. 'I hope they're not late.'

Then we looked at each other when the table was laid. No chutney.

'We can't have a curry without chutney.'

'They do in India sometimes, it's a British idea really. You know Major Gray's Mango Chutney.'

'Well, I want chutney. What on earth can we do?'

Eventually we did have a chutney of a very superior and unusual kind. We soaked sultanas, raisins, chopped glacé fruits, and chopped lemons and oranges in Marsala wine, then after a few hours, when the fruit was fat and plump, we added brandy. It was a wonderful chutney which everybody ate lavishly. I shudder to think what orthodox non-drinking Indians would have thought of it.

I heard nothing from Constantine and in a way it was a relief. Mimi and I were getting on very well. I was earning a little money, and the drink bill was considerably less. I felt much healthier and had stopped being sick. In fact I had got used to the idea of pregnancy; somehow 'God would provide', as they always said in Ireland. Luca always kept me leftover pasta and scraps for Flotow, which I would collect daily. Pinky rushed in one day when I was there, crying:

'There's some gorgeous men coming to Positano in a few days' time. They're in Sorrento at the moment.'

Luca and I looked at each other. The Italian grapevine was very strong and he had heard nothing.

'I'll ask at some of the hotels,' he said thoughtfully.

Meanwhile, quite unexpectedly, Constantine arrived, 'for a few days', he said, to see how I was. He seemed quieter than usual and, when I asked how the book was going, all I got was a casual 'all right'.

Then the 'gorgeous men' arrived. Pinky dashed in to ask if he could borrow my black lace blouse for the evening at the Buca, to which I readily agreed. Curiously, that evening the Buca was deserted when the four men entered. Just us, a few locals with some Swedish girls and an elderly Italian painter. They were dressed in pale khaki drill trousers with smart shirts and cravats, almost as though it was summer, not the end of November, They seemed to us to have a strange way of talking, addressing each other very formally. Each sentence started Sar . . . or Su . . . then they would correct themselves and heartily slap one another on the back saying something like:

'What'll you have Bill (or Jack)?'

The locals eyed them suspiciously, as did Luca. I saw him disappear to the telephone in the back and when he returned he was smiling. Mimi had put on some records, which cheered the place up. One of them came over to Mimi to ask her to dance, but she said promptly:

'Why don't you ask Pinky? He's a much better dancer!' He eyed Pinky disconsolately, who was standing nearby, fetching in my lace blouse.

Luca beckoned me and I followed him. He was longing to tell someone his news.

'They're all policemen,' he said. 'They're here to find out where the English are getting the money from to live here. That's why Alex and the others have driven off.' We laughed quietly, conspiratorially.

'I'll tell Mimi and Con. We'll have some fun with them.'

And fun it was too, quite lucrative fun as it turned out. Con and Mimi had played cards together since childhood, and were both extremely good at bridge and poker. They seemed to know just by looking at each other what cards the other one had. For several days they played cards with the policemen and won quite a lot of money. Then, when a cunning question was aimed at them as to money, Con said in his most English voice:

'Oh, it's no use asking us anything. We're Americans. I was born in Lenox, Mass. That's my sister.' Which of course was true.

Shortly afterwards the policemen moved on, sadder and no wiser. I often wondered how they accounted for the losses on their expense sheets. It certainly cheered us up during the long winter evenings.

Constantine stayed much longer than he had intended, mainly I think because he enjoyed Mario Prodan's company. Together they thought of a film for the Holy Year, which was to be in 1950, and many days he would walk up to Mario's house in the hills to work with him on it. They both talked about it incessantly, and because he was working after a fashion, Constantine's behaviour towards me was reasonable. It was easy to work here, he said. Casa Solatia had too many people in it now. I resisted asking who was there. Then one morning he asked if I had the big suitcase he had borrowed. Gerry had taken it back to Rome and Riette was supposed to bring it round to me.

No, she didn't; but I could pick it up when I went back.

'You wouldn't like to go up and get it, would you? I think I'll leave Solatia; everything's getting too complicated.'

No, I wouldn't like to go and get it. What was the hurry anyway?

'Well I'll go, then. I want to see the GI people about transferring my grant. I think I'll go to Paris, then maybe on to England. Pity you're pregnant. It's come at a very bad time.'

He said this as though the pregnancy was parthenogenetic.

'I'm not staying in Italy if you're going back to England. You might have talked to me about it.'

He kicked at a hole in the carpet, walked to the window, and said:

'It's only just occurred to me, actually. I think I'd do better there with my book coming out next year. I might be able to sell my new novel, which is all but finished. I do love you, darling, but we seem to be getting deeper into a morass of drink and debt.'

'I don't owe anything, and I only occasionally get drunk when everything seems too much. It's a funny way of loving someone, to rush off and leave them when they're carrying your child.'

'From all I've heard I'm not even certain it is mine,' he said. This really incensed me. I almost shouted:

'From whom? From Gerry, I suppose, who ever since I refused to go to bed with him has hissed untrue gossip at you? For heaven's sake, be reasonable; check the dates if you like, but don't ever say such a thing to me again. If you do, everything is finished between us, damn you.'

He left abruptly and I heard later from Luca he had taken the bus to somewhere. I should have known; he always had to have a plausible excuse if he wanted to do something of which I would disapprove, to stop him feeling too guilty.

Mimi was very loyal, urging me to stay with her. She would write to her mother, who would send some money, she was sure. She became quite protective towards me, very kind and thoughtful, almost too much so, stopping me having more than two or three glasses of wine at a time, and also restricting herself. She also decided that where she lived was not suitable for me, not warm or comfortable enough. Cleverly she negotiated winter rates for us both at an hotel near the top of Positano. The hundred steps were too much for me! I was very touched, finding myself very close to her. In the closed circle of one's emotions, one tends to discount other people's. She, too, had had to leave the husband she loved. I grew to love her. Luca, her lover, was very kind too; he was very fond of Flotow, unusually so for a young Italian man. His strong sturdy body, the age-old face betraying its Greek origins, and the puckered smile all appealed to me. His determination to have his own restaurant was realized within five years.

Some weeks later, in December, Constantine arrived back to Positano with my suitcase, intending I think to return to Capri and possibly pack up, but I insisted he stayed a little to discuss any plans. I had begun to realize the foolishness of staying on alone, possibly unable to work, certainly to act, no proper medical attention, or indeed any sort of attention. However, there was Flotow. I wouldn't leave him with Mimi lest she start drinking again when I had gone; we could never have afforded quarantine fees and I hated the thought of having him put down. We were discussing it one day when Mario called. He stroked his beard, looked thoughtful, then said:

'I'll take him; he's a most lovable animal. Cissie will love him; we've just lost our old dog. Come on, boy, walkies.'

When Constantine was leaving for Rome, I went as far as Sorrento with him. From the bus in Positano we saw Mario standing with a contented-looking Flotow on the lead. He bent down to pat him, then gave us the thumbs-up sign. It was my last glimpse of my companion of many years, but he was to have a happy life until the end of his days.

It had been arranged that Con would spend some days in Rome before going on to Paris, where he would wait for me at the old Hotel Montana. If he wasn't there at the time he would also leave a letter at the Café Flore. Would I go to Anacapri and collect a few things of his he had left with Tony Paanaker? I had left most of my possessions in Rome, and these I had to pack up too. He would leave me half his GI money at the American Express for the journey. It seemed comparatively simple. Mimi was sad at the idea of my going, and toyed with the idea of coming too, but I pointed out I didn't know where I would end up, as I couldn't stay indefinitely at my mother's tiny flat in Chelsea. The thought of going back to Anacapri hung over me and depressed me utterly.

It was a cold and windy day in January when I took the ferry from Sorrento to Capri. The seas were high; the boat looked very small as I looked out of the window of the Excelsior Vittoria Hotel where I was having some coffee. Soon I would go down in the old hotel lift to the harbour, but I felt apprehensive and unwell. This I put down to going back to the place where we had been so unhappy, from where I had left with Mouche that horrible morning which seemed so long ago when she had had to be put down. As I picked up the empty canvas bag I had brought, knife-like pains shot through my stomach; my head and legs ached. Was this what was called psychosomatic? I wondered. Pulling myself together, I went downstairs and on to the boat; it smelt horribly of oil which made me feel queasy, so I had a brandy in the bar. There were a few Italians there and a young American man who smiled at me.

As we got away from land I began to feel very sick. I had never felt seasick in my life, going to and from India, to America in the winter on a small steamer, even during a typhoon in the Indian Ocean. Nevertheless I was horribly sick then. The pains in my stomach increased.

'You look very pale. Are you all right?' asked the young American. 'Can I get you something?'

He ministered to me during that short journey; I learned he was going to say goodbye to his girlfriend, one of Edwin Cerio's daughters, before going back to America. He was very much in love and very sad. When we arrived he insisted on seeing me to the bus, even saying where he would be later on if I felt ill again. The Cerio girl was fortunate, I thought, as I took leave of him.

Tony Paanaker, in contrast, seemed even more repulsive than I remembered. He rolled his frog-spawn eyes at me, putting forward propositions 'if I stayed on'. The lunch was interminable. Poor Ilda the maid, whom he had taken over from Con, looked quite cowed and nervous. I took what I could carry, for the books weighed heavily, saying I would come back sometime for the rest. I searched and searched for the slim volume of Merimée's stories I had taken from Peter in Paris, but I never found it, which distressed me further. The walk to the bus tired me immensely; the twirl of Paanaker's stick and the rhythm as he kept putting it down jarred my head. The journey back seemed interminable and in between trying to rest in the bus I was only thankful I wouldn't have to get down all those steps to the old room at the Buca.

Mimi took one look at me and put me to bed. I was racked with pain and had a fever, but the nearest doctor was in Sorrento, an hour away at least, even if he came at once. Mimi went off to get Assunta – that kind, large, motherly woman – who bathed my forehead and gave me some sweet-smelling herb tea to drink, muttering comforting phrases I didn't understand. Later that night I lost the baby which had caused such contention. Assunta said prayers over it, wrapped it up carefully and departed, leaving me clean and comfortable. She would be along in the morning after the *bambini* had gone to school. I slept.

For several days I rested, feeling drained. I ate but little, thinking I would give several years of my life for a cup of Irish tea. I could almost smell the turf burning under the blackened kettle in the kitchen, and the warm aroma of soda bread taken from the range, spread when hot with golden country butter. As I gazed out over the sea, I came to hate it, wishing it was the green, so-green pastures of my home, horses nibbling peacefully, the mist-enshrouded hills in the distance. That's what I would do – go back to Ireland for a while. One extra person in that house never mattered: I could look after the soft-nosed, nuzzling horses, help on the land. But, even as I thought it, I knew it was a fantasy. I would never be able to lift and carry heavy bales of straw and hay, lift milk churns or any of the most essential things. They would give me love, wonder how long I was going to stay, and ask, where was my husband? Had I met any 'fillum' stars or made my fortune in the lands beyond the avenue gates?

Mimi interrupted my reverie, sounding just like her mother, saying:

'It's just like Con, going off just when we want him; *and* we don't know where he is. I wonder if he's still in Rome. Shall we try and ring up someone?'

On very bad, indistinct lines we rang Ann, who had seen him once, but knew nothing more. Then we rang the Tompkinses, and Peter said he'd rescued him from the contessa who owned the Anacapri house. Apparently she wanted some money, and as her lover was chief of police in Naples, well . . . you know. He thought he'd left, but couldn't be sure. Mimi said she'd send a telegram to Paris but I scoffed at the idea, knowing how the ones from Capri to Rome got scrambled. However, send one she did, announcing it proudly.

'What on earth did you say?' I asked.

'I said the calf had slipped and you couldn't travel for a few days. I sent it to the Flore.'

I burst out laughing:

'Oh, Mimi, in the unlikely event of his ever getting it he won't understand it.'

Then we both laughed until the tears rolled down our cheeks, but afterwards I felt much better.

In Rome, Ann welcomed me at the apartment when I arrived from the train. It looked so cosy and charming that I felt many pangs of regret at having to leave it. She had made some enquiries and thought Con had stayed much longer than a few days, more like a week, but she had no idea where he'd been living. She remarked on how thin I was, so I had to tell her what had happened.

'Are you sure you can make the journey?' she enquired. 'Stay a little longer until you feel stronger.'

'If I do I'll probably never go back, Ann. I think I'd better go; I can always come back if things turn out better. I'll go and see what there is at the American Express across the road tomorrow.'

My agent had been telephoning every day; apparently I had missed all sorts of offers, which I wouldn't have been able to take in any case.

I looked at the electric sewing machine which Dylan Thomas had once tried ineffectively to pawn, realizing I couldn't carry it. So finally I sold it to a contessa's English nanny, the name 'Singer' working magic.

My money stretched to a second-class ticket, but not a couchette, with a little over; so I borrowed something from Peter to have enough to stay over in Paris if our meeting went awry. Packing up was difficult, for I didn't want to take things Ann was using; it consisted mainly of personal items I wouldn't like to be without and a few clothes, anything which would fit into the old secondhand Revelation case I had bought in New York. On my last night, Reinhard and Bendi came to dinner. Bendi was very excited about a job he had got in, of all places, Tahiti, so the mood was festive. The thought of England with no friends was depressing, but I put it aside. Peter drove me to the station, efficiently dealing with everything. It was a sad leave-taking, especially so without Flotow. I was determined to come back.

As I settled in my corner seat, I hoped some of the other passengers would leave before we crossed the frontier; otherwise we would have very little room to stretch out and sleep during the night. I started to read the Thurber book I had brought from Bermuda, conjuring up my meetings with him; the laughter, warmth, anticipation and love Constantine and I had shared there. Unaccountably John Donne's lines came into my head:

> I long to talk with some old lover's ghost,
> Who died before the god of love was born.

Did I still love Constantine? If I didn't, why was I leaving this beautiful country I felt at home in and going back to England? Would we be able to live peacefully – I dared not think of the word 'happily' – again? I still had a battered kind of love left, I decided, but I was hurt and bruised, both physically and mentally. Maybe a few days in Paris with Con would bring us closer together, for his fondness for that city equalled mine. My thoughts whirled round incessantly, punctuated with maybe's and ifs.

If only Con could write again, I knew other things would fall into place. I looked out at the harsh February light which made the fruit trees of Tuscany stand out like regiments of well-trained soldiers; every scrap of ground was diligently cultivated, here and there a farmhouse with its vineyard, the vines twisted and bare, waiting for the sun of spring to clothe them in pale green leaves. Florence, the city of gold, containing enough beauty to last several lifetimes. The noise of the engine seemed to hammer out: 'why leave, why leave, come back, come back . . .' – through the Emilia Romagna with its fertile land tucked under the mountains; Parma, its cheese, pale gold honeycombs of pleasure, the whey-fed pigs making the pale rose ham, paper-thin slices of sweet tenderness. It was making me very hungry, and realizing I had had no lunch I gathered up my things and made my way along the crowded train to the restaurant car. That too was very full, and in hurrying to get one of the two vacant seats I was thrown by a jolt in the train almost on to a man's lap; my book went flying across the table. The man picked it up and closed it, looking at the title before handing it back to me.

'Thurber,' he said almost to himself. 'I haven't read him since I was in America just before the war. He's a very amusing writer, isn't he? Are you American?'

I took the book and sat down.

'No, I'm not. If anything, I'm Irish.'

This was said a little ungraciously, for I was annoyed at stumbling, the contents of my travelling bag were strewn about on the floor, my purse had rolled out of sight and I felt panicky.

'Here you are,' he said. 'I think that's everything. It's amazing how far things will roll, isn't it?'

As he sat down, I looked at him, smiled and thanked him very much. He was an Englishman, about fifty years old, fair thinning hair over a kindly but undistinguished face. He was easy to talk to and we talked of Thurber, my meeting him in Bermuda and many things, as we lingered over our coffee. I was turning over in my mind whether I had enough Italian money for a sandwich (the last taste of Parma ham) and some fruit as well as to last me until we reached Paris, when he asked me to join him at dinner.

After dinner I felt exhausted. Realizing I would have to sit up all night, I mentioned I must get back to my seat, otherwise people would be spread over it.

'Don't you have a couchette?' he enquired. 'You can't possibly sit in a compartment full of people. You look very tired and pale. Wait a minute.' It was comfortable in the restaurant car and I was almost asleep when he came back.

'It's all fixed, come along.'

'But no, what about you?'

'Don't worry, please. I'd be most happy if you would take the compartment the steward is preparing for you. See you in Paris in the morning.'

I don't know where he slept, but after a comfortable night I didn't see him in Paris in the morning. I took a taxi to the Montana; Monsieur had left two days ago, no there was no letter. It was then about nine-thirty in the morning so I left my luggage, then walked to the Café Flore, where I would have breakfast and think what to do.

Although the Flore looked very much the same, all the faces were alien to me there. Pascal had retired and there was no message for me.

'Deux oeufs sur le plat, s'il vous plait, avec du pain et café.'

When it was served, the taste took me back ten years. When Peter and I had any money, that is what we had for breakfast at the Flore. We could boil or fry eggs at home, but we didn't have any of those lovely little stainless-steel dishes to cook them this way. How grandly Pascal would serve them, beaming with pleasure, sometimes a curl of sweet, crisp bacon added. Automatically I broke the still-warm fresh *baton* of bread and dipped it first in the orange yolks as we always did. Why did they taste so much better in France? Was it the good Normandy butter they were cooked in? I wondered if he and Mary were living in Paris, and thought how perfect it would be if that enormous hunched-up figure walked through the door. Cautiously I counted my money to see if I had enough to spend a night in Paris, with perhaps a bowl of soup tonight, and to telephone my mother. After all it was almost ten years since I had seen the armoured cars full of German soldiers rattling down the streets, and before I started on the long bicycle ride to St Jean de Luz for England. Almost without thinking, when I left the Flore I found myself turning into the rue du Bac, then on through to the rue de Bellechasse which crossed it. I stood outside the building where Donald Maclean's apartment had been, the apartment Peter and I had shared and left Paris from, albeit at different times. The brass plate containing the bells had very different names; the window I used to look from had an unfriendly face which seemed to tell me to go away and not waste my time there. I turned into the Boulevard St Germain until I came to the rue des Saints Pères. On the corner of the turning I bought a bag of hot chestnuts, asking the seller if the Hôtel des Saints Pères was still there.

'Mais oui, mademoiselle.' He said it as though I had asked if Notre-Dame was still there.

As I went on walking, I thought: if they have room number seven, I'll stay there overnight. The hall was as I remembered it, the brass clock with the loud tick, heavy curtains and large, old furniture. Yes, number seven was free and I could afford it. The huge, downy brass bed still dominated the room. I moved to touch the left-hand knob at the top of the bed. It still wiggled and came off easily when I lifted it. I heard myself saying:

'If we get separated during the war I'll leave a message for you under that knob.'

I had forgotten, though, and there was no message, except the welcome of the silent over-furnished room. That was all a grief ago.

———

How very different the French bourgeois atmosphere was, even from some English hotels, where those of a similar class were often still imbued with a rakish Regency air; or sometimes a slightly erotic Edwardian muskiness hung about the embossed walls and the tasselled curtains. Illicit love and memories of *Fanny by Gaslight* were not too far away. On the fringe of memory was Dostoevsky's account of a summer month in London, from which he fled in horror at the licentiousness on and off those gracious streets, some with rural-sounding names like Haymarket.

The hotels of Europe filled my mind. Was the first one clear? Yes. I was a five-year-old child recovering from measles in the darkened room, a screen around the bed, endless dishes of bread-and-butter pudding; so that for many years it was impossible to taste it without thinking of that room and the half-light. Then the pleasure when the screen was removed, the blinds raised, several people standing around the bed asking the question:

'Will she be all right to travel so far?'

Being warmly dressed despite the July sun, scarf wrapped round the face so that only the eyes showed, and seated on cushions with a rug, in the 'dicky' at the back outside part of the open tourer, which had a seat, usually reserved for children 'because the air is good for her'. On to the boat at Dover, standing on the quay and watching the car swung high in the air, on a crane, to be put on board.

Whisked away to a cabin, the tickly scarf and coat taken off, then some biscuits and a glass of milk. Watching the glasses and decanter on the wall swinging in a brass holder; the sleep-inducing effect. Excitement of the arrival at Calais, fright lest the car be swung into the sea, then snug in the small seat in the 'dicky', not even missing the little King Charles spaniel, Yetty, who usually sat alongside. The funny pointed houses with turrets, but not as big as in the fairytale book. Driving on the other side of the road.

The pointed-roof hotel seemed very large, as did the bedroom up the stairs. Biggest of all was the bed, and so high, a little stool was there to stand on, to help you reach the top. The fairytale book, which had been taken away when the measles were bad, was beside the little girl, me, and I was happy.

Later a large bowl of creamy soup with chunks of all the vegetables I liked, melting butter trickling over the top forming the shape of a dog's head. Stirring it about so that other shapes formed, and then drinking it from the large spoon. That was my first, never-to-be-forgotten memory of an hotel, for as I got better the others on that journey to the south were obliterated by the fun of travelling.

There were the rabbit-warren hotels with endless corridors where the White Knight or the Red Queen might be expected to appear, and sometimes did, especially if it was Rosa Lewis's extraordinary Cavendish Hotel in Jermyn Street, with its unorthodox owner.

Clearest of all in the glass of memory is the sweet ecstasy of first love in the old, shabby Paris hotel: the sagging bed, peeling wallpaper, the view of the higgledy piggledy Paris rooftops from the spattered, never-cleaned windows; the brightly coloured print of Napoleon, a pretty watercolour of someone's dream garden.

Even now it all seemed very real to me as I sat, alone, apprehensive as to what would happen in the future after I reached London.

———

The next day, as the train rattled through the French countryside on its way to Calais, I thought of the kind Englishman who had bought me a sleeper then disappeared. Catch a Frenchman or an Italian behaving like that! Maybe England wouldn't be so bad after all.

Surprisingly I met him again on the boat, which made my journey to Victoria Station very pleasant. As we were leaving the barrier in the dimly lit station, the slender, graceful figure of my mother emerged from the shadows.

'Where's Constantine? Isn't he with you?' she asked.

'I've no idea. I thought you might know. Didn't he phone?'

My new friend insisted we had a drink before parting, during which we arranged to meet him at lunchtime the next day. However, the next day I wasn't able to meet anyone; the doctor was called and said I had a serious infection and must go to hospital as soon as possible. He would call an ambulance. We had been waiting for several hours when the telephone rang. It was my grandmother, who said quickly:

'You're wanted by the *News of the World*. Take this down.'

My immediate thought was that Constantine was in some sort of trouble, and at that moment I didn't feel able to cope. I said I would ring back, and put the phone down. It rang again almost immediately, simultaneously with the arrival of the ambulance.

'You must listen. You're wanted in the unclaimed money column. You're to ring this number.'

The ambulance men were in the room. Quickly I asked my mother to ring the number, then to come to the hospital to tell me about it. As I came out of the anaesthetic haze I saw my mother's face; she was talking:

'. . . said it's a will that was made in 1872 and you're one of the last descendants. It's several thousands, but he wouldn't tell me exactly. Isn't it exciting? Do hurry up and get well.'

PART FIVE

England and Ireland

CHAPTER FORTY-TWO

England in 1950 seemed a very different place when I left the Chelsea hospital. There were new words to be learnt, such as 'cosh boy', the cosh being a home-made heavy stick like a super-truncheon; other accoutrements such as bicycle chains, broken milk bottles, 'flick' knives and knuckledusters were displayed in photographs of the 'cosh boy's' armoury. 'Spiv' was another word new to me which my fellow patients assured me meant 'diddler'. For instance, I was told the time-honoured costermonger often held a matchbox concealed in his hand, with a Cox's pippin apple, when crying: 'Lovely ripe Cox's: hear the pips rattle!' My mother had mentioned a nice fat chicken she had bought in Soho, only to find smoke pouring from the oven when cooking it. It had been tightly stuffed with newspapers to give the illusion of plumpness. Crime, which had dropped considerably during the war, owing I suppose to most men being drafted into some service, had risen dramatically. This was blamed by a large number of the population on the wireless (as the radio was called) serial *Dick Barton, Special Agent*, which had been running uninterrupted since 1946, the year I had left England.

The Archbishop of York enlarged on the 'moral chaos', and the Bishop of Exeter said chastity had never been held in lower esteem since the reign of Charles II. Again, large numbers of the population laid this at the door of the American Dr Kinsey, with his *Report on the Sexual Behaviour of the Human Male*, an instant bestseller, a strange bedfellow of the numerous war books. Indeed a friend told me that after her charwoman had glanced through the book, she remarked:

'Men is beasts, Mrs Watkins!'

Norman Mailer's war book *The Naked and the Dead*, commonly known as 'the effing book' was severely slammed for its obscenity by the *Sunday Times*, who called for its withdrawal.

The BBC now employed an 'expert' psychiatrist to answer everyday problems; psychiatry was popularly accepted. T. S. Eliot's play *The Cocktail Party* had as the central figure Sir Henry Harcourt-Reilly, a cross between a psychiatrist and a priest, perhaps a symbol of the era. There should be nothing to hide, or maybe no place to hide it.

So much I had learned or read during my stay in hospital. However, later, certain things were as I remembered them in England. Petrol was still rationed. The meat ration for instance was one shilling's worth per week. Milk came off the ration while I was in hospital, but cream was impossible to find in the city. The five shilling limit for restaurant meals was still in force.

The beauty of Chelsea Embankment still bewitched me; the atmosphere in the small shops and pubs was as friendly and inviting as I remembered it. The Crossed Keys pub in Lawrence Street, where I had spent many pleasant hours in wartime, now served excellent food, as did some other pubs. In fact, for good unpretentious English food it was hard to beat them. Although for the first time for some years I had no dog, I walked my mother's in Battersea Park; it was not in the least like the sun-filled Pincio Gardens, but had its own melancholy, austere English charm and beauty. This beauty was enhanced by the open-air exhibition of modern sculpture which galvanized me into excitement when I came upon it set in a green grove in the park. For the first time I saw Henry Moore's sculptures, having previously known only his fantastic drawings of London tube or basement shelterers from the bombs. They opened my mind to a new world of form and dimension. I loved walking about Chelsea on my own, even though I was trying not to think of the immediate problem of 'where was Constantine?'

Con had telephoned several times while I was in hospital, but hadn't visited me. I gathered he had been staying with Patrick O'Donovan, the writer, but had left saying he was going down to Harold Scott's cottage for a while. Harold was an old and valued friend, an extremely good actor, very much in demand for certain parts, but I had no idea where he lived now, or indeed where the cottage was. Meanwhile we went down to see the country solicitor in Chelmsford to find out about my inheritance. This proved very simple once my passport had been examined; and subsequently when the bonds, stocks and shares were forwarded to my old bank beside the Chelsea Town Hall, I had the brief yet glorious moment of saying: 'Sell them.' It was a comforting and miraculous feeling to have money in my pocket and a cheque book for the first time for nearly five years. I enjoyed my largesse immensely: a present for my grandmother's char who had seen the notice, and for favoured members of the family. Some days I felt like Caitlin Thomas who, when Augustus John (well known for his meanness) gave her ten pounds, tucked a fiver in the pocket of a sleeping tramp she passed in a Soho doorway. I found a few friends' telephone numbers in an old address book, all of whom warned me against extravagance. Now, they said, was the time to strike out on my own, go back to acting, make a new life for myself. But the newly found game of spending money was most attractive. Their clichés fell on unheeding ears. I discussed the problems with my mother, who flatly refused to give any advice, helpful or otherwise.

'I haven't made much success of my marriage,' she said. 'I'm the last person to ask.'

An old friend, who had loved me for many years, pressed his case even more strongly. He had written several very successful books and painted a future life together which sounded almost too idyllic. My thoughts about Constantine were ambivalent. Some days I missed him so as to feel only half a person; other days a hard knot of resentment rose up in my body like a malignant tumour. There was still no word from him.

Every day I thought about him and discussed with myself what it was about him that produced such turmoil in me. It was not so much a sexual attraction, for many times I found his sexual drive too fierce, with never a sign of tenderness to heighten by contrast the moments of pure passion. After seven years of marriage it was still like Mrs Patrick Campbell's 'hurly burly of the *chaise-longue*', not the 'peace and quiet of the double bed'. Sexual understanding had not come with the years; his sexual powers were as violent as during the first months of our love. It was not so much sexual dissatisfaction for me, but that the friendship and camaraderie we still shared at other times simply disappeared in bed. I loved him as much for his power of using words, for his writing, the lucidity of his prose: that is where his sexual understanding lay, not in his physical actions. I was as hungry for his genius to emerge as another woman might be for her man to make a lot of money. Any woman connected with a creative person will tell you the same thing. The work and the man are inseparable, and the woman plays the secondary role no matter how much love there is. When the creative person is unable to work, life is nigh impossible on both sides. The dreadful void for the artist is often filled with deadening drink, or the quest for other women who do not see, or even want to see, what lies behind the curtain which is drawn down over that void.

These thoughts ran haphazardly through my mind; they were there the day I casually met Harold Scott in the King's Road, Chelsea. His cottage was on Romney Marsh, he was going down for the day next week, and would I like to come too?

The primitive cottage was set in the flat, secretive Marsh country, cold winter winds sweeping in from the sea, the skies brooding over past scenes of murky death and smugglers' tales. As we walked on the long, narrow, squelchy path to Jackson's Cottage, as it was called, I noticed some hardy, long-coated sheep huddled along one side of the house, seeking shelter, their breath coming out almost like smoke. From time to time they stamped their feet and coughed hoarsely.

Constantine looked very young, a cherubic smile on his face, as he opened the door.

'How wonderful to see you, darling. You too, Harold. I'm getting weary of these consumptive sheep coughing outside the window.'

There was a large fire of wood in the small shepherd's room, making it warm and giving out the smell of apples burning. A wooden table was covered with typing paper and it was obvious Constantine had been writing.

'Only sausages and baked beans, I'm afraid, and a few bottles of beer. How long are you staying?'

When I said I was going back with Harold his face darkened. I could sense his disappointment, but I didn't see how I could stay there with no change of clothes or indeed anything else.

During the afternoon Harold said he wanted to call on some people in the village, so when we were alone I asked Con if he had got Mimi's telegram in Paris. He hadn't asked why I was in hospital – so as far as he knew I was still pregnant.

'Telegram? No, I didn't get any telegram. What was it about? I had practically no money by the time I got to Paris so I thought I'd better get to England as soon as possible.'

I told him what it had conveyed; he looked thoughtful, then asked:

'Why are you going back with Harold? Don't you want to live with me any more? Admittedly I haven't much to offer, but I'm writing again and *The Iron Hoop* is due out with Cassell anytime now. I can probably get some money from Desmond Flower on this book, which is almost finished.'

I realized he didn't know about the money I had inherited, so, minimizing it, I recounted the strange and unexpected story. If anything he looked a bit annoyed, and his mood changed from one of coaxing to aggression. In minutes we were into a hellish scene in which accusations were shouted from both sides, some true and some untrue. When Harold came back and said we must be starting for the train, I was torn between reconciliation and a desire to leave at once. In my heart I knew there wouldn't be a reconciliation for many murderous hours.

A few days later a letter arrived from him: not at all apologetic, but saying he wanted us to 'build a new and sensible life' together; that everything he wrote, he wrote for me, because he loved me; 'we were the same person'. He could never again live through the chaos and misery of last year, and without me his work would count for nothing. Would I please come down again? I went down for about a week and we lived the life of the nineteenth-century peasantry – collecting wood, trimming oil lamps, filling stone hot-water bottles, rising and going to bed very early. Meanwhile Constantine wrote all day while I busied myself with the never-ending process of keeping warm, cooking simple soups or stews, and reading. I took long walks garbed in a duffle coat I found behind a door, wellingtons and woollies, and I thought and thought. We were careful with each other, stifling unkind thoughts or resentment, trying desperately to achieve even a gloss of the harmony we had once known. It was impossible for me to go on staying in my mother's small house, so it was agreed I would go back to London and look for a flat in Chelsea which we could both share and then see how things worked out.

I found a flat on the top floor of a pleasant house on Cheyne Walk, overlooking the river, just past Whistler's house. It was bright, and that part of Chelsea concealed no ghosts for either of us. It was near enough to stroll along the embankment to pubs we knew like the Crossed Keys, the King's Head and Eight Bells, and the Pier. Acquaintances would nod greetings which made us feel as if we had come home. One evening just before we moved in we went to the Crossed Keys to eat and a large brown poodle came over and nuzzled my arm. He was a proud, handsome dog who seemed unattached to anyone except us.

'He reminds me of Flotow,' I said. 'Isn't it strange that as soon as we arrive a brown poodle so like him should come over to me?'

The dog continued to sit by my side, nudging my arm from time to time. We got up to leave. Turning round, I saw a few tables away Barney and Sue Fawkes, whom we had last seen in Bermuda before they were married. Sue's sister, Natalie, had bought one of Mouche's puppies when we were at Cheriton, Sue and Barney having taken him over. No wonder I thought the dog, called Beau, was like Flotow; he was his brother! The Fawkeses had that day moved into another flat in Cheyne Walk, and we all marvelled that Beau had remembered his foster-mother over the years. For he had left me when he was three months old and seen me only a few times in New York. The Fawkeses were delighted to have Constantine to stay for the short time before we moved. It was good for our relationship to be able to meet in the atmosphere of love and warmth which Barney and Sue exuded.

Once into Cheyne Walk we began to look for old friends such as Diana Graves, who was acting again. One lunchtime Constantine brought Peter Ustinov back for a meal. They had first met when Constantine was seventeen and was at the Barn Summer Theatre in Shere. Estelle, his girl then, was acting Clytemnestra in Racine's play and Constantine was translating *Britannicus* for her to play Agrippina in later on. The theatre, as the name implied, was a converted barn. The semi-professional actors lived in an old farm building.

Constantine had enjoyed being treated as a coming prodigy, then felt very deflated, he told me, by the arrival of Peter Ustinov, who at the age of sixteen had produced, written and acted in his own play there.

'And as long as I live,' Constantine would remark, 'Peter will always be one year younger than I am.'

Peter was fantastically good company that morning. He kept us enthralled by detailing the plot of his play *Love of the Four Colonels*, acting almost all the parts. Although I later saw it staged, it is that day's performance I remember with the greatest pleasure.

The Six Bells pub in the King's Road looked remarkably unchanged when I looked in one morning, the mahogany gleaming, the brilliant green of the billiard table showing through the hatch behind the bar just as it had always done. Only Curly was missing, the Irish barman who had been killed in 1941 when the pub was bombed. It had a strange effect on me, even more so when I saw, sitting in the corner where we had both sat so often in the past, Peter Rose Pulham. As usual he was making notes on a sketching block, so he did not see me sit down opposite him. I knew he would look up in annoyance at having a stranger at his table, and he did. Then his face softened into a broad smile as he said:

'Pussy, how clever of you to appear just now.'

'I thought you lived in France. What on earth are you doing here? Is Mary here too?'

'Yes, I do, but I'm over to arrange my exhibition at the Redfern Gallery in a few months' time. I've had a lot of exhibitions in London since you left, Pussy, and some in Paris. Pity you've just missed one at the London Gallery. Mary's still in France. But let's talk about you. Let's spend the day together, there's so much to say, isn't there?'

Constantine didn't seem at all pleased when I rang, but agreed rather grudgingly. Peter was in one of his few exuberant moods when I got back and had ordered Pimms to drink. 'A sort of celebration,' he said. We had a glorious day. First to the back bar of the Café Royal, where we found Dylan Thomas who seemed surprised to see us together. He asked after Constantine and told me Caitlin had had a baby boy they called Colm the previous July. He had great hopes of an extensive American tour to read his poetry in a few weeks' time. He was extremely excited about it. Then we had an excellent lunch at L'Etoile which went on for some time while we reminisced, explored each other's ideas and felt very happy. It was like ten years ago when we were in love, as if for a day we had been transported back in time. We both knew it would end at midnight and there was no magic except what we were making ourselves.

Then we had to go to the Colony Rooms, an afternoon drinking club, as Peter wanted to see Francis Bacon. What about Constantine? I thought, and said so. He waved his hand.

'Nonsense, he can let you go out for a day. After all, he snitched you from me all those years ago, he can't possibly complain.'

———

Desmond Flower of Cassell was a kind and friendly man, who entertained us several times. He suggested that a lot of our worry in the past could have been lessened if Constantine had had an agent. When told of the disastrous effect of the original agent's letter, in Bermuda, he told Constantine to get in touch with Pearn, Pollinger & Higham (now David Higham Associates), whom he was sure would be helpful. They were, too, and remained his agents all his life.

The Chelsea flat was fine for a short stay but not for permanent living. I suggested finding a house in the country, not too far from London.

'Not that stockbroker belt,' said Constantine immediately. 'I know, let's try Hertfordshire. Estelle and I had a little cottage there once.'

So we looked and looked, but found nothing we felt was right. We asked in pubs and country hotels; somebody suggested that nearer the Essex border was better. So we went to Bishop's Stortford to an agent who sent us to look at houses in Much Hadham. A good rural name, we thought. A friendly publican sent us to call on the Levy Teasdales who lived in a pleasant house there, and so we found what we were looking for. Stephen Thomas, who had been Sir Nigel Playfair's stage manager at the Lyric Theatre, Hammersmith, held it in trust for his son Billy. It was called Sacomb's Ash and we were to live there for nearly ten years.

CHAPTER FORTY-THREE

The name Sacomb, we were told, was a corruption of 'Saxon combe', which might have been true. It was in a hamlet called Allen's Green, consisting of a score of dwellings, mostly farmworkers' cottages, a small school, a wooden church, and a pub which sold only beer. None of these had electric light although London was only twenty-eight miles away. There was no shop, no bus and no telephone kiosk, so it was truly rural, and apart from the modern house of the farmer Mr Knight, who also cultivated mushrooms, it was as it had been for many years. The nearest shops were three and a half miles away at Sawbridgeworth, but the larger town, Bishop's Stortford, was over six miles. We had no car so it meant bicycling, which I enjoyed.

The house was a quarter of a mile from the hamlet at the end of a twisting no-through road, set in its seventeen acres, ten of which were rented to the farmer. To the back and side were very large flat fields of corn. Along one side of the house was an oblong pond surrounded by willow trees. There were nine rooms, one an addition the opposite side to the pond. The outside of the house was half-pargeted, that is plastered, with traditional designs incised on to it. A small lawn in front was bounded by a beech hedge, with a beautifully shaped walnut tree in the middle with a bench round it. The rest of the land available to us was a half-acre paddock, a large orchard with lofty and well-built barns, loose boxes and an exercise yard; then a huge lawn which we subsequently made into a croquet pitch. Overgrown flower borders enclosed it, beyond which was a walk between a long hazel hedge with an eighty-year-old mulberry tree to the right and a lot of rough land. This was encircled by a hedge layered intricately by two of the villagers. Also, unusual for that time, a big boiler centrally heated the house. It was remote, pleasant of aspect and peaceful. I paid the rent for a year to ensure that peace.

The indigenous villagers were a strange folk; old grudges were harboured and many of them had never ventured far from Allen's Green. One family, in which the mother had died some years before, hated their father, even going so far as when his cat was run over to string it up in the bicycle shed so that 'when the old bugger puts his bike away tonight he'll walk into it!' They thought this a great joke. I urged some of the almost grown-up sons of that family to go to London, even for the day; they went to the zoo and told me the wild animals frightened them, so they came home. They seemed quite content to go to the pub and play darts endlessly. I never saw them with any girls.

There were, of course, exceptions – notably Len and Minnie Rix who ran the pub, Rixie, as he was called, also having a job elsewhere. Old Bob, a relative of Minnie's, lived with them and he went as far as to make the sign of the index and little finger extended against the evil eye when certain people came in. Then there was Old Lil and Old Herb who lived together next to the school of which Old Lil was caretaker. Apparently the job went to the senior widow, which might have accounted for their unmarried state. Herb must have been fine looking as a young man, for even at seventy he was tall and upright, with very good manners. Lil was small and dark with very merry twinkling eyes which must have fluttered a few rural hearts in days gone by. Next to the church lived Mrs Howe and her husband George, a happy little man whom I never saw without a smile. He and Herb worked for the farmer and Mrs Howe was a loyal and good helper in the house all the time we were there. The others were in general small, dark, round-headed people, whom the local doctor swore were true ancient Britons, the Romans having gone up the river Stort without stopping to colonize the small hamlets on the way. It's a theory I like to believe. Halfway down the lane was a small thatched cottage in which lived Bert and Jane Wellstead with their small son. The husband was a small, sad-looking man, born a Rothschild, but who changed his name to his mother's maiden name, for as he said:

'Who wants to know a poor Rothschild?'

He lived a curiously introverted and almost secret life, which largely excluded his wife and son. Jane was to become a steadfast friend of mine over the years. She lived the life of a country woman, growing flowers, vegetables and tending animals such as goats and Chinese geese with which Bert, from time to time, arrived home. Opposite the Queen's Head pub were two thatched cottages made into one, where Andrew and Elizabeth Foster-Melliar lived, Elizabeth being Irish born. They, too, were to figure in our lives in many ways. There was also Kathleen Fraser who was to become Constantine's typist; she lived with an enormous number of dogs and cats.

Although there was a little furniture in Sacomb's Ash, it was far from furnished, so we bicycled to auctions all over the place, and my grandmother produced many things, as she had during the war when we were married. Georgette, Constantine's mother, had left some of her pretty furniture in store in London when she returned to America, and that was also given to us. So gradually we were able to make an attractive home with some of our own things for the first time. We explored the nearby villages, mostly by walking across the fields behind the house. Green Tye was the nearest, about two miles away, and boasted a pub and a few houses, but nothing else. However, it was a pleasant walk; the pub was bright and clean, frequented by the villagers.

The village further on was Perry Green, which was bigger, with some larger houses, no shops but a pub called the Hoops. It was here one Sunday morning that we met Michael O'Connell, who had built himself a story-book house nearby in a little copse which he had cleared himself. Attached to it was his long, low workroom, for he was an expert tie-dyer of cloth, having gone as far afield as New Guinea and West Africa to learn his craft. He also perfected resist-dyeing, where the pattern is painted on the cloth with a thickened paste, preventing the dye from penetrating where the paste protects it. Some of his designs were spectacular and adorned offices such as the Time-Life Building in London. He was a kind and interesting man. In this small colony of interesting people there was also a painter and his wife, a fashion designer, who lived on the outskirts of Perry Green. Outside the pub there was a wooden table and benches where we sat when the weather was fine. It was on such a day that we saw coming towards us a man of about fifty, of medium height, with a very jaunty, quick walk. He was talking volubly to a tall white-haired man who had difficulty keeping up with him. Behind them was a small dark woman with Slavic features talking to a pretty English-looking girl. As he approached he smiled a greeting and entered the small pub. It was the first time we met the sculptor Henry Moore and his wife, Irina, who lived almost opposite, with Carl Sandberg the director of the Stedelijk Museum in Amsterdam, and Susan, a girl who helped to look after Mary Moore, their small daughter.

We became good friends with the Moores, spending some time in each other's houses. Irina intrigued me; she seemed so very self-contained, although it was obvious she thought deeply. Her slightly Asiatic cast of feature added to the strangeness. She was small, with slanting brown eyes and close-cropped grey-black hair. Apart from Henry and their Mary, her only other visible interest was in collecting cacti, which were housed in a separate greenhouse. She often talked to me of their early years, having met Henry when she was a student at the art college, and their extreme poverty to begin with, sometimes living on cheap oranges bought from a stall late on Saturday nights. She had been determined not to have any children while Henry was struggling for recognition, deciding to wait until she was forty years old. This she did, in the perfect way Irina managed her life; they both adored Mary. Irina couldn't remember her parents in Russia, as during the Revolution she had walked many miles with other children until they had found sanctuary in Switzerland. Then she was either adopted or looked after by an English family. This was only said briefly, never elaborated on, and Irina was not the kind of person you asked questions of.

Henry seemed the opposite type of person – smiling, outgoing and full of fun, with a delightful giggle.

'Irina's quite right about those early years,' he said once. 'My first big sale was when Selfridges had an exhibition on their roof garden, and somebody accidentally knocked my sculpture over!'

He told me he thought his feeling for form came from the time he was a child in Yorkshire, the youngest of seven children.

'My mother worked so hard for us, father was a miner, and she had awful rheumatism in her shoulder.' He paused for a moment as if reflecting, then went on: 'She used to say, "Come on, Henry boy, give my old shoulder a rub." Yes, I can remember the feel of the rounded bone.'

Going round his large studio was always interesting and I noticed on shelves a collection of odd-shaped stones, some piled one on top of another. They almost looked like small Moore sculptures, they were so rounded and beautiful. It was a great part of the country for odd-shaped stones, so I started collecting them too. Behind the house was the 'engine path', so called for a huge steam traction engine which went up to do the ploughing of the two huge fields on either side. This path was a good hunting ground for these odd stones. Often I would find one to give to Henry, and some for myself. I still have one which resembles a minute Moore standing figure.

To begin with, our life here was like a convalescence; we both wanted to avoid any of the horrors of the previous years, and we took pains to study each other's sensitivity. However, we knew that to ensure this, Constantine must finish his novel and then decide what else he wanted to do. I was more than willing to make everything as easy as possible. *The Iron Hoop* was published in England and had excellent notices. He did finish the next novel *Cousin Emily*, and Desmond Flower accepted it happily; but there was a paper shortage at the time, so no date was yet given for its publication. Before he had time to worry about what he would do next, Con's agent telephoned asking if he would, or could, translate a book from German into English. The publisher was Allan Wingate and the book, *The Burned Bramble*, was by Manès Sperber.

Manès Sperber was a remarkable man born in Zablotow, a small town in the Ukraine. He had studied under Alfred Adler, the Viennese psychologist, and became a professor of psychology at the University of Berlin. Pre-Hitler, he held high posts in the German Communist Party, then after 1933 he went underground and finally left Germany. In 1937, after the Moscow Purge trials, he left the Communist Party and became a fugitive from both the Gestapo and the NKVD. Manès now lived in Paris with his wife Jenka and their son, Dan. His book (the first of a trilogy) was about the Communist movement in Western Europe and the betrayals of its heroes. It was a fascinating book, and although Constantine hadn't spoken much German since the war, he was convinced he could do it.

'After all,' he said, 'one needs to be able to write well in one's own language. I can always look up words in a dictionary.'

Our house was furnished in all but our books, which we had left in Italy, and we missed them as much as anything.

'I would like my dictionaries now,' remarked Constantine, 'and so many other things, my manuscripts and notebooks particularly. You remember what Norman always said: "Never throw any work away; you never know when it will come in useful." I might even be able to finish the Douglas book in the sanity of the English countryside.'

It was decided that I would go back to Italy to collect our things, as well as to repay all the kind people who had lent me money during those last months.

————

My thoughts were very confused as the train rumbled across Europe to Rome. I felt at home in Italy and I loved certain people who had given me warmth, and indeed their love, which had sustained me through days of bleakness, endless dark tunnels of misery. Despite the years of unhappiness and pain I had experienced in Italy, I looked forward to being in La Bella again. I pushed away the soul-clinging mire and thought instead of those sunny mornings when I set out for work, the murmur of 'Bella bionda' from the first good-looking man I encountered, and the automatic clutching of the genitals as he passed me, to avert any impotency from the blue-eyed girl who *could* possess the evil eye. This superb blend of paganism and Christianity was what attracted me about Italy, and particularly Rome, not only in the layers of earth but also in the people. I thought of Samuel Rogers's remark, penned in 1820:

The memory in Rome sees more than the eye.

Probably the only other place I felt like that about was Ireland.

The Tompkinses had moved from the via Gregoriana to a beautiful apartment on the top floor of an old house in the via Margutta, for years the street where painters and writers lived. It had a glorious view, and was high enough up to muffle the street noises. A young man was sitting on the terrace typing, and he was introduced as Pabst's son who was staying with them. Instantly my thoughts went back to the time I had met his father, the hopes and fears I experienced then, but I said nothing for I knew that if such opportunity should occur again, I would not return to England. When I visited my apartment in the Piazza di Spagna it was to find Ann had left; some said she had married an Italian and gone to Canada, but nobody really knew. Sybille Bedford now lived there. She looked so happy and comfortable that unfairly I almost resented her being there. The signora had taken my things, she told me, but I was welcome to any books I saw of mine. I picked out a few favourites which she would keep for me until I was leaving.

After a few days I went down to Positano before going to Capri for the books Paanaker still had. Mimi was drinking very heavily again, delighted to see me, but somehow vague when I suggested to her that she come back to England with me and stay for a while at Sacomb's Ash. Not now, she might come next year, maybe . . . Luca found me some large sacks to put the books in when I collected them from Capri. What few possessions we'd had apart from books seemed to have disappeared.

Back in Rome, Peter had said I couldn't possibly take books in the sacks as some would get cut open or stolen; so he got packing cases from somewhere, and these were filled, then nailed down and labelled. He was to bring me to the station to deal with the officials, who apparently could be capricious about non-personal luggage. Somehow the nailed-down cases made my decision to go back irrevocable. I had spent the last evening, way into the early hours, with Reinhard, and we both knew we were unlikely ever to meet again. That part of my life was over, sealed into its own secret compartment.

On the journey homewards I realized that Constantine and I were going through an uneasy peace; we were not really behaving quite spontaneously with each other. What was it Georgette had said in Bermuda?

'I know everything will be all right between you both because you laugh so much together.'

There had been precious little laughter over the past year and I knew it was as much my fault as Constantine's. If your relationship with yourself is honest and understood, then, no matter what, your relationship with other people falls into place. I had mistrusted myself many times and been full of suspicion and near hatred. There was one way to sort out my thoughts and that was to go soon to my family in Ireland for a while. The rain like soft mist, the smell of wet earth, even the pace and attitude to life would calm the many turbulent feelings that coursed through me.

CHAPTER FORTY-FOUR

It was some months later when I stood leaning over the old bridge at Killaloe, looking up the Shannon River to Lough Derg. As I looked at the Lake Hotel where my father had been living before he died I wondered if there was any more beautiful place in the world: a serene, peaceful beauty now, the watery sunlight casting pale shadows, the puffy clouds fast moving, giving rapidly changing colours to the hills and the lake. No wonder Ireland was difficult to paint, the colours changed so frequently. The Dalcassian Kings knew what they were about when they sited the royal seat here. I had just left the twelfth-century cathedral, attributed to King Donal Mór O'Brien, now Church of Ireland, marvelling again at the rich romanesque doorway. Was it really the entrance to King Murtagh O'Brien's tomb, nearby the shaft of a cross with runic and ogham inscriptions? So much had taken place here, it was impossible to sort out fact from legend, but the magic remained.

It was the same kind of magic as I had found in India, yet the countries were vastly different to live in – two countries which had cast a never-to-be-forgotten spell over me with their mysticism, fatalism and religious strength, whether one had belief or not. The sages of Ireland and India, the guru and the priest, both gave consolation to those in need. There were the cruelties and the kindnesses, the superstitions and the fears, the catastrophes of famine and wars. Now they both had their independence from the British Empire. Was it because of all these similarities that the colours of the Indian flag were the same as those of Ireland's?

I remembered the first time I came to Ireland at the age of about seven. My aunt Roberta, known as Bobby, who lived but ten miles from this spot, had remembered that my father had another daughter whom she wanted to see. I was sent for from my convent during the school holidays; not that I was a neglected child, merely that I had insisted on staying for some weeks after term had finished. For I felt far happier with the ebullient South American girls and the Italians who never went home than I did as an only child with my grandmother. I worshipped a girl named Cordelia de Freitas, the eldest of about four sisters, who was much older than I was. She had promised we would put on a costume play, written by her, and we would have very colourful clothes, made by the younger nuns. It was wonderfully exciting; we seemed to have the run of the school and spacious grounds, for the nuns, too, adored Cordelia and let her do many things forbidden to us. She had enormous flashing eyes which rolled as she told us of the carnivals which went on for some days and nights in her native town. However, I think some of it must have been hearsay for I cannot imagine a strictly brought-up South American girl being allowed to wander the streets day and night.

It was fortunate that my aunt's request came just after the play had been performed, otherwise I might have refused to go. County Clare in Ireland seemed a long way away and none of my immediate family was able to accompany me. So a courier was found from the best travel bureau to take me to Dublin. The courier must have thought it a cushy job, for, when we got on the boat, he spent most of the time in the bar, telling me his 'tummy was upset'. At night I was handed over to a kind stewardess, who tucked me up in what I thought was a queer bed, then brought me hot cocoa. The following morning the courier's tummy seemed even more upset for he could hardly stand, clutching on to the walls to help himself along.

'You'd better hold on to me,' I said, but when he did I too nearly fell down – he was a very heavy burden for a seven-year-old to carry. Going down the gangplank was the worst, for he lurched from side to side until I was frightened I might fall through the ropes. His face was very red and he kept coughing. Passengers behind were saying:

'Imagine that poor little child with that drunken man. Someone ought to do something.' But nobody did.

My new uncle and aunt met me. They were smiling, then my uncle Terry laughed and said:

'You're a great little girl to have handled that so well,' and he patted my head. 'Do you want to stay in Dublin tonight with us, or be getting down to your cousins? They're about the same age as you. You'd best stay with us, I think, and go down on the morning train. I'll ring your uncle Jack to meet you.'

Uncle Terry put me on the train in care of the guard, a common occurrence in the 1920s and 1930s and very thrilling it was. There were often dogs and other animals such as chickens or pigeons to be talked to. I sat on a small tip-up seat in the guard's compartment, and when the train stopped at stations I was allowed out on the platform with the guard until he blew his whistle, then waved his flag for the train to move on.

The train stopped at Limerick Junction which, in true Irish fashion, is in fact in Tipperary. It was just a junction and there was no one to meet me. The stationmaster was fond of children and pressed a cup of hot strong sweet tea into my hand. I'd never had tea before; the nuns brewed their own kind of weak beer which we were given at mealtime, with milk for breakfast and supper. I didn't like the tea at all, so I just sipped it.

'Too hot, is it?' he asked. 'Have some more milk.'

Luckily another train was coming through so we ran and took back the gates.

After what seemed a very long time to me the old AC car drove up.

'Have you been here long?' Uncle Jack asked. 'There was a man looking at a horse so I couldn't get away.'

I couldn't think what he meant; why was he looking at a horse? Why not ride it? I thought how my grandmother would have disapproved – 'It's just as easy to be punctual as late' – but it never was and never has been for my Irish relations.

Never could I have imagined how wonderful it would be as a child in Ireland. Cordelia and her play were soon forgotten as I learnt to ride, a special pony being designated just for me, played wild games with my boy cousins, climbed huge trees, often without shoes on, and went to race meetings. I reflected how much life had improved since those early days, for an unforgettable memory is of us children sitting on one of the farm carts they used to have at country race meetings, eating oranges and throwing the peel on the ground. A group of ragged children appeared from nowhere, gathered up the peel and ate it avidly. To a well-fed child like myself it made a lasting impression. A job I loved was naming the foals: when I was about twelve years old I was handed the studbooks and told to make a list of names for the horses appropriate to their breeding. I became quite good at this and even today I find myself doing it if I glance through a race card.

But my familiarity with horses and race meetings was to cause me trouble when I was about eleven. We were allowed to make small bets of about a shilling when our own or friends' horses were running, so when I went back to school I continued it, putting on bets with the gardener. For some time I was very careful, never exceeding my pocket money, but the day came when I won the fantastic sum of thirteen pounds, four shillings and sixpence. There was chocolate fudge all round and a healthy balance left. However, a few weeks later my luck plunged and I lost nearly fifteen pounds. The gardener kept coming to me saying I must pay. But how? It was an astronomical amount for a child in those days. Finally I asked him for the name and address of the bookmaker, and in my childish hand I wrote saying my daughter was at present abroad but would settle the debt on her return, a form of letter I had glimpsed written by several of my uncles.

Alas, the next thing I knew, I was in the Mother Superior's office together with the gardener and my mother. The letter was on the Mother Superior's desk. There was no denying it and I didn't attempt to. Sadly, I was asked to leave 'because I had a bad influence on the other girls'. In Ireland, where I was sent until another suitable school could be found, I was treated like a heroine.

We were allowed to do almost anything; there were few restrictions that might have stifled our initiative and imagination. In Ballybunion on holiday, one of my young cousins, while we were paddling and swimming, bought and sold donkeys on the beach making himself a handsome profit. He is now a rich man – and no wonder.

Whenever we felt ill, or had the slightest thing wrong with us, it was referred to as 'growing pains', which made sense to me as daily I grew taller. The cure was always the same: bowls of hot, creamy-white onion soup and afterwards, before going to sleep, hot whisky with lemon and funny little black things with a spicy taste when you bit them, which we were told were cloves. I was even given this 'cure' when I cracked some ribs after a fall when riding. To a certain extent I was treated by the boys as a foreigner, therefore with a mixture of awe and good-natured disdain. There were so many things I didn't know about Ireland which my cousins were quick to capitalize on. Sometimes their plans didn't come off, but at other times I fell straight into the trap.

One day in the early 1930s, after my father had taken us to see his sister at Ballymackey, we were returning home by O'Brien's Bridge. As often happens in Ireland we could see a group of young men standing and talking on the bridge as we approached. We were sitting in the back with a good view. My cousin Desmond grabbed my arm and hurriedly whispered:

'When we go past the men, put your head out and shout "Up the Blueshirts!"'

This I did and the car was immediately pelted with large stones, one cracking the celluloid of the side window. My father stopped the car, getting out in a fury.

'What the hell . . .?'

Straight away I told him what I had called out, not however mentioning who had prompted the act. Staring at my cousins, he said:

'Of course you couldn't know, but O'Duffy had his headquarters at Killaloe during the civil war a few years ago, so he isn't popular here now he's head of the Blueshirts. I wonder what put the idea in your head anyway.'

(General O'Duffy led the Blueshirts, a mildly Fascist party in Ireland, which is said to have gone to fight in the Spanish Civil War six-hundred-strong and to have returned with six hundred and one!)

We were expected, or rather the boys were, to help with the haymaking, so all the farm machines were at our disposal to drive about the place, which is why no doubt I was attracted to an Austin Seven open tourer when I was about sixteen. It cost five pounds, so I bought it, to find out later that this very cheap price was because the brakes hardly worked at all. This didn't deter us one bit, for we stopped by driving into either a soft hedge or a haystack, and slowing down was done by all the passengers putting their feet out and dragging them along the road. We had cousins in Clarina, the other side of Limerick, and to get there I had to drive along the quay, which was flat, just in case we ran into too much traffic in the main street. It was always great fun at Clarina, the home of the Craigs, one of the twin boys being Harry Craig, later known as H. A. L. Craig. He wrote poetry and was to become a well-known film scriptwriter and author of many BBC documentaries.

We were very late getting back one day and my aunt was standing wringing her hands at the open avenue gates. We had got up a good speed down the hill on the approach, so there was no possibility of stopping quickly. She saw what was happening and nimbly jumped on to the verge, astonishment on her face, as we made for the safety of the hay barn.

———

When I had arrived a week before, it was as if I had left only recently. The atmosphere and love were the same. The Virginia creeper sprawled all over the house, almost obscuring the windows. I was taken up to the room that had been mine, looking out over the park and Slieve Kimalta, the 'Hill of the Sorrows', in the distance. Old Trixie, the grey mare, was to be seen munching placidly with the other mares and young horses. I looked around the room.

'What beautiful murals!' I exclaimed.

My aunt Bobby looked puzzled; then I realized the 'murals' were young, lacy strands of Virginia creeper which had grown up over the roof, grown down the chimney and fanned out over the walls like the espaliered fruit trees in the walled garden of pre-war years. It looked lovely and my aunt said:

'I hadn't the heart to cut it down.'

She turned and looked searchingly at me, critically I thought.

'What's happened to your skin?' she asked.

I ran my fingers over my face. 'Is it dirty from the journey?'

'No, it's the colour, a sort of biscuit-brown.'

'I have lived in hot places for four years, you know, auntie. It's suntan. Don't you think it's rather nice?' I pulled up my sleeve to show my brown arms, but she looked doubtful.

'I don't know, I'm sure. You used to have such beautiful white skin.'

Later, during my stay I was to lunch with a local historian in Limerick who was a family friend. My aunt came into my room as I was getting ready and said:

'I've arranged that lunch should be early, it's nearly ready now.'

'But I'm going out to lunch, I told you. Have you forgotten?'

Again she looked sad, hesitated, then said: 'You'd better have a little something, dear. It wouldn't do to go out with a man alone and eat too much!'

My father's words came back to me: 'Every time I go back to Ireland, it's still fifty years behind the times.' This was the first time I had been back to Ireland since I had married in 1944, as it was almost impossible to get over during the war.

My historian friend, Michael, was also an amateur genealogist and seemed to know a lot about the FitzGibbon family.

'The FitzGibbon house is not far from here, you know. It's called Mountshannon, a ruin now like so many others. There's an old man who is alive in Limerick who was a boy when Lady Louisa FitzGibbon had the duns in and it was sold up. You ought to call on him. His father was head groom there. He loves to talk about it. I've got an idea Lady Louisa's farm bailiff's daughter lives out Ballyneety way; Greene Barry, I think the name is.'

Like many Irish people he was fascinated with the past, filling me with such enthusiasm that I, too, began to think of them as people recently gone, not shadowy figures from long ago.

'You ought to go to Castleconnell too, it's only a few miles from your uncle's house. The church there is full of memorials to members of the FitzGibbon family. One of the family had a house there by the Donass Falls. I think cousins of your family had one adjoining, so you see you might still have met your husband over a hundred years ago.

'Coolbawn House there is going to be a hotel. Kitty and Adza should do well with it, during the salmon fishing season. Adza's a fine looking girl, and capable too.'

I looked at him with astonishment. 'Adza, did you say?'

'Yes, Adza.' After a moment he looked equally astonished. 'Of course, she must be a relation.'

Never in my life have I heard of anyone else being called Adza; it had to be my sister, whom I hadn't seen for years.

We weren't brought up together, but during our childhood Adza's mother, Kitty, who had been a singer, often took us – the 'two little girls' – away on holidays. She was an expansive, passionate woman with a deep love of the theatre. The holidays were always unusual and exciting. Heredity must count for something, for as we grew up we shared the same enthusiasms and ambitions: a love of the theatre, a love of good food, and travel. With such common interests it was always easy when we did meet to take up almost where we had left off, even though our childhoods had been so very different. We also shared the same sort of ingenuity and sense of humour.

Some years later, when Adza decided to sell the hotel, it was an inclement time of year; guests were scarce, but this didn't daunt her. She was great friends with the cast of a touring company which was playing at the Limerick Theatre. They were all engaged to play their part in the sale, for she invited them to be her guests when the prospective hotel buyer came. The bar was full, drinks and lunch being on the house.

'What'll you have, Charles? Same again?'

'Thanks, Aidan. Maybe we should get the menu and the wine list to make sure the wine's the right temperature.'

'Two gin-and-limes, please,' said the two young ladies next to them. Other orders came thick and fast. The lunch was long, lingering and delicious. The buyer looked impressed.

'You've a good clientele, haven't you? Is it regular, or just casual trade? Will they be here long?'

The sale went through; the evening's performance of the play had an additional sparkle; everyone was content.

————

Once I start thinking about Ireland it is not only of people but of places: the bicycle ride from Ballylickey up the long winding hill to the Pass of Keimaneigh (the deer's pass), the glacier-washed rock enclosing it; the merry tinkle of the stream, the mountain sheep and, incredibly, a raven uttering its sad cry; then on to Gouganebarra, a still, shining mountain-hemmed lake with its tiny island and the shrine to St Finbarr, the first bishop of Cork in the sixth century; Dinny Cronin's simple, bare pub (the scene of some of Sean O'Faolain's stories), draughts of Guinness, bacon, eggs and potato cakes, then waking up in the cold, crystal clear air, feeling more sparkling than after champagne; the field of gentians near Inchigeela, so impossibly blue they dazzled the eyes.

Dublin: the crowded pubs where the sound of people talking was like several hives of contented bees. The late-night sessions which went on in the back rooms of small hotels, talking, talking all the time, the glasses filled regularly. Sean O'Faolain, the biographer and brilliant short-story writer, delightful, witty and malicious, his alert blue eyes moving quickly as he went from subject to subject. Old Joe Hone (biographer of Yeats) and his wife Vera, Joe so absent-minded I remember a lunch at their house where he ate the string tied round the asparagus as well as the vegetable, without noticing. Then Arland Ussher, whose tall, spare mien decried his nature, for underneath that shy, hesitant exterior was the most agile of brains and the most passionate of hearts. He wrote exquisite prose, and was also a Gaelic scholar, having translated *The Midnight Court* in the 1920s, and other Irish books. When I first met him, his book *The Face and Mind of Ireland* had been published to great critical acclaim. John Betjeman wrote of it: 'It is penetrating, as entertaining as a thriller, witty, but not chatty, catty, but not unbalanced . . .'

In the early 1950s when I was there, he had just finished a book about the Jews, to be called *The Magic People*, which became one of my favourites. He was fundamentally a philosopher, hence his *Journey Through Dread*, a study of Sartre, Heidegger and Kierkegaard. But then he was working on studies of Bernard Shaw ('Emperor and Clown'), W. B. Yeats ('Man into Bird') and James Joyce ('Doubting Thomist and Joking Jesuit'). It was called *Three Great Irishmen*.

In company Arland hardly spoke at all and many found him dull, but with one or two loved friends he was not only very talkative, but very entertaining. His almost ascetic appearance and introverted manner did nothing to prepare you for either his thoughts or his behaviour, both of which were extremely unconventional. He was a little over fifty when I first met him and hardly resembled the red-haired, sensual young man Augustus John had painted. We both found pleasure in each other's company, for he talked very openly to me, often late at night in a dim room, the only other sound perhaps the crackling of a fire and the constant hiss of a match as he lit yet another cigarette. Our meetings were rare, but in between there were many letters. It was almost a love affair by letter, for there were times over the thirty years that we shared a great affection. Arland admired George Moore very much, having known him in the 1920s, and he once said he felt about me the way George Moore had about Lady Cunard.

There were other journeys, each one memorable, and some with Constantine, who, after my recounting stories of the FitzGibbon family, wanted to find out more, to write a book about them. This was to be *Miss Finnigan's Fault*.*

* Cassell 1953.

We met the old Limerick man who as a young boy had held the horses outside Mountshannon. He vividly described the last ball Lady Louisa, Constantine's great-grandmother, gave while the duns were in the house playing cards.

'Millions!' he mumbled through toothless gums. 'Every window was flaming with great gas bowls. She spent more money in twenty years than Queen Victoria in her whole lifetime!'

I visited Miss Greene Barry, who had inherited a few of the FitzGibbon paintings from her father. She was a charming sensitive woman, who hinted that we might like some of the paintings, but alas she was unable to make us a gift of them. Through her solicitor I bought a pleasant portrait of the Second Lord Clare, Lord Byron's close friend at Harrow of whom he wrote in his poem 'Childhood Recollections'.

> Friend of my heart, and foremost of the list
> Of those with whom I lived supremely blest . . .

Some three weeks before Byron died he wrote a letter from Missolonghi to Clare, saying: '*I hope you do not forget that I always regard you as my dearest friend and love you as when we were Harrow boys together.*'

In the basement of the Limerick library I discovered the bronze panels depicting scenes from the disastrous battle of Balaclava in the Crimea, which had decorated the sides of Macdowall's statue of the young Hussar, Viscount FitzGibbon, the statue having been tipped from its place on Sarsfield Bridge, Limerick, into the Shannon, during the Civil War. I photographed them.

Now I reflected how very curious it was that, although Ireland and her people had known but little peace, or indeed prosperity, the atmosphere could calm and bring such hope to troubled hearts; not only to the inhabitants, but also to others from across the seas.

CHAPTER FORTY-FIVE

The peace and hope I had experienced in Ireland were still alive when I got back one early summer's day to Sacomb's Ash. The catkins on the hazel hedge, dusted with yellow powder, tossed a welcome in the zephyr-like breeze. Constantine greeted me with delight, saying what a lot of work he had done on the translation of Manès Sperber's book. He was looking forward to finishing it as he had an idea for another novel. The only thing missing to me in that shining, charming house was my dog. The parting with Flotow was still very vivid in my thoughts.

Our life assumed an order it had seldom had before: Constantine worked all morning, thene broke off to walk down to the pub, or across the fields; he worked again in the late afternoon until dinner time. Since petrol coupons were no longer needed after May 1950, the first time for eleven years, friends usually drove down for the weekend. We had a pin or firkin of beer at weekends from the pub and a little wine, but no spirits unless somebody brought a bottle. The five-shilling meal limit in restaurants had been lifted in May too, also the points system for canned meats, but fresh meat was still very scarce; there were, however, good country chickens, rabbits and fish to be bought. Even so, many foods were impossible to get in the country, and I would go up to London to Soho and buy some of the things I had been used to in Italy. I spent days experimenting with cooking dishes so that the huge larder was full of food for the long weekends. There was goat's milk and cream to be got from Mrs Pugsley in the village and I made goat's cheese, at that time little known in England except by well-travelled gourmets.

Most Sunday evenings we would have a large cold buffet of pâté, quiches, poultry or tongue, with a tureen of hot soup and baked potatoes. It was then regularly open house for local friends like the Foster-Melliars, and Henry and Irina Moore, together with our guests.

The flat countryside produced exceptional sunsets; in summer we would sip our drinks on the large lawn, watching the changing colours, while the scent of stocks, tobacco plants, roses and lilacs pervaded the air, an added delight. The rapture of the early days in Bermuda or Italy was gone; it was a more sedate pleasure now, for we had changed. There was so much to be done; the large garden had to be planted, then kept under control. Constantine made the back lawn his special duty, by rolling it constantly, weeding, and scattering grass seed, so that in some months it looked very fine, making a splendid almost full-size croquet lawn. Neither of us had ever gardened before, but our flowers and vegetables seemed wonderful. Most of my knowledge came from my nearest neighbour Jane Wellstead who could make a dry stick grow, or so it appeared to me. The large orchards bore great crops of apples, pears, plums, and the rarer greengage.

Some of the hard fruits I stored on fruit-racks in the huge black barn, and it was there one evening, when going out to collect some fruit, that I saw some rats performing an extraordinary feat. One rat was lying on its back holding a large apple on its stomach with its four legs, while another rat pulled him along by the tail to their nest. I stood fascinated for some minutes, neither animal taking the slightest notice of me. We decided a cat might be a good idea to prevent the rats coming into the house, and luckily Kathleen Fraser, Constantine's typist, had a litter of half-Persian kittens, from which we chose a pretty little female we called Jocasta. Also looking through the advertisements in *The Times* one morning I saw a standard poodle puppy for sale, in Cornwall. I went up to London to fetch her and somehow felt I knew her at first sight. She reminded me so strongly of that brown puppy with us in Bermuda. It was extraordinary to find, on looking at the pedigree, that she was in fact Mouche's granddaughter.

There was always something new going on in London, only an hour away by train. Peter Rose Pulham held a successful exhibition at the Redfern Gallery; one of his paintings, 'La Salle des Pas Perdues', is still so alive in my memory. Those that weren't sold were bought by the French surrealist painter André Masson. Ealing Film Studios were well on the way to making extremely good popular English films – *Passport to Pimlico* with Margaret Rutherford and *Kind Hearts and Coronets* with Alec Guinness playing six or seven parts were assured successes. Alec Guinness was now becoming established as a fine actor in films such as *The Lavender Hill Mob* and *The Man in the White Suit*, which portrayed characteristically British types instead of the Hollywood model. The drabness of wartime and post-war food was much altered with the launching of some small owner-run restaurants and country pubs. There was the bistro-like Ox on the Roof in the King's Road, Chelsea, which amongst good French bourgeois dishes also served snails steaming hot with garlic butter. The first *Good Food Guide* was started by Raymond Postgate, a fine outspoken man, who earlier had written an article for the *Leader* magazine called 'Society for the Prevention of Cruelty to Food'. I would often lunch at one of these new places, perhaps with my friend Diana Graves, who always had her flat full of interesting people.

Constantine, too, refound friends he had known at Oxford, some of whom came for weekends. It was a full life.

When the translation was finished, Constantine was going to Paris to see Manès Sperber, who worked in a publishing company and couldn't get away to come to England. Con insisted I go with him, an invitation I naturally didn't refuse.

The Sperbers lived at that time in a flat near the Porte de Versailles. Manès was a small man, grey-haired, with rather thoughtful stern brown eyes and a most determined mouth. He spoke good but accented English, quickly but forcefully. He gave the impression that he would not change his mind easily but would be a loyal friend. Jenka, his wife, was Estonian, large in build with an attractive, kind face and an easy manner. She too spoke English well, with less of an accent than her husband. Manès was very pleased with the translation and, after giving us some wine, he started to talk about the book and other matters of interest. They were stimulating to be with, Jenka a good cook, Manès an excellent host; they became good friends, even lending us their apartment when they went on holiday. They both drank very little – Manès had always been afraid of the comrades with him who drank, for he said they were the first to crack. I think Constantine's consumption of Pernod, wine and sometimes cognac after dinner rather alarmed him. He loved the cinema and we saw many French films. Constantine couldn't enjoy *M. Hulot's Holiday* with Jacques Tati, so he got up and walked out. Afterwards Manès was astonished:

'But where can he be? Why did he leave the cinema?'

I assured him I thought Constantine would be at the nearest café and I was right. However, there were times when I too was worried by Con's behaviour after consuming too much alcohol. Although he held his drink well, it always had much more effect on him (although strangers would not perhaps have noticed anything) because for a big man he ate very little, only small amounts of everything, not minding if he missed a meal. I never once heard him say he was hungry, especially if he was drinking.

Together we wandered about Paris, the city we both loved and had spent so much time in years before. We explored each other's childhoods in a way which hadn't been possible earlier. The Place des Vosges, colonnaded and exquisite, the Place Royale with the King's Pavilion on the south side; an imaginative nun had told me as a child about the duellists in the gardens in former times, and had shown me where Camille Desmoulins had plotted with his friends during the French Revolution. Another day we went to Passy to see if Constantine could find any trace of the old Russian lady who had looked after him for a while when he was a child.

'She must be dead by now, for she seemed old to me when I was about eight. But children are notoriously bad about adults' ages, aren't they? It's like houses you thought were enormous, but when you go back they are quite small. I adored her; she wore a bright red wig, saying her hair had fallen out with fright during the Russian Revolution, and she used to tip it over one eye to make me laugh.'

Alas there was no trace at all, nobody remembered her, though she was alive in Constantine's heart. As we walked through the streets past the Musée Clemençeau, we saw the Musée du Vin which Con said made him feel thirsty, so we stopped for a drink.

'Are we near that extraordinary school you went to, darling?'

———

The taste of Rome had been heady for my father on that journey back from India, so when he suggested we visit other European capitals before returning home, Manny and I were delighted. We were at last in Paris, but a day's journey from England, when unpredictably my father announced to me:

'I think you'd better go to a finishing school for a bit.'

Furiously, I answered: 'Really, after racketing around Europe with two middle-aged roués, to be sent back to school is a bit much.'

Manny joined in with my father against me as I protested vociferously: 'Manny, you've soon forgotten I stood up for you over the papal audience, it's a funny way of thanking me.'

He looked a bit sheepish as my father continued: 'You've still a few rough corners to be rounded up.'

So off I went, after saying I would only stay for a term, to an exclusive school for young ladies. I have to admit it was far better than any other establishment I had been to; there was more freedom. Still it was school, a word that had become anathema to me. As at my convent, the girls came from many parts of the world and, as before, it was the foreign girls I felt most at home with. We were taught many things I had learnt in India such as placement at table, etiquette, deportment and flower-arranging. Once a week we were brought out to Passy to a middle-European ex-queen of a country which had disappeared after the First World War, who gave classes in 'behaviour'. I think we were all expected to marry into minor royalty or the nobility, an ambassador at least, for the classes were very stringent.

The ex-queen lived in a detached house of quite humble proportions. We were received in a room of moderate size – in no way could it have been called a *salon* – with a small dais at one end on which was a carved chair, called the 'throne'. She was a forceful elderly lady, grey-haired, with very large, dark flashing eyes and a domineering manner. Several young, thin girls lived there too; these were referred to as 'ladies in waiting'; they looked frightened of her. It seemed to me that whatever language one spoke, she would answer in a different and usually alien one, which encouraged quick thinking. She would have parties just for us students at which all the food tasted horrible, for we had to be be taught to cope with any situation all over the world. If, when eating, very fragile pastry crumbs were dropped, we lost points in our tests. To this day I seldom ever make crumbs when eating; also, I can still walk backwards beautifully, without bumping into anything, so rigorous was our training. Alas it was never completed, for true to my word I left after a term; but often those curious lessons come back to me, given by the sad old lady who was waiting for the 'old days' to return.

Now, when Con and I went to look, the discreet brass plate that had adorned the column by the gate was gone. The house looked different; the curtains hanging up at the windows would never have been approved by the ex-queen. I was pleased to think that perhaps she had not lived to see the aftermath of the war, when the map of the world had changed yet again.

As we had a weekend to spare we went down to stay with Peter and Mary Rose Pulham. They lived about an hour's journey from the Gare du Nord but quite in the country. Valmondois was a large house of nearly thirty rooms, very sparsely furnished but beautifully situated. How Mary entertained large numbers of people with the primitive cooking arrangements is a mystery, but she was an excellent hostess, and had become a very good cook.

Peter was painting well, telling me of a series of paintings he had in mind, large canvases of the four seasons. The horse's skull I had gone to such pains to find for him during the war was still there; the secondhand easel my mother had given him about the same time was in daily use. It was a pleasant, relaxing few days with old friends, in a region of France neither of us knew. Peter and Mary looked well and happy – a perfect ending to our visit to France.

CHAPTER FORTY-SIX

One of the things I liked most about Sacomb's Ash was its wild life. There were some very beautiful birds, not all approved of by the farmer, but I enjoyed them: brightly coloured woodpeckers, called 'yaffles' by the locals, both the red and green variety and the spotted woodpecker; pink jays with pale blue eyes talked loudly in the trees; bullfinches, green finches, yellowhammers, flocks of noisy field fares in the winter. All flew about in numbers and fed on the lawn. My mother, who was very fond of birds, caught a young raven with a damaged wing which I nursed back to health in the stables. It was the time of Lorenz's book, about birds, *King Solomon's Ring,* and I read that corvines should be called by the first sound they made. So the raven was called Ark; when I freed him after about nine months, I would call his name in the garden and for some time afterwards he would circle round my head waiting for a piece of meat. The farm labourers looked up in surprise the first time they witnessed this.

There was a young hare who used to come and sit with me as I hung out clothes; at first I took it to be a little brown dog. There was a badger set in the spinney and one night we went down at dusk to watch the young badger cubs playing, an enchanting sight. At that time there were plenty of rabbits too, including black ones breeding in the wild. The land around us was rich with pheasants and red-legged partridge, and many of the small American owls hooted through the night. They were not much more than six inches high. There were nightingales too, and bats fluttered through the air on warm summer evenings. A beautiful vixen and her mate wandered nonchalantly along the engine path, and once, when I was walking along it with Minka, who was in season, I saw the brush of the dog fox in the corn field as he waited for us to return. I looked after a deserted cub for some time before releasing it; he too visited us for a little while. A solitary water-hen made her nest every year at the bottom of one of the willow trees around the pond, but her eggs were always unfertile. One morning, looking out of the bedroom window I saw something dart quickly at the top of the walnut tree – some red squirrels, delightedly taking the top nuts for their store. I wonder how many of these animals remain today.

My small inheritance didn't last very long, but it gave us nearly eighteen months of security and pleasure. Constantine, too, was making a certain amount of money from his translations and books. My grandmother died of pneumonia one cold January day, in her ninetieth year, refusing to let me come and see her as she lay ill, saying she wanted me to 'remember her, as she had been'. Could I ever forget the taste for adventure and originality she had given me as a child? She had got me out of the convent in Bruges I hated; 'an unhealthy place for a child, with all those smelly canals.' My first aeroplane flight with Alan Cobham's circus; her beach pyjamas at over seventy in the French resort; the party in the bedroom when a guest leaned on the hot-water basin and it came away from the wall, cascading water everywhere:

'Let me handle this,' she had said. 'You all go back to your rooms.' She had handled it so well, we got better rooms and preferential treatment.

She bought me my first sailor suit with a sailor's cap, HMS *Tiger* on the ribbon around it; I sat so proudly with it on, next to Deare the chauffeur in the Ford V8. Impossible to forget. She left me a small amount of money in the will 'to enjoy' (underlined); the small pieces of furniture and her mother's little sewing basket ('*You* will appreciate it') are with me to this day.

———

Over the years many people came to visit us at Sacomb's Ash, as they had in Bermuda. One of the first to appear unexpectedly was Derek Verschoyle, who had left the Diplomatic Service and was starting a publishing firm. I was delighted to be able to return some of his hospitality of Rome days. We met Nigel Dennis the writer, who was a tall, dark man with a craggy face, deep-set brown eyes and a slightly hooked nose. Every Sunday he would come to dinner bringing with him his meat ration, usually giving it to me, with the words:

'If it's no good to you, give it to Minka.'

But during the time meat was rationed, it was very useful. At that time he lived in a pleasant cottage with some land where he grew vegetables and soft fruits – these he also shared with us. It was in a wood at Broxbourne, a very secluded and rural situation, with a magnificent selection of trees including the beautiful hornbeam. One day Nigel took me for a walk in the wood and as we came into a clearing and looked over the top of some high bushes we saw a group of about twelve people in green cloaks, dancing in a circle. We watched for about a minute, then he said:

'I think we'd better leave them to it. I did hear something about a witch's coven roundabout here. Maybe that's what it is.'

Nigel never drank alcohol, yet such was his personality that it was never noticed. He was an interesting person to talk to, having been at a progressive school in Germany, and after a variety of jobs becoming assistant editor of the *New Republic* magazine; later he joined the staff of *Time* magazine as contributing editor and reviewer of English and Continental books. He was planning to write his famous satirical book *Cards of Identity* when we first met him, so each week we would get a bubbling account of its progress. When it was produced as a play at the Royal Court Theatre with the young Joan Plowright playing a leading role, it received a good response.

Harold Scott frequently came down, often with his daughter, or with a young actor or actress. Harold bought six terraced cottages in the village, all occupied at a nominal rent, except one which he let to friends. This became known in the village as Scott's Lot. The Wakemans, who were living in Florida, were coming to Europe for a few years, and they rented the Foster-Melliars' cottage one summer whilst they were on holiday. It was a good summer with them. Surprisingly, too, Peter Rose Pulham arrived one day saying he and Mary had separated; could he stay? Of course. For me it was a gentle memory of once-upon-a-time. He stayed with us for some months, once looking after the house while we were away researching Constantine's Irish book.

One weekend at a large luncheon party Derek Verschoyle said:

'You're always giving us such delicious meals, Theo, why don't you write a cookery book?'

'But who would publish it?' I asked.

'I would. I'm just starting up as a publisher.'

No more was said at that time, so I quickly forgot about it, but a few weeks later he rang me, saying:

'How are you getting on with the cookery book?'

We discussed what form it should take and I suggested I write recipes from all the countries I had lived in, adapted to what was available in England then. It should be mentioned that in the early 1950s in England there were very few cookery books being written by women; the only names I can remember are Elizabeth Craig, Marguerite Patten, Fanny Craddock and Elizabeth David, who had published *Mediterranean Food* and *French Provincial Cooking*, although there were several books by well-known chefs. I enjoyed researching and writing for I had found that too much domesticity did not give me enough mental stimulation. With the money I got for the advance I bought a beautiful gouache by Henry Moore which I treasured. That first book, *Cosmopolitan Cookery in an English Kitchen**, went into several editions and was to start me on a new, absorbing career.

* Derek Verschoyle, 1952.

Alas, Derek's publishing firm didn't last all that long; he commissioned a book from Peter Rose Pulham about his life in the Indre district of France; Denis Johnston's *Nine Rivers from Jordan*, my own and others. By the time my second book was ready he was in bad straits; the writers on the list were transferred to André Deutsch, for whom I wrote five books in all. Deutsch became the most prolific publisher of cookery books and it was due to his publicity and good reviews that I was asked to do freelance articles for the *Daily Telegraph* and *Harper's Bazaar* and broadcasts on the BBC. As I got a little more money I bought a small bronze from Henry, who generously allowed me to take several home to make my choice.

Although at first Constantine was pleased with my moderate success, as time went on he seemed to resent anything that gave me even a slight independence. When I went to London to see a publisher or editor he was always very bad-tempered when I got home, and if I missed the six o'clock train and took the fast later one, there were often violent scenes, with accusations of infidelity. My denials only seemed to inflame him, so I learned to say nothing. I was never allowed to spend the night in London alone, even with my mother, who Con said harboured and encouraged my lovers. It was extremely unpleasant to live with; the remoteness of our house didn't help for there was nowhere to escape to except the garden, not an attractive proposition on a winter's night. However, I was determined not to give up my days in London – even the hated dentist got more visits than ever before! For the first time in my life I became secretive and introverted. I devoted more and more time to writing; short stories, ghost stories mostly, a play which was produced by the BBC, more cookery books and a novel, later published by Dent and made into a television play. I converted a small room off the drawing room into a writing room and library for myself, although my hours of work were restricted to after dinner when Constantine was reading or listening to the radio.

I was always delighted when the BBC wanted to see me, for afterwards I would go to the George pub nearby to have drinks with the exceptional people who were writing for the features programme: Louis MacNeice, the Irish poet, tall and commanding, with a satirical wit which amused me; he once described Dylan Thomas's visits to London as like 'a sort of Welsh night-bomber'; Bertie Rodgers, another Irish poet, so quietly spoken that the beautiful prose he used when talking was like soft, exquisite music. He was probably the first person to present a well-known character through the memories of people who had known him or her. When Norman Douglas died I was asked to contribute my memories to a similar programme. My cousin Harry Craig, whom I had last seen as a boy in Ireland, was often there; Dylan too sometimes. Afterwards we might go to a nearby Italian restaurant, then inevitably to the afternoon drinking club, the ML. It was very difficult to conceal my exuberance when I arrived home.

Fortunately I am a resilient person, for there was another reason for unhappiness. I had several distressing miscarriages, one resulting in peritonitis which required a long operation. I thought how much pleasanter, and in a way easier, to have had a healthy, bouncing baby. It took me some time to recover both physically and mentally, for I could not help remembering the never-to-be baby that lay forgotten in Italian earth. Constantine had a pathological hatred of sickness, so he always went away at the worst time of my illness, getting my aunt or someone down to look after me, and returning as soon as I was getting better.

He translated not only the other two books of Manès Sperber's trilogy, but many more from German and French. He also wrote a book of his own every year, so it was not entirely lack of work which made him restless, but the knowledge that he was not writing the kind of books he had set out to write. He produced one short novel about a disastrous holiday in Italy which led to tragedy, a readable book but lacking the beauty of the earlier novels. Carl Forman did take an option on it for a film, and for a week or so we lived in a cloud of thousands of dollars; then silence, for ever.

Several ideas were explored, sometimes started but never finished; he was drinking more and I feared a recurrence of what had happened in Italy. He ate even less than usual and seemed discontented in the country, making frequent trips to London, hiring the local taxi to drive him there, having it wait, then returning sometimes late at night. He justified this by saying the taxis to and from the stations were expensive, the trains at all the wrong times, and really it didn't cost all that much more to go up in comfort. So it was perhaps fortunate that about this time he met Giles Playfair again, son of Sir Nigel Playfair of the old Lyric Theatre, Hammersmith.

Giles was a good friend of Diana Graves, who no doubt brought them together once more. Giles had been a barrister but had given it up as he hated prosecuting people, he told me, and had written four books by now – one about his father (*My Father's Son*), a biography of Kean the actor, his experiences in Singapore at the radio station there, and lastly a theatrical novel (*The Heart of Fame*). Apparently years before when Constantine was about nineteen they had talked of a book Giles thought of writing about the little countries of Europe, the really little countries like Andorra, Monaco and Liechtenstein, where Giles had been with his father, and San Marino. He hadn't ever written it as unfortunately 'the war got in the way'. He and Constantine decided then it would be good for them to collaborate on such a book, but as they both lacked even an elemental knowledge of cameras, I was to come too, as official photographer. Cassell agreed to publish the book and accordingly lent me a Rolliflex camera, which was fortunate as it was like the camera Peter Rose Pulham had shown me how to use during the war. It was to be a momentous journey.

On a late April day in 1953, we set sail in a wine-boat, the MV *Grebe*, from Southampton for Bordeaux. The days before Constantine and I had spent with Sue and Barney Fawkes, he now Rear-Admiral, Flag-Officer Submarines, at their pretty Queen Anne house nearby. As we had had a late night we decided to have a siesta before looking around the little ship. We were both lying naked on our bunks when the first officer knocked briefly, then looked in. Unperturbed, he said:

'Oh, turned in, have you? The captain thought you might like to see the radar.'

When I remarked to Con that it was an unorthodox introduction, he replied:

'Oh, don't be silly. They're used to people resting at odd times with all those watches they have to keep.'

Steaming up the Gironde River in the early morning was a pleasant ending to the first stage of a delightful trip. However, at Toulouse we found the road to Andorra was still closed by snow. So we went down by train to L'Hospitalet near the Andorran border, spent a few noisy nights, uncomfortably – as Constantine said, 'like a wood-louse inside a banjo' – amongst what we were told later on were probably smugglers. From there we took a car for about four miles, and with just rucksacks walked another two or three miles to the frontier.

Andorra, past the control post, seemed just a simple street with shacks, a café, then huge mountains in the background. We had been told a bus would take us on from here, but alas there was no bus on the blocked road, no way of getting there except to walk around the mountains. The snow was waist-high and there were times during those three hours when I was certain I wouldn't make it; our rucksacks were like millstones, the camera round my neck like lead. Then, miraculously, a guardian appeared, astonishment on his face. No one, he said, except those on skis or snowshoes had ever come over the pass before when the snow was like this. At least we gained some pleasure from being pioneers. We still had a perilous drive, with Constantine and Giles on kitchen chairs sliding about in the back of a van to Les Escaldes. I had frostbite in my toes, but after a sulphur bath from the natural sulphur spa waters which made me smell of bad eggs for days, we explored the primitive charms of Andorra. Getting out was as difficult as getting in. There was no question of going back the same way except through Spain, for which I had no visa. I was given a pass by the Episcopal Viguier of Andorra (both Spain and France have joint claims), which was torn up without being examined. After endless bureaucracy and a lecture for daring to enter Spain without a visa, I was allowed to enter Urgel. We had to go back by a long route to L'Hospitalet to collect our luggage before going on to Monaco. There we would stay with the Wakemans, who were now living at Antibes.

It should have been a most pleasant reunion, and to begin with it was, but somehow Margaret Wakeman and Constantine were antipathetic. Everything was argued about, and their four-year-old son's constant habit of lifting out Con's ice from his Pernod, sucking it, then putting it back brought about a monumental row between them. We left for Monte Carlo to continue the research for the book.

Gambling has always attracted me; it has taken great willpower sometimes to say 'no more' to myself. The ornate, legendary casino at Monte Carlo was too tempting. Giles and I bought a small amount of chips while Constantine looked on disdainfully before striding off to the *salles privées* to play baccarat. Giles soon lost his money and went off to buy some more chips, whilst I put mine first on 3, which came up, so I moved it all to number 7; that came up too. In a brave gesture I put the whole lot on number 21, when I saw Giles was beside me again. When that won, too, I was all set to go on, but he clutched my arm and said:

'Stop now, Theodora, please. I'm Scottish and you're Irish. Believe me, you'll lose it all. Let's go and cash it in, then go to the bar.'

I had won what was to me then a considerable amount of money – about three hundred pounds. But I still wonder, should I have banked more on my winning streak that night? Constantine had lost quite a bit when he joined us and suggested I take us all to a nightclub, which of course I did.

Liechtenstein was even more expensive than Monte Carlo, beautiful to look at in the mountains, but truth to tell rather boring. San Marino was the most lovable of them all, making up to a large extent for the rigours we had encountered on the way. In fact Giles decided to stay on there for a few weeks. As we had let our house to friends for a specified time, we didn't know quite where to go, finally deciding, as we were travelling by train, to go to stay with Peter Rose Pulham at Conives in the Indre for a while. He had gone to live there after his final separation from Mary. Although he seemed quite content and extremely pleased to see us, I was quite shocked by the primitive conditions he was living in, above the stables in the old groom's quarters. All right for June, perhaps, but not for the winter. Until we came he had been eating nothing but bread and garlic, with a little cheese, washed down with a lot of wine. He had almost no money, but was writing the book for Derek Verschoyle, part of which I brought back with me. I left feeling very concerned for him.

Giles came to stay with us while they were writing *The Little Tour.** I was pleased, for he acted as a sort of buffer between Constantine and myself. Also he was an amusing person and very kind. I don't think the book – although I found it very enjoyable – was really what the publisher had envisaged; it wasn't a travel book as such, for instead of telling people where to go, if anything it told them where not to go.

When it was finished and Giles left to live in London, the house seemed empty without him. The problem arose once more of what Constantine wanted to write next.

He had done nothing much with the Norman Douglas material, except after Norman died in 1952, he put together a little book of photographs of Norman from his early years to the end, with a long essay about him. I suggested he turn the whole thing into a novel, incorporating his own experiences with Norman's life. I still think it would have made an excellent book, written from the heart, but it was never attempted. When Nancy Cunard was writing her book about Norman Douglas she would come down to stay so that she could hear about him from Constantine.

Never having met her, but knowing of the legends surrounding her, I was apprehensive before our first meeting with Nancy. That tall, emaciated figure, with incredibly bright blue eyes, hair swathed in a chiffon scarf, countless necklaces and bangles jangling on a long, thin neck and stick-like arms. 'Cunard covered in ectoplasm,' she once remarked to me; her clothes, of an earlier fashion, enveloped her thin body, flowing out behind her, and concealed the most enchanting warm-hearted woman. Not for nothing had she been the mistress of the best minds of her generation and characterized by Aldous Huxley in *Chrome Yellow*. The high, light, slightly gabbling voice would talk until three or four in the morning, changing from English to French to Spanish as the night wore on, and the subjects changed so rapidly it was sometimes difficult to follow. When I brought up her breakfast in the morning, the cat would be on one side, Minka on the other, something they never attempted with other guests. 'I love these *animalitos*,' she would say. How she hated her mother, whom she always referred to as 'her ladyship'. Naturally we talked of George Moore, who had loved her mother for so many years. She told me he had once said to her:

'You're my daughter, I hope!'

* Cassell, 1954.

Nancy said the story going about that he had once asked to see her in the nude was quite garbled. What he had asked her was if he could see her *back* without clothes.

I would sit in the bedroom chatting with her. She seemed to wear the same kind of clothes in bed as out; the chiffon scarf was always in place. We discussed many intimate details of her life, and I grew to love Nancy. She was kind and helpful to me in many ways, especially with one of my books, for she got her cousin Sir Victor Cunard to lend me precious papers from his library. We had long, lovely lunches at the Café Royal together. Although the Café was not the same as I remembered it, I had the feeling Nancy always would be.

She arrived, late, one bleak November Sunday evening. Some guests we had in the house had stayed on, as they were anxious to meet her. In her breathless voice she told us that Dylan Thomas was seriously ill in New York, news which stunned Constantine and myself; only a month ago I had seen Dylan in the George, where he had told me excitedly that Stravinsky had asked him to be his librettist for the new opera he was writing in America. We listened to the late news on the radio, which gave little hope. About two o'clock in the morning we were still talking quietly when there was a loud, persistent tapping at the window. It was a windy night so I thought one of the long branches of the climbing rose outside had come adrift. I pulled back the curtains, to see that it was a robin pecking hard at the glass. When I opened the window he flew on to the sill, looked at us and flew out again. In Ireland a bird in the house means a death. I turned to face the others in the room.

'Dylan's dead,' I said flatly.

Everyone said I was being melodramatic, but the next morning, November 10th, 1953, the newspaper announced his death.

Later his wife Caitlin was to write to me from Laugharne: 'You and Constantine are two of the few people who have any conception of what we meant to each other: it was all, and now it is nothing!'

CHAPTER FORTY-SEVEN

Living with a temperamental writer for some years is very different from a life with a man who spends most of his day away from home. For one thing, he is there all the time, except perhaps for a few weeks a year. There is no business partner or secretary to vent displeasure on; every nuance of feeling is directed at the one person who is present. With an emotional man this can be very exacting. You try to understand the rapidly changing moods but it's not always possible; you interject with your own, invariably a mistake. After over twelve years you may fall into the trap of complacency. But marriage is far from being a race where you eventually come into the straight: there is no finishing post and it is at the point when you think you know someone that you become lazy and fall. Neither person is really to blame, for the gap opens slowly and you do not realize what has happened. It is only noticeable during a period barren of creativity.

After Constantine had finished his book about the July Plot to kill Hitler,* he was emotionally exhausted. He had researched for over a year and we had been in Germany several times for him to talk to the widows of those few brave men, but the grimness and irony of the story only added to his exhaustion. At the time I thought his bitterness was directed at me, whereas in reality it was against inhumanity and I was the sole recipient of his anger. The witticisms I thought of fell very flat; my ability to make him laugh had gone.

You forget that the day once started with laughter, as now you sit silently waiting perhaps for the postman to bring the magic letter which would put back the smiles again. It is a very gradual process, like an unsuspected disease which one unhappy day manifests itself. The physician is yourself until you realize your knowledge doesn't go far enough; you are no longer on the register. You look up at the once-cherubic face, now stern, trying to think of some untrivial thing to say; you stare at the china bee on top of the honeypot wishing it would come to life to make a diversion. Instead you take the dirty crockery to the kitchen and look out of the window at the countryside as desolate as your heart. The smiles are reserved for strangers, and they no longer come from the heart.

It was an unhappy time in other ways. Dear Peter had died suddenly at

* *The Shirt of Nessus*, Cassell, 1956.

Conives in May at the age of forty-five. I had received many sad letters from him over the years about his continued lack of money, and had sent what little I could spare to buy him food, as by now I had almost nothing of my own left. He could not sustain himself. The warning signs had been there, for his vision had been badly impaired during the winter, but I knew little of what those symptoms meant. The cold, too, must have been frightful in that dilapidated outbuilding with just a tiny wood-stove in the kitchen. Towards the end, unable to afford canvas or wood, he painted on fallen roof slates, charming, sad and evocative little pictures, one of which Mary gave me later on. Despite his great talent and innovation, both as a photographer and a painter, like so many before him he had to wait for recognition until after his death. Now he lives on through his work in many museums and private houses. He was a brave man, an exceptionally good friend, one to whom I owe a lot.

Mimi had been to England a few years back and was drinking very heavily again. In June 1956, the American Hospital in Paris telephoned to say she was a patient there suffering from alcoholic poisoning. Constantine went over to bring her back to England. He put her into a nursing home in London in the charge of a doctor who specialized in an alcohol-revulsion cure, which in short meant she was given alcohol all the time from early morning on, together with pills which made the taste repulsive and brought on sickness. Afterwards she came down to stay with us, a frail-looking ghost of what she had once been. I loved having her there; we worked in the garden together and cooked meals as we had done in Italy. Whether Constantine thought I was spending too much time on her I don't know, but after a week or so he said he couldn't work properly with her there, wondering if she would be nipping out to the pub. In fact, she showed no inclination to go down to the bare pub and drink beer.

However, my aunt in Chelsea was very fond of Mimi and she said she would take her in there, she had plenty of room. In the basement of her house lived the young unknown Sean Connery, then with little money, playing small parts on the stage and in films. Sean and Mimi got on well together, sharing meals of spaghetti Mimi had cooked. He knew about her drinking, and one night when she came in and he thought she had started again he was very angry with her. He made her give him the doctor's name and telephoned him.

It must have been a lonely time for her as she had been out of England for so many years – most of her friends had dispersed. We would meet when I came up to London, and although she was looking much better I could see she was getting restless. She had had a disastrous affair which had worried all of us, leaving her sadder than she had ever been.

'I must get it out of my system,' she said. 'I'm writing a novel all about it. If only I could find a cottage in the country. There are too many ghosts in London.'

She went down to stay with her sister Fanny in Kent, finally finding a cottage in the same county. She finished her novel, which was full of imagery, strange but confused. It didn't seem publishable then, but I think with a little editing it would have been. She telephoned Constantine, frequently asking him to lend her money 'until her allowance arrived', which he always refused to do. Then early in February 1957 she telephoned again saying she was ill, he must help her. He rang her doctor in the country, who said she had a bad liver complaint and was under treatment. At last she rang in desperation, first my aunt, who wasn't in, then Constantine, asking him to send a car to bring her to London as she felt ghastly. The scene is etched in my memory:

'Mimi's always "crying wolf"; I just haven't the money to indulge her whim to come to London.'

He refused to send the car.

On February 20th, 1957, a hospital telephoned to say she was dead. She was a little over forty years old. The love and tenderness she had shown to me in Positano, the naughty days and nights we had spent together, the charm, beauty and gaiety were gone for ever.

My mother and I went down to collect her clothes and the finished novel. Constantine refused to have any of them in the house; the novel he burnt, saying 'it was too personal'. I tried to snatch it from the flames, succeeding in rescuing only a few pages, which are today more evocative of Mimi than her photograph is.

Constantine had loved Mimi. They were the nearest of the four children, not only in age but also in personality. Late at night he would tell me he felt guilty about turning her away; but what use is remorse? Instead of being warned by her death, he too began to drink more – spirits, which up till then we hadn't kept in the house, were bought lavishly, and as they were consumed, the aggression increased. I tried to dissuade him, saying that drink only increased the mood he was in: if he was miserable it made him maudlin or aggressive, and if he was bubbling, his mood developed into euphoria. He always agreed, then poured himself another large whisky, and so it went on.

Money was getting short again. Unless Con wrote another book we would be perilously broke. Perhaps it was because of all this that I was not aware of what was happening; I was so relieved when his mood changed, I encouraged him to go on the long walks he was taking, also his increasing visits to London. For about two months he was as he had been when we first came to Sacomb's Ash. I was quite unprepared one Sunday evening when the Tompkinses, who'd stayed the weekend, were to drive home to London and he suddenly announced he would go with them. He wrote me a cheque for ten pounds, saying he didn't know when he would be back; to which I bitterly replied that ten pounds wouldn't last very long. Then he left, hardly saying a word to me. I walked down with Minka to the pub, crowded with locals swilling beer, and I felt out of place as everyone enquired where he was. Some friends drove over, which helped, but it was a melancholy night. I had no idea where Con had gone, why, or for how long. All night I wondered, but I was not in doubt for long. The following afternoon he telephoned saying he was coming home that evening, would I order a taxi? His voice had the stern inflection of some months earlier.

He came into the drawing room, walked up and down saying nothing for some minutes, then took up his customary position leaning his arm on the bookshelf.

'I went to London to meet C.' Here he mentioned the name of a woman friend of mine. 'We were going away together. However, she didn't turn up.'

Before I could even register my astonishment, he went on:

'But if in the future she would change her mind, I shall go.'

'Meanwhile you will stay here?' I asked.

'Of course. Where else would I go?'

The words didn't register with me. My brain seemed to stop taking in signals. I went out to the kitchen to prepare the dinner. Why did he have to tell me? I asked myself. Never would I have thought of it; and if I had I would equally quickly have dismissed it as being absurd. Why inflict unnecessary pain? He followed me out, drew some beer from the barrel, then looked at me.

'I've had other affairs,' he started, 'but I still loved you. Maybe I do now, I simply don't know.'

He seemed to be using me as a sounding board, not realizing the wounds he was inflicting. Then with all the insouciance he could muster, he said:

'What's for dinner? I'm hungry.'

It was the first time I had ever known him express such a thought. After dinner he went to play the gramophone.

'Oh, damn, I'd forgotten it was in London being mended. I could have picked it up.'

Quickly I said:

'I'm going to London tomorrow for a few days, I'll get it.' This was one time when I felt he was unable to stop me going.

My mother was a very calming influence. 'Of course it's a shock, but I suppose it's bound to happen in any marriage, and it's usually one's best friend. I can't see why he had to tell you, though. He must be quite insensitive to your feelings. Anyway it's lovely to have you for a while, I never see you these days. Let's have a drink.'

It might seem as if I was making a lot of fuss about something which happened all the time, but ours had never been a marriage of convenience. The only point to living the way we had was to be held together by affection and trust. My mother was quite right about infidelity in marriage but there are many different kinds. Sexual relationships outside marriage should remain the concern of the two involved people. To flaunt an affair is an expression of sadistic behaviour, which I think is wrong. If it is a question of loving another very deeply, then one ought to leave, allowing the wife or husband to make another life. It is very different if one is separated through force of circumstances, as happened so frequently during the war. I had not been blameless in that respect, but it has remained my own secret. Constant infidelity which isn't felt to be satisfying unless it is boasted about expresses frustration, hostility and resentment.

———

It was difficult to know quite what to do in my present situation. I had almost no money, so I couldn't go to Ireland, which would have been one solution. London was difficult too, for I kept meeting friends who knew us both. My mother sensibly pointed out that I couldn't just walk out leaving everything, including my dog, Minka.

'You'd have to go back sometime. Better to do it soon and make up your mind when you see how things are,' she said wisely.

Constantine had telephoned every day to know when I was returning, as he missed me. After about a week I decided to go back and see what the situation was between us. I collected the repaired gramophone and telephoned Peter and Jerree Tompkins to tell them of my decision, for they had been wonderfully helpful. Peter's last words to me were:

'He'll be pleased you're back, but be warned, he'll find something to lose his temper about before the evening's through.'

He was quite right; luckily it wasn't with me, but with the gramophone, which although better now needed a new sapphire stylus. Constantine was very euphoric that evening, saying he had been asked to rewrite a film script for Orson Welles, which he could do easily while doing a book of his own. It could lead to getting his own film option taken up again.

'We can look for a new house too, if you like,' he told me excitedly later. 'Aunt Olive's giving us all five thousand pounds. I had a letter from her this morning. What do you think?'

I thought how Mimi would have enjoyed that money, how she might have had better treatment a few months before and not now be lying in a Kent churchyard, but I didn't voice these thoughts. Somehow his words didn't penetrate my consciousness. Occasionally a phrase would be clear and loud, followed by an excited mumble. I felt hollow and empty, fixing my eyes on the calm ethereal beauty of my Henry Moore painting.

'. . . don't you think so?' I heard his voice questioning me. 'When you've finished your book?'

Yes, that is what I would do, finish the book that was two-thirds written, then I would have a little money and maybe a new commission.

It was getting late on this warm summer's night. Even with the windows open there was no wind.

'I'll take the dog round the garden before I go to bed,' I said, then: 'Shall I sleep in the blue room?'

He laughed. 'Good heavens, whatever for? I'll come round the garden with you, wait a minute.'

The little owls hooted from the paddock and the scent of the tobacco plants was almost overwhelming as we strolled around the back lawn, yet I felt like a stranger walking with another stranger. And I wished that it was so, for I no longer knew what to expect from this man who looked like Constantine, yet behaved very differently. I tried to recollect what he had been like when I had first met him in 1943, but that man, too, was a stranger from the one who walked beside me. Would he make love to me tonight? I hoped not for I felt so cold inwardly, as though my skin was filled with sawdust, dry and useless. In the dark of the garden in a confused way I tried to put my thoughts into words, but they sounded so banal I stopped mid-sentence. I tried once more, but he stopped me, saying:

'Come on, darling, Minka's been out long enough. Let's go to bed.'

Constantine's ability to change his moods with unpredictable rapidity was a contributing factor to being able to go on living with him. For they were genuine changes, not assumed for effect; he believed in them himself and transmitted that belief to me. Now he was determined to find another house, to settle down and start afresh. We went all over the immediate countryside looking at houses, but there was always something wrong with them: too small, too ugly or wrongly situated to please him. At last we found a perfect house at Letcombe Bassett in Berkshire. Admittedly it was very large, but the rooms were beautifully proportioned, the gardens delightful. There was even a very fine old mulberry tree under which, it was reputed, Dean Swift used to sit to write. Alas, when at the behest of my aunt we had it surveyed, it proved to have wet rot, dry rot, and the death-watch beetle amongst other things. Constantine said he couldn't possibly live in a house that 'ticked' all the time. In any event, he bought Sacomb's Ash, but by the time the sale was complete he was saying it was too 'cottagey' and was alternating between planning to rebuild or taking a flat in London and using it as a weekend refuge. He did neither.

During this time he was writing short stories and also translating, for the first time into English, the beautiful long poem *The Cornet* by Rainer Maria Rilke. This he dedicated to his aunt, Olive Antrobus, as a gesture to thank her for the handsome gift. Vernon Watkins the great Welsh poet, friend of Dylan's and of ours, read the manuscript, making several suggestions some of which Constantine accepted. The film script for Orson Welles was finished and approved. Eventually when it was made it seemed quite different from what I had read and it had another title, so no doubt it was rewritten yet again. Con's book *The Blitz** and a translation of La Rochefoucauld's *Maxims* had been published, to critical acclaim. Once more friends came for the weekend, the Sunday evening buffet was brought back, and to my knowledge he never deliberately saw the non-eloping lady again.

Henry Moore enjoyed being with Constantine and liked talking to him. When Henry was asked to be chairman of a committee for a sculpture personifying the horrors of Auschwitz, it was Constantine who went with him on that grim journey. Therefore it was not entirely a surprise, when a large sculpture of Henry's was being exhibited in Paris, that Henry suggested we both accompany him and Irina.

The Moores always travelled separately as long as Mary was a child, lest there be an accident. We all met up in Paris. They were delightful to be with – Henry full of energy, determined to see as much as he could; Irina, always calm, compliant and serene. Going round museums with Henry was an unforgettable experience, his quick sculptor's eye pointing out things I had never before realized. Striding through the Louvre behind him, down the long hallway where Henri III used to ride up and down on a camel, through the Rubens room, we went quickly, but not too quickly, for from time to time he would stop to look at something he wanted to see again. Then upstairs to the Egyptian room, where the pace slackened considerably until he stopped beside a wooden carving a little over three feet high of a tall man with his arm around a woman's shoulder.

'Look,' he said. 'Look at the movement in it. You feel the sadness, they are going from somewhere they do not want to leave.' He walked slowly round to the back of the carving. 'Look at how the man has his arm about the woman's shoulder. In that arm is love and tenderness which have lasted over five thousand years.'

* Allen Wingate, 1957.

We went to Rodin's house, and walking round Henry would show you why Rodin was such a good sculptor. We all forgot we were in a museum. Looking at a portrait head, he said:

'I wonder how much that one weighs.' Immediately he started to lift it up. Burglar alarms rang, custodians gathered, while Henry stood shamefaced, like a little boy scrumping apples, as Constantine explained who he was: handshakes and smiles instead of stern faces. Then on to the Musée de l'Homme, Henry stopping in front of a primitive drawing:

'Oh, Picasso's been here. You can see the influence.' Then as we went further, he would stop from time to time, again saying:

'They've *all* been here, look at that!'

We discovered the Musée Guimet, where upstairs we found the most exquisite small pieces of pre-Grecian sculpture from some part of Afghanistan, mostly heads, but of such vitality, gaiety and life that we stood amazed. The day when we went to see Henry's sculpture was also memorable, for as we walked around it, he put out his hand and stroked the long, rounded thigh. At once the custodian approached, telling him he mustn't touch the exhibits. He put his hands behind his back immediately, standing with chastened expression, not saying a word.

However, it was not all culture. There were delicious meals at Drouant's restaurant in the Place Gaillon, where the Academie Goncourt always met; La Laperouse and La Closerie des Lilas in Montparnasse, where Verlaine usually drank, or maybe a small café if Henry was in a hurry to get to another place. He also wanted to go to the Moulin Rouge which he had heard so much about, but that proved a little disappointing to him, so we went on to a small *boîte*, where we ate. It was amusing when a chic, pretty woman came on to do her turn, for Henry at once loudly said in his slightly Yorkshire voice:

'That's not a woman; the shoulders are all wrong!' As it turned out, he was quite right.

We also accompanied Henry to Dublin. A piece of his sculpture had been bought by subscriptions from admirers of his work in Ireland, and he wanted to choose a suitable site in St Stephen's Green. He showed as much interest in the early Celtic gold work in the National Museum as he had in museums in Paris. The Horse Show seen from the presidential box entranced him, and I thought how well he fitted into the many parties that inevitably followed. 'Surely,' I said, 'with a name like Moore, you must have some Irish blood?' But he didn't know of any.

I never remember any time we spent with Henry and Irina Moore that didn't create an atmosphere of happiness and understanding.

CHAPTER FORTY-EIGHT

Writing is a solitary occupation. Not only does it entail sitting alone and putting your thoughts on paper, but a large part of every day and some nights is spent in sifting, analysing and ordering those thoughts. There are some fortunate people who have the facility to do this quickly, even able to dictate into a machine, but for most writers this is not possible. So I understood the desire Constantine had to see friends at the weekend, for he was a very gregarious person, and I encouraged it.

It was probably due to this solitary life with me in the country that offers to write more film scripts attracted him. Also the money was extremely good, paid on completion of work and not months later in arrears, as book royalties are. After the preliminary script was written, there were script conferences, which brought him into enjoyable contact with people who had lively minds. To begin with, some of these conferences were held at Sacomb's Ash, but as time went on and the finished script became more pressing, they were held in London. At first he would stay with friends, often arriving back late Friday evening with several people not always known to me. Then on Monday he would return with them for another working week. During this time his own work, a novel he was outlining, was pushed aside.

Several of my books had gone into second impressions, one into paperback, and I was working on another, so I was quite pleased to be able to devote this much time to writing. I read omnivorously in the evenings, went for walks with Minka, and planned food for the weekend. A novel was forming in the back of my mind, for which I made notes. The peace and quiet of the countryside were very comforting. This way of life would continue for some months, until Constantine would telephone and say he couldn't get back for the weekend; I should expect him perhaps the weekend after. After I'd finished my book, the days seemed very long, for often I was entirely on my own after Mrs Howe left at lunchtime until she came the next morning. Occasionally I would make a brief visit to the Foster-Melliars or to Jane Wellstead, otherwise I saw nobody.

I took the opportunity to go over to Ireland, as I had a little money from the book I had just delivered. Emotionally I was still insecure, so I wanted to see friends, to be on neutral ground in a pub or a restaurant, rather than be in the close-knit cocoon of my family. I was afraid of questions that I couldn't answer, of telling half-lies to those I loved. Arland Ussher had been staying with us on his way back from China some months previously, and had asked me to stay with him and his wife when I came over. Arland's wife, Emily, was looking after their grandchild, so Arland entertained me.

Together we wandered about Dublin, Arland showing me places I had never seen, like the Brazen Head Tavern in Bridge Street, the oldest in Ireland I think, where the United Irishmen met and Robert Emmet the patriot used to go; out to Marino to see the exquisite eighteenth-century casino built by Vierpyl in 1762 for the Earl of Charlemont, looking almost like a surrealist picture surrounded by a housing estate; to St Michan's Church, near the Four Courts, on the site of the first church of Norse Dublin in 1096 – the vaults have contained bodies for centuries without showing signs of decomposition, owing to the walls' construction of magnesium limestone, which absorbs moisture; the 'Lucky Stone' of St Audoen's Church in High Street, founded by the Normans and dedicated to St Ouen of Rouen in France. All of this was taken at a leisurely pace, Arland being a charming and erudite companion. It reminded me a little of my walks with Norman Douglas, a man Arland admired very much. So as we were strolling along I would recount some of my meetings with him.

There would be pleasant stops for a drink or food: the back bar of Jammet's; the Dolphin with its delicious grills; the Red Bank restaurant, which for years as a child I had thought was a bank, when my father used to leave me in the car and nip in; Neary's pub with the bowls of gas along the counter; Davy Byrne's, the pub James Joyce writes about in *Ulysses*; and others. We met friends of Arland's including Brendan Behan, who seemed very fond of him. They joked and talked together, often in Irish.

Usually we had dinner at the house, but on my last evening Arland mentioned a bistro-type restaurant called La Taverne which had newly opened. It was owned and run by a friend I had last seen in Paris, Leona Ryan. It had good cheap food and wine, and a pleasant atmosphere rather like a Continental café. We were finishing dinner when Arland looked round the room and said:

'Oh! There's George over there. I must bring him over to meet you.'

He came back accompanied by a fairly tall, slender man of about thirty-five, with fine features.

'This is George Morrison. I've known him since he was about six years old,' said Arland. 'You'll have a lot in common, for he's making a film.'

They sat down and I looked at the young man opposite me. The sensitive, thin face with a broad forehead was dominated by the large blue-grey eyes, one moment with a sad, thoughtful expression, contradicted by deeply etched laugh-lines at the corners. When I asked him about his work, the eyes grew even larger, soft and deeply expressive. He had long fingers on his well-shaped hands, hands he used in a very graceful way when talking.

After a little while Arland said he must be getting back; he had promised Emily he wouldn't be late. Maybe he saw a slight disappointment in my face, for he went on:

'You stay for a while with George. He'll look after you and find you a taxi later on.'

I asked George more about the film, which I gathered was an epic feature about Ireland from the turn of the century until just before the Civil War in 1922, using old newsreels.

'But surely there weren't many such films?' I asked. 'How is it possible to find enough to make a feature-length film?'

He looked at me, the large eyes smiling:

'My cutting room is only a little way off. Why don't you come and see some of it on the moviola?'

Looking through the small viewing aperture and seeing scenes of real events in Dublin at the time of the 1916 Easter Rising, I couldn't believe I was actually looking at what had always been, to me, stories told by my father, uncles and aunts. I felt very excited.

'They are all running or walking at a normal pace,' I said. 'Other old films I've seen show people scurrying about. Why are these different?'

In his soft voice he explained to me the elaborate process he was using for the first time in a long film, and how since his twenties he had been to many places in Europe, cataloguing film of Irish interest. It was from this catalogue that his idea for the film had developed. Again his face changed completely as he talked with dedication about his art. We arranged to meet for lunch the next day with Arland, before I left later to catch the plane home. It was a cold, damp November day, which made me dread leaving the friendliness of Dublin to go back to an empty Sacomb's Ash. They both accompanied me to the airport, waiting as I left for the plane. However, the plane did not leave that night owing to fog in England, so we were returned to the departure lounge to await further news. George was still there, and sat with me until they announced there would be no more flights that night; I'd have to return in the morning.

I booked a room at the Gresham Hotel, which was almost next door to the check-in office. George and I had drinks and a sandwich in a pub before I went back to the hotel. I thought I had better telephone Constantine, who had rented a flat in Bloomsbury from Sonia Orwell, George Orwell's widow. There was no reply. In the morning I spoke to someone I took to be a cleaning woman, leaving a detailed message with her.

The fog had closed London Airport so we flew to Manchester, then on by a crowded slow train to Euston. To my surprise Constantine was there to meet me, but as I quickly realized, he was very drunk. We went back to Sonia's flat in Percy Street which was very untidy, the bathroom and bedroom littered with make-up and women's clothes which I took to be Sonia's. It was far from a happy homecoming, for he was quarrelsome and aggressive, so much so that I slept in a small spare room, determining to go back to Sacomb's Ash the next day. Before doing so I went to buy some food to take back home, and coming back to the top-floor flat I passed an elderly woman opening the door to her flat on the lower floor. She smiled at me, hesitated a little, then said:

'Do you know when Mrs FitzGibbon is coming back? I want to ask them down for drinks; you too, if you'd like to come.'

I packed quickly and left a note saying where I was going, and that the woman in the flat below wanted him to call.

Seldom, if ever, have I spent a more solitary time than I did then. The weather was damp and harsh, with frequent fogs which muffled sounds outside but seemed to intensify them in the house. Boards creaked, doors groaned as they opened, winds whipped the isolated house making the lath and plaster tremble; the cat's large eyes opened even wider and her tail twitched as she sat in front of the fire. Minka seemed constantly on the alert, staring at me, going frequently to the front door and sniffing underneath it.

Behind the house was a very overgrown lane, once a carriageway to Green Tye, so Mrs Howe told me. One terrifying night, standing in the kitchen I heard loud moaning coming from that direction. The dog growled, then the noise stopped and I continued preparing my dinner. It started again, softer than before, but working up to a crescendo. It sounded like a large animal such as a cow in pain. I decided that's what it was and I wondered if I should telephone the farmer. Then I realized there were no cows nor cattle anywhere near the house – only the vast ploughed fields waiting to be sown with corn. The melancholy noise continued as I waited, knowing I must go out with the lamp to see if I could help. The sounds were intermittent as I pulled on trousers and a sweater, then lit the lamp. Minka and I stumbled through briars, fallen branches and stones for some time but found nothing. However, that night I took the two animals up to my bedroom and pulled a chest across the door.

Sometimes the fog was so dense I lost my way going down to the pub, ending up in a ditch, so that I would put the lead on Minka and let her take me. There were nights when I would wake up cold with fear. I worked for most of the day on my novel, not knowing whether what I was writing was good or bad, but I felt compelled to keep on. The characters became my friends. When they were happy, I shared it with them. When Constantine occasionally came home, they were kept out of sight.

Just as suddenly as he had left to live in London, Con returned, a little before Christmas 1958. His moods were still very changeable: during the daytime he was usually a pleasant companion, but as the evening came he often became aggressive for no apparent reason. He sometimes questioned me about events of long ago.

Once he said: 'I'm a trained interrogator, you know.' And as he stood over me, looking down from his great height, his eyes full of hostility, I was frightened. This constant interrogation became an obsession with him. Then the next morning he would behave as if nothing had happened. To say it was confusing is to understate how I felt. I wondered if I had imagined these scenes, perhaps misunderstood them, or had I dreamt them?

At this time he was working with the ex-Ealing film director Charles Crichton who had made *Hue and Cry* and many other successful films. He had a charming, amusing personality, very easy to work with, and I enjoyed the days and nights he spent with us. They were working on a film called *Graziella*, a 'vehicle' as it was called for the one-time Parisienne cabaret singer Juliette Greco. There were trips to Paris to see Daryl Zanuck the producer, with whom she was living, which Constantine enjoyed. There were never any rows between us when they were in the house. I began to feel there was something lacking in my behaviour which made me increasingly awkward and nervous when we were alone together. I longed always to be in the company of other people, but as time went on even that didn't prevent the most shattering scenes of violence and humiliation. I found it hard to disentangle the reality from the enveloping fog of emotional insecurity which surrounded us both. Sometimes the sound of voices was as clear as that of a blackbird on the lawn. At other times words that were said became unnaturally loud and distorted, or seemed to merge into each other, as though we were both being moved very rapidly on a revolving stage. There were occasions when I felt like the onlooker and not a participator. My health became affected. I would pray that there would be a miraculous end to this torment.

In June 1959 there was some respite. Constantine was beginning to work on a new novel, concerned with England under Fascist rule. I didn't like what he outlined to me, but said nothing. I don't think he was very enamoured with it, for later he changed it to being under Communist rule and it became *When the Kissing had to Stop.** I hoped desperately he would work off some of his aggression in the book, which he did to a certain extent.

* Cassell, 1961.

Earlier in the month I had bought a small secondhand car, which made me feel much freer. News came from Ireland that my aunt was ill, and was asking to see me. I went over for a week, spending some time with her until she seemed to be getting better, then a few days in Dublin where I gave a dinner party for some of my friends, including George. My mother had been staying at Sacomb's Ash to look after Constantine, and was still there when I got home. We sat together in the June sun under the walnut tree; I felt refreshed and wished for this contentment to continue. The little car was a help, for if I saw signs of boredom I would suggest driving out to visit friends. There were still quarrels but not the destructive scenes of earlier months. If only, I thought, there was some way of knowing exactly what triggered them off.

A little over two weeks after I returned from Ireland, three people whom neither of us knew very well came down to lunch. Proud of my new acquisition, after lunch I drove them all around the country; after a swim at a friend's pool we stopped frequently at pubs or hotels for drinks. However, I was very careful and all day I only had two beers. It was a pleasant, easy day which we all enjoyed. I drove two of them to the station, the other woman preferring to stay with us. Once home, I remember the relish with which I said:

'Now I'm going to have a real drink, my first today.'

It was then about ten-thirty at night. The three of us talked for about an hour. Constantine left the room and after a little while I went out to look for him. As I opened the kitchen door he shouted something at me, but it was too late, I was in the room. He was standing naked by the central heating boiler, burning his clothes. He had done this several times before and I knew he would be in a fury afterwards. When he came back, fully dressed in other clothes, he started a menacing attack on me. The other woman protested, saying I had been very good to them all that day. I knew it wouldn't stop that night, so I excused myself to go to bed. He followed me to the dressing room where I intended to sleep, still haranguing and pushing me so that I banged my head against the washbasin. Then he left. My heart was beating very fast; I felt helpless, wondering when it would all cease.

Quietly I slipped out the back door with Minka to the car, but it wouldn't start. Over and over I tried. I would go somewhere, anywhere, away from that accusing voice. Then I saw his figure looming up out of the darkness.

'Just as well it won't start,' he said. 'You'd only crash and be more of a nuisance.'

I went back to the house and upstairs into a spare room. Eventually I must have fallen asleep from exhaustion. It was very quiet when I woke in the morning, sunlight coming through the window, although I had no idea of the time. I tiptoed along the corridor to get my toothbrush from the dressing room on the far side of our bedroom. Quietly I opened the door to go through, but stopped at once as I saw two heads on the pillow in our large bed. Downstairs the kitchen clock said nine-fifteen; the tick sounded unnaturally loud in the large kitchen as I put on the coffee pot. Despite the warmth I was trembling. All I wanted to do was to get away. Once more I tried to start the car in the garage – it was as dead as I felt. I walked round the garden with Minka, praying:

'Please, God, let me get away before they wake up.'

When I got back to the house, Constantine was having his breakfast as I went to telephone the local taxi driver to take me to a nearby hotel. We did not speak to each other. Upstairs I packed a few things in the empty bedroom. A voice from the spare bedroom called:

'Is there any coffee?'

I replied there was some downstairs.

Constantine looked up as I came down the stairs. Before he could say anything I said:

'I'm going to Gilston Park for a few days. I want to think everything over. There's plenty of cooked food in the larder. Please don't forget to feed Jocasta. I'll take Minka with me.'

Gilston Park was a sham-Gothic hotel set in very beautiful grounds; I wandered down to the lake with Minka and the hotel dog, the wild thoughts tumbling about in my head like autumn leaves swept hither and thither by a cruel wind. One part of me wanted to say forgive, the other knew there was no end to the hurt and humiliation that could be inflicted. Perhaps a few days alone here, in these peaceful surroundings, would enable me to come to a reasonable answer, would stop me feeling like a puppet in the hands of a mad puppet-master.

Walking back up the gentle green slopes towards the oak-panelled, antlered room used as a bar, I was much calmer. Minka darted ahead of me at the open french windows. I looked up; there at the bar were Constantine, Elizabeth Foster-Melliar and Con's companion of the previous night. They looked like any Sunday-morning drinkers, chatting and laughing together.

'Hullo, darling, we came over to have drinks with you.'

Another stormy scene was the last thing I wanted, so I joined them, talking mostly to Elizabeth. Then I said I must have my lunch as the dining room would soon close.

'The *boeuf à la mode* you left us was delicious, a superb soft jelly,' said the woman.

I smiled briefly, then I left.

That evening I telephoned my mother, who said I could come to her, but she thought London was not the answer. I should get right away for a little. What about Ireland? Wasn't it much cheaper than England?

As I left the phone box, Constantine was in the hall saying he wanted to talk to me. Over drinks I told him I must go away for a month at least. No longer could I stand this life of destruction; we must both think very seriously about any future life together and he must give up drinking spirits if I was to return soon. He left and I was glad, for I was being pulled first one way, then the other, until I no longer knew what I wanted. Over dinner I decided to telephone Arland Ussher in Dublin, to see if he could find me a small flat there.

'Oh, I'm no good at that sort of thing, Theodora. I'd have to ask someone to do it for me. Why don't you get in touch with George about it?'

'But, Arland, I've only met him three times, and I don't even know his phone number. I can't impose myself like that.'

'Nonsense. He's very good at doing that sort of thing. Wait a minute, I'll give you his number. He won't mind, I assure you.'

Arland was quite right. George sounded as if he was finding homes for people all the time. Maybe he was, I knew so little about him. I explained it mustn't cost more than five pounds a week and it must have a small patch of garden for Minka. I spent the next day alone in an agony of indecision. Constantine rang asking if I was determined to go away; when I said I was, he began shouting, accusing me of going to a lover. Then surprisingly he said he had got an old friend down to be his housekeeper, and he was spending the next day in London. It seemed obvious that he expected me to go. I knew that whatever I did had to be done at once; it was like severing a gangrenous wound.

The next day I went back to pack a few clothes. I only took my personal belongings, a few books, Peter's painting on the house slate, and a small print I had bought when I was sixteen. I looked lovingly and longingly at my Henry Moore painting but decided it might leave a mark on the wall, which would be a constant reminder. Anyway, I'd probably be coming back. It was the only home we'd ever had of our own.

George rang that evening to say he was on the track of a small house. Did I like cooking on gas or electricity?

There were more meetings with Constantine which merge into a haze of sadness in my memory. At the end of the week I left Gilston Park and went to my mother's flat. That night George rang me there, told me he had found a not very nice little house, and would I like him to come over to accompany me to Ireland? As I surveyed the assorted luggage and regarded the now elderly Minka, the thought of transporting them all by train and boat dismayed me. I willingly accepted his offer. I told Diana Graves, my truest friend, what I was doing, mentioning George's kind offer. In her husky voice she said:

'Darling, would you like a second opinion? If so, bring him over!'

On Sunday July 19th, 1959, one week since I had left for Gilston Park, I went back to Ireland, never to return to Sacomb's Ash. This was not entirely my own decision, for someone I had never known had replaced me. I never again had the Henry Moore hanging on my wall, nor indeed could I recline in my *chaise-longue*, or drive my little car. Yet, ultimately, Constantine and I were to be the best of friends, and in future days of crisis and unhappiness it was to me he always turned.

I was frightened, unhappy, and unsure of myself when I arrived in Ireland. I did not know what kind of reception my family in County Clare would give me. They seemed so untouched by the banalities and brutalities of the sophisticated life. I need not have worried; the family that was determined enough to coin their own money a century ago had their own original views on everything.

'Why didn't you tell us?' they asked. 'And why did you not come back to us before this?'

My future was very uncertain for some months, but the tenderness, care, and love given to me by George gradually restored my emotional security. That we had no money to speak of hardly mattered, for the relationship we built up was bound by common interests as well as by affection. We were able to work together in complete harmony. As only children, we had both known what inner loneliness can be felt, but at last it was shared and understood. I could not have visualized the hours of research and work my life-giving career of writing would take – or the heartbreaking struggles of helping George to make original films without money. Nor could I ever have imagined the years of happiness that were ahead of me.